THE CHARACTER OF INTERNATIONAL LAW

Professor Robert Cryer was a foundational voice in modern international criminal law. This book celebrates his character, his life, his work, and his influence.

The book is a Festschrift of love and admiration for a character that is dearly missed. Fittingly, the book also continues to voice the many conversations that Rob started. It thereby doubles as a critical examination of the life of international law.

The book constellates 17 expertly-authored chapters nurtured by four editors through five distinctive sections, each of which reflects on the character of international law. These sections, presented as acts, are: discipline and borders, (re)imagination and continuity, violence and reckoning, acoustics and storytelling, and friendship and kindness.

A wide gamut of touchpoints dovetails into a beautifully eclectic medley. These include criminal law, the law of war, music and harm, gender-based violence, nuclear weapons and artificial intelligence, law after war, the crime of aggression, drones and targets, the domestication of international law, and the role of law in inter-state relations. The book journeys to many places, including Japan, Bosnia and Ukraine, while reflecting on the role of teaching and mentorship in the life of international law.

The Character of International Law

A Festschrift for Rob Cryer

Edited by
Emma J Breeze
Mark A Drumbl
Gerry Simpson
and
Marianne L Wade

•HART•
OXFORD • LONDON • NEW YORK • NEW DELHI • SYDNEY

HART PUBLISHING

Bloomsbury Publishing Plc

Kemp House, Chawley Park, Cumnor Hill, Oxford, OX2 9PH, UK

1385 Broadway, New York, NY 10018, USA

Bloomsbury Publishing Ireland Limited, 29 Earlsfort Terrace, Dublin 2, D02 AY28, Ireland

HART PUBLISHING, the Hart/Stag logo, BLOOMSBURY and the Diana logo are trademarks of Bloomsbury Publishing Plc

First published in Great Britain 2025

A catalogue record for this book is available from the British Library.

A catalogue record for this book is available from the Library of Congress.

Library of Congress Control Number: 2025942500

ISBN: HB: 978-1-50998-337-7
ePDF: 978-1-50998-339-1
ePub: 978-1-50998-338-4

Typeset by Compuscript Ltd, Shannon

To future ripples

Foreword by Professor Robert Cryer's Family

As we have continued to reflect on the inconceivable loss of Rob, we have found solace in the way his friends and colleagues remain enthusiastically dedicated to the promotion of his legacy. Not only is this reflected in their advocacy of Rob's contribution to the academy but also their friendship, support and insight into a life well led. He and his colleagues embody for us the true meaning of collegial endeavour and the stimulating impact that has on confidence, creativity and the exchange of ideas and insights.

We celebrate this volume as further recognition of the broad contribution Robert (as we know him) has made, and continues to make, to the areas of scholarship he so loved. We are touched by the genuine affection shown by the contributors towards a figure who was much more than an outstanding academic and scholar, but one who was also an outstanding human being who always gave of himself unstintingly and with unselfish warmth and generosity.

The organisers, editors and authors have through their efforts delivered successfully on their joint objective to integrate and synthesise the key themes of both Rob's life and work. They have produced not just a remembrance, but an erudite and important contribution to legal scholarship that will provide ripples of inspiration for others, an aim Robert would wholeheartedly endorse. Such ripples are like those produced by skimming stones on calm waters, an art in which Robert was skilled, both in reality and metaphorically.

We send our best regards to all those involved in the production of this volume and to its readers who we hope will be inspired to skim their own stones and generate their own ripples arising from the many challenging insights and stimulation to be found in the chapters that follow.

Figure 1 Robert skimming stones, 23 June 2018 in Betws-y-Coed, Wales. Taken by Sudeshna Bhattacharya

Figure 2 A cartoon of Rob teaching the International Humanitarian Law LLM course in Nottingham, drawn by Rogier Bartels in 2003 whilst sitting in class

Acknowledgements

As editors, we warmly thank all the contributors. The book is yours, you are the book. After all, 'What is the city but the people' (Shakespeare, *The Tragedy of Coriolanus*, Act 3, Scene 1). Warmest appreciation to everyone who participated in the conference but did not submit papers. Through your words and deeds, thoughts and charms, you meaningfully contributed to the event and your fingerprints – evident yet untraceable – are all over this Festschrift. Above all in this space is Sudeshna, whose grace, dignity and love for Rob(ert) served as a galvanising force, and Rob's lovely family.

Thanks to everyone who helped organise the conference, notably, the initial committee comprised of the editors along with Adrian Hunt, Andrew Sanders, Isobel Roele, Solange Mouthaan and Javier Eskauriatza. Thanks to the University of Birmingham, the University of Warwick, and Washington and Lee University for funding the event.

Thanks to the committed and punctilious team of student research assistants at Washington and Lee University, School of Law, who helped bring this book over the finishing line: Susan Wanjugu, David Tall, Blair Brown, Kate Risser and Will Vardy.

Thanks to all colleagues not at the conference or who did not write for the book but who were very present to offer helpful suggestions to us along the way – notably, Barbora Holá, Kirsten Fisher, Sam Cole, and the innumerable staff of the University of Birmingham who lost a close friend and have supported us in this endeavour in manners great and small.

And we personally and individually give thanks to others in our lives who helped make this possible through their generosity and kindness. Mark thanks his wife Michelle for the bottomless well of support, and their sons Paul and Luke for enlivening each day; Gerry thanks his nephew, Liam, for care and support; Emma thanks her dad, Bob, for always asking the right questions and those others that continue to inspire; Marianne wishes to express her gratitude for seeing this book become a reality, and her hope that the process that led to it remain the hardest (in any way) professional undertaking. In addition to the above, she expresses thanks to all the conference organising committee, speakers at memorial events for Rob and co-editors; she notes it her part without the many words and gestures of shared goodwill. Enormous thanks to Adrian, Emma B and Javi in the first days and weeks. Rob was many things to many people, and part of her family. Her mother Yvonne gave great comfort finding the perfect, if heartbreaking, words to express that. Boundless thanks to Julian, Izzy and Rosie who lost him too, but who all gave everything they could to make sure she also honoured 'work Rob'. She knows it cost quite a bit.

Mark took the cover photo. In it, we see friendship and solidarity; how colour remains over and through the weathering of time.

Contents

Notes on Contributors

Rogier Bartels is a Legal Officer at the International Criminal Court and Senior Researcher at the University of Amsterdam.

Neil Boister is Professor of Law at the University of Canterbury, New Zealand.

Emma J Breeze is Assistant Professor of International Criminal Law at the University of Birmingham Law School.

Eoin Campbell is a pupil barrister at No 5 Barristers' Chambers, Birmingham, UK.

Mark A Drumbl is the Class of 1975 Alumni Professor of Law and Director, Transnational Law Institute, Washington and Lee University, US.

Javier S Eskauriatza is Assistant Professor of Criminal Law at the University of Nottingham.

Adrian Hunt is Honorary Associate Professor at the University of Birmingham Law School.

Agnieszka Jachec-Neale is Chair of the UK Group, International Society for Military Law and Law of War.

James Lee is Professor of English Law at the Dickson Poon School of Law, King's College London.

Solange Mouthaan is Associate Professor in Law at Warwick University.

Raphael Oidtmann is Adjunct Lecturer in International Law at the University of Mannheim, Germany.

Alexander Orakhelashvili is Professor of International Law at the University of Birmingham Law School.

Stoyan Panov is Lecturer in International Law and EU Law at University College Freiburg, University of Freiburg, Germany.

Paul Roberts is Professor of Criminal Jurisprudence at the University of Nottingham.

Shagufta Sen is a Doctoral Candidate at the Faculty of Law, University of Delhi, India.

Gerry Simpson is Professor of International Law at the London School of Economics.

David Turns is Senior Lecturer in International and Operational Law at the Swedish Defence University, Stockholm.

Elies van Sliedregt is Professor at Tilburg Law School, University of Tilburg, the Netherlands.

Sergey Vasiliev is Professor of International Law at the Faculty of Law, Open University, the Netherlands.

Marianne L Wade is Reader in Criminal Justice at the University of Birmingham Law School.

Notes on the Editors

Emma J Breeze is Assistant Professor of International Criminal Law at the University of Birmingham. Her work has been featured in *OpinioJuris* and *Dagbladet Information*, as well as the *Journal of Conflict and Security Law*. She has contributed to several edited collections, including 'Healthcare in Conflict: Legally Protected, Physically at Risk' in John Tingle et al, *Research Handbook on Patient Safety and the Law* (Edward Elgar, 2023). She is currently writing the monograph *Know Your Enemy: Intelligence Standards, Technology and Preserving Life* (Hart Publishing, 2025).

Mark A Drumbl is the Class of 1975 Alumni Professor at Washington and Lee University, School of Law, where he also serves as Director of the University's Transnational Law Institute. He has authored *Atrocity, Punishment, and International Law* (Cambridge University Press, 2007), *Reimagining Child Soldiers in International Law and Policy* (Oxford University Press, 2012) and *Informers Up Close: Stories from Communist Prague* (Oxford University Press, 2024, with Barbora Holá). He has also co-edited three other volumes on child soldiers, aesthetic theory and international prosecutions, and children and violence.

Gerry Simpson is Professor of International Law at the London School of Economics. He is the author of *Great Powers and Outlaw States* (Cambridge University Press, 2004, winner of the American Society of International Law Annual Prize for Creative Scholarship in 2005) and *Law, War and Crime: War Crimes Trials and the Reinvention of International Law* (Polity Press, 2007), and co-editor (with Kevin Jon Heller) of *Hidden Histories* (Oxford University Press, 2014) and (with Raimond Gaita) of *Who's Afraid of International Law?* (Monash University Press, 2016). His most recent book is *The Sentimental Life of International Law: Literature, Language and Longing in Global Politics* (Oxford University Press, 2021). He is now writing a book on the Cold War and a meditation on nuclearism entitled *The Atomics: My Nuclear Family at the End of the Earth*. He is also a Fellow of the British Academy.

Marianne L Wade is a Reader in Criminal Justice at the University of Birmingham, Birmingham Law School. She also leads the Violence, Crime and Justice research theme there, is a fellow of the Institute for Global Innovation, and a member of West Midlands Police Counter-Terrorism Reference Group. Her activities focus on cross-border criminal justice cooperation and particularly related developments within the EU, including crimes of terrorism and trafficking human beings and their prevention, investigation and prosecution at a national, regional and global level.

Figures

1

Introduction
To Remember and Smile

EMMA J BREEZE, MARK A DRUMBL, AND GERRY SIMPSON

Remember me when I am gone away,
Gone far away into the silent land;
When you can no more hold me by the hand,
Nor I half turn to go yet turning stay.
Remember me when no more day by day
You tell me of our future that you plann'd:
Only remember me; you understand
It will be late to counsel then or pray.
Yet if you should forget me for a while
And afterwards remember, do not grieve:
For if the darkness and corruption leave
A vestige of the thoughts that once I had,
Better by far you should forget and smile
Than that you should remember and be sad.
Christina Rossetti, 'Remember', 1849

THE ROSSETTIS – the entire family – repaint the formality of the British Victorian years in florid and delightful Italianate colours. Winsome and wanting, in words and brush strokes, they burrow into and map onto what it means to be alive. They are wonderful Brit-misfits. As for Christina Rossetti, well, she favours the smile over the frown. So for her, in 'Remember', it is better to forget and smile than it is to remember and be sad.

But Christina's is not the only way. There are other paths and possibilities and permutations. Ours, here, is to both remember and smile.

OVERVIEW: THE GENEALOGY AND TAPESTRY OF THIS PROJECT

This celebration of Professor Rob Cryer's life doubles as a memorial to Rob and as a distinctive and original contribution to those disciplines and sub-fields (international humanitarian law, international criminal law, legal theory, penal law, criminology and public international law) to which Rob devoted much of his academic life. The idea is not to create a smorgasbord of high-quality disconnected essays, but, instead, to commission serious writing capable of being moulded into a coherent and unified piece of work. This collection, then, offers a view of international law as a structure of thought, a jurisprudential tradition, a language of punishment and reckoning, a diplomatic style, and a congeries of sub-disciplines with shared pre-occupations and ways of thinking and seeing. Rob's own methodological certainties, his ethical commitments and his versatility form the animating spirit behind the book.

This book's title is an obvious play on the word 'character'. It refers, of course, to Rob's own character, a character full of character we might say, and one who stamped his identity on the various fields in which and with which he engaged. Rob's career coincided with the lifespan of contemporary international criminal law and a particular style of international law itself, which began in the halcyon immediate post-Cold War years. Character also refers to something general, perhaps elusive. When we talk about the 'character of international law', we gesture towards an indefinable quality associated with its overall effects on the world, its reputation and its grand projects. This is a book about the life of law and about a life in law that inspired many lives in law.

Rob passed away from lymphoma at the age of 46 on 3 January 2021. He was a pillar of the international law community – a veritable character indeed. Following his death, memorial services, commemorative ceremonies, and multiple blog postings and obituaries were written and held. Many of these transpired in virtual spaces as his death coincided with one of the most difficult stretches of the COVID-19 pandemic.

Amid this tumult and grief, a group of eight scholars assembled to think hard about kindling something bright. We committed to organise an event that would celebrate Rob as a friend, to be sure, but also his rich scholarship, his role as an intellectual inspirer and his fingerprints on the pages of international law. We set up a website to honour Rob, issued a call for papers and got the word out. At this point, it had become possible to hold a conference in person. Gathering and creating community was central to our wishes.

The responses to the call for papers were overwhelming. Some contributors got to know Rob through his teaching, others through his words and the glint-gleam in his eyes, and many 'through the pages' – so to speak – of his many publications.

In the spring of 2023, we assembled a conference programme for an event which was held on 29–30 June 2023, at the University of Birmingham Faculty of Law.[1] The lead organiser of our efforts, and indomitable host, was Rob's

[1] https://www.rob-cryer-scholarship.com. Throughout this book, we as editors refer to Rob as 'Rob'. As far as individual contributors go in their chapters, we as editors have eschewed a standardised approach. We have elected to allow contributors the flexibility to refer to Rob in whichever way

Birmingham colleague Dr Marianne Wade. Marianne delivered a stellar opening lecture on 'Rob the Person'. Rob had taught at Birmingham for many years. The conference was entitled: 'Robert Cryer: A Life in Law and a Law unto Himself'. Its goal was to 'channel this loss, those missings, into this event, that celebrates his oeuvre, research, mentorship, teaching, insights, idiosyncrasy, laughter, vim, and wit'. Panels were sited in time and location: Rob in War, Rob in Tokyo, Rob in the Classroom, Rob Undisciplined, Rob beyond Space and Place, and Rob in Britain. The event was funded by the University of Birmingham, the University of Warwick, and Washington and Lee University.

The conference was a huge success. Each presenter received considerable feedback on their presented work. Discussions extended far beyond the formal sessions. At the end of the conference, Gerry Simpson and Mark Drumbl convened a plenary session to synthesise common threads that emerged and, in an operational sense, discuss future paths. A strong group consensus emerged in enthusiastic support for a Festschrift. In addition to Gerry, Mark and Marianne, Dr Emma Breeze joined the editorial team. A former PhD student of Rob's, and now an insightful scholar of law, war and technology, Emma took on a lynchpin role in the production of the book.

As editors, we have identified five crucial themes, or acts, that bind the 17 chapter-contributions while also sensibly sorting them. These are: (1) Discipline and Borders; (2) (Re)Imagination and Precision; (3) Violence and Reckoning; (4) Acoustics and Storytelling; and (5) Friendship and Kindness. Throughout, Rob's scholarship is a central thread. As such, this is a book about Rob as a character, but also about the character of international law. It is a substantive project. The first act unfurls interdisciplinarity through a series of essays concerned with the relations between Rob's various fields and spheres, and his influence upon or within them. The second act takes up Rob's rare combination of imagination and precision in relation to pedagogy, criticism, discipline formation, and historical revision. In the third act, Rob's special interest in violence and its consequences provokes a sequence of essays touching on targeted killing, the criminalisation of aggression, selectivity in international criminal law enforcement, and the regulation of autonomous weapons. In the fourth act, a group of scholars consider the ways in which Rob and other international lawyers go about writing on the subject. How is international law expressed? How does it convey moral convictions? How does it narrate 'our' hopes for the world and 'our' sense of justice, along with who, exactly, forms part of the 'our'? These essays, then, consider the acoustics of international law and the literary and emotional life of international law. Finally, in the fifth concluding

they are comfortable. All contributors had different relationships with him. In our estimation, this move reflects the diversity of the book's multiple source threads as well as the personally felt impact Rob and his legacy have, and continue, to have.

act, the book expands the aperture of international law to take in friendship or friendly relations with essays on kindness, inheritance and collegiality.

Albeit vividly addressed in the fifth act, this book brims with themes of friendship, love, amity, conviviality and conversation. As editors, we are guided in our own sentiments by the friendship between Dante and Virgil as unwrapped in *The Divine Comedy*. Dante, to be sure, treks from inferno to purgatorio and then to paradiso. During the long and arduous slog, he encounters many souls and sights and sites. For much of the journey, he is accompanied by Virgil, who acts as his guide. Virgil is nurturing and positive, supportive and leading, wise and never wobbly. *The Divine Comedy* is a tale of many things, and companionship is among them, notably the connection between Dante and Virgil. They journey side by side. Dante learns throughout. But then, in Canto XXVII, they reach the top (the end) of purgatorio. This is the Earthly Paradise. Arriving here is the goal of all the lost souls in transit in purgatorio. Dante's paradiso is a virtuous garden of beauty and grace and propriety. Upon reaching the end (the top) of purgatorio, Virgil slowly begins to part ways with Dante. Virgil then bids Dante farewell:

> When the stairway was all sped beneath us,
> And we were upon the topmost step
> On me did Virgil fix his eyes
> And said: 'Son, the temporal fire and the eternal,
> Hast thou seen,
> And art come to a place where I, of myself, discern no further.
> Here have I brought thee with wit and with art;
> Now take thy pleasure for guide.

In Canto XXIX, when faced with challenges anew in Earthly Paradise, Dante turns to Virgil for enlightenment. Dante is struck by the 'fair pageant flaming forth' by the streams. Reflexively, 'full of wonderment I turned me to the good Virgil'. Virgil is still by his side, so to speak, but is fading away. Virgil offers no counsel. This is a first. All that the fading Virgil can offer is 'a face not less charged with amazement'. Dante then navigates alone the seven virtues, three by the right and four by the left. Dante manages. He perseveres.

Then, in Canto XXX, Dante faces yet another challenge. This is from the ancient flame. Pierced and frightened, Dante turns to Virgil. He tells Virgil how he is trembling. But the fade is complete. Virgil is no more. Yet Dante is prepared. Indeed, Virgil has left him power and grace, elegance and strength. Virgil does so through his parting gift – his words and his faith, his presence – festooned 'with wit and with art'. Because of Virgil, Dante's own pleasure – his own wishes and wants – serve him well as a guide though his long, and increasingly less arduous, journey.

God Bless you Rob! And thank you for your legacy of wit and art, of words and deeds, of laughter and love. We are all emboldened and enriched.

THE ROADMAP OF THIS BOOK

After Rob died, there was, among his peers, colleagues and friends, an acute and widespread sense of loss. But it quickly became apparent – and this was especially palpable at the conference held in his honour in Birmingham – that just as his death had brought in its wake feelings of loss, his life and work had bequeathed to us a tremendous experience of gain, of having gained, of addition and of enhancement.

There is much to be said about Rob (we merely scratch his surfaces in the obituary that follows this introduction and in an earlier valedictory essay by one of us ('Godspeed, Rob' by Mark in *Opinio Juris*),[2] but for these present purposes, we want to say something about the essays that follow.

Looking back to the moment when it was decided to assemble a set of chapters from the papers and presentations given in Birmingham two years ago, we doubt that we could have envisaged such a rich array of interventions on subjects dear to Rob from people who in various ways and to varying degrees hold Rob dearly in their hearts and their heads. The truth is that Rob has taken up residence in our work, in our minds, and in the manifold fields to which he contributed so masterfully.

The authors here each tell us about the character of their chosen fields and about the character of Rob's work in those fields. The title, of course, as we have already mentioned, also alludes to Rob's outsize character, his melodic forms of life and scholarship, and the ineffable sense that he and his many interlocutors not only nudged international criminal law along, but on occasions also changed the character of the whole enterprise.

The chapters vary in length and form. Some are literary, others are academic; some dig deeply into law, others into feelings and experiences, and many into both. All around, and around all, we have decided to treasure individual authorial voice and build a unified yet eclectic book that values contribution and community and respects the form of friendship and association each contributor has with Rob. Throughout, we also have been guided – to the extent possible – by what we imagine Rob would (might?) do, say or think. On this note, Marianne Wade's chapter in this volume offers a dynamic and poignant contribution.

Rob was an exacting wordsmith. On this note, he recognised that international criminal law has, as Timothy Waters remarks, 'long since departed from a lay understanding of criminality [and] that its categories are abstract, esoteric, hyperprecise and multivariate'.[3] On the other hand, Rob also revelled

[2] http://opiniojuris.org/2021/01/04/godspeed-rob.

[3] TW Waters, 'The Persecution of Stones: War Crimes, Law's Autonomy and the Co-optation of Cultural Heritage' 20(1) *Chicago Journal of International Law* 62–97 at 97 (also noting that: 'Even when the usual names for crimes appear, they are qualified, rendered as exemplars of some more essential, Platonic category: murder *as a crime against humanity*, rape *as a war crime*').

in the beauty of the English language, in literature and art, and treasured music, as Agnieszka Jachec-Neale observes in her contribution to this volume. Rob's transgressivism and lack of form, coupled with his knowledge of multiple forms, infuses the way in which we chose to edit this volume and the authenticity we bring to this project of memory and commemoration. Rob was also a cosmopolitan thinker. He delved into the bottomlessness of the Second World War, in which, as Rick Atkinson notes, 'there will always be more to write',[4] and also the novelty of new methods of warfare and the sediment of the domestication of the law of war in the laws of England and Wales. He was a polyglot of ideas and form, of content and space. And, so too, are the essays we compile here for him. In the vein of words, and their creation, contributors herein deploy terms that convey Rob's spirit – words such as 'Robism' and 'Cryeresque' – that shall live on in the collective lexicon of shared memory.

To be clear, we have assembled chapters in groupings. As editors, we have identified commonalities. We also have facilitated, and encouraged, individual chapters in terms of how they speak with each other; this largely takes the form of extensive cross-reference, interactive citation and, most centrally, mutual engagement and discussion.

Here, now, we summarise in greater detail each of the five Acts in which we have gathered the 17 contributions, along with a brief synopsis of each individual chapter. The purpose of this is to offer a primer for this edited volume as a whole and a freestanding snapshot of what is to follow. The Acts are preceded by this introduction, obviously, and then by Gerry Simpson's obituary for Rob. Taken together, these constitute the first two chapters of this book.

ACT I: DISCIPLINE AND BORDERS

This first Act is primarily about relationships, to wit, those between disciplines as well as those emerging beyond any such boundaries. As Adrian Hunt comments in his chapter, Rob was keen to be recognised as a Chair in international and in criminal law. Rob's scholarship was deeply cross-disciplinary. Act I considers these fluidities and connections. Rogier Bartels begins by bringing us a discussion on the relationship between international criminal law and international humanitarian law, presenting the practical application of both and the need for precision and clarity. He also highlights the significant impact Rob had on the professional application and interpretation of international humanitarian law (IHL) by the International Criminal Court (ICC). He then shifts the discussion into collective criminality, introducing the relationship between the domestic and the international. Finally, this Act closes with consideration of the

[4] A Mohler, 'War, Revolution, and the American Story: A Conversation with Historian Rick Atkinson', 19 November 2020, available at https://albertmohler.com/2020/11/19/rick-atkinson.

application of international law within English law: Alexander Orakhelashvili offers a detailed analysis of the law of war in England and Wales.

Chapter 3: Rogier Bartels, 'The Interplay between International Humanitarian Law and International Criminal Law: Rob Cryer's Contribution to the Understanding of War Crimes Law'

This chapter focuses on the relationship between IHL and international criminal law (ICL). Bartels points to the distinction and particular specialism of Rob's findings here, such that this is IHL and ICL rather than merely an interrelationship. This nuance is key to the rest of this chapter and reflects keenly upon Rob as a scholar 'fluent' in both fields. Bartels takes the approach that IHL was written to be applicable on the battlefield and not in the courtroom, and discusses how Rob's work influenced many ICL practitioners. The chapter demonstrates how Rob's scholarship contributed to a better understanding of what war crimes should entail. At the same time, it critically discusses certain instances where those working in ICL did not apply the same care and how such findings may affect the application of IHL on the battlefield.

Chapter 4: Adrian Hunt, 'Limits to the Notion of General Principles of Criminal Liability in International Criminal Law: The Case of Individual Criminal Responsibility for Collective Criminality'

Taking up this idea of legal interrelationships, Hunt builds upon work undertaken by the author in co-authorship with Rob. Hunt presents the importance of the general part of (international) criminal law, and why this was important to Rob, Namely through its role in establishing what conduct is deemed criminal and what is not. The chapter examines the implications of the UK approach to the enactment of the Rome Statute of the ICC and, specifically, how this relates to collective criminality. It analyses and contrasts different modes of collective criminality in England and Wales with key general principles commonly applicable in ICL. Through discussions of areas of convergence and divergence, this chapter considers what these mean for conceptions of a 'general part' in the field of ICL and consequent implications for concepts of justice and responsibility.

Chapter 5: Alexander Orakhelashvili, 'Laws of War as Part of English Law'

This chapter furthers the analysis of the challenges presented by the interrelationship of legal disciplines by focusing on the status of IHL in UK law, especially The Hague Conventions and Geneva Conventions, in line with the doctrines of statutory interpretation and statutory transformation of treaties. It raises several issues about fundamental doctrines of English law, considering specifically the use of the royal prerogative in the areas covered by IHL treaties. Orakhelashvili comments on how the scholarship and dialogue with Rob has influenced this work. This chapter covers topics such as the status of war prisoners, the right to angary, belligerent occupation and enemy alien rule.

ACT II: (RE)IMAGINATION AND CONTINUITY

This second Act considers the ways in which whole sub-fields of international law are brought into existence through acts of intellectual imagination, scholarly precision, and not only how Rob has influenced previous students and scholars, but also how this work may continue to do so 'by proxy'. Paul Roberts begins this Act by reflecting on the genesis and development of international criminal justice as a distinct disciplinary field, located in a fragment of institutional history and providing insight into Rob's early teaching and practice. Raphael Oidtmann moves us forward as he reflects upon and engages in pedagogical discussion on the characteristics that make a superb legal educator. He ponders the experiences of Rob's students, supervisees and mentees, and considers the concepts of intellectual guardian and role model. Marianne Wade provides an account of the reimagining of a module impacted by the COVID-19 pandemic; whilst Rob's role in this module was truncated by his death, the module prevailed, and the author reflects on how these conversations continue long after Rob has fallen silent by imaging what he would be saying and thinking and feeling. Finally, Neil Boister concludes the Act by analysing the scholarship surrounding the International Military Tribunal for the Far East (IMTFE, or Tokyo IMT) and the 're-igniting' of interest in the 'Tokyo' trial. Boister and Rob co-authored several volumes on these trials. This chapter sheds light on the bewildering array of research both before and after Rob's intervention.

Chapter 6: Paul Roberts, 'Envisioning International Criminal Justice'

This chapter considers and celebrates Rob's early contributions as an international criminal justice pioneer. Rob's monograph on *Prosecuting International Crimes* (2011) and a clutch of articles informed policy and theorising driving the normative development and practical implementation of ICL and shall continue to do so. Roberts puts it brilliantly in his own words: 'Rob Cryer lived the intellectual history of international criminal justice in its modern disciplinary incarnation, and I was fortunate to be one of his earliest travelling companions on the metaphorical road "from Nuremberg to Rome".' In this chapter, Roberts takes readers on this journey in the form of a law school oral history.

Chapter 7: Raphael Oidtmann, 'Rob Cryer and the Art of Teaching (International) Law'

This chapter considers the role international law academics might play as they reimagine their field in their capacities as teachers and mentors to future generations of students, academics and practitioners. Oidtmann initially engaged with Rob through his textbook. Here, by focusing on three areas – that of an academic teacher and educator, as a mentor and supervisor, and as an intellectual guardian and role model – Oidtmann pays tribute to Rob's considerable presence and lasting impact.

Chapter 8: Marianne L Wade, 'Principle or Pragmatism? Misogyny as Genocide'

This chapter narrates Wade's experience preparing an international criminal law course module with Rob. This journey was truncated by Rob's death. Still, the module went on. In this chapter, Wade poignantly imagines how Rob would have been and what he would have said in the classroom, notably on the intersection of international criminal law and the horrors of sexual violence, whether occurring in times of 'war' or times of 'peace'.

Chapter 9: Neil Boister, 'Remaking the Tokyo Tribunal: Robert Cryer and the Revival of Scholarship on the Tokyo Trial'

Boister provides an account of how Rob took the initiative to re-ignite legal and historical scholarship on the IMTFE in co-authoring the seminal monograph *The Tokyo International Military Tribunal: A Reappraisal*. The chapter also sets out how a new wave of scholarship on the trial 'discovered' the extensive Japanese literature on the subject and describes the subsequent flowering of scholarship in the last 15 years. It asks readers to consider whether scholars have exhibited neutrality and precision in approaching the trial.

ACT III: VIOLENCE AND RECKONING

This Act weaves Rob's scholarship through terrains of violence and the aspirations of reckoning. Act III begins with one of Rob's signature critiques of ICL, namely, selectivity. Here, Elies van Sliedregt considers Rob's early work on these sneaky selectivities and how these in turn to inform and influence her own work. The third Act is progressed by Shagufta Sen, who addresses a current challenge for the crime of aggression, itself a focus of Rob's work in selectivity, namely autonomous weapons systems. Stoyan Panov enriches the analysis of the crime of aggression as initiated by Sen. Panov focuses on Rob's approach in his scholarship on seeking accountability through prosecuting leaders and reflects upon how this knowledge base may be applied to the Russia-Ukraine war. The Act is concluded by Javier S Eskauriatza, who unspools Rob's approach to the jus post bellum as exemplified in Rob's 2012 article on the topic. Eskauriatza analyses the debate over this aspect of reckoning, or resolution, and offers a delightfully Cryer-esque reading and critique of this topic.

Chapter 10: Elies van Sliedregt, 'Tribute to Rob: Selectivity in ICL'

This chapter addresses a pillar of Rob's scholarship, namely, selectivity in international prosecutions. In his book *Prosecuting International Crimes. Selectivity and the International Criminal Law Regime* (2005), Rob addresses not just selectivity in prosecution but also selectivity in the parameters of criminal responsibility, which he calls 'selectivity by stealth'. This chapter applies Rob's clever theoretical construction to current developments in ICL.

Chapter 11: Shagufta Sen, 'Envisioning Targeted Killings and the Crime of Aggression in the Age of Autonomous Weaponry'

In the age of emerging and disruptive technologies, the ability of weapons to autonomously identify targets raises concerns regarding the use of force. This chapter assesses such methods, including drones. Sen places these methods within conversations about the crime of aggression, which constituted a major centrepiece of Rob's work, beginning with his scholarship on the IMTFE. The chapter considers Rob's work in the age of artificial intelligence, while undertaking the daunting task of identifying the myriad challenges that inhere in 'justified targeted killings'.

Chapter 12: Stoyan Panov, '"Prosecuting the Leaders": Reflections on the Prohibition and Prosecution of the Crime of Aggression in International Law'

This chapter deepens the analysis of the crime of aggression foreshadowed by Sen. In comparison to war crimes, crimes against humanity and the crime of genocide, the crime of aggression has not been widely litigated before contemporary international or hybrid tribunals or domestic courts. Panov focuses on recent trends in the prosecutability of international crimes, including in the context of the war in Ukraine and the creation of potential new tribunals. He anchors his analysis around Rob's take on the intertwined nature of the political and legal aspects of the prosecution of international crimes, and Rob's quest to craft new avenues for accountability.

Chapter 13: Javier S Eskauriatza, 'Robert Cryer and the *Jus Post Bellum*'

This chapter honours and reflects on Rob's extensive scholarship by engaging in a detailed and 'close-up' analysis of Rob's published work on the *jus post bellum* (to wit, the law after war). Eskauriatza recalls the detailed discussions he had with Rob regarding these topics. Eskauriatza beautifully continues this conversation throughout this chapter. He charts the course of scholarship in the area and considers Rob's thoughts on related theoretical and practical considerations. On this note, this chapter has a similar dialogic rhythm to that of Wade.

ACT IV: ACOUSTICS AND STORYTELLING

This Act constellates thoughts about Rob as musician and Rob as raconteur. It begins by unlocking the place of music in Rob's work and in law generally. As many souls who encountered Rob's will recall, music was a significant personal passion. This fourth Act starts with Agnieszka Jachec-Neale, who explores the influence of music on Rob's scholarly practice. Whilst finding few explicit references to music, melody rings clearly throughout Rob's work. Jachec-Neale magically considers these aesthetics, sounds and words throughout her chapter. Eoin Campbell carries this fourth Act forward by ruminating about Rob's work on the crime of aggression. Fusing the doctrinal aspects (as introduced earlier by Panov), Campbell assesses recent conflicts, and considers how music and the power of language have been leveraged by both sides in promoting or rebuking the resort to war. Campbell riffs off the musical notes of anti-war songs to further unwrap the role of emotions in storytelling. The memory of Rob as storyteller, and musician, continues with two interlocutors imagining a trial that never was but should have been – of the US use of atomic weapons in Nagasaki – and place Rob's scholarship intertemporally at the centre of their conversation. In this chapter – which is presented as a combined short story, play and epistolary diary – Mark A Drumbl and Solange Mouthaan pivot to one of the central themes of this book – namely, the value of amity – and share some ruminations about how we, as human beings, ought to be with each other.

Chapter 14: Agnieszka Jachec-Neale, 'Diving into Noise and Bringing Clear Melody'

This chapter explores the profound influence of music in Rob's life and its subtle integration into his scholarly work. Jachec-Neale investigates Rob's scholarship. She identifies three specific and clearly references instances of music. That said, along her journey, she discovers a wealth of melody. This chapter emphasises Rob's literary craftsmanship, the symphony of his authorship and his ability to elegantly (and at times punchily) merge rigorous legal analysis with broader implications of justice, ethics and humanity.

Chapter 15: Eoin Campbell, 'Music and War: The Themes from Anti-war Music and the Impact They Have'

Authored by a former student of Rob, this chapter reflects upon the author's learning from Rob and addresses the power of language and emotion in law, as well as the role of music in providing a platform for emotive language both for war or anti-war cries. Campbell unwraps how language can affect the reactions of states to uses of force. This chapter considers the specific language of rock music, of which Rob was a fan, to explore how the sounds and lyrics of 'anti-war' can be used to emotively advocate against the use of force.

Chapter 16: Mark A Drumbl and Solange Mouthaan, 'Tokyo IMT: Another Sequel to a Prequel'

This chapter presents as a fictional, yet factual, thought experiment in which the Tokyo IMT has welcomed an additional trial. Proceedings are ongoing against US General Leslie Groves for dropping the atomic bomb on Nagasaki. Prosecutors claim this is a war crime (indiscriminate, inhumane and excessive). The US defence is one of necessity. This creative critical fabulation features two characters in Tokyo – a Canadian law clerk and an Indonesian bartender – who discuss the trial and invoke Rob's work on selectivity, colonialism and war crimes to set the legal and moral frame. The journey continues through a dyad of epilogues in which an interlocutor, an imagined descendant of one of the authors, subsequently comes to wander through Japan. This chapter places contributions by Boister, Campbell, van Sliedregt and Sergey Vasiliev (who appears in the fifth Act) in newly imagined spaces.

ACT V: FRIENDSHIP AND KINDNESS

What would a 'kind' international law look like? How did Rob embody kindness in his friendships and in his friendly relations with the discipline itself? Are friendship and kindness partly communicated (along with sense of universal collegiality) through a textbook tradition, this being a mode in which Rob worked with panache and which led to profound results? This final fifth Act explores these ideas and queries what a law of friendship would look like. Emma Breeze and David Turns open the Act by returning to Rob's 2002 article on the 'Fine Art of Friendship' and reflecting upon his call for considering our friends during episodes of armed conflict. They import the discussion into contemporary conflicts, particularly Ukraine-Russia, and revisit Rob's important work. The role of friendship and value of collegiality is also taken up by James Lee, who reflects upon the textbook tradition of academia. Lee highlights how Rob's collegiality aided the development of textbooks far beyond the expected disciplines, and analyses how the textbook and doctrinal traditions remain valuable for legal scholarship. This Act is brought to a close by Sergey Vasiliev. This chapter returns to Japan, and the IMTFE, specifically the judgment of Dutch Judge Bert Röling, who Rob in his own scholarship described as a 'dignified dissenter'. Vasiliev takes readers on a kaleidoscopic journey towards themes of fairness, humility and collegiality, highlighted by Rob on Bert, and now by Vasiliev on Rob. Vasiliev closes, as this book must, by saying goodbye to a dear friend.

Chapter 17: Emma Breeze and David Turns, 'A Fine Art of Friendship Revisited'

Revisiting Rob's 2002 article analysing the early months of the war in Afghanistan, Breeze and Turns reflect on Rob's thoughts on friendship in armed conflict. They apply IHL to contemporary conflicts, primarily Russia-Ukraine. They critically consider how of certain aspects of IHL could promote, and indeed place obligations upon, this kind of relationship. The hope is, as was the case in Rob's original piece, that a refocus on friendship and its obligations can promote positive change in the application of IHL during conflict.

Chapter 18: James Lee, 'Cryer, et seq: The Collegial Character of Legal Scholarship'

This chapter reflects upon two of Rob's key contributions to the academy: first, his collegiality; and, second, his scholarship. This chapter does so by honouring Rob's great contributions to the textbook tradition. However, Lee goes further and also reflects upon the past, present and future of the common law textbook. He connects this to current debates within the legal academy and the judiciary, particularly in the UK over the nature and value of different forms of legal scholarship. This chapter accordingly connects to that of Oidtmann as well.

Chapter 19: Sergey Vasiliev, 'Rob and Bert in Tokyo'

This elegy – an exercise, as the author puts it, in mourning, coping and letting go – is an effort at remembering and re-reading Rob's work on the IMTFE and in particular his essay on the 'dignified dissenter' in Tokyo, Judge Bert Röling. The work takes us through three core themes: fairness and fairmindedness, humility and collegiality, and independence and integrity. These are explored in depth with Vasiliev reading Rob's read of Bert.

CONCLUSION

The book then is a mirror turned towards us as readers, writers and thinkers. It explores the connections between technique and passion, memory and narrative, fact and fiction, the earthly and the mystical, time and movement, poetry and music, prose and law, authenticity and strategy, the possible and the feasible, encountering and gazing, closings and openings, as well as humour and justice. Rob in his work endeavoured to expand the epistemology of international law – namely, from where do 'we' know what 'we' know about international law. He hoped to make international law more international. He was deeply committed to academic freedom. All these threads, too, are woven together this volume.

Mostly, however, this is an attempt to remember Rob and to do so with a smile.

Assembling this book has been a joy. And here we are. Here we have it. Perhaps Rob himself put it best, while thinking about the twentieth anniversary of the International Criminal Tribunal for the Former Yugoslavia (ICTY), when at a legacy conference he ended his remarks with this off-the-cuff pearl in his own distinctive style: 'And to finish off, I just simply want to say that what is written about is not forgotten.'[5]

[5] R Cryer, *20 Years of the ICTY: Anniversary Events and Legacy Conference Proceedings* (UN, 2014) 42, available at www.icty.org/x/file/Press/Events/2013/20_Years_of_the_ICTY_en.pdf.

2

Obituary for Rob

GERRY SIMPSON*

PROFESSOR ROBERT CRYER, who died at 46 on 3 January 2021, was an international law polymath and bibliophile, an inspirational teacher, a selfless academic administrator, an adored colleague, one of life's great enthusiasts, and a thoroughly decent and golden-hearted human being who had no time for the hierarchies that define so much of our daily existence.

His work on international criminal law – informed by his facility with criminal law itself, his surefootedness around legal theory and his range as a generalist international lawyer – was expansively illuminating, technically capable, quietly witty, clear-eyed, corrective and bluntly authoritative. It will stretch down the generations. He leaves behind his life-partner, Sudeshna, his parents, his brother, a generation of bereft PhD students and colleagues, an emptier professional space, and a Rob Cryer-shaped hole at the heart of our field (I recently looked at the page that the University of Birmingham established for him after he died. The sheer number of people who wrote condolences, their keenly felt sense of loss palpable, is astounding. This collection itself was occasioned by an event held in Rob's honour at Birmingham where, again, Rob's absence – or should that be presence – was vitally felt).[1]

Rob himself was a vivacious, life-affirming soul. Darryl Robinson has written about corresponding with Rob before meeting him and then struggling to reconcile the tweedy, pipe-smoking academic image he had conjured in his mind throughout the correspondence, with the raging actuality of Rob in his heavy metal glory (Rob, the planet's only lover of both Iron Maiden and the *rationae personae*/*rationae materiae* distinction). As Darryl put it so tenderly, writing about that first encounter: 'Throughout the evening, my mind wildly reeled at just how far my long-held inferential assumptions had missed the target. My brain struggled to catch up to the vastly superior Rob Cryer before me.'[2]

* This is a modified and updated version of an obituary that originally appeared in the *British Yearbook of International Law* (2023), available at https://doi.org/10.1093/bybil/brad012.

[1] For a comprehensive list, see the Robert Cryer Publication Archive at www.rob-cryer-scholarship.com. On the conference, see also Vasiliev, ch 19 in this volume.

[2] D Robinson, 'In Memoriam: Robert Cryer' (2021) 19(2) *Journal of International Criminal Justice* 235.

Rob Cryer completed his LLB at Cardiff before joining the University of Nottingham in 1995 where he read for his LLM before signing up to work, under the supervision of Nigel White and Dino Kritsiotis, on a PhD concerning the problem of selectivity in international criminal law. He completed his thesis in 2001. He went on to positions at Manchester and Nottingham as a lecturer before, in 2007 when he was only 32 years old, becoming a Chair of International and Criminal Law (the 'and' was very important to Rob) at the University of Birmingham (where he subsequently served as Head and Deputy Head of School).

Rob will be remembered for many things. This festschrift and the various symposia in his honour are full of testaments to the largeness of his personality, his enterprise, his conviviality, his eccentricities. To read these and the tributes online is to experience again the loss of this deeply companionable, intensely social person.

Rob *was* a scholar first and foremost, but he made some singular contributions to other aspects of the practice of international law. He was on the British delegation at the International Criminal Court (ICC) negotiations and he helped write the world's first treaty on the prevention and punishment of crimes against humanity. Despite knowing what life was like in the sausage factory, he continued to possess an unshakeable faith in the future of a legal order that he himself helped bring into being.[3] He taught a generation of officers in the Army Legal Services the rudiments (and more) of international humanitarian law and international criminal law. As Major General Alex Taylor, Director Army Legal Services, has written: 'His enthusiasm for the subject, degree of pragmatism in practical application and his almost encyclopaedic knowledge of the reference material will be remembered by many.'

Here, though, I want to reflect on his work as a scholar (not always, I appreciate, separable from these other sides of Rob). Rob was an industrious academic, publishing several influential books in the field, notably, *Prosecuting International Crimes: Selectivity in the International Criminal Law Regime* (2005); (with Håkan Firman, Darryl Robinson, Sergey Vasiliev and Elizabeth Wilmshurst) a number of editions of *An Introduction to International Criminal Law and Procedure* (2019) and (with Neil Boister) *The Tokyo International Military Tribunal: A Reappraisal* (2008), as well as an formidable array of articles and chapters.[4] These range from his final written pieces working through the distinctions in practice between the concepts of *jus cogens* and international crime to essays on the relationship between international humanitarian law and

[3] R Cryer, *Prosecuting International Crimes: Selectivity and the International Criminal Law Regime* (Cambridge University Press, 2009). Paul Roberts makes the point in ch 6 in this volume that Rob's career as an academic coincided more or less with the modern institutional life of international criminal law itself.

[4] Other books include R Cryer and C Henderson (eds), *The Law on the Use of Force and Armed Conflict* (Edward Elgar, 2017) and A Cassese et al, *The Oxford Companion to International Criminal Justice* (Oxford University Press, 2008).

war crimes law to studies of complicity to an early essay on the law of friendship to chapters on drug crimes, air power, terrorism, reprisals, the Security Council and numerous case notes, reviews, favours for friends.

It is impossible to do justice, then, to Rob's writing here, but I do want to touch on three or four of his major contributions.

Prominent among those was his instrumental role in recuperating the Tokyo War Crimes Trial as one of the field's formative and most misunderstood moments.[5] A number of the authors in this collection return to Tokyo as a way of continuing that work and marking Rob's importance in bringing Tokyo into the light.[6] The book he and Neil Boister wrote on the trial is a definitive, monumental, scholarly achievement. As Neil describes it, Rob was made aware (by Neil) in 2003 that the University of Canterbury was in possession of the New Zealand judge's personal records of the trial. This set in train a project (archival, synthetic and conceptual) to place Tokyo alongside Nuremberg as one of international criminal law's two mid-century, foundational events. Neil recently described Rob's prodigious memory, his Olympic-standard reading practices, his all-night writing marathons and his commitment to accuracy. All of that is reflected in this mighty book and in Rob's many other essays on the subject.[7]

Tokyo has always been dismissed as an inferior sibling when it comes to the post-war trials of major war criminals. But then Rob had an affection for international law's outsiders. One such figure was Georg Schwarzenberger. He and I often spoke of Schwarzenberger and his modified legal realism. In the early days of our fascination with this neglected figure, I recall chatting to him about Schwarzenberger's long-forgotten book on the Nazi state and international law.[8] As soon as the conversation ended, I looked for the book online and discovered that there was a single second-hand copy available on AbeBooks. I ordered it immediately. Rob called me the following week to say he had tried to purchase it, but that there were no copies left anywhere in the world. Omitting to inform him that I had beaten him to the punch, I told him he could borrow my copy. Years later, I was asked to write a biographical essay for the British Institute of International and Comparative Law project on British international lawyers. I suggested Schwarzenberger, but was told a week later that Rob – serving up his cold revenge – had nabbed that subject already.[9] Which is a very good thing

[5] For a 'critical fabulation' of the Tokyo Trial, see Drumbl and Mouthaan, ch 16 in this volume.

[6] See Drumbl and Mouthaan, ch 16 in this volume; Boister, ch 9 in this volume; Vasiliev, ch 19 in this volume.

[7] N Boister and R Cryer, *The Tokyo International Military Tribunal: A Reappraisal* (Oxford University Press, 2008). See also R Cryer, 'Japanese War Criminals: The Politics of Justice after the Second World War by Sandra Wilson et al. (review)' (2020) 46 *Journal of Japanese Studies* 510; R Cryer, 'The Tokyo IMT and Crimes against Peace' in LN Sadat (ed), *Seeking Accountability for the Unlawful Use of Force* (Cambridge University Press, 2018).

[8] G Schwarzenberger, *International Law and Totalitarian Lawlessness* (Jonathan Cape, 1943).

[9] R Cryer, 'International Law and the Illusion of Novelty: Georg Schwarzenberger' in R McCorquodale and J-P Gauci (eds), *British Influences on International Law, 1915–2015* (Brill, 2016) 458.

because his essay is such a fluid, benevolent exploration of Schwarzenberger's work and life that also turns out to be a study of the whole field.

Ioannis Kalpouzos, I think, captures the essence of this essay and Rob's work more generally when he says:

> Fundamentally, Rob's Schwarzenberger article is also an example of how far-reaching and potentially radical critiques of the international law field can be developed from a sceptical, inductive and methodologically constrained – in Rob's case positivist – position. Indeed, while Rob consistently wrote from the field's mainstream, his rigorous and decidedly non-celebratory exploration of the intersections of doctrine and (institutional) politics constitutes, for me, an incredibly rich resource for understanding and critiquing international criminal law, the law of war, and international law in general.[10]

Rob's major monograph – on selectivity (drawn from his doctoral thesis) – was a rather masterful piece of work demonstrating that rarest of qualities: youthful wisdom. In a review of the book, Mark Drumbl, later to become a dear friend of Rob's, called it a 'must-read for those concerned about the quality, provenance, and content of international criminal justice'. Returning to it for this obituary, the reader is able to identify some very distinctive Rob-isms. There are the now-familiar distinctions between safe and unsafe tribunals, between different forms of selectivity, and between civil and common law. There is the Schwarzenberger-inflected history chapter where Rob, in an antiquarian mood and shedding light in dark corners, takes us back to Xenephon, to the Maharabharata to the Romans, to the Battle of Hastings, to the law of chivalry and, inevitably, to Peter von Hagenbach. What strikes me now is the way in which these historical moments are made to work as avatars or analogues for more recent developments (von Hagenbach and *Tadic*, Grotius at *Nuremberg*, Lorimer and jurisdiction, Vitoria and Lauterpacht). It's a rich piece of history-writing and one that places the origins of international criminal law not at Nuremberg, but in Versailles two-and-a-half decades or so earlier (this has become a commonplace view, but when Rob was writing, it was an unusual move).

As for the present day, well, not many people would compare, for example, the new international economic order with the then-embryonic International Criminal Court. Rob's reminder is salutary though. Projects really do wither and die. Rob is too much of an optimist to think that international criminal justice will meet the same end as international economic justice; yet, the gesture of placing them in conversation is already a provocative one. But it is 'far too early to write off the regime as doomed', Rob says of international criminal law.[11] Instead, he recognises the unlikelihood of it having come into any sort of existence in the first place. The mood is one of cautious optimism. A system

[10] I Kalpouzos, 'In Memoriam: Robert Cryer' (2021) 19(2) *Journal of International Criminal Justice* 235.

[11] Cryer (n 3) 328.

of justice but not a global one. A court but not necessarily a busy one. A shift in sensibility but not, perhaps – at least not yet – a revolution in human affairs. What Rob emphasises is the prospect of normalisation. There will come a day, according to Rob, when calls for accountability through prosecution and trial will be entirely unexceptional.[12] Meanwhile, we have to put up with selectivity or contraction in the applicable law in order to secure the existence of a court at all.[13]

As usual, Rob was prepared, even in his first book, to speak his mind, even against the current. He was happy, too, to criticise senior judges when he thought they had got it wrong. In 'Aggression at the Court of Appeal', he took the Court of Appeal to task for its failure to understand how a customary international legal norm came into being (later berating himself for being too harsh at the end of this essay).[14]

In 'Déjà vu in International Law', a lengthy review article for the *Modern Law Review*, Rob turned his sights on Martti Koskenniemi, one of the acknowledged masters of the field.[15] As ever, Rob begins in a generous frame of mind. Much of the best work published in recent years, he notes, has been written by scholars related to what he terms, in an old-fashioned phrase, 'the critical legal movement'. Koskenniemi, with his apology/utopia-indeterminacy thesis, seemed to belong to this tribe, but in the book under scrutiny, *The Gentle Civiliser of Nations*, the author, according to the reviewer, wants to show us what is worth defending in international law. As Rob writes: 'Koskenniemi's road onwards, or backwards, is a surprising one: formalism' (here, and I am guilty of reading between the lines, one can detect a certain degree of gleeful delight in Rob's voice).[16] The other fish he wants to fry here is the absence in Martti's *The Gentle Civiliser* of much reflection on British international law. Here is not the place to go into the detail. Instead, I would simply suggest that Rob was, at least, a British (English) common law international legal positivist. And he was very keen in some of his work to trace this tradition, feeling himself to be part of that tradition and responsible for, and to, it.

Rob, himself never ceased to be a student (in the strongest sense of that word) of the discipline and at the same time he was committed to it as a pedagogical practice. This is amply illustrated by his dedication to the textbook genre and his compiling of a number of useful documentary collections. The various editions

[12] This was one of these matters on which Rob and I agreed (we disagreed on whether this naturalisation marked a positive development).

[13] Cryer (n 3) 330.

[14] R Cryer, 'Aggression at the Court of Appeal' (2005) 10 *Journal of Conflict & Security Law* 209, 230. The offending line was as follows: 'When dealing with such a serious matter, more ought to be expected from the Court of Appeal and, it is to be hoped, more can be asked of the House of Lords when it comes to deciding the question.' See M Paparinskis and M Wong, 'In Memoriam: Robert Cryer' (2021) 19(2) *Journal of International Criminal Justice* 235.

[15] R Cryer, 'Déjà Vu in International Law' (2002) 65 *Modern Law Review* 931.

[16] On Rob and the crits, see also Vasiliev, ch 19 in this volume.

of the primer he wrote with Elizabeth Wilmshurst, Darryl Robinson, Håkan Firman and Sergey Vasiliev represent a body of rigorous, technically adept, historically informed work that for many, many students is *the* introduction to the field. The doctrine is carefully explicated, the debates fairly presented: Rob's voice of temperate conviction present throughout. What a pleasure it is to teach with a textbook rather than against it.

I might finish with the words of his friend and co-author of later iterations of that textbook, Sergey Vasiliev:

> Despite being an accomplished and renowned scholar, Rob was organically non-hierarchical … I think it is people like Rob who make academia worth staying in, despite all its problems: its toxic competitiveness, creeping commercialization and bureaucratization, inattention to mental health issues and persistent lack of diversity across the board. Rob was the embodiment of human decency, integrity and solidarity – the principles and values that, if pursued more doggedly and uncompromisingly, would make academia a better place. We are indebted to him for countless lessons in kindness and humility.[17]

Sergey is one of the many people who told me that Rob had called them in November 2020. In each case, Rob had thought up some pretext and phoned for a casual chat. In my case, he contacted me on a mid-winter morning to say that he had been thinking of the final lines of a book I had written. We spoke about George Steiner, about Judaic and Greek conceptions of tragedy, about the defence of superior orders, about the last time we had seen each other; the last time, it turned out, we would ever see each other (in a pub (of course) in Nuremberg (of course)). He seemed in good spirits. He made a glancing reference to his illness and the fact that these lines of mine had somehow helped him understand it better. When I put the phone down, I felt unaccountably euphoric. This is what academic life can be like – gossipy, intellectually liberating and morally serious. I thought: 'I must see more of Rob'.

[17] S Vasiliev, 'In Memoriam: Robert Cryer' (2021) 19(2) *Journal of International Criminal Justice* 235.

Act I

Discipline and Borders

3

The Interplay between International Humanitarian Law and International Criminal Law

Rob Cryer's Contribution to the Understanding of War Crimes Law

ROGIER BARTELS*

INTRODUCTION

ROB CRYER'S SCHOLARSHIP transcends legal disciplines. His academic interests went far beyond just international criminal law (ICL). Rob may be known foremost for his work on international criminal justice, but I first got to know him in 2003 as an international humanitarian law (IHL) enthusiast, when he taught the IHL course I took as part of my LLM at the University of Nottingham. Indeed, those familiar with Rob or the full breadth of his writings are well aware of his passion for IHL. He nonetheless became a household name in the field of ICL.

In addition, he was also known for being somewhat 'unconventional' within that field. I recall in this regard an international criminal law event taking place on a warm summer day in the second half of the 2000s, on an overcrowded top floor of a building in The Hague, the town where I worked and lived. Rob was scheduled to speak at this event organised by the Grotius Centre of the Leiden University. I had told some colleagues who joined me at the event how great a person Rob was and – perhaps based on his eloquent writings – they must have had a somewhat different image in their minds of what he would be like. Rob was preceded by Antonio Cassese – 'Nino' for those in the international criminal justice field. Nino, who was already in his early seventies and dressed in a grey suit with a light-blue shirt and dark-coloured tie, spoke in his

* Rogier Bartels is a Legal Officer at the International Criminal Court (ICC) and a Senior Researcher at the University of Amsterdam. The views expressed in his contribution are his own and do not (necessarily) reflect those of the ICC.

usual calm and reserved, almost reticent, fashion. Then Rob came on; without a suit jacket, wearing a purple silk(-like) shirt that – for usage by Rob – was far too thin and therefore too quickly showed dark sweaty patches, bellowing into the microphone that was still set at the highest volume for the previous speaker's soft, already somewhat frail voice. My colleagues initially wondered whether this 'English football hooligan' was the same 'Rob Cryer' that I had been raving about, only to subsequently be amazed by Rob and the persuasiveness of the arguments put forward – both during his presentation and over pints later that day.

It was a true pleasure to discuss IHL and ICL matters with Rob through the years, over a pint or by email. His untimely passing is a great loss for international law and he will be missed. However, as is fortunately the case with academics, Rob will live on in his published works and continue to influence those in the legal field, both academics and practitioners. In this contribution, I will address a specific aspect of Rob's impact, namely on the law relating to war crimes. Rob used to tell me that, like it was for me, IHL was his 'first love' and that although he happened to have ventured into ICL because that was where the career opportunities lay, he always kept – as one does with first loves – IHL close to his heart.[1]

IHL and ICL may be related branches of public international law, but, as will be discussed next, they are distinctly different and being knowledgeable in one of these fields does not mean that one has knowledge of the other. Rob was one of the few scholars who was truly 'fluent'[2] in both fields. In 2014, in a book dedicated to Peter Rowe, Rob wrote about '[t]he relationship of international humanitarian law and war crimes'.[3] He noted that whilst the interrelationship between international human rights law and IHL had received significant attention in scholarship,[4] the interplay of IHL and ICL had not been the subject of a similar level of 'investigation'. By pointing to two pieces that I wrote a few years

[1] Using language that exemplifies his writing style, and with a healthy dose of 'self-reflection' on the field that made him a famous scholar, Rob wrote that: 'International criminal law is neither what God is to the religious nor what parents are to young children. It provides neither an explanation for everything nor makes everything alright; it is a bad idea to treat it as a panacea for all ills.' R Cryer, 'The Role of International Criminal Prosecutions in Increasing Compliance with International Humanitarian Law' (2014) 44 *Israel Yearbook of Human Rights* 247, 247.

[2] 'Fluent' in the same sense as Françoise Hampson referred to herself as being 'bilingual', ie, being able to speak human rights law and IHL: F Hampson, 'Relevance for the Prosecution of Violations of International Humanitarian Law' in L Maybee and B Chakka (eds), *Custom as a Source of International Humanitarian Law* (International Committee of the Red Cross, 2006) 103, 103.

[3] R Cryer, 'The Relationship of International Humanitarian Law and War Crimes: International Criminal Tribunals and Their Statutes' in C Harvey, J Summers and ND White (eds), *Contemporary Challenges to the Laws of War: Essays in Honour of Professor Peter Rowe* (Cambridge University Press, 2014) 117–18.

[4] Indeed, many books and articles have been written about the interplay between international human rights law and IHL, as well as on whether IHL is the *lex specialis* during armed conflicts, including by Rob himself: R Cryer, 'The Interplay of Human Rights and Humanitarian Law: The Approach of the ICTY' (2009) 14 *Journal of Conflict and Security Law* 511. For a recent overview of the scholarship on this issue, see K Fortin, 'The Relationship between International Human Rights

before, he observed that '[o]nly very recently has there been any systematic study of the interplay between these two closely related areas of law'.[5] This reference is a good indication of how Rob was. He was very generous towards younger scholars and did not consider it necessary to only refer to the already-established names. What Rob omitted to mention was that he himself in his own research addressed many aspects of the relationship between IHL and ICL. Moreover, his work on ICL matters is written with a keen eye for any (potentially negative) consequences for IHL.

Indeed, in his publications on ICL, Rob showed a genuine understanding of IHL. Since his work is so widely read by those working at the international criminal courts and tribunals, Rob has influenced, and contributed to, the understanding of war crimes law by these practitioners. In the present contribution, I will highlight the value of Rob's work in this regard. I will first address the interplay between IHL and ICL more generally, followed by a discussion of the risk of viewing IHL issues through a criminal law lens, integrating ample references to Rob's views on the matter, and will finish with some thoughts on his enduring impact on war crimes law and those who practise in this field.

IHL v ICL

IHL, initially referred to as the laws of war, and more recently as *jus in bello* or the law of armed conflict, is significantly older than ICL, since the latter emerged out of modern international criminal justice.[6] IHL and ICL have been said to 'represent two extremes in the making of international law'.[7] IHL is applied during armed conflicts and wars, in a 'world of madness and emotion', but ICL develops far away from the hostilities, in a 'world of order and

Law and International Humanitarian Law: Taking Stock at the End of 2022?' (2022) 40 *Netherlands Quarterly of Human Rights* 343.

[5] Cryer (n 3) 118, referring to R Bartels, 'Discrepancies between International Humanitarian Law on the Battlefield and in the Courtroom: The Challenges of Applying International Humanitarian Law during Criminal Trials' in M Matthee et al (eds), *Armed Conflict and International Law: In Search of the Human Face: Liber Amicorum in Memory of Avril McDonald* (TMC Asser Press, 2013) 339; R Bartels, 'Dealing with the Principle of Proportionality in Armed Conflict in Retrospect: The Application of the Principle in International Criminal Trials' (2013) 46 *Israel Law Review* 271.

[6] The first multilateral humanitarian law treaty dates back to 1864 (Convention for the Amelioration of the Condition of the Wounded in Armies in the Field of 22 August 1864). After a failed attempt following the First World War to set up a tribunal to try the German Emperor Wilhelm II, international criminal justice did not conceived until the International Military Tribunals at Nuremberg and Tokyo were set up after the Second World War, but ICL as a body of law was only created with establishment of the ad hoc tribunals in the 1990s, and even more so with the adoption of the Rome Statute for the International Criminal Court and the Rules of Evidence and Procedure by the Relevant States.

[7] SR Ratner, 'Sources of International Humanitarian Law and International Criminal Law: War Crimes and the Limits of the Doctrine of Sources' in J d'Aspremont and S Besson (eds), *The Oxford Handbook of the Sources of International Law* (Oxford University Press, 2017) 912.

reason'[8] – that is, during long diplomatic processes and in the courtrooms of international institutions, thereby allowing for the benefit of hindsight.

IHL and ICL are not one and the same. Rob cautioned that 'there is a risk of identifying one with the other, even though the norms of one are not coterminous with the norms of the other'.[9] IHL was drafted to be applied on the battlefield, not in a courtroom. Indeed, it was not meant to serve as an 'international equivalent of a comprehensive national criminal code'.[10] Instead, during armed conflict, IHL aims to regulate the conduct of hostilities and to protect those who are not, or are no longer, taking part in hostilities: the wounded and sick, prisoners of war and civilians. Restrictions are therefore placed on warring parties, but the drafters of IHL have always been mindful of the reality of warfare and have left room for the necessities of war. In fact, one has to accept that 'war is a brutal business' and that unless all armed conflicts are eradicated, 'one must accept that the purpose of the body of law that purports to regulate combat is to limit human suffering, not to eliminate it'.[11] If one were to view IHL otherwise and expect it to fully prohibit any casualties or damage to civilian buildings, the law would be ineffective.

Although IHL is a body of *law*, it is usually applied in practice by members of the armed forces or armed groups – that is, persons who are not lawyers. Those deciding on the use of armed force may receive legal advice from military lawyers, but commanders normally are not trained lawyers themselves. As such, the preventative rules of IHL must be straightforward. Moreover, violations of many IHL rules do not constitute war crimes, and those rules may better be considered as 'instruction norms'.[12] Indeed, as Rob observed, 'prosecutions for war crimes can never be considered a means of ensuring compliance with all of international humanitarian law for the simple reason that such prosecutions cannot be for the full panoply of international humanitarian law rights and responsibilities'.[13]

Logically, then, IHL provisions differ from those found in a criminal code and do not include elements of crimes. Criminal law, at least in the courtroom,

[8] ibid.

[9] Cryer (n 1) 247. He explained that IHL and ICL 'to a considerable extent, overlap, but the provisions of international criminal law are in fact somewhat narrower than those of humanitarian law, 'and it is an error to conflate them entirely'.

[10] W Fenrick, 'International Humanitarian Law and Criminal Trials' (1997) 7 *Transnational Law and Contemporary Problems* 26.

[11] W Fenrick, 'Crimes in Combat: the Relationship between Crimes against Humanity and War Crimes', paper for Guest Lecture Series of the ICC Office of the Prosecutor (5 March 2004) 2.

[12] See R Bartels, 'Discrepancies between International Humanitarian Law on the Battlefield and in the Courtroom: The Challenges of Applying International Humanitarian Law during Criminal Trials' in Matthee et al (n 5) 339, 341; see also P Gaeta, 'The Interplay between the Geneva Conventions and International Criminal Law' in A Clapham, P Gaeta and M Sassòli (eds), *The 1949 Geneva Conventions: A Commentary* (Oxford University Press, 2015) 739–40.

[13] R Cryer, 'The Role of International Criminal Prosecutions in Increasing Compliance with International Humanitarian Law in Contemporary African Conflicts' in H Krieger (ed), *Inducing Compliance with International Humanitarian Law: Lessons from the African Great Lakes Region* (Cambridge University Press, 2015) 188.

is applied by lawyers. Moreover, the parties in a criminal trial must have resort to clear rules proscribing the alleged unlawful conduct. The principle of legality requires this, and it also makes sense practically. After all, the statutes of international criminal courts and tribunals are not setting out the law that belligerents must comply with, because these rules are found in IHL. Substantive ICL is therefore not an autonomous body of law that happens to be based on IHL, but instead it is an accessory to it.[14]

Rob himself advocated for developing a so-called war crimes law. He observed that 100 years ago, it was suggested that one need not 'enumerate exactly what may now be considered war crimes or violations of the laws of war' because '[t]he list will change from time to time, by the addition of new offences and the omission of those now so considered'.[15] Yet, according to Rob, nowadays one can indeed 'no longer … be so lackadaisical' and 'a more in-depth analysis of the question is needed'.[16] In my scholarship, I have tried to provide such in-depth research, often relying on Rob's work in doing so,[17] as have others researching these issues.[18] Rob's views in that regard are discussed next.

THE RISK OF IHL BEING SEEN THROUGH AN ICL LENS

War crimes law should therefore logically be interpreted with a close eye on the law upon which the violations are based.[19] Yet, for reasons that are inherent to the nature of criminal trials, namely the aim of the parties to achieve a conviction or an acquittal and the general desire to avoid impunity for undesirable behaviour, pronouncements go unpunished, pronouncements on war crimes made in ICL may not actually represent the branch of law that was allegedly

[14] M Sassòli, 'Humanitarian Law and International Criminal Law' in A Cassese (ed), *The Oxford Companion to International Criminal Justice* (Oxford University Press, 2009) 111, 117–19.

[15] E Colby, 'War Crimes' (1925) 23 *Michigan Law Review* 482, 482. For the purposes of the present study, it is interesting to note that Colby was not keen on the prospect of having some form of ICL. When commenting on the 1922 proposal by the International Law Association to create an international criminal court to try war criminals, he wrote: 'War crimes will persist. But the laws of war must also persist. International prosecutions will shatter the stability of those laws and offend laws and offend state dignity more than will dependence on national responsibility.' E Colby, 'War Crimes and Their Punishment' (1924) *Minnesota Law Review* 40, 45–46.

[16] Cryer (n 3) 118.

[17] In my PhD thesis, for which Rob was intended to be a member of the reading committee, entitled 'From the Battlefield to the Courtroom (and Back): The Interplay between International Humanitarian Law and International Criminal Law', Rob is the most referred to and cited author – with more citations than, for example, Theodor Meron and William Fenrick, two practitioners who also have expertise in both IHL and ICL.

[18] See, eg, M Faix and O Svacek, *ICC Jurisprudence and the Development of International Humanitarian Law* (Palgrave Macmillan, 2024), in which seven different works by Rob are cited. See also discussions in Sen and Panov, chs 11 and 12 in this volume respectively.

[19] See G Werle, *Principles of International Criminal Law*, 2nd edn (TMC Asser Press, 2009) para 964, referring to the ICTY, *Prosecutor v Dusko Tadić* (Decision on the Defence Motion for Interlocutory Appeal on Jurisdiction) ICTY-94-1-A (2 October 1995) para 81.

violated – or, at least, what humanitarian lawyers and armed forces consider the law to be.[20]

ICL, as an independent body of law, has developed greatly since the 1990s and has, through the numerous judgments of the international tribunals and courts, such as the International Criminal Tribunal for the former Yugoslavia (ICTY), contributed to the enforcement of IHL in general, but also to the development and clarification of the substance of IHL.[21] The significant influence of ICL on the development and clarification of IHL is perhaps best shown by the countless references to the case law of the tribunals in the International Committee of the Red Cross's authoritative study on customary IHL.[22]

In recent times, states have been unable to agree on and adopt significant IHL treaties, leaving it other actors, including international criminal courts and tribunals, to take on the task to clarify, and thereby develop, IHL.[23] The increasing role of ICL in the formation of IHL highlights the need of those working at international criminal courts and tribunals to understand IHL. Yet, criminal law pronouncements on the rules applicable to the conduct of belligerents during armed conflicts often appear to have viewed IHL through the lens of ICL.[24] Indeed, as Rob was also mindful of,[25] not all 'clarifications' by such courts and tribunals have simplified, or indeed clarified, IHL. Whilst certain rulings might be understandable from a criminal law point of view, the impact on IHL when applied on the battlefield, instead of in the courtroom, could lead to confusion and to a blurring of the (usually) clear and basic rules of IHL. With regard to the

[20] With regard to the aforementioned ICTY's findings on belligerent reprisals in *Kupreškić* (and similar findings in the *Martić* case), the UK Ministry of Defence's *Manual of the Law of Armed Conflict* states that it 'is unconvincing and the assertion that there is a prohibition in customary law flies in the face of most of the state practice that exists. The UK does not accept the position as stated in this judgment'. UK Ministry of Defence, *The Manual of the Law of Armed Conflict* (Oxford University Press, 2004) 420–21.

[21] See, eg, S Darcy, *Judges, Law and War: The Judicial Development of International Humanitarian Law* (Cambridge University Press, 2014); see also C Greenwood, 'The Development of International Humanitarian Law by the International Criminal Tribunal for the Former Yugoslavia' (1998) 2 *Max Planck Yearbook of United Nations Law* 97.

[22] J-M Henckaerts and L Doswald-Beck, *Customary International Humanitarian Law, Volume 1: Rules* (Cambridge University Press, 2005). On the impact of the ICRC's Customary IHL Study, see R Cryer, 'Of Custom, Treaties, Scholars and the Gavel: The Influence of the International Criminal Tribunals on the ICRC Customary Law Study' (2006) 11 *Journal of Conflict and Security Law* 239.

[23] Many IHL topics, such as the application of IHL to cyberwarfare, have been addressed by groups of experts. As observed by the present author, 'role of States in the formation of IHL has become more limited. Instead of a State-driven process, the contemporary clarification and development of IHL is done by non-State actors. The role of States is reduced to either accepting or rejecting the prospective developments of IHL and any consequential impact on their sovereignty leaving it for States to either agree or disagree with such developments'. R Bartels, 'The Relationship between International Humanitarian Law and the Notion of State Sovereignty' (2018) 23 *Journal of Conflict and Security Law* 461, 486.

[24] See R Bartels, 'A Fine Line between Protection and Humanisation: The Interplay between the Scope of Application of International Humanitarian Law and Jurisdiction over Alleged War Crimes under International Criminal Law' (2017) 20 *Yearbook of International Humanitarian Law* 37.

[25] R Cryer, '*Prosecutor v Galić* and the War Crime of Terror Bombing' (2006) 2 *Israel Defence Forces Law Review* 75.

trial judgment in *Galić*, Rob observed that the trial chamber's treatment of the rules related to targeting, as included in Additional Protocol I of 1977:

> [W]as something of a problem, because it allowed the majority [of the trial chamber] to blur the distinction between the first and second part of Article 51(2), and thus come up with a hybrid crime that drew upon both parts, rather than dealing with the question of whether the second part, itself, reflects a separate offense.[26]

He favoured a more careful approach to IHL, such as the one by the *Krnojelac* Trial Chamber, which adopted, in Rob's words a 'more (although not perfectly) sophisticated approach',[27] when it held that:

> In attempting to define an offence or to determine whether any of the elements of that definition has been met, the Trial Chamber is mindful of the specificity of international humanitarian law. Care must be taken to ensure that this specificity is not lost by broadening each of the crimes over which the Tribunal has jurisdiction to the extent that the same facts come to constitute all or most of those crimes.[28]

However, such a careful approach has not always been followed by international criminal courts and tribunals.[29]

As international courts, crowded by international lawyers, have always extensively relied on scholarship and academic commentaries to their statutory framework, it is important that such scholarship accurately reflects IHL. It is therefore vital to have academic commentaries from persons like Rob, who write authoritatively about ICL, but do so with a constant understanding of IHL and how war crimes law should operate. Possibly because IHL was his 'first love', Rob's work never interpreted IHL aspects through a criminal law lens. He had a thorough understanding of IHL and always showed a keen insight in the need to ensure that IHL remained workable for those who must apply it in practice, namely members of armed forces.[30]

At the same time, Rob believed in the idea of international criminal justice, and that war crimes law ought to be effective. He noted, for example, that the IHL principle of proportionality had been 'particularly badly dealt with' in the Rome Statute, reflecting that 'proportionality is a concept that is difficult to apply, but that is no excuse for raising the threshold for liability'.[31] He also considered that a strict interpretation of the chapeau of Article 8 of the

[26] ibid 90.

[27] R Cryer, 'The Interplay of Human Rights and Humanitarian Law: The Approach of the ICTY' (2009) 14 *Journal of Conflict and Security Law* 511, 526.

[28] *Prosecutor v Krnojelac* (Judgment) ICTY-97-25-T (15 March 2002) para 181.

[29] See Cryer (n 27); see also R Bartels, 'The Interplay between International Human Rights Law and International Humanitarian Law during International Criminal Trials' (2018) 12 *Journal of Human Rights & International Legal Discourse* 44.

[30] See, eg, R Cryer, 'The Fine Art of Friendship: *Jus in Bello* in Afghanistan' (2002) 7 *Journal of Conflict and Security Law* 37. This work is discussed further by Breeze and Turns in ch 17 in this volume.

[31] R Cryer, *Prosecuting International Crimes: Selectivity and the International Criminal Law Regime* (Cambridge University Press, 2005) 277.

Rome Statute, according to which the ICC has jurisdiction over war crimes 'in particular when committed as part of a plan or policy or as part of a large scale commission of such crimes', would collapse the definition of war crimes into that of crimes against humanity and would result in the prosecution having to prove these additional elements, whilst such elements are not present in the customary law on which the jurisdiction over the offence was asserted.[32]

In his work on the Tokyo Tribunal,[33] Rob noted that many of the judges and prosecutors of both the Nuremberg and Tokyo Tribunals had fought in one or two world wars and had observed military operations first-hand, whereas '[t]he ICTY, ICTR, and ICC are staffed, largely although not entirely, by civilians. Although some have seen military service, the judges are, in vast majority, from civilian walks of life'.[34] Indeed, nowadays, the likelihood of judges or legal staff of international criminal courts and tribunals having first-hand experience of what happens on the battlefield, or otherwise having experience with military operations, is limited. Knowledge of these matters must therefore be acquired in a different way. Moreover, IHL and ICL have different rationales and objectives.[35] Practitioners in either of these fields tend to approach legal issues from a different perspective. Those working in international criminal justice must therefore be mindful that one's perspective, as retributive or instead as protective, shapes the scope and outcome of one's approach.[36] Thus, it is all the more important that the academic writings read by those working in the field of international criminal justice do not approach war crimes matters merely from a criminal law perspective.

In his publications on ICL, Rob's writing on war crimes or related matters showed a real understanding and appreciation for IHL. His work is widely read by ICL practitioners, and thereby he has contributed to the (correct) understanding of war crimes law by those working at international criminal courts and tribunals.

[32] ibid 268.

[33] See N Boister and R Cryer, *The Tokyo International Military Tribunal: A Reappraisal* (Oxford University Press, 2008); see also R Cryer, D Robinson and S Vasiliev, *An Introduction to International Criminal Law and Procedure*, 4th edn (Cambridge University Press, 2019). These are also reflected upon further by Boister and Vasiliev in chs 9 and 19 in this volume respectively.

[34] R Cryer, 'International Criminal Justice in Historical Context: The Post-Second World War Trials and Modern International Criminal Justice' in G Boas, W Schabas and MP Scharf (eds), *International Criminal Justice: Legitimacy and Coherence* (Edward Elgar, 2012) 145, 186.

[35] IHL aims to regulate warfare and thereby to mitigate the suffering resulting therefrom (eg, D Fleck, *The Handbook of International Humanitarian Law* 2nd edn (Oxford, Oxford University Press, 2008) 11), whereas the war crimes part of ICL seeks to counter the impunity of those having violated the rules of IHL in such a manner as to give rise to individual criminal responsibility (eg, R Cryer et al, *An Introduction to International Criminal Law and Procedure*, 2nd edn (Cambridge, Cambridge University Press, 2010) 1).

[36] See also C Jenks, 'Law as Shield, Law as Sword: The ICC's Lubanga Decision, Child Soldiers and the Perverse Mutualism of Direct Participation in Hostilities' (2013) 3 *University of Miami National Security and Armed Conflict Law Review* 107.

CONCLUDING THOUGHTS

Judicial findings of international courts and tribunals in a specific case only relate to one or a few suspects,[37] but – as recalled above – these judgments have a significant influence on the development of IHL. International criminal justice must address horrendous atrocities, often committed in times when IHL failed to achieve its aim, namely to mitigate suffering in times of armed conflict whilst permitting the warring parties to achieve their military goals, but one must not forget that for every such criminal case, there are many situations where IHL does work – precisely because of the realism built into this law.[38]

In trying to foster a proper understanding of IHL amongst international criminal lawyers and a realistic 'war crimes law', Rob influenced many of those working in ICL. As such, he contributed to a better understanding of what war crimes should entail. It testifies to his academic neutrality that he was referred to by all sides and participants. The 294 references to his work I found in the internal ICC database of filings and decisions[39] were citations by the prosecution, the defence, the lawyers representing victims and – also often – by chambers. By the prosecution, the defence, the lawyers representing victims and – also often – by the chambers.[40] Besides cherishing the memory for who he was as a person, we therefore also ought to be grateful for Rob's bearing on the legal field – one that likely will endure and help to keep international criminal justice realistic, and ensure that the ICL impact on IHL does not reduce this body of law to one that can no longer fulfil its intended purpose.

[37] Naturally, the findings also 'relate' to the victims of the alleged crimes.

[38] See, eg, 'IHL in Action: Respect for the Law on the Battlefield' (International Committee of the Red Cross, 2024), www.icrc.org/en/document/ihl-action-respect-law-battlefield.

[39] This number concerns references up to 2021 and does not include documents related to amici curiae briefs Rob submitted together with other academics. Since 2021, there will have been many more references made to his work in filing before the ICC or decisions and judgments.

[40] Naturally, not all these references related to Rob's work on war crimes law, but they include many references to international criminal procedural issues.

4

Limits to the Notion of General Principles of Criminal Liability in International Criminal Law

The Case of Individual Criminal Responsibility for Collective Criminality

ADRIAN HUNT

INTRODUCTION

Rob Cryer wrote that:

> The general principles of criminal liability matter. Being a primary aspect of the 'general part' of criminal law, and applying across the board to criminal offences in international criminal law, the general principles of liability tell us a great deal about the justifications for criminalising conduct.[1]

By 'general principles of criminal liability', Rob means what in domestic criminal law systems is often referred to as the 'general part', which we might define as 'those doctrines, rules and definitions that are not essentially tied to any specific offence or set of offences'[2] and usually apply to all offences. Though special part offences may sometimes admit exceptions to or qualifications of certain general part doctrines, this should usually be a conscious decision of a legislature or court informed both by consideration of the rationale for the particular rule, and a justification for departing from it in the individual case. Thus, general principles of criminal liability comprise 'not only directly justiciable general

[1] R Cryer 'General Principles of Liability in International Criminal Law', in D McGoldrick et al (eds), *The Permanent International Criminal* Court (Hart Publishing, 2004) 233.

[2] RA Duff, *Answering for Crime, Responsibility and Liability in the Criminal Law* (Hart Publishing, 2009) 3.

rules … and rules concerning general exceptions … but also their underpinning rationale'.[3] It follows then that Rob in drawing our attention to the fact that general principles of liability matter is not simply saying they matter because they determine, in a practical or instrumental sense, in what circumstances criminal liability will be imposed on individuals for their conduct. They also matter because – insofar as those principles involve a system which serves to distinguish between criminal and non-criminal conduct and different types of involvement in criminal conduct – they signal both why certain conduct is criminally wrongful and, by establishing an internal hierarchy of different types and levels of wrongfulness, why some conduct is considered more seriously wrongful than others.

In any system of criminal law, these 'doctrines, rules and definitions' – along with exceptions, qualifications and rationales – comprise a broad and complex set of matters whose abstract principled bases will be much debated, and whose implementation in practice will rightly give rise to scholarly critiques focusing on normative coherence and/or instrumental feasibility. Throughout his scholarly work, Rob engaged insightfully and authoritatively with these debates. He was particularly anxious to do so because of his concern that the general principles of liability had received far less attention from international lawyers than the definition of specific offences: 'And much of what [had] been written on the general principles of liability has been based upon an international law, rather than criminal law perspective.'[4] Being a superb criminal and international lawyer, Rob was ideally equipped positively to assist in repairing such a deficit. Although most of his published work was in the field of international criminal law, Rob's expertise – as a scholar, researcher and teacher of postgraduate and undergraduate students at Nottingham, Manchester, Birmingham and Oxford – encompassed domestic criminal law, comparative criminal law, theory of criminal law, transnational criminal law, general international law, public international law, theory of international law, international humanitarian law and probably much more besides. As his friends will all have been aware (because Rob was wont to tell them at least once), when appointed to his Chair at Birmingham, although the School suggested he be 'Professor of International Criminal Law', Rob suggested that his preference was that he be appointed as 'Professor of International and Criminal Law', and this was the Chair to which he was appointed. This reflects the fact that, to Rob, the doctrinal frameworks, theoretical foundations and paradigmatic debates in criminal and international law were central to the endeavour of articulating and developing the discipline of international criminal law, and to his own preoccupations as a researcher, and his conception of himself as a scholar in substantive terms.

[3] AP Simester and S Shute, 'On the General Part in Criminal Law' in S Shute and AP Simester (eds), *Criminal Law Theory Doctrines of the General Part* (Oxford University Press, 2002) 2.
[4] Cryer (n 1).

My contribution to this collection seeks briefly to highlight one set of issues concerning general principles of liability in international criminal law of which Rob was well aware, had thought a lot about, and which he and I touched on in passing in a piece we co-authored on criminal liability for collective crimes in common law countries.[5] There we noted that when the UK came – in the International Court Act 2001 – to incorporate into domestic law the criminal offences identified and defined in Articles 5–8 of the Rome Statute of the international criminal Court (ICC), the Act did not provide that the general principles of liability applied by the ICC would be applied by British courts in determining liability for these crimes. Instead, the Act provides that: 'In determining whether an offence under this Part has been committed the court shall apply the principles of the law of England and Wales.'[6]

Questions therefore arise as to what the implications are of adopting this approach. Drawing upon this previous work with Rob on 'collective criminality' in England and Wales, my concern is primarily to focus on what Rob might have termed criminal law issues of justification rather than international law questions of strict legal obligation, though I may touch on the latter in addressing the former. For the purposes of this exercise, I first briefly identify some of the key features of the general principles which constitute some of the different modes of collective criminality in England and Wales, and explore the ways (if any) in which they differ from cognate principles applicable in international criminal law. The chapter proceeds to reflect briefly on what such divergences mean for conceptions of a 'general part' in the field of international criminal law and consequent implications for concepts of justice and responsibility within the field.

MODES OF COLLECTIVE CRIMINALITY IN ENGLAND AND WALES AND THE ICC STATUTE COMPARED

Joint Principals and Co-perpetration

Article 25(a) of the Rome Statute provides that a person shall be criminally responsible and liable for punishment for a crime within the jurisdiction of the Court if that person:

> Commits such a crime, whether as an individual, jointly with another or through another person, regardless of whether that other person is criminally responsible.'

The second and third legs of this formulation have given rise to recognition by the ICC of forms of co-perpetration through control of an organisation, where

[5] R Cryer and A Hunt, 'Les formes de responsabilité pénale individuelle our des crimes collectifs en droit Anglo-Saxon' in O de Frouville (ed), *Punir Les Crimes de Masse: Entreprise Criminelle Commune ou Co-action?* (Anthemsis, 2012) 73–105.

[6] International Court Act 2001 (ICA 2001), s 56.

crimes committed by members of the organisation are attributable to them where certain conditions of control exist.[7] Furthermore, the ICC has also recognised forms of indirect co-perpetration attributing criminal responsibility to horizontally connected organisation leaders for crimes committed by members of organisations for which one of them is vertically responsible.[8]

In contrast, the idea of joint principals in England and Wales is much narrower. The criminal law of England and Wales places considerable emphasis on the notion of voluntary choice. In part, this arises from a strict and narrow approach to causation, the leading case on point declaring[9] that:

> The criminal law generally assumes the existence of free will. Generally speaking, informed adults of sound mind are treated as autonomous beings able to make their own decisions how they will act ... Thus [X] is not to be treated as causing [Y] to act in a certain way if [Y] makes a voluntary and informed decision to act in that way rather than another.

Thus, both (or more) joint principals must act together to produce the *actus reus* jointly. For co-perpetration, each must commit some part of the *actus reus* themselves. The law does not recognise the expansive forms of co-perpetration developed by the ICC from Article 25(a) noted above. Insofar as large-scale commission by collective action is criminalised in the general part of the law of England and Wales, it is done through the standard forms of secondary/accessorial liability and/or inchoate offences.

Secondary Participation/Accessorial Liability

The basis for secondary or accessorial liability in its traditional form is set out in a nineteenth-century statute[10] which criminalises aiding, abetting, counselling or procuring the commission of an offence. The *actus reus* can take various forms, but, with the exception of procurement, there is no need for any aiding or abetting to be substantial or significant. If there is factual assistance, or the principal receives the abetment, that suffices. Indeed, in certain circumstances, omissions suffice for liability so long as the secondary party had a power or duty to control the actions of the principal.[11] This may be thought to have some overlap with command responsibility in international criminal law, but it should be noted that omissions have only, so far, been held to amount to complicity where the secondary party is present at the scene of the offence, which is quite a limitation on it.[12] In any event, specific provision is made in the International

[7] *Prosecutor v Katanga and Ngudjolo Chui* [2008] ICC PTC I, [500]–[510].
[8] ibid; *Prosecutor v Lubanga* [2007] ICC PTC I.
[9] *Kennedy (No 2)* [2007] UKHL 38.
[10] Accessories and Abettors Act 1861 (AAA 1861) s 8.
[11] *Du Cros v Lambourne* [1907] 1 KB 40.
[12] *Tuck v Robson* [1970] 1 All ER 1171.

Court Act 2001, which expressly incorporates command responsibility,[13] as per Article 28 of the Rome Statute as a form of accessorial liability for the purposes of domestic prosecution of Article 5 offences.[14] For all other circumstances, it is the traditional principles of England and Wales which apply.

Turning to the traditional principles for the mental element of complicity, the basic rules are that the secondary party must intend to aid, abet, counsel or procure the principal's conduct; they must know the essential matters/facts of the offences aided, abetted etc; and they must intend that the principal carry them out with the requisite *mens rea*. As for knowing the essential matters that make up the offence, it is not necessary that every fact be known, nor is it necessary that a defendant knows the conduct in question is a crime. However, the traditional position was that they must know the essential matters which constitute the offence which the defendant is intending to assist or encourage and intend to aid and abet that.

These traditional principles expand the scope beyond the very narrow confines of joint principals. Although they require direct and explicit connections with the action of the principal in terms of the accessory's conduct, and their intentions and knowledge in respect of the object of their aiding, abetting etc, the fact that there is no requirement that this be substantial, significant or essential to the commission of the crime by the principal catches many different forms of contribution. Nonetheless, without more, the traditional principles of England and Wales were unlikely to operate to attribute criminal liability in respect of behaviour not somehow directly aided/abetted etc. in some way. Thus, of particular importance was the judicial expansion of accessorial liability in situations referred to as joint enterprise/common purpose liability[15] where the substantive law was developed so that a person would be liable as an accessory for a principal's commission of Crime B, if the secondary party and the principal entered into a 'joint enterprise' to commit Crime A, and the secondary party foresaw the possibility that the principal would commit crime B. This was the version of the law at the time of the enactment of the international criminal Court Act 2001, but this has now been rejected by the decision of the UK Supreme Court in *Jogee*,[16] where the Court declared the 'error was to equate foresight with intent to assist'[17] and held that in addition to an agreement between the parties on a common criminal design, the accessory must *intend* to assist the principal in the commission of crime B (not merely *foresee* that it might happen).

[13] ICA 2001, s 65.

[14] ibid s 65(4). See the discussion in R Cryer and O Bekou, 'The Core Crimes and ICC Cooperation in England and Wales' (2007) 5 *Journal of International Criminal Justice* 441, 446.

[15] This expansion was first made by the Judicial Committee of the Privy Council in *Chan Wing-Siu v The Queen* [1985] AC 168 and was developed in later cases, including most significantly by the House of Lords in *R v Powell and R v English* [1999] AC 1.

[16] *R v Jogee* [2016] UKSC 8.

[17] ibid [87].

The position prior to *Jogee* did bear similarities to the law of joint criminal enterprise in international criminal law before the tribunals and its attenuated accessorial equivalent in Article 25(3)(d) of the ICC Statute. However, it should be noted that, in spite of these similarities, all the cases that dealt with this form of liability in England and Wales did so on the basis that both parties were present at the scene of the crime, whereas for other manifestations of complicity the courts traditionally took the view that presence or absence does not matter in relation to complicity.[18] Furthermore, when the relevant case law of the ICC is considered, it is clear that there can be overlap between cases in terms of the expansive form of direct and indirect forms of co-perpetration which the ICC regime recognises and forms of complicity pursuant to a common plan as set out in Article 25(3)(d) and, in the case of the former, an acceptance that the common plan does not need to be to commit a crime, but awareness of the risk that implementing the common plan (which is specifically directed at the achievement of the non-criminal goal) will result in the commission of the crime.[19] Furthermore, the England and Wales version, being a form of complicity, required that the perpetrators (ie, those who pull the trigger) had to be members of the joint criminal enterprise, whereas this is not an essential factor in all versions of joint enterprise in international criminal law. What is thus very notable is that the (conscious or otherwise) ideal-type of joint enterprise in the England and Wales context was a relatively small group, often engaging in relatively spontaneous violence, rather than a situation of system or macro-criminality.[20] The change effected by *Jogee* serves to reinforce that position in practice. This means that this part of the general principles of the law of England and Wales will catch a very different type of offender than would be the case applying the equivalent principles from international criminal law. Arguably, this is not a mere instrumental difference, but one which reflects a different approach in principle as to what the relevant criminal wrong is.

Inchoate Offences

The law of England and Wales recognises general inchoate offences which either are not provided for in the Rome Statute or, to the extent that they are, are recognised only in a much more limited and restricted form. Thus, there is no generally operating equivalent of the British inchoate crime of conspiracy in international criminal law for war crimes or crimes against humanity, and although the International Criminal Tribunal for the Former Yugoslavia (ICTY) and International Criminal Tribunal for Rwanda (ICTR) statutes criminalised

[18] *R v Rook* [1993] 2 All ER 955.

[19] *Prosecutor v Lubanga* [2007] ICC PTC I, 348.

[20] On the latter, see A Nollkaemper and H van der Wilt (eds), *System Criminality in International Criminal Law* (Cambridge University Press, 2009).

conspiracy to commit genocide,[21] the offence is not included in the ICC Statute.[22] The British offence consists of agreeing with any other person or persons to pursue a course of conduct which, if the agreement is carried out in accordance with their intentions, will necessarily amount to or involve the commission of any offence or offences by one or more of the parties to the agreement.[23] This bites much earlier than complicity, since the offence is committed as soon as agreement is entered into and, of course, there is no need for the offence agreed to be committed, or indeed for any steps to be taken towards completing it.

Furthermore, in addition to conspiracy (and attempt),[24] the law of England and Wales recognises a collection of (relatively new) inchoate versions of assisting or encouraging offences, which are in effect forms of attempted complicity. This is a complex set of offences, but significantly (and controversially) they cast the net very wide.[25] Thus, one version of the offence criminalises doing an act capable of encouraging or assisting the commission of an offence or offences, believing it will encourage a person to commit the conduct constituting the offence(s), whilst being reckless as to whether they will do so with the requisite fault for the offence(s).[26] Even more controversially perhaps, the law of England and Wales permits various forms of double-inchoate liability. So, for example, it is an offence to do an act which is capable of assisting or encouraging others to conspire with or do an act which is capable of assisting or encouraging others to commit an offence or offences.[27]

In principle, then, all these inchoate offences apply to the Article 5 of the Rome Statute offences when prosecuted before British courts and, as noted above, they contemplate criminal liability attaching to inchoate versions of those offences which simply do not exist for the purposes of prosecution before the ICC.

IMPLICATIONS FOR THE NOTION OF GENERAL PRINCIPLES OF CRIMINAL LIABILITY IN INTERNATIONAL CRIMINAL LAW

The brief survey of the law in England and Wales demonstrates that the approaches available in the general part within the domestic British context are in certain key respects significantly narrower, and in others broader, than those applicable

[21] See also Article 3(b) of the Genocide Convention.

[22] R Cryer, H Friman, D Robinson and E Wilmshurst, *An Introduction to International Criminal Law and Procedure*, 3rd edn (Cambridge University Press, 2014) 381.

[23] 'Or 'would do so but for the existence of facts which render the commission of the offence or any of the offences impossible': Criminal Law Act 1977, s 1.

[24] Section 1 of the Criminal Attempts Act 1981 criminalises 'doing an act which is more than merely preparatory to the commission of the offence' with the intention to commit the offence.

[25] Serious Crimes Act 2007 (SCA 2007), ss 44–48.

[26] ibid s 46.

[27] See D Ormerod and J Child, *Smith, Hogan and Ormerod's Essentials of Criminal Law*, 5th edn (Oxford University Press, 2019) 270, which very usefully sets out the various possibilities and combinations of double-inchoate offences available in Table 11.9.

in the international criminal law context. Domestic law has a categorically different approach to perpetration – a difference which is one of principle and has the practical consequence that by definition limits the range of conduct which can be aided, abetted, counselled or procured. Although accessorial liability expands the scope of collective criminality caught, and this was especially so before the *Jogee* decision, there remained and remain important differences of detail between the British and ICC systems, some which may lead to very different forms of criminal liability being applied to persons in comparable situations in each system. These differences no doubt reflect nuances of the discrete systems themselves, but may be significant when the treatment of the same set of facts/circumstances is compared in respect of the different ways in which it will be handled by each system. Perhaps the same point might be made about the role which inchoate offences play in the English system in facilitating an expansive approach towards 'collective criminality'. However, here we can say very clearly that the English regime includes a range of types of liability which are simply not available in any form whatsoever to the ICC prosecutor and Court. They are applied as a piece within the criminal law in general without any thought to accepted norms in the field of international criminal law or whether as a matter of principle international crimes require any different approaches.

Therefore, even though the definition of the international criminal law offences prosecutable in British courts may be the same, the differences in the relevant general principles mean that in effect, individual criminal liability may be unalike depending on whether the individual is prosecuted in a domestic court, applying domestic general principles to Rome Statute offences, or in the ICC (or other analogous forum) applying the relevant general principles of international criminal law to those offences. Furthermore, any changes, qualifications and enhancements made to the British general part applying across the board will apply to international criminal law crimes without any consideration of whether particular or unique requirements might justify treating them differently.

This is not necessarily a situation of British exceptionalism in the face of an otherwise universal uniform approach, since the Rome Statute does not require that a particular approach to implementation be adopted (and indeed states have not adopted such an approach). The statute is concerned with the jurisdiction of the ICC and is not framed in the same way as transnational criminal treaties which require states to implement them through their national law in accordance with specified provisions in those treaties. Nor is it necessarily inconsistent with any of the other strict legal requirements of the ICC regime, or the underlying principles upon which it is based. The Rome Statute provides that the Court's jurisdiction 'shall be complementary to national criminal jurisdictions'[28] and the complementarity regime there established gives priority to national criminal

[28] Article 1.

proceedings through a range of specific and interrelated mechanisms.[29] Thus, Article 17 provides that a case is inadmissible before the ICC where it is being investigated or prosecuted by a state which has jurisdiction over it, or has decided not to prosecute where that decision is not characterised by 'unwillingness' or 'inability' to do so. 'Case' for this purpose encompasses both the person and the conduct,[30] and as regards the latter, the jurisprudence indicates that this is concerned with substance – ie, imposition of criminal responsibility for substantially the same conduct – rather than legal characterisation.[31] As such, the extent to which the British regime may characterise the criminal responsibility arising in a different way is not necessarily a problem in terms of the strict legal requirements and is not inconsistent with the internal logic of this system as explained by Philippe Kirsch, the ICC's first President: 'if a national judicial system functions properly, there is no reason for the ICC to assume jurisdiction'.[32] Insofar as the British regime may catch behaviour which is not caught at all by the ICC regime, whilst some may point to it as the legitimate exercise of domestic sovereignty in the realm of criminal law, it may, as Rob Cryer has noted, constitute an 'illegal assertion of jurisdiction under international law' if not supported by some other treaty or customary rule.[33]

However, even if it does not, it should give us some pause for thought concerning claims to universality, and approaches to general principles within that context, from the prospective of criminal law theory, and rule of law considerations bearing upon consistency and substantive fairness. For example, in principle there is a key difference between imposing criminal liability on the basis of conduct which constitutes completed and inchoate offences, since in the case of the latter, liability arises for engaging in that conduct without the harm or substantive offence intended or feared necessarily being realised.[34] There may be less of a principled concern where liability arises by way of complicity as distinct from perpetration in common law systems which do not adopt a separate regime for those considered accomplices when compared to principals, but the same would not be the case for systems which do treat them differently. Furthermore, insofar as general principles of liability encompass rationales for their application, and an internal logic as between different types and modes of liability, the reasons or justifications for imposing liability are connected with

[29] In addition to Article 17 discussed in the text, here we may also note that Article 53 limits the power of the Prosecutor to begin investigations where Article 17 admissibility criteria are met, and Article 18 provides that where initially he concludes they are met, the Prosecutor shall 'defer to the States investigation' if having been notified by the prosecutor that he proposes to investigate, the state informs the prosecutor that it is undertaking an investigation of nationals or others within its jurisdiction with respect to crimes referred to in Article 5.

[30] *Prosecutor v Lubanga*, 10 February, ICC PTC I [31].

[31] *Prosecutor v Gaddafi and Al-Senussi* [2013] PTC I, ICC PTC [85].

[32] P Kirsch, 'Keynote Address' (1992) 32 *Cornell International Law Journal* 437, 438.

[33] Cryer (n 1) 234.

[34] JJ Child and A Hunt, 'Inchoate Offences' in P Caiero et al (eds), *Elgar Encyclopaedia of Crime and Criminal Justice* (Edward Elgar, 2024).

the claim being made about the specific form of wrongdoing being alleged. It is an issue of fair labelling both in terminology and substance.

Therefore, one view is that it might be preferable, both for reasons of principle and pragmatism, if, when enacting the International Court Act 2001, the UK had followed the approach used in New Zealand[35] and adopted the Rome Statute's provisions on general principles of criminal law for the purposes of prosecuting Article 5 offences in British courts. Of course, it is true that this would involve treating those offences differently from others in the British criminal law field and, as such, would give rise to claims of internal inconsistency as between offenders. However, arguably it is a better solution where whatever approach one adopts is likely to lead to some anomalies. As Rob Cryer noted:

> Unlike in domestic law, where the traditional image of a criminal is the primary perpetrator, such as the person who pulls the trigger, in international criminal law, the paradigmatic offender is often the person who orders, masterminds, or takes part in plan at a high level. This also reflects the fact that international crimes tend to occur against a backdrop of collective criminality.[36]

So, the argument may go, it is preferable and *justified* to employ the discrete system of general principles of liability in the international criminal law which have been developed with that context in mind. It would essentially be an example of 'special part' exception to the general part rules created for good reason. It could also be pointed out, at least within the British context, that the specific recognition of command responsibility in the International Criminal Court Act 2001 reflects in principle the need to make specific adjustments with the context of international crimes in mind. Furthermore, taking the system of criminal law of England and Wales as a whole, we may note that special part offences focused on collective and associational criminality already exist, including participating in the 'criminal activities' of an organised crime group,[37] and membership of a proscribed terrorist organisation.[38] The latter offence in particular departs (controversially) from the spirit of accepted principles, since mere membership is criminalised without any necessity of proving any link to any particular substantive offence or harm. Special provision for forms of collective criminality for the core international crimes would therefore be far from unprecedented and, unlike some of the domestic efforts, would at least be tied into a system which, though imperfect, has been constructed and developed with those very specific forms of large-scale and grave criminality in mind.

[35] International Crimes and International Court Act 2000 (ICICA 2000), s 12.

[36] Cryer et al (n 22) 353.

[37] Serious Crime Act 2015, s 45. 'Criminal activities' is defined as activities constituting an offence for which the penalty is seven years or more where the activity is carried on with a view to obtaining (directly or indirectly) any gain or benefit (which need not necessarily be financial). 'Participating' is defined as taking part in any activities which the person knows or reasonably suspects are criminal activities of an organised crime group, or will help an organised crime group to carry on criminal activities.

[38] Terrorism Act 2000 (TA 2000), s 11.

Not all will agree with such a proposal, not necessarily due to reasons of national small-mindedness, but rather because, as Rob Cryer's own scholarly work demonstrates, the framework of general principles in international criminal law is underdeveloped when compared to the extensive development of principles at the domestic level, and certain aspects of the ICC regime are less extensive than customary law, or the approach which the ICTY and ICTR countenance.[39] Rob has also noted that 'the provisions of the Rome Statute for inchoate crimes are highly parsimonious … it means that there are inchoate crimes worthy of criminalisation that are not covered'[40] and, further, 'where the Rome Statute has used language based on the Model Penal Code (MPC), there has been a failure to understand that the MPC was a careful balance between principal, complicity-based and inchoate offences. To take one without the other upsets the balance'.[41] This indeed is true. However, the English general part is not itself such a paragon of balance and coherence as to be unable to tolerate or accommodate appropriate adjustments or exceptions where there is a good reason for doing so in the case of specific type of offences. This is a fact of which Rob was very aware, given his background and expertise in domestic criminal law mentioned above. Furthermore, the issue here is not the internal coherence of domestic law on the one hand or the wants of the international system on the other; rather, it is the coherence of domestic criminalisation of international crimes *as part of* the international system of international criminal law. This issue of coherence can be approached from the perspective of instrumental and principled coherence in a criminal law sense rather than as a matter of international law obligation. The problem, as Rob himself explained, was that the general principles of criminal liability in England and Wales may be:

> [S]omewhat unsuited to dealing with large scale criminality … In many ways, this is not a surprise, for the most part, such jurisdictions have not had to deal with such offences many times. Indeed, some of the major advances in the Civil law world, such as Roxin's theorisation of system criminality only came about when German criminal courts prosecuted Nazi crimes in the 1960s.[42]

Therefore, it is not surprising that the general principles of criminal liability in England and Wales do not target the same wrongs generally as is the case with international criminal law. However, what is surprising is mechanistically applying those domestic principles where both the substantive and declared object of the exercise is, as a minimum, to criminalise domestically the same wrongs which international criminal law criminalises.

[39] See particularly R Cryer, *Prosecuting International Crimes Selectivity and International Criminal Law Regime* (Cambridge University Press, 2005).

[40] Cryer (n 1) 251.

[41] ibid.

[42] Cryer and Hunt (n 5) 104–05.

5

Laws of War as Part of English Law

ALEXANDER ORAKHELASHVILI

INTRODUCTION

THE APPLICATION OF general (customary) or treaty-based international law in the English legal system involves the constitutional relationship between courts and Parliament, including the interpretation of legislation and assessment of Parliament's legislative intention. While customary international law is generally (though not without occasional obstacles) regarded as being incorporated into English law, it is often assumed that treaties do not apply directly on the domestic plane.[1] This chapter proposes to verify some assumptions that are at times advanced as part of the 'dualist' tradition or constitutional 'orthodoxy' in the UK. It proceeds through the example of one specific area of international law: the laws of armed conflict.

For about 12 years, Rob Cryer has been a friend, colleague, mentor and, overall, a brother figure to me. Regardless of several academic disagreements, he was massively supportive of my academic career and development, one discrete aspect of which was an opportunity to regularly pick his brilliant legal and analytical mind on complex questions of international law as well as English public and criminal law.[2] Both he and I felt rather passionate on how various aspects of international law could operate in the English legal system. When starting as an early career academic at Birmingham, I had (re)discovered this area. Rob was rather insightful on analytical and practical aspects of these matters as well as on certain unpublicised matters on which he would at times gracefully utter that he 'ha[d] no footnote', and at times he would go further and reveal some discrete detail. If that would be about some untoward motive or factor that had led to adopting certain decisions in this area, he would be rather obviously uncomplimentary about that. This chapter on the operation of laws of war in English law – an area that has witnessed the overriding of certain prejudices against the direct domestic effect of international treaties without

[1] See, eg, A Orakhelashvili, *Akehurst's Modern Introduction to International Law*, 9th edn (Routledge, 2022) ch 4.

[2] For more on Rob's collegiality see, among others, Lee, ch 18 in this volume.

statutory transformation – is merely a small way in which I could thank Rob for his enormous support that not many academics would be able either to match or to repay.

DIRECT INCORPORATION OF THE LAWS OF WAR

The use of the incorporation doctrine regarding the laws of war has been premised on the positivist approach to international law, at least from the First World War onwards. In *Marie Glaeser*, the Admiralty Court (sitting as the Prize Court) decided to 'regard the [1856] Declaration of Paris … as a recognised and acknowledged part of the law of nations, which alone is the law which this Court has to administer'. In this area, and unlike creating or developing common law by precedent, the Court was not meant to pre-empt the process of consensual creation of the rules of international law. It could:

> [O]nly enunciate what it conceives to be the law of nations. If any matter of international law in controversy between nations requires to be settled by international convention, this Court cannot antecedently declare the controverted doctrine to be a part of international law.

In the same positivist spirit, the Court emphasised the jurisprudentially obvious distinction between the underlying social interests and the rules of law that apply to state conduct or regulate those social interests. The Court specified that there is no direct relation 'between guarding the safety of this commerce upon its course across the oceans in the common interest of the nations, and giving protection by special rules of international law to persons or companies who invest their moneys in shipping ventures'.[3]

A year later, the Court in *Odessa* held that the relevant international law was directly applicable on the domestic plane and that 'the law to be administered here is the law of nations, i.e., the law which is generally understood and acknowledged to be the existing law applicable between nations'. Earlier precedents handed down by domestic courts on the subject matter of the litigation in question should be treated as guides to lead and not as shackles to bind.[4]

The Privy Council in the same case has also endorsed the direct effect of international law and its impact on relevant English law. The Privy Council said that international law acknowledges the right of belligerents to seize enemy property regardless of what English law might otherwise consider to be an undue hardship to the property owner: 'War must in its very nature work hardship to individuals, and in laying down rules to be applied internationally to circumstances arising out of a state of war it would be impossible to avoid it.' Domestic law should not endorse any position that interferes with the belligerent right of

[3] *Marie Glaeser* [1914] P 218, 233.
[4] *Odessa* [1915] P 52, 61.

capture which is recognised under international law, but it can, subject to that right, lay down the rules aimed at avoiding 'as far as may be any loss to innocent parties'.[5]

As McNair has explained, 'the principle that treaties such as the Declaration of Paris and the Hague Conventions are binding upon a Prize Court without statutory authority was accepted without question and without reason given'.[6] Functions of prize courts in Britain have been traditionally exercised by the Admiralty Court. Prize courts apply international law which binds the Crown on the same terms as common law. As explained, '[f]or the purpose of the inquiry how far international law is part of the law of England, a British prize court stands … on the same footing as any other English court'. Since the eighteenth century, prize courts have regularly acknowledged the position of the law of nations as part of the common law.[7] It was said by the Privy Council in *Zamora* that: 'The Crown has no power by Order in Council to prescribe or alter the law which Prize Courts have to administer, even where that law is imperfectly ascertained and defined.' Therefore, 'an Order declaring a blockade will prima facie justify the condemnation of vessels attempting to enter the blockaded ports, but will not preclude evidence to show that the blockade is ineffective, and therefore unlawful'. This latter question fell to be ascertained by reference to international law. In practice, the approach endorsed in the prize court hardly differs from that endorsed in other English courts.

In *Krupp*, the Chancery Court addressed Article 23(h) of the 1907 Hague Regulations, which prohibits '[t]o declare abolished, suspended or inadmissible the right of subjects of the hostile party to institute legal proceedings'. With regard to the German ordinance that forbade transmission of funds to Britain and purported to cancel all liability for agreed interest during suspense of payment during the First World War, the Court said that, before the war, it was held universally across Europe that Article 23(h) made it unlawful for any state party to the Hague Convention 'to declare any right of action unenforceable or suspended by reason of the outbreak of war'. However, the German ordinance plainly intended 'to penalize particular classes of persons, and incidentally to injure the enemy countries to which these persons belong'.[8] English courts would not recognise the German ordinance 'so far as it operates to extinguish all German liability for conventional interest, as being one which is not conformable to the usage of nations'.[9]

In *Porter v Freudeberg*, the Court of Appeal has again admitted the direct effect in English law of Article 23(h) of the Hague Regulations.[10] The Court

[5] *Odessa* [1916] 1 AC 145, 161.
[6] AD McNair, 'When Do British Treaties Involve Legislation?' (1928) 9 *British Yearbook of International Law* 59, 64.
[7] H Reason Pyke, 'The Law of the Prize Court' (1916) 32 *LQR* 144, 151–52.
[8] *Krupp* [1917] 2 Ch 188, 192.
[9] ibid 194.
[10] *Porter v Freudenberg* [1915] 1 KB 857, 877–78.

held, in contrast to *Krupp* (see above), that the situation before it was not the one addressed by that provision. The Court adopted a rather literal – or seemingly at least somewhat pedantic – construction of Article 23(h) and declared that the old English law rule regarding the enemy aliens was not abrogated by that clause because the Regulations did not require this. Article 23(h) was therefore 'ineffectual because it only prevents some executive authority from declaring that rights of action are suspended, extinguished, or inadmissible'. Thus, there was no conflict between the Hague Regulations and English law, and, consequently, unlike the cases addressed above, no need to adjust the latter to the former. Article 23(h) had no application to England where there was no room for a declaration along the above lines. Instead, '[b]y the existing law of the country the mere fact of war operates *ipso facto* to suspend any rights of action which at the time of the outbreak of war any alien enemy may possess'. On that interpretation, Article 23(h) would apply to a declaration made by a belligerent party regarding a particular armed conflict or a category of enemy nationals, typically upon or after an outbreak of an armed conflict, but it would not apply to provisions of English law that operated regardless of the relevant armed conflict. Overall, the practice of English courts validates the conclusion that 'in the view of municipal courts the Hague Regulations cannot now be denied enforcement in the municipal sphere' just because no legislation has been enacted to implement them domestically.[11]

INTERNATIONAL LAW AND THE ROYAL PREROGATIVE

Historically, the scope of the royal prerogative in foreign relations has been shaped by the need to enable the Crown to act in the capacity, or within the limits, determined by international law. Sir William Blackstone has said that prerogative operates to enable the Crown to exercise its entitlements under international law.[12] As Chitty pointed out two centuries ago, '[t]he King cannot change by his prerogative of war, either the law of nations or the law of the land, by general and unlimited regulations', and consequently anything the government does by prerogative has to comply with the relevant international law, in terms of the type of or the manner in which the government's relevant measures are undertaken.[13] For instance, and along the above lines, a belligerent occupier's authority is created, or delegated to the state, by international law, and then acknowledged by domestic law and courts.[14] English law incorporates the

[11] F Morgenstern, 'Validity of the Acts of the Belligerent Occupant' (1951) 28 *British Yearbook of International Law* 291.

[12] W Blackstone, *Commentaries on the Laws of England in Four Books* (JB Lippincott Company, 1893) 251–52.

[13] J Chitty, *A Treatise on the Law of the Prerogatives of the Crown* (Butterworth & Son, 1820) 50.

[14] Morgenstern (n 11) 321.

law of occupation accordingly (the same way as the law of prize or blockade discussed above).

In *Egypt Commercial Estates*, the Court of Appeal held that the right of angary, ie, to using or destroying, subject to indemnification, a neutral state's property present in the belligerent state's territory, under general international law could operate domestically as an element of the royal prerogative. Thus, international law weighs in determining, on the domestic plane, where the relevant prerogative power derives from and what it relates to. To illustrate:

> [A] State has by International Law the right to seize the property of neutrals found within its territory, on payment of compensation. The benefit of that right rests in the Crown as the executive of the country, and conversely, the benefit of the compensation rests in the owner of the property. *There ought therefore to be a prerogative right* of the Crown to seize the property in accordance with the rules of International Law and a right in the owner to recover compensation for its seizure. (Emphasis added)[15]

A prerogative right thus operated as conferred by (and subject to the requirements of) public international law, as opposed to being identified through more concrete evidence available under domestic law.

Atkin LJ outlined a choice between the two options. One option was a wide construction of the Defence of the Realm regulations to imply the right of seizure in them, while another option was to give domestic effect to international law which permits that seizure. As the right of seizure is accompanied by the requirement of compensation, Atkin LJ was not prepared to interpret the Defence of the Realm regulations so as to avoid the award of compensation. Therefore:

> [W]here there is a well recognized conditional power to seize the property of neutrals agreeable to international usage, it would be wrong, unless no other construction is possible, to construe general words in domestic legislation, so as to confer a similar power over the goods of neutrals absolved from the condition of paying compensation, and on that ground not consonant with international usage.[16]

And this is exactly the outcome that Lord Atkin's further passage endorses:

> [O]ne of the conditions of the right of angary as recognized by international law is that full compensation shall be made to the neutral owner. I see no reason for holding that our municipal law recognizes the right to seize, but rejects the obligation to compensate.[17]

What follows from this is that the content of the war prerogative is directly informed by international law, and its impact on private rights and on the outcome of litigation is also determined based on international law. What the Court does is premised on the domestic recognition of the underlying rules of

[15] WI Jennings, 'The Right of Angary' (1927) 3 *CLJ* 49, 57–58.
[16] *Commercial and Estates Company of Egypt v Board of Trade* [1925] 1 KB 271, 293–94 (Atkin LJ).
[17] ibid 295–96.

international law. Therefore, the incorporation doctrine applies in this area in the way that the calculus of rights and obligations set by international law ought to be reflected in decisions of national courts, both regarding substance of the matter and prerogatives of the Crown.

THE DOMESTIC EFFECT OF THE 1949 GENEVA CONVENTIONS

In the area where an international treaty has been made a subject of domestic legislation, controversies could arise as to the extent to which the treaty is applicable on the domestic plane.[18] The 1957 Geneva Conventions Act has been adopted in the context of the UK's ratification of the 1949 Conventions on the laws of war.[19] Section 1 of the Act creates a criminal offence from grave breaches of Geneva Conventions. Sections 2–6 relate to prosecution of that offence. These sections do not expressly incorporate other specific provisions of the Conventions. The 1995 War Crimes (Amendment) Act has extended the approach adopted in the 1957 Act to the 1977 Additional Protocols.

Both the 1957 and 1995 Acts are subject to ordinary methods of statutory interpretation to identify what Parliament's intention was when these Acts were adopted, and how the meaning of the relevant legislative enactments should be identified. When adopting these Acts, Parliament would no doubt have been aware that the legal system has already been operating on the premise that treaties in the area here under consideration do not typically require statutory transformation into English law. Nevertheless, the discourse on the 1949 Geneva Conventions has at times witnessed suggestions to the opposite effect. One view is that the 1957 Geneva Conventions Act does not make the 1949 Conventions part of English law in their entirety. In support of such constitutional 'orthodoxy', the High Court in *Cheney v Conn* cited a reference, in *Constitutional Law* by Wade and Phillips, to '[t]reaties which, for their execution and application in the United Kingdom, require some addition to, or alteration of, the existing law'. The Court thus identified the 1957 Act as one that makes amendments to UK law and concluded that UK law is hence amended to the extent of particular provisions of the Geneva Conventions to which the Act expressly refers.[20] The Court added that '[t]he title and the preamble relied on do not make the Geneva Convention statute', because the opposite view would endorse the conclusion that the Crown has amended the domestic law by simply ratifying the Geneva Conventions.[21] However, this distinction is somewhat pedantic because in both

[18] For discussion of this, see Hunt, ch 4 in this volume.

[19] I know from Rob Cryer that the 1957 Act was adopted as the UK government felt that this arrangement should be made before the tenth anniversary of the adoption of 1949 Geneva Conventions.

[20] *Cheney v Conn* [1968] 1 WLR 242, 246.

[21] ibid 247.

cases, the real question is what Parliament had intended by adopting the 1957 Act – domestication of some or of all provisions of the Conventions – and what interpretative elements help to identify the intention of Parliament. What the Act's title and preamble states is an empirical fact that can guide towards identifying Parliament's intention as to adding to or amending the pre-existing domestic law. The point made by Wade and Phillips was about the overall need for statutory transformation of certain treaties rather than the identification of legislative intent in specific cases.

Cheney v Cohn does not go far beyond making the above claim, not least because of the legislative context that the case was addressing, namely a putative conflict between the 1957 Act and the 1964 Finance Act. This issue would probably have to be resolved the same way regardless of how many provisions of the Geneva Conventions exactly would operate directly as part of English law because a later statute would ordinarily prevail over the earlier one, owing to the implied repeal doctrine. Moreover, *Cheney v Conn* involved a rather eccentric claim that the construction of nuclear weapons is illegal because their use would conflict with the Geneva Conventions. The claim would have been hardly tenable under the Geneva Conventions, and no specific provision was cited before this Court. Hence, an argument regarding the scope of statutory incorporation of a treaty was not a key argument required to defeat that claim.

By reference to *Cheney v Conn*, Rowe and Meyer argue against McNair's point of view that 'a treaty relating to the conduct of war automatically becomes part of English law in the absence of an enabling Act'. They continue that '[*i*]*n any event*, the creation of new criminal offences requires domestic legislation. This is what the draftsman did in 1957 by including the grave breach provisions in the Act itself. The 1995 Act follows the same pattern' (emphasis added).[22]

This is a rather curious viewpoint because it presupposes a rather far-reaching outcome that, with the 1957 Act, Parliament not only stated its position on specific treaties involved in that case but also revised, by some implication, the approach that the overall legal system had adopted to the relevant international treaties beforehand, and thus unilaterally changed the distribution of authority as between courts and Parliament. This is too far-reaching a view to be sustained.[23]

Therefore, the weightiest argument that can be advanced in favour of the restrictive view of statutory incorporation of treaties in relation to both the 1957

[22] P Rowe and MA Meyer, 'The Geneva Conventions (Amendment) Act 1995: A Generally Minimalist Approach' (1996) 45 *International and Comparative Law Quarterly* 476, 477–78. Rowe and Meyer also suggest that the scope of the 1995 Act is generally co-extensive with how they see the scope of the 1957 Act, though they admit that the 1995 Act touches upon aspects other than criminalisation. However, and for our purposes at least, the scope of the 1995 Act is meant to replicate the scope of the 1957 Act, whatever that scope in fact is. Hence, I do not focus on the 1995 Act any further here.

[23] See also A Orakhelashvili, 'Parliamentary Sovereignty before and beyond Brexit' (2021) 15 *Vienna Journal of International Constitutional Law* 435.

and 1995 Acts is that the lack of express reference to substantive provisions of the Geneva Conventions (or those other than dealing with grave breaches) in sections 1–8 of the 1957 Act manifests the legislator's intention to rule out the domestic effect of those provisions. That would be an assertion based only on one element of statutory interpretation that is not validated by other elements relevant to interpretation. However, it would hardly be a rewarding exercise in statutory interpretation to treat this matter as one of mutually exclusive pointers that could, on their own, facilitate the conclusion that the legislator's intention directs us to one outcome instead of the other one. This view of 'pointers' is discredited, especially after it was rejected in *Al-Skeini* (having been upheld by dissenting Lord Bingham only), where it was held that treaty provisions not expressly mentioned in the relevant legislation can still be considered to have been domesticated by that legislation.[24] Following this approach, the legislator's intention could be identified more productively if the design and structure of the entire 1957 Act is taken into account and prioritised in the analysis.

The long title of an Act of Parliament is regarded by courts as a guide to legislative intention. Bennion explains that while not being the sole factor in interpretation or determinative of the meanings of specific provisions or prevailing over them, the long title is regarded in case law as 'the plainest of all guides to the general objectives of a statute'. It can be resorted to both when the particular provision is or is not ambiguous.[25] The choice of the 1957 Act's long title is quite telling and indicative of its legislative purpose. It does not validate the view that the Act only relates to criminalisation. Instead, it is formulated on more broad terms as '[a]n Act to enable effect to be given to certain international conventions done at Geneva on the twelfth day of August, nineteen hundred and forty-nine, and for purposes connected therewith', such as 'to make certain amendments in the law'. It could thus be understood that Parliament has performed two different, if interrelated, things: incorporating the 1949 Conventions and additionally providing for criminalisation of relevant acts as part of 'purposes connected therewith'. Nor is the long title of the 1957 Act put on such restrictive terms as is, for instance, that of the 1991 War Crimes Act ('An Act to confer jurisdiction on United Kingdom courts in respect of certain grave violations of the laws and customs of war committed in German-held territory during the Second World War'). The 1957 Act's short title, according to section 8, is simply 'The Geneva Conventions Act', as opposed to it being presented on more restrictive terms, such as 'prosecution of certain offences (or war crimes) Act', and this is clearly in contrast with the fact that the Act's substantive provisions are precisely about criminalisation and prosecution of relevant wartime offences. Hence, if Parliament wants to legislate on procedural or criminalisation issues alone, it has ample means at its

[24] *Al-Skeini v Secretary of State for Defence* [2007] UKHL 26, paras 16 and 22.

[25] F Bennion, *Statutory Interpretation* (Butterworths, 1997) 560, 652.

disposal to manifest its intention accordingly. Section 1 is titled 'Grave breaches of scheduled conventions'. The entirety of the four 1949 Geneva Conventions are scheduled with the 1957 Act, and the 1977 Additional Protocols are similarly scheduled with the 1995 Act. This scheduling was clearly not done for the purposes of mere public awareness, because the content of the Conventions is in the public domain anyway. Moreover, nothing in the text or schedules of the 1957 Act contradicts the purpose stated in the long title. Therefore, it would be unwarranted to conclude that the express provisions of the two Acts by some (and inevitably strong) implication exclude the domestic effect of anything included in the Conventions. Therefore, the outcome is that the Geneva Conventions have been fully incorporated into English law. This outcome is less far-reaching in comparison to one endorsed in earlier decisions regarding the Hague Regulations where legislative intervention was not involved at all.

THE DOMESTIC APPLICATION OF THE GENEVA CONVENTIONS AND THE ROYAL PREROGATIVE

In *Rahmatullah*, the domestic effect of the Geneva Conventions arose again before the Supreme Court.[26] The appellant in the case, Mr Rahmatullah, was transferred to US forces after being detained by British forces in Iraq in February 2004. He was then transferred out of Iraq without the UK being officially made aware of it. This was in breach of Article 45 of the Third Geneva Convention (GC3). The key issue in the case was the legal basis on which the UK had to make representations to the US about the return of Rahmatullah to the British authorities. The appellant applied for a writ of habeas corpus requiring the UK to seek his return or at least demonstrate why it could not do so. The Court treats these issues separately such that the Geneva Conventions provide the criteria for determining whether the appellant was lawfully detained, while habeas corpus operates as a consequential remedy available under English law,[27] one operating 'as of right', as Lord Scarman had put it in an earlier case.[28] Indirectly at least, the Court's approach also reflects adversely on any possible plea of non-justiciability, as the Court directly embraces treaty provisions not expressly incorporated as the basis on which the UK government's responsibilities are to be assessed and does so in the very context of the UK government's relations with a foreign government.[29]

The Supreme Court took the direct effect of the Geneva Conventions for granted, as '[t]he illegality in this case centres on the UK's obligations under

[26] *SS FCO v Yunus Rahmatullah* [2012] UKSC 48.
[27] ibid paras 74–76.
[28] ibid para 41.
[29] ibid para 53. Incidentally, the foreign act of state doctrine was also found inapplicable, owing to the central importance of the Geneva Conventions.

the Geneva Conventions'. Lord Kerr's leading speech refers to section 1(1) of the Geneva Conventions Act 1957, which makes it an offence for any person to commit, or aid, abet or procure the commission by any other person, of a grave breach of any of the Geneva Conventions. An unlawful transfer or confinement of a person constitutes a grave breach under Article 147 of the Fourth Geneva Convention (GC4) and therefore a crime under the 1957 Act. Thus, Lord Kerr concluded, the UK had to obtain a commitment from the US that prisoners transferred by British forces to the US army would be treated in accordance with GC3 and GC4.[30] However, *Rahmatullah* was not a criminal law case, and the Supreme Court was not dealing with the prosecution of any crime per se (to which, according to some views, the effect of the 1957 Act may be limited); it concerned, more broadly, the domestic effect of 'unincorporated' provisions of GC4 to determine the responsibility for and consequences of Rahmatullah's transfer.

The case also involved 2003 Memorandum of Understanding (MoU) between the UK, the US and Australia, and it enhanced the legal basis for the UK to demand Rahmatullah's return.[31] Lord Kerr held that 2003 MoU was to be implemented in accordance with GC3, GC4 and customary international law.[32] Thus, owing to the effect of Article 45 GC4, and quite independently of the 2003 MoU, the UK remained under a continuing obligation to take such steps as were available to it to ensure that Rahmatullah was treated in accordance with the Conventions and, if necessary, to demand his return. This obligation applied to the stages of transfer and of events after it.[33] It is therefore clear that *Rahmatullah* does disapprove of the *Cheney v Conn* 'orthodoxy' or narrow view on this matter. The premise on which the Supreme Court has acted could be either that laws of war treaties are domestically applicable without or regardless of any statutory incorporation, or that legislation specifically referring to a treaty's certain provisions, but not to its other provisions, will nevertheless be regarded to have domestically incorporated the relevant treaty in its entirety.

It is also against this background that Lord Phillips was rather vocal about whether it was open to 'Mr Rahmatullah [to] invoke in domestic proceedings the obligations of the United Kingdom under the Geneva Conventions' and about what it means in this context 'that section 1(1) of the Geneva Conventions Act 1957 makes it a criminal offence to be party to a "grave breach" of any of the Geneva Conventions'. Lord Phillips thought that these issues were important, but, unfortunately, they had 'not been addressed on this appeal'.[34] Nevertheless, Lord Phillips did not dissent from the Court, but wrote a concurring opinion instead.

[30] *Rahmatullah* (n 26) para 6.
[31] ibid para 17.
[32] ibid para 3 (Lord Kerr).
[33] ibid paras 11, 39.
[34] ibid paras 106–07.

A somewhat different perspective from that of the majority was adopted by Lady Hale and Lord Carnwath in their dissenting opinion about the relationship between the Geneva Convention and the MoU. They focused on factual features of the case, namely the issue of the government's actual control over the applicant, and held that the Convention did not as such give the government the control over the appellant for the purposes of habeas corpus, especially as 'the USA, unlike the UK, did not regard GC4 as applicable to the applicant, because of his alleged Al-Qaeda links'. Hence, they thought that 'the 2003 MoU is central to this issue' and was designed specifically to ensure that the UK retained control over the continuing legality of the detention. Nevertheless, 'the UK was the original detaining power', on which basis 'as such it has continuing responsibilities under GC4'. Their Lordships' conclusion was that 'the court should not rest on an inconclusive response [from the US], but should require the resubmission of the request in terms specifically relying on the UK's continuing responsibility under GC4 and its continuing rights under the MoU'.[35] Moreover, Lord Kerr's lead opinion also says that there still 'was ample reason to believe that the UK government's request that Mr Rahmatullah be returned to UK authorities would be granted'.[36] Obviously, the Convention did not go as far as requiring the impossible over and above Article 45 requirements, and the MoU was an aspect of whatever was possible or realistic in this context. It is submitted here that control over the appellant and the domestic effect of a treaty are two different issues. The latter is a normative issue of legal regulation, and the former is about whether, on the facts of the case, the agent or stakeholder in question has the capacity to do or omit doing anything that would contravene requirements operating under the Geneva Conventions and hence to be held to have violated them. The MoU was one of the ways in which UK's compliance with the Convention could be actualised. This way, the Convention had a continuing and robust regulatory effect on the government conduct.

DOMESTIC APPLICATION OF TREATIES AND THEIR IMPACT ON THE EXERCISE OF STATUTORY AUTHORITY

The *Al-Jedda* decision of the Court of Appeal[37] has endorsed the direct and somewhat reinforced effect of the 1907 Hague Regulations in English law, not simply as a guidance to determine the legality of the underlying state conduct, but also to influence the interpretation and application of section 40 of the British Nationality Act 1981, as well as of Security Council Resolution 1483 (2003), which dealt with the governance of Iraq after the 2003 US-led invasion of that country. Under section 40 of the 1980 Act, the Home Secretary could

[35] ibid paras 118, 122, 131.
[36] ibid para 40.
[37] *Hilal Al-Jedda v Secretary of State for the Home Department* [2012] EWCA Civ 358.

withdraw British citizenship from a dual UK and foreign national, provided that such a decision would not render the relevant person stateless. The matter was, quite simply, whether Iraqi domestic legislation (including, for our purposes, that enacted under the post-invasion provisional Governing Council) could be relied upon before English courts with the effect that Al-Jedda's Iraqi nationality was restored and therefore deprivation of the UK nationality would not have made him stateless.

The Court of Appeal's starting premise was that 'international law prohibits an occupying power from making fundamental changes to the laws of the occupied territory'.[38] That outcome followed from 'Article 43 of the Hague Regulations [which] is reinforced by Article 64 of the Fourth Geneva Convention'.[39] These provisions from the two treaties establish the 'normal limits of the international law of occupation' and are premised on:

> [T]he idea of the continuity of the legal system applies to the whole of the law (civil and penal) in the occupied territory and that there is no reason to infer, from the fact of express reference only to penal law, that the occupying power is not also bound to respect the civil law of the country.[40]

Hence, these two provisions confirm that 'it would be contrary to international law for an occupying power to make fundamental changes to the law of nationality of the occupied territory'.[41] The Iraq Governing Council decision had gone over and above these limits permitted to the belligerent occupier under international law.

Again, the Court of Appeal used provisions of the Hague Regulations that have not undergone statutory incorporation at all, and of the Fourth Geneva Convention which are not expressly referenced in the relevant sections of the 1957 Act. According to international law, Al-Jedda's Iraqi nationality was not restored and deprivation of his British nationality under 1980 Nationality Act would lead to his statelessness.

CONCLUSION

The above analysis has demonstrated that there is at least one area of application of international law in the English legal system which shows that certain 'orthodox' preconceptions about the domestic effect of treaties are not validated by the experience of this legal system. What is also important is that the outcome as to the direct effect of the laws of war operates similarly across the range of

[38] ibid para 50.
[39] ibid para 53.
[40] JS Pictet, *The Geneva Conventions of 12 August 1949 Commentary – IV Geneva Convention Relative to the Protection of Civilian Persons in Time of War* (ICRC, 1958) 335.
[41] *Hilal Al-Jedda* (n 37) paras 53–54, 67.

issues arising under domestic public law and common law in general, whether relating to the scope of underlying legal rights, to selection of applicable sources of law or to the range of the government's prerogative rights. Outcomes reached in specific cases are guided by the similar constitutional rationale that weighs in favour of giving direct domestic effect to international humanitarian law treaties. In addition, I have endeavoured to use here the positivist legal methodology in an impartial and evidence-based manner to which Rob Cryer was himself accustomed and recommended to others. In respect of this and many other areas of international law, he will remain for many of us a prominent example of carrying out rigorous and impartial legal research, without fear or favour.

Act II

(Re)Imagination and Continuity

6

Envisioning International Criminal Justice

PAUL ROBERTS

INTRODUCTION: DAYDREAM BELIEVERS

INTERNATIONAL CRIMINAL JUSTICE is, first and foremost, a work of visionary idealism. For most of the twentieth century, the primacy of ideals was self-evident: in the absence of live international criminal prosecutions or other concrete institutional embodiments, on either side of the *sui generis* post-Second World War tribunals, coherent conceptions of international criminal justice lived only in the fertile imaginations of law reformers, planners and dreamers.[1] Frenetic institutional innovation and rapid normative development during the 1990s[2] transformed international criminal law into a living, breathing, censuring and sanctioning system of international penal justice. Thirty years on, it is easy to lose sight of just how recently all this impressive juridical architecture existed, for the most part,[3] only in the minds of prophets and visionaries.

My contribution to celebrating Rob Cryer's extraordinary life's work in this memorial volume is concerned with the genesis of international criminal justice as a distinct disciplinary field, chiefly in response to global events and responsive institution building in the 1990s and 2000s. The discussion is anchored in one fragment of local institutional history: the launch and development of the LLM in International Criminal Justice and Armed Conflict at the University of Nottingham. Rob Cryer was intimately involved in this pioneering venture

[1] TLH McCormack, 'From Sun Tzu to the Sixth Committee: The Evolution of an International Criminal Law Regime' in TLH McCormack and GJ Simpson (eds), *The Law of War Crimes: National and International Approaches* (Kluwer, 1997); G Schwarzenberger, 'The Problem of an International Criminal Law' (1950) 3 *Current Legal Problems* 263.

[2] For an engaging tour d'horizon, see GJ Bass, *Stay the Hand of Vengeance: The Politics of War Crimes Tribunals* (Princeton University Press, 2000).

[3] The doctrinal corpus of international criminal law, such as it was, had to be reconstructed from miscellaneous suppression conventions and fragmentary municipal legal practice. See LS Sunga, *The Emerging System of International Criminal Law* (Kluwer, 1997).

and, especially in subsequent years when he also taught on the programme, actively shaped its content. In light of the novelty of the subject matter and its fresh conceptualisations and innovative modes of delivery (described below), this formative influence could not fail to animate Rob's teaching philosophy and spur the discipline-generative body of scholarship he had already begun to produce.[4]

David Sugarman suggests that legal (auto)biography 'not only appeals to a universal human interest in gossip, but answers a need within us to understand each other better'.[5] Mitigating undeniable risks of narcissism and sentimentality, I aim to synthesise more general lessons from this personal memoir. The progressive, organic and programmatic 'disciplining' of international criminal justice is a case study in the evolution of specialist legal sub-fields. It exposes the institutional preconditions for successful disciplinary formation and resilience, and showcases, in particular, the value to scholarship of research-led teaching. The following account draws on contemporary documentation (my filing cabinets), digital archive (my computer files) and first-hand testimony (personal memories), in the manner of law school oral history.[6] Rob Cryer lived the intellectual history of international criminal justice in its modern disciplinary incarnation, and I was fortunate to be one of his earliest travelling companions on the metaphorical road 'from Nuremberg to Rome'. This chapter tells the tale of how this somewhat unexpected journey began and unfolded, and what, with the benefit of hindsight, it taught me about pedagogy, collegiality, scholarship and jurisprudence.

DREAM, DREAM, DREAM: INVENTING INTERNATIONAL CRIMINAL JUSTICE

Curriculum formation and development in university-based legal education retain an enigmatic quality. Aside from box-ticking review exercises and endless redrafting of pro forma module 'specifications' and 'learning outcomes' (recited in *nomenklatura* Dalek), it is rarely discussed with much intellectual seriousness. Undergraduates studying law in the UK might easily presume that orthodox taxonomies of legal material neatly packaged into discrete 'subjects'

[4] R Cryer, 'A Commentary on the Rome Statute for an International Criminal Court: A Cadenza for the Song of Those Who Died in Vain?' (1998) 3 *Journal of Armed Conflict Law* 271; R Cryer 'The Boundaries of Liability in International Criminal Law, or "Selectivity by Stealth"' (2001) 6 *Journal of Conflict and Security Law* 3; R Cryer, 'A "Special Court" for Sierra Leone?' (2001) 50 *ICLQ* 435. For further discussion, see van Sliedregt, ch 10 in this volume.

[5] D Sugarman, 'From Legal Biography to Legal Life Writing: Broadening Conceptions of Legal History and Socio-legal Scholarship' (2015) 42 *Journal of Law and Society* 7, 8.

[6] *cf* L Dingle, 'Legal Oral Histories in the Cambridge ESA: Some Examples of Researching Personal, Institutional and Social Developments' (2019) 19 *Legal Information Management* 192; G Parry, 'Is Legal Biography Really Legal Scholarship?' (2010) 30 *Legal Studies* 208; F Cownie, *Legal Academics: Culture and Identities* (Hart Publishing, 2004).

have existed, more or less in their currently recognisable form, for many decades if not centuries. Academic law tends to live in the now, with pervasive disciplinary amnesia.[7]

The standard law school curricular sub-divisions betray few hints of their deliberate creation through the modern 'textbook tradition'.[8] These texts were written by scholar-teachers seeking to cater to rapidly expanding university-based legal education, a project which gathered momentum in the wake of the influential Robbins Report in 1963[9] and was further catalysed by the creation of another cohort of 'new' universities after 1992.[10] The sprawling, undisciplined realities of law in practice had to be reduced, reordered and repackaged to meet the pragmatic demands and pedagogical objectives of law teachers and their students. And so, the familiar law school diet of 'criminal law', 'law of contract', 'torts' and the like came into being, selectively sampling primary materials and only faintly echoing the day-to-day realities of legal practice.

The value and importance of placing law in context,[11] and of associated pedagogical developments such as clinical legal education,[12] are nowadays taken as read in UK law schools. In this atmospheric sense at least, 'we are all socio-legal now'.[13] Yet no reductive criticism of traditional law teaching is implied. On the contrary, the vision, skill and industry of these textbook-writing disciplinary architects should be recognised and celebrated. If law school were merely professional 'trade' education, designed and delivered as training for legal practice, it would barely deserve its place in the modern university. My point is simply that the disciplinary contours of contemporary legal education are more recent and selective than most law students ever appreciate, and few law teachers typically pause to acknowledge. After all, the entire system of university legal education,

[7] P Goodrich, 'R.I.A. to R.A.E.: Aporia and Amour Propre in the Legal Academy' (2006) 15 *Social & Legal Studies* 129.

[8] D Sugarman, 'Legal Theory, the Common Law Mind and the Making of the Textbook Tradition' in W Twining (ed), *Legal Theory and Common Law* (Wiley-Blackwell, 1986).

[9] Committee on Higher Education, *Report* (Cmnd 2154, Her Majesty's Stationary Office, 1963) (describing the immediate need for expansion in university places as 'an emergency of the same importance as the emergency produced by demobilisation after the last war and demanding the same type of extraordinary measures to meet it').

[10] Further and Higher Education Act 1992, s 77. The term 'new' university was recycled throughout the course of the twentieth century to apply to successive phases of development in British higher education. The University of Nottingham, formally founded in 1948, is arguably the oldest 'new' British university, closer in time to the 1960s plate-glass and concrete campuses than to the nineteenth-century civic 'red bricks'.

[11] R Pound, 'Law in Books and Law in Action' (1910) 44 *American Law Review* 12; KN Llewellyn, 'Law and the Social Sciences – Especially Sociology' (1949) 62 *Harvard Law Review* 1286.

[12] R Cranston, 'Law and Society: A Different Approach to Legal Education' (1978) 5 *Monash University Law Review* 54.

[13] F Cownie and A Bradney, 'Socio-legal Studies: A Challenge to the Doctrinal Approach' in D Watkins and M Burton (eds), *Research Methods in Law*, 2nd edn (Routledge, 2017); *cf* R Collier, '"We're All Socio-legal Now?" Legal Education, Scholarship and the "Global Knowledge Economy" – Reflections on the UK Experience' (2004) 26 *Sydney Law Review* 503.

at least in the common law world,[14] was constructed essentially from scratch from the late nineteenth century onwards.[15]

Curriculum development has, in reality, always been a routine and continuous part of law teaching. New law school 'subjects' have been added to augment the curricular core on a rolling basis, responsive to the changing complexion of law in politics, society and culture.[16] Family law, employment law, European law, environmental law, public international law and human rights law readily spring to mind as significant additions to UK law schools' disciplinary offerings during the post-Robbins period. An emergent specialism in international criminal justice would later follow a similar institutional dynamic and trajectory.

When I first encountered Rob Cryer at the University of Nottingham in the mid-1990s, there was no International Criminal Court (ICC), the jurisdictional competence of United Nations Security Council ad hoc tribunals remained highly contentious,[17] and the International Criminal Tribunal for the Former Yugoslavia (ICTY) had yet to conclude a single trial. Having graduated from the LLM in International Law and Armed Conflict in 1996, Rob had begun his PhD research on international criminal prosecutions,[18] which he would eventually work up into his first published monograph.[19] In those days, any mention of international criminal law would typically be met with blank expressions from all but a handful of specialists. When trying to explain his research topic in casual conversation, Rob sometimes mentioned the post-Second World War Nuremberg and Tokyo international military tribunals.[20] This popular reference might garner some flicker of recognition, but only at the risk of being mistaken for a legal historian. Certainly, beyond the realms of public international law,

[14] D Sugarman, 'Making Respected Gentlemen out of Law Professors: A Commentary on Albert Venn Dicey, Can English Law Be Taught at the Universities?' in I Löhr, M Middell and H Siegrist (eds), *Kultur und Beruf in Europa* (Franz Steiner Verlag, 2012); RC van Caenegem, *Judges, Legislators and Professors: Chapters in European Legal History* (Cambridge University Press, 1987).

[15] W Twining, *Blackstone's Tower: The English Law School* (Sweet & Maxwell, 1994) (observing that 'the modern English law school is in most important respects a post Second World War creation', with the caveat that '[a]s late as 1900 most of the academic subjects we know today had either barely been accepted in the university or had not been invented'); S Sheppard, 'Casebooks, Commentaries, and Curmudgeons: An Introductory History of Law in the Lecture Hall' (1997) 82 *Iowa Law Review* 547.

[16] Also see Wade, ch 8 in this volume.

[17] C Warbrick and P Rowe, 'The International Criminal Tribunal for Yugoslavia: The Decision of the Appeals Chamber on the Interlocutory Appeal on Jurisdiction in the *Tadic* Case' (1996) 45 *ICLQ* 691 (observing that '[t]he significance of the decision of the Appeals Chamber cannot be underestimated' and asking rhetorically: 'What if it had reached the opposite conclusion? Would the lights have been turned out and the microphones switched off?'); H Fox, 'The Objections to Transfer of Criminal Jurisdiction to the UN Tribunal' (1997) 46 *ICLQ* 434.

[18] Completed as R Cryer, *Towards an Integrated Regime for the Prosecution of International Crimes* (2000), available at: https://eprints.nottingham.ac.uk/11305.

[19] R Cryer, *Prosecuting International Crimes: Selectivity and the International Criminal Law Regime* (Cambridge University Press, 2005).

[20] This proved to be an enduring research interest: see N Boister and R Cryer, *The Tokyo International Military Tribunal: A Reappraisal* (Oxford University Press, 2008).

'Nuremberg'[21] was regarded as an arcane topic of merely antiquarian interest. I was insulated from this widespread misconception only through accidental proximity with Nottingham's well-established tradition in teaching and research on the international law of armed conflict. I had it directly from Hilaire McCoubrey[22] that individual criminal responsibility for war crimes was a topic of contemporary legal salience, if only in the jurisdictionally discrete and – as a law school subject – marginal context of military justice.

Disciplinary specialisms may arise from law teachers' imaginative responses to events in the world, but they develop, thrive and endure only through institutionalisation. Concrete expressions of institutionalisation are manifold and, for the most part, mutually reinforcing. They include specialist modules, degree programmes, journals, societies and associations, research centres and, of course, textbooks and other dedicated resources to support teaching and its dissemination across the sector. Ideally, all of this pedagogic and discipline-forming activity will be underpinned by high-quality research and innovative scholarship, but there is no guarantee that scholarship will translate into curriculum development or that law teaching will be research-led. Harnessing synergies between research and teaching requires self-conscious choices and directed efforts. It presupposes an inclusive conception of scholarly activity in which postgraduate students, and preferably undergraduates too, are regarded as an integral part of the university research environment, making valuable contributions to the wider research ecosystem and culture.

For a masterclass in how to institutionalise a new disciplinary specialism, one need look no further than the development of human rights law at Nottingham, led by David Harris.[23] When I joined what was then the Department of Law in 1993, Harris and his colleagues were in the process of setting up what became Nottingham's flagship Human Rights Law Centre (HRLC).[24] This was closely linked to the teaching of bespoke LLM modules and a new degree pathway.

[21] JE Persico, *Nuremberg: Infamy on Trial* (Penguin, 1994); T Taylor, *The Anatomy of the Nuremberg Trial* (Little, Brown & Co, 1993). The historical 'Nuremberg' encompassed much more than the famous trial of high-ranking Nazis and political and military leadership: see M Lippman, 'The Other Nuremberg: American Prosecutions of Nazi War Criminals in Occupied Germany' (1992) 2 *Indiana International and Comparative Law Review* 1.

[22] McCoubrey left Nottingham for Hull in 1995 to assume a professorship and found the Centre that now bears his name. His death was, like Rob's, tragically premature: see N White and E Myjer, 'Editorial' (2000) 5 *Journal of Conflict and Security Law* 131; R Burchill, ND White and J Morris (eds), *International Conflict and Security Law: Essays in Memory of Hilaire McCoubrey* (Cambridge University Press, 2005).

[23] Behind which stretches a much longer departmental history establishing Nottingham's reputation as a 'legal textbook factory'. Landmark contributions to student-orientated publications include: H Street, *The Law of Torts* (Butterworths, 1955); JC Smith and JAC Thomas, *A Casebook on Contract* (Sweet & Maxwell, 1957); JC Smith and B Hogan, *Criminal Law* (Butterworths, 1965); DJ Harris, *Cases and Materials on International Law* (Sweet & Maxwell, 1973); SH Bailey, DJ Harris and BL Jones, *Civil Liberties: Cases and Materials* (Butterworths, 1980); PF Smith and SH Bailey, *The Modern English Legal System* (Sweet & Maxwell, 1984). Prominent additions to this roster since the early 1990s are too numerous to list.

[24] See www.nottingham.ac.uk/hrlc/about/index.aspx.

Although this postgraduate provision built directly on the success of Nottingham's existing LLM in International Law, a conscious decision was taken to badge both the Centre and the LLM as 'human rights law', rather than 'international human rights law', to ensure that 'human rights' would not be interpreted narrowly as a sub-specialism within public international law (PIL). The prescience of this decision would be emphatically vindicated within five years by the advent of the Human Rights Act 1998, by which time nobody could seriously think that 'human rights' was a topic of interest exclusive to international lawyers.[25] Its deliberately expansive conceptualisation and inclusive agenda attracted me to participate in the HRLC's inaugural planning meetings, despite having no PIL background whatsoever. The expanding research portfolio of the Centre and the instant success of the LLM degree programme were soon reinforced by a pioneering textbook[26] and a dedicated *Human Rights Law Review*,[27] originally published in-house by Nottingham University Press and subsequently adopted by the Oxford University Press.[28] LLM programmes are excellent breeding grounds for talented and inspired PhD students, who in time replenish and expand the ranks of legal scholars and law teachers, replicating the best features of their own student experience and enriching the disciplinary corpus with new ideas, courses and publications. One law teacher's module is, at best, a cult of personality with a temporal horizon delimited by an individual's academic career. However, once institutionalised and disseminated through degree programmes, textbooks, journals and centres, disciplinary specialisms become endowed with stabilising characteristics of mass, vitality and endurance, somewhat reminiscent of evangelical religions.

In this intellectually stimulating and creative environment, it soon occurred to me that there could and should be more to criminal law teaching in the Department beyond the conventional parameters of the undergraduate core module[29] and the more penology-orientated undergraduate elective on criminal justice and the penal system.[30] The LLM in Human Rights Law afforded an accommodating structure

[25] *cf* the range of topics surveyed in H Fenwick, R Masterman and G Phillipson (eds), *Judicial Reasoning under the UK Human Rights Act* (Cambridge University Press, 2007); A Mowbray, *Cases, Materials, and Commentary on the European Convention on Human Rights*, 3rd edn (Oxford University Press, 2012).

[26] DJ Harris, M O'Boyle and C Warbrick, *Law of the European Convention on Human Rights* (Oxford University Press, 1995). Now see D Harris, M O'Boyle, E Bates and CM Buckley, *Harris, O'Boyle, and Warbrick: Law of the European Convention on Human Rights*, 5th edn (Oxford University Press, 2023).

[27] Launched in 2001: see www.nottingham.ac.uk/hrlc/publications/humanrightslawreview.aspx.

[28] See www.academic.oup.com/hrlr. Now in its 24th volume, the current Editor-in-Chief is Dominic McGoldrick, and scholars with a Nottingham connection remain very well represented on the Editorial Board.

[29] See also P Alldridge 'What's Wrong with the Traditional Criminal Law Course?' (1990) 10 *Legal Studies* 38; N Lacey, C Wells and D Meure, *Reconstructing Criminal Law: Text and Materials* (Weidenfeld, 1990); C Sumner (ed), *Censure, Politics and Criminal Justice* (Open University Press, 1990).

[30] M Cavadino and J Dignan, *The Penal System: An Introduction*, 2nd edn (Sage, 1997); A von Hirsch and A Ashworth (eds), *Principled Sentencing: Readings on Theory and Policy*, 2nd edn (Hart Publishing, 1998).

for injecting elements of criminal justice into masters-level teaching. As originally conceived and first offered in 1996, my 'Comparative Criminal Justice' module was a (benign) trojan horse for smuggling material on penal theory and domestic criminal process into an overarching degree programme, still at that point styled the 'LLM in International Law'. With the benefit of classroom experience, and in response to jurisprudential developments in the wider world, the module offerings progressively became more relevant, focused and conceptually coherent. I split off the theoretical material into a dedicated module on the Philosophical Foundations of Human Rights and Criminal Justice.[31] The criminal process content forked in two directions. First, a module on Fair Trials, Human Rights and Criminal Justice took criminal adjudication as a locus for productive engagement between overlapping, though still largely siloed and estranged, 'criminal justice' and 'human rights' literatures.[32] A second module on comparative criminal justice limped on for a while with small but enthusiastic cohorts, before being rebranded, refreshed and relaunched in 2009 as 'Globalisation and Criminal Justice'.

Co-taught with Dirk van Zyl Smit, and as a consequence tilted more towards transnational criminal justice, penal systems and policy transfers, the 'Globalisation' module ran for six years.[33] From my perspective, it was highly successful both as a vehicle for expanding disciplinary horizons and recruiting healthy numbers of students. An average of 5–10 annual enrolments for 'Comparative Criminal Justice' instantly became 25–30 for 'Globalisation'. The power of effective (including intramural) advertising in postgraduate legal education should not be underestimated; no matter how engaging and relevant a module's content, coverage and approach, students will never experience it unless they are first enticed to walk through the door. Leveraging events in the news is one surefire way of generating student interest: our module specification name-checked Julian Assange and the WikiLeaks scandal, then attracting widespread media headlines.[34] Whilst a globalisation-orientated syllabus promised to 'investigate issues that cut across national borders and territorial boundaries and shed new light on the fundamental questions of contemporary criminal justice, in theory, policy and practice', the module retained substantial comparative elements

[31] In fact, it was originally just 'Philosophical Foundations of Criminal Justice', but after several years, I realised that (Western) moral and political philosophy could provide a shared foundation for human rights more broadly conceived, without necessarily filtering the arguments and analysis through a narrower penal lens. The rebranded module was more inclusive and expanded student choice (and, in a sense, repaid some of my debt to the broad conception of 'human rights' that had opened the door to criminal justice teaching on the LLM in the first place).

[32] The same methodological premise inspired P Roberts and J Hunter (eds), *Criminal Evidence and Human Rights: Reimagining Common Law Procedural Traditions* (Hart Publishing, 2012).

[33] It was cut short at the height of its popularity when Dirk moved on to become Head of School.

[34] See, eg, A Ward, 'Swedish Prosecutors Seek to Interview WikiLeaks Founder', *Financial Times*, 26 August 2010; C Philp, 'New Spying Claim against Assange: WikiLeaks Founder Could Be Extradited to US', *The Times*, 24 December 2011. Now see J Lawless, 'WikiLeaks Founder Assange Starts Final UK Legal Battle to Avoid Extradition to US on Spy Charges', *The Independent*, 20 February 2024.

carried over from legacy teaching. This design feature will not surprise readers already convinced that comparative perspectives and methodology must be integral to robust transnational, international and global analytical frameworks. My own experience during these first two decades of masters-level teaching was that I never had any difficulty in encouraging student engagement with comparative topics and literature, *provided that the label itself was downplayed or, preferably, avoided altogether*;[35] which does, alas, tend to corroborate comparative legal scholars' frequent complaint that ill-informed preconceptions of their subject drive students (and other scholars) away.[36] At any rate, 'globalisation' as an organising concept appears to have captivated parts of the postgraduate student market that 'comparative criminal justice' evidently could not reach.

The final seminar of the 'Comparative Criminal Justice' module in its original format was interrogatively titled 'International Criminal Justice?' At this embryonic stage, my thinking on the subject had barely progressed beyond formulating that question. I had noticed a recent uptick in literature putting the prospect of systematising international criminal justice on the agenda for discussion. By now fully immersed in his doctoral research, Rob was a receptive sounding board and expert informant, sharing his already voluminous knowledge of the history of international criminal proceedings and pointing me in the direction of additional reading material.[37] I was also curious about the place of European law in this novel configuration, since it was obvious that neither EU law[38] nor European human rights law[39] could be considered parts of domestic criminal law as conventionally conceived. Institutionalisation of disciplinary innovation is always a team game, and at Nottingham, I was fortunate to be surrounded by colleagues with expertise in just about every aspect of international law. In particular, Nigel White had written his PhD under David Harris'

[35] One student memorably told me at the end of the term that they had been amazed by how interesting and relevant comparative criminal justice turned out to be, having chosen the module originally because 'it was the only option timetabled on Friday afternoons, when I needed to be on campus anyway'.

[36] *cf* VV Palmer, 'Insularity and Leadership in American Comparative Law: The Past One Hundred Years' (2001) 75 *Tulane Law Review* 1093; B Markesinis, 'Comparative Law: A Subject in Search of an Audience' (1990) 53 *MLR* 1; G Frankenberg, 'Critical Comparisons: Re-thinking Comparative Law' (1985) 26 *Harvard International Law Journal* 411.

[37] Prescribed reading for the seminar included: R Bhattacharyya, 'Establishing a Rule-of-Law International Criminal Justice System' (1996) 31 *Texas International Law Journal* 57; TLH McCormick and GJ Simpson, 'A New International Criminal Law Regime?' (1995) 42 *Netherlands International Law Review* 177. See also C Warbrick, 'International Criminal Law' (1995) 44 *ICLQ* 466; P Akhavan, 'Punishing War Crimes in the Former Yugoslavia: A Critical Juncture for the New World Order' (1993) 15 *Human Rights Quarterly* 262.

[38] R Guldenmund, C Harding and A Sherlock, 'The European Community and Criminal Law' in P Fennell, C Harding, N Jorg and B Swart (eds), *Criminal Justice in Europe: A Comparative Study* (Oxford University Press, 1995). Now see K Ambos, *European Criminal Law* (Cambridge University Press, 2018).

[39] B Swart and J Young, 'The European Convention on Human Rights and Criminal Justice in the Netherlands and the United Kingdom' in P Fennell, C Harding, N Jorg and B Swart (eds), *Criminal Justice in Europe: A Comparative Study* (Oxford University Press, 1995).

supervision[40] and was already an established authority on UN institutions and collective security law;[41] moreover, my contemporary Dino Kritsiotis specialised in international humanitarian law (IHL). When I broached with Dino and Nigel the possibility of launching an LLM in International Criminal Justice, both wanted to hear more. The proposal was intellectually coherent, inasmuch as 'penal justice', 'policing', 'criminalisation', 'criminal responsibility' and so on could serve as unifying themes and analytical heuristics comfortably encompassing both domestic and international criminal proceedings. However, to avoid confusing and wasteful duplication, the new programme would inevitably supersede the established degree specialism in International Law and Armed Conflict. In other words, Dino and Nigel had vested interests in existing LLM teaching, whereas I had nothing to lose and everything to gain from major structural redesign. Some effort would naturally be required to persuade colleagues to share my vision and to turn theoretical hunches into an elaborated plan for a deliverable programme.

A charm offensive was launched and, with a few minor hiccoughs and temporary setbacks along the way, the campaign was won. As memorialised in a report to the departmental (general) meeting in October 1997, '[a]fter lengthy and wide-ranging discussion, a meeting of relevant teachers … concluded that the proposal to relaunch the LLM in International Law and Armed Conflict as an LLM in International Criminal Justice and Armed Conflict was supported on intellectual, educational and pragmatic grounds'.[42] With the Head of Department's support,[43] the proposal was duly approved in full committee and authorised to be advertised for commencement in the autumn of 1998. It would comprise six modules, split evenly between 'criminal justice options'[44] and 'armed conflict options',[45] and would require candidates to choose at least one option from each side of the conjunctive '[i]n order to retain the intellectual integrity and coherence of the new degree'. Mirroring the institutional evolution of the fledgling international criminal tribunals themselves, we were up and running.

[40] ND White, *The United Nations and the Maintenance of International Peace and Security* (Manchester University Press, 1990).

[41] H McCoubrey and ND White, *International Law and Armed Conflict* (Ashgate, 1992); ND White, *The Law of International Organisations* (Manchester University Press, 1996); H McCoubrey and ND White, *The Blue Helmets: The Legal Regulation of UN Military Operations* (Dartmouth, 1996).

[42] *Proposal to Modify an Existing Specialist LLM: LLM in International Criminal Justice and Armed Conflict*, University of Nottingham, Department of Law, 30 October 1997.

[43] Geoffrey Morse, a company and tax lawyer with no particular interest in international criminal justice, but a keen sense that if junior faculty were not encouraged and supported in their aspirations, they could easily take them somewhere else. I would almost certainly have left Nottingham within five years without the opportunities afforded by LLM teaching.

[44] The criminal justice options included: International Criminal Justice; Comparative Criminal Justice; and Philosophical Foundations of Criminal Justice.

[45] The armed conflict options included: International Humanitarian Law; International Law of the Use of Force; and Collective Security Law.

IMPLEMENTATION: 'HOW YA GONNA HAVE A DREAM COME TRUE?'

The start of the 1998–99 academic year was especially keenly anticipated. The Statute for the ICC had been successfully concluded at the Rome Conference in July 1998. Rob Cryer had been in Rome for the duration, as an observer attached to the UK delegation, and returned from summer vacation brimming with enthusiasm and armed with cloak-and-dagger tales of last-minute negotiations on textual amendments between national delegations huddled in hotel rooms. By all accounts, the final acts of the Rome Conference were chaotic[46] and ultimate success in producing a treaty was by no means guaranteed.[47] Meanwhile, events in the Balkans were unfolding rapidly and regularly featured on evening news bulletins.[48] The ICTY had concluded its first contested trial in 1997,[49] but the appeal proceedings in *Tadic* were still ongoing and the trial chamber's verdict and sentence would not be confirmed until 1999.[50] In September 1998, Rwandan local politician Jean-Paul Akayesu was convicted of genocide after a contested trial lasting 20 months.[51] This was the first trial verdict to be handed down by the International Criminal Tribunal for Rwanda (ICTR) based in Arusha, Tanzania, and a landmark in international criminal jurisprudence.[52] The following month, Chile's former dictator, General Augusto Pinochet, was arrested in London in response to an international warrant alleging systematic state torture, precipitating the most high-profile extradition proceedings in many years.[53] On and off campus, a palpable buzz surrounded anything related to international criminal justice. Addressing the incoming cohort of LLM students during Induction Week in September 1998, Dino quipped that, whereas Nottingham's postgraduate programmes always aspired to be cutting-

[46] I Tallgren, 'We Did it? The Vertigo of Law and Everyday Life at the Diplomatic Conference on the Establishment of an International Criminal Court' (1999) 12 *Leiden Journal of International Law* 683; M Cherif Bassiouni, 'Negotiating the Treaty of Rome on the Establishment of an International Criminal Court' (1999) 32 *Cornell International Law Journal* 443.

[47] DJ Harris, 'Progress and Problems in Creating an International Criminal Court' (1998) 3 *Journal of Armed Conflict Law* 1.

[48] See, eg, T Judah, 'Serb Mayor's Suicide Ends Key War Trial: UN Shamed as Man Charged with Deaths of 260 Hospital Patients in Croatia Hangs Himself after Alibi was Destroyed', *The Independent*, 30 June 1998; T Walker, 'Peace in Jeopardy after Radicals Gain Ground in Bosnia', *The Times*, 17 September 1998; 'NATO Intervention is a Necessity, Not an Option', *The Independent*, 12 October 1998; M Woollacott, 'Noose Tightens for the Architects of Evil', *The Guardian*, 13 December 1998; R Cornwell, 'NATO Delivers Final Warning to Milosevic', *The Independent*, 19 January 1999.

[49] *Prosecutor v Tadic*, IT-94-1, Trial Chamber Judgment [1997].

[50] *Prosecutor v Tadic*, IT-94-1-A (Appeals Chamber), [2002] 9 IHRR 1051.

[51] *Prosecutor v Jean-Paul Akayesu*, ICTR-96-4-T, [2002] 9 IHRR 608.

[52] Particularly in relation to rape and sexual violence: see A Adams, 'The Legacy of the International Criminal Tribunals for the Former Yugoslavia and Rwanda and their Contribution to the Crime of Rape' (2018) 29 *European Journal of International Law* 749.

[53] *R v Bow Street Metropolitan Stipendiary Magistrates ex parte Pinochet Ugarte (No 3)* [2000] 1 AC 147, HL; N Boister and R Burchill, 'The *Pinochet* Precedent: Don't Leave Home Without It' (1999) 10 *Criminal Law Forum* 405.

edge, with the launch of the LLM in International Criminal Justice and Armed Conflict, we had anticipated the cut!

To the best of my knowledge, this was the first LLM in International Criminal Justice (ICrimJ) to be offered in the UK – and possibly anywhere in the world. Certainly, we were not aware of any models to emulate. Our course design and module content were innovated from the ground up. The first iterations of module seminars posed foundational questions of disciplinary constitution, normative purposes and juridical basis: what were ICrimJ's motivating ideas and ideals?[54] What is an international crime?[55] How can the (putative) existence of universal criminal jurisdiction be squared with traditional conceptions of state sovereignty?[56] What had been the UN's contribution to the project thus far?[57] What had international criminal tribunals achieved to date, and how might they develop in future?[58] Where did (international) human rights law fit into this blurry picture?[59] What about the potential contribution of supranational legal entities such as the EU?[60] Or the status of domestic criminal processes applying international norms or claiming international authority?[61] Of course, we had many more questions than answers. But formulating the right questions with focus and precision is, generally, more than half the battle in intellectual labour.

[54] SR Ratner, 'The Schizophrenias of International Criminal Law' (1998) 33 *Texas International Law Journal* 237; GP Fletcher, 'The Law of War and its Pathologies' (2007) 38 *Columbia Human Rights Law Review* 517; S Cohen, 'Crime and Politics: Spot the Difference' (1996) 47 *British Journal of Sociology* 1.

[55] G Abi-Saab, 'The Concept of "International Crimes" and its Place in Contemporary International Law' in JHH Weiler, A Cassese and M Spinedi (eds), *International Crimes of States: A Critical Analysis of the ILC's Draft Article 19 on State Responsibility* (EUI/De Gruyter, 1989); A Pellet, 'Can a State Commit a Crime? Definitely, Yes!' (1999) 10 *European Journal of International Law* 425; NHB Jørgensen, *The Responsibility of States for International Crimes* (Oxford University Press, 2000).

[56] WB Cowles, 'Universality of Jurisdiction over War Crimes' (1945) 33 *California Law Review* 177; J Paust, 'Universality and the Responsibility to Enforce International Criminal Law' (1989) 11 *Houston Journal of International Law* 337.

[57] GH Oosthuizen, 'Some Preliminary Remarks on the Relationship between the Envisaged International Criminal Court and the UN Security Council' (1999) 46 *Netherlands International Law Review* 313; T Howland and W Calathes, 'The UN's International Criminal Tribunal: Is it Justice or Jingoism for Rwanda? A Call for Transformation' (1998) 39 *Virginia Journal of International Law* 135; O Schuett, 'The International War Crimes Tribunal for the Former Yugoslavia and the Dayton Peace Agreement: Peace versus Justice?' (1997) 4 *International Peacekeeping* 91.

[58] JE Alvarez, 'Rush to Closure: Lessons of the *Tadic* Judgment' (1998) 96 *Michigan Law Review* 2031; P Akhavan, 'Justice and Reconciliation in the Great Lakes Region of Africa: The Contribution of the International Criminal Tribunal for Rwanda' (1997) 7 *Duke Journal of Comparative and International Law* 325.

[59] M Cherif Bassiouni, 'Human Rights in the Context of Criminal Justice: Identifying International Procedural Protections and Equivalent Protections in National Constitutions' (1993) 3 *Duke Journal of Comparative and International Law* 235.

[60] GA Bermann, 'Taking Subsidiarity Seriously: Federalism in the European Community and the United States' (1994) 94 *Columbia Law Review* 331; C Harding, 'The Identity of European Law: Mapping Out the European Legal Space' (2000) 6 *European Law Journal* 128; E Baker, 'Taking European Criminal Law Seriously' [1998] *Crim LR* 361.

[61] TLH McCormack and GJ Simpson (eds), *The Law of War Crimes: National and International Approaches* (Kluwer, 1997); H Arendt, *Eichmann in Jerusalem: A Report on the Banality of Evil* (Penguin, 1994).

Forty-one students formally enrolled on the ICrimJ module. LLM seminar classes were notionally capped at 30 students (most attracting fewer than 20 enrolments), but excluding enthusiastic subscribers above an arbitrary quota would have been excessively formalistic, and largely self-defeating, in this evangelical phase of popularising the module. For its inaugural seminar, scheduled in a draughty set of crumbling prefab classrooms lyrically styled 'Cherry Tree Buildings',[62] it was literally standing room only. Curious PhD students, miscellaneous Law Department researchers and window-shopping masters students yet to finalise their options swelled the attendees to well over 50. The crackling electric atmosphere in the room exceeded anything I have ever experienced in teaching, either before or since. It had always been our intention for seminars in this module to be 'triple-headed' by Dino, Nigel and me. For this inaugural occasion, we were joined at the head of the classroom by two doctoral students, or 'special guests'. The first was Neil Boister, then in the process of submitting his PhD on 'The Suppression of Illicit Drugs through International Law',[63] supervised by David Harris. Rob Cryer, supervised by Dino and Nigel, was the second.

Team-teaching in seminars was a vital part of the module design. On the premise that international criminal justice itself represented an unprecedented amalgam of international law and criminal law, the idea was that our own classroom conversations would mimic and enact evolutionary interdisciplinary encounters among previously disparate literatures, jurisprudence and theoretical frameworks. Roughly speaking, Nigel would represent the perspective of a UN institutional lawyer, Dino would advance the agenda of IHL, and I would speak for criminal law and criminal justice. This 'tournament of ideas' format, notwithstanding some pedagogical risks, served marvellously well as a vehicle for orchestrating lively discussion and wide-ranging debate worthy of our contentious subject matter. Dino, less comfortable than I am with philosophical argumentation, might tut-tut at my 'pulpit' moralising in advancing normative claims about penal justice. I would respond in kind, swatting away his (deliberately)[64] provocative remark that 'international law owns the intellectual property to international criminal justice' as tendentious disciplinary imperialism. Anxious claims to proprietorship were rife at the time.[65] Beneath

[62] Also known as 'the cowsheds', the Cherry Tree Buildings were demolished in 2004 as part of a comprehensive programme of campus modernisation, though some of the eponymous cherry trees were saved and can still be viewed in blossom to this day, if you know where and when to look.

[63] Available at: https://eprints.nottingham.ac.uk/11121; see also N Boister, *Penal Aspects of the UN Drug Conventions* (Brill, 2001).

[64] Dino assures me.

[65] 'For many decades, the study of international criminal tribunals was the jealous preserve, the mascot almost, of international lawyers … who kept the discipline of international criminal law alive, when the more worldly inclined would have dismissed it as a quaint irrelevance': see F Mégret, 'The Politics of International Criminal Justice' (2002) 13 *European Journal of International Law* 1261. This is part of a larger story about the disciplinary identity of public international law, which was then experiencing existential anxiety about the prospect of 'fragmentation' into discrete regimes and

the veneer of theatre, these exchanges were profoundly educational, not least for the teachers. Over the course of a term, I graduated from a position of near-total ignorance to a plausible *flâneur* of international law. Team-teaching this module was, incidentally, enormous fun.

The danger, of course, was that we might spend two hours jousting with each other while the students never got a look in. There may be *some* pedagogic value to spectating clashes between disciplinary perspectives thrown together in unfamiliar configurations, but active engagement is undoubtedly preferable. By my recollection, there was always at least a solid core of any given year's cohort with the diligence in preparation and confidence in self-expression to ask questions and get involved in seminar discussions. Dead air was unknown; the two-hour slot usually flew by. The calibre of students taking this module should be stressed: many have since embarked on distinguished careers in international legal practice or academia, including several who now teach their own versions of international criminal law and justice modules.[66]

That said, the unusual dialogic format did not suit every student who was exposed to it over the seven years in which multi-headed teaching was retained. One disgruntled class member wrote in a course evaluation that the teachers seemed to lack basic lecturing skills and should 'write out the main points on the whiteboard'! Some students were also perplexed by my standard disclaimer: 'I am not an international lawyer'. Did this not surely imply that I was unqualified to teach the module? But my impression is that the majority of students, on balance, did take away the primary messages (which we continually underscored in the classroom): the entire field was under construction, its parameters and content were hotly contested, and nobody was yet a bona fide expert in the interdisciplinary scholarship that its mature evolution would entail. Triple-heading or even double-heading seminars is resource-intensive. To its external credit in my estimation, the Law Department underwrote a significant chunk of this investment, and the remainder the teachers volunteered as fair quid pro quo for the fringe benefits we derived from professional development and stimulus to further research. Double-heading seminars was retained, with rotating personnel, until the 2005–06 academic year. Limited staff availability was the immediate driver behind its abandonment, but with the module now into its eighth year and boasting an evolved syllabus and course materials, team-teaching in seminars had, in any event, mostly served its intended purpose.

consequent loss of normative and disciplinary coherence: see also Report of the Study Group of the International Law Commission, *Fragmentation of International Law: Difficulties Arising from the Diversification and Expansion of International Law*, A/CN.4/L.682 (13 April 2006).

[66] Notably, Annika Jones at Exeter Law School: https://experts.exeter.ac.uk/21713-annika-jones; Hemi Mistry at Nottingham: www.nottingham.ac.uk/law/people/hemi.mistry; Roisin Mulgrew at the Irish Centre for Human Rights, University of Galway: www.universityofgalway.ie/our-research/people/law/roisinmulgrew; and Yassin Brunger at Queen's University Belfast: https://pure.qub.ac.uk/en/persons/yassin-brunger.

For its third iteration during the 2000–01 academic year, the LLM's international criminal justice offering underwent a major structural upgrade. The material comprising the original core module was reorganised and expanded into two new modules: (roughly) functionally differentiated into Foundations of International Criminal Justice, taught in the first term, and Principles of International Criminal Justice in the second. As well as expanding to accommodate the now rapidly accumulating primary sources and secondary literature, this framework afforded more seminar time for closer examination of doctrinal substantive and procedural international criminal law, alongside conceptual questions (what is 'international criminal justice'? Can a state commit a crime? What is international criminal jurisdiction?), institutional history ('From Nuremberg to the Hague') and international politics (are the Security Council's powers appropriate and legitimate? Should the US join the ICC?) towards which our initial focus had gravitated. The twin Foundations and Principles modules became the compulsory backbone of the LLM degree, obviating the need to insist that students study IHL or collective security options in order to preserve the overall coherence of the programme.

When Nigel White's teaching hours significantly reduced on becoming Head of School, Rob Cryer was his obvious replacement in the international criminal justice triumvirate. Rob co-taught Foundations of International Criminal Justice with Dino and me in the 2001–02 and 2002–03 academic years, and with Olympia Bekou and me in the following 2003–04 session. Olympia, Dirk van Zyl Smit and I designed and originally taught the companion 'Principles of International Criminal Justice' module, but it existed in this format only for two years. Olympia and Rob inherited the module content and rebranded it as 'International Criminal Law', which continues to be taught, with a predominantly juridical focus, on the contemporary LLM. Rob and Olympia concomitantly developed a new undergraduate optional 'International Criminal Law' module, which proved an instant hit and continues to thrive with large student enrolments – topping three figures in some years. In addition to introducing hundreds of Nottingham undergraduates to the specialist field of international criminal law, the experience of collaborating with Olympia in crafting and delivering this module undoubtedly influenced Rob's future teaching and scholarship, and represents a major strand of Rob's enduring institutional legacy at Nottingham.

Meanwhile, on the LLM, I persevered in teaching Foundations of International Criminal Justice, eventually single-handedly, until the 2010–11 academic year. With Olympia (and later Sandy Sivakumaran)[67] minding the doctrinal side of the shop, I reimagined the 'Foundations' module as an interdisciplinary exercise in conceptualising and researching international criminal justice. This final

[67] S Sivakumaran, *The Law of Non-International Armed Conflict* (Oxford University Press, 2012).

iteration of the module considered international criminal justice from the overlapping perspectives of global politics and international relations, jurisprudence, penal philosophy, historiography and criminology. It culminated in reflections on genocide as a liminal theme, melding together jurisprudence[68] and legal process,[69] historical[70] and criminological[71] context, survivor testimonies,[72] representations in art, literature[73] and popular culture,[74] and concluding with tentative thoughts on constitutive (inter)disciplinary questions of taxonomy,[75] scope,[76] focus[77] and ethics.[78] The module was rewarding to teach and reliably attracted over 20 students, yet I gave it up in the end – partly to concentrate on other things, but also because I sensed that I was becoming too far estranged from the institutional fabric and burgeoning jurisprudence of international criminal law and process. In the 12 years since we had launched the LLM, international criminal justice had blossomed into a full-fledged disciplinary specialism, with

[68] D Fraser, *Law after Auschwitz: Towards a Jurisprudence of the Holocaust* (Carolina Academic Press, 2005); JE Alvarez, 'Crimes of States/Crimes of Hate: Lessons from Rwanda' (1999) 24 *Yale Journal of International Law* 365.

[69] MA Drumbl, *Atrocity, Punishment and International Law* (Cambridge University Press, 2007); L Douglas, *The Memory of Judgment: Making Law and History in the Trials of the Holocaust* (Yale University Press, 2001); H Arendt, *Eichmann in Jerusalem: A Report on the Banality of Evil* (Penguin, 1994).

[70] O Bartov, 'Defining Enemies, Making Victims: Germans, Jews and the Holocaust' (1998) 103 *American Historical Review* 771; DJ Goldhagen, *Hitler's Willing Executioners: Ordinary Germans and the Holocaust* (Alfred A. Knopf, 1996); RJ Evans, *Telling Lies about Hitler: The Holocaust, History and the David Irving Trial* (Verso, 2002).

[71] W Morrison, *Criminology, Civilisation and the New World Order* (Cavendish Publishing, 2006); R Dallaire, *Shake Hands with the Devil: The Failure of Humanity in Rwanda* (Arrow Books, 2004).

[72] Y Vashem, 'Survivor Testimonies', available at: www.yadvashem.org/collections/testimonies.html; CW Mullins, '"He Would Kill Me with His Penis": Genocidal Rape in Rwanda as a State Crime' (2009) 17 *Critical Criminology* 15.

[73] T Borowski, *This Way for the Gas, Ladies and Gentlemen* (Penguin, 1992); P Levi, *The Drowned and the Saved* (Abacus, 1991).

[74] A Spiegelman, *The Complete Maus* (Penguin, 2003); P Levi, *The Black Hole of Auschwitz* (Polity Press, 2005); W Morrison, '"Reflections with Memories": Everyday Photography Capturing Genocide' (2004) 8 *Theoretical Criminology* 341.

[75] GS Yacoubian Jr, 'The (In)Significance of Genocidal Behavior to the Discipline of Criminology' (2000) 34 *Crime, Law and Social Change* 7.

[76] M Glenny, *McMafia: Crime without Frontiers* (Bodley Head, 2008); J Sheptycki and A Wardak (eds), *Transnational and Comparative Criminology* (GlassHouse Press, 2005); V Ruggiero, N South and I Taylor (eds), *The New European Criminology: Crime and Social Order in Europe* (Routledge, 1998).

[77] DO Friedrichs, 'The Crime of the Century? The Case for the Holocaust' (2000) 34 *Crime, Law and Social Change* 21; K Ericsson, 'Rape, Love and War: Personal or Political?' (2011) 15 *Theoretical Criminology* 67.

[78] K Jaspers, *The Question of German Guilt* (Fordham University Press, 2001); R Hilberg, *Perpetrators, Victims, Bystanders* (HarperCollins, 1992); A Norrie, 'Albert Speer, Guilt, and "The Space between"' in M Matravers (ed), *Punishment and Political Theory* (Hart Publishing, 1999); Z Bauman, *Modernity and the Holocaust* (Polity Press, 2000).

its own courses, textbooks,[79] journals,[80] treatises,[81] institutional structures and frontline practitioners, industriously generating ever more voluminous material for scholars to consume, editorialise and critique. This was no longer a safe space for *flâneurs* and dilettante theorising; jurisprudential muscle is built up and maintained only by putting in the doctrinal hard yards.

Beyond satisfying native curiosity in a set of juridical puzzles, my engagement with international criminal justice had been motivated by three primary considerations. First, I was determined that it should be conceptualised as a genuinely interdisciplinary – or, at least, multi-disciplinary – enterprise rather than as a sub-field of PIL. My modest contributions to the early literature stressed the salience of penal theory[82] and criminological perspectives.[83] Initially, this argument encountered some resistance and miscomprehension,[84] but it seems to be widely acknowledged nowadays, at least by perceptive observers.[85] Second, it occurred to me that whereas international criminal justice in its design phase was largely the preserve of diplomats and international lawyers, expertise in the practical conduct of criminal litigation would be at a premium once real-life criminal trials were underway. This quickly became received wisdom amongst those with direct experience of international criminal trials.[86] Third, I thought it important

[79] By the time that a secondary wave of 'companions' and 'handbooks' started to appear, the disciplinary deal was sealed: see, eg, A Cassese, *The Oxford Companion to International Criminal Justice* (Oxford University Press, 2009); BS Brown (ed), *Research Handbook on International Criminal Law* (Edward Elgar, 2011); WA Schabas and N Bernaz (eds), *Routledge Handbook of International Criminal Law* (Routledge, 2012); K Heller, F Megret, S Nouwen, J Ohlin, and D Robinson (eds), *The Oxford Handbook of International Criminal Law* (Oxford University Press, 2020).

[80] Brill's *International Criminal Law Review* first appeared in 2001, edited by Michael Bohlander and dedicated to 'the exciting task of establishing a forum for the exchange of ideas and opinions in the growing discipline of international criminal law': 'Editorial' (2011) 1 *International Criminal Law Review* 1, 3. Oxford University Press's *Journal of International Criminal Justice*, led by Antonio Cassese as Editor-in-Chief, was launched two years later with ambitiously theoretical and interdisciplinary aspirations. '[I]nternational criminal justice cannot be allowed to become a ghetto of public international law: indeed, the issues it raises are also of great interest to human rights experts and criminal lawyers, comparativists, proceduralists, penal philosophers, and criminologists': 'Editorial' (2003) 1 *Journal of International Criminal Justice* 1.

[81] A Cassese, P Gaeta and JRWD Jones (eds), *The Rome Statute of the International Criminal Court: A Commentary* (Oxford University Press, 2002); K Ambos, *Treatise on International Criminal Law* (Oxford University Press, 2013).

[82] P Roberts, 'Restoration and Retribution in International Criminal Justice: An Exploratory Analysis' in A von Hirsch et al (eds), *Restorative Justice and Criminal Justice* (Hart Publishing, 2003).

[83] P Roberts and N McMillan, 'For Criminology in International Criminal Justice' (2003) 1 *Journal of International Criminal Justice* 315.

[84] Despite professing allegiance to interdisciplinarity (and, in all probability, borrowing from me its warning against propagating intellectual ghettos) in its founding 'Editorial', the *Journal of International Criminal Justice* still managed to publish our 'For Criminology' article (with no prior notification) under the performatively othering subtitle of 'The Contribution of Other Disciplines to International Criminal Law'! Disciplinary preconceptions and assumptions operate at the level of 'unconscious bias': formative, pervasive and difficult to shake.

[85] MA Drumbl, 'Toward a Criminology of International Crime' (2003) 19 *Ohio State Journal on Dispute Resolution* 263; R Jamieson (ed), *The Criminology of War* (Ashgate, 2014).

[86] PM Wald, 'Running the Trial of the Century: The Nuremberg Legacy' (2006) 27 *Cardozo Law Review* 1559; P Murphy, 'No Free Lunch, No Free Proof: The Indiscriminate Admission of Evidence

to stress that interdisciplinary learning is a two-way street. International criminal justice should benefit from the accumulated wisdom of more established legal disciplines and scholarship at the domestic level,[87] but it may just as surely repay the compliment by enriching traditional strands of jurisprudence and legal theorising.[88] The injection of international perspectives should encourage legal scholarship and teaching to cast off their statist blinkers and adopt a more cosmopolitan outlook.[89]

A fourth preoccupation revolved around devising an original conceptualisation of 'international criminal justice' capable of accommodating the disparate variety of norms, processes and jurisdictions with a plausible claim to inclusion in its disciplinary orbit. For this mapping task, I proposed 'seven concentric circles of international criminal justice'.[90] Questions of disciplinary taxonomy and organisation naturally occupy teachers of novel subjects with no textbooks or conventional syllabi to guide them. As disciplinary specialisms become institutionalised over time, such questions may be regarded as transitional and increasingly superseded. My longstanding view is that periodic reflection on constitutive disciplinary taxonomies is essential for the continued salience and intellectual vitality of the disciplines.[91] For example, I think it would be regrettable if broad, interdisciplinary conceptions of

is a Serious Flaw in International Criminal Trials' (2010) 8 *Journal of International Criminal Justice* 539; R May, D Tolbert, J Hocking, K Roberts, BB Jia, D Mundis and G Oosthuizen (eds), *Essays on ICTY Procedure and Evidence in Honour of Gabrielle Kirk McDonald* (Kluwer, 2001).

[87] P Roberts, 'The Priority of Procedure and the Neglect of Evidence and Proof: Facing Facts in International Criminal Law' (2015) 13 *Journal of International Criminal Justice* 479.

[88] P Roberts, 'Mr. Seferovic's Pigeons: A Brief Encounter with International Criminal Justice' in P Behrens (ed), *Contemporary Challenges to Criminal Justice: Liber Amicorum for Ralph Henham* (Hart Publishing, 2023); P Roberts, 'Why International Criminal Evidence?' in P Roberts and M Redmayne (eds), *Innovations in Evidence and Proof: Integrating Theory, Research and Teaching* (Hart Publishing, 2007).

[89] P Roberts, 'Confronting the Challenges of Cosmopolitan Criminal Jurisprudence', Inaugural Lecture, University of Nottingham, 10 September 2010; P Glenn, 'Cosmopolitan Legal Orders' in A Halpin and V Roeben (eds), *Theorising the Global Legal Order* (Hart Publishing, 2009). For worked illustrations, see D Giannoulopoulos, *Improperly Obtained Evidence in Anglo-American and Continental Law* (Hart Publishing, 2019); J Hodgson, 'EU Criminal Justice: The Challenge of Due Process Rights within a Framework of Mutual Recognition' (2011) 37 *North Carolina Journal of International Law and Commercial Regulation* 308; JD Jackson and SJ Summers (eds), *Obstacles to Fairness in Criminal Proceedings* (Hart Publishing, 2018); P Roberts, 'Normative Evolution in Evidentiary Exclusion: Coercion, Deception and the Right to a Fair Trial' in P Roberts and J Hunter (eds), *Criminal Evidence and Human Rights* (Hart Publishing, 2012); K Ambos, 'The Transnational Use of Torture Evidence' (2009) 42 *Israel Law Review* 362; M Langer, 'From Legal Transplants to Legal Translations: The Globalization of Plea Bargaining and the Americanization Thesis in Criminal Procedure' (2004) 45 *Harvard International Law Journal* 1.

[90] P Roberts, 'Comparative Law for International Criminal Justice' in E Örücü and D Nelken (eds), *Comparative Law: A Handbook* (Hart Publishing, 2007).

[91] *cf* P Roberts, 'Rethinking the Law of Evidence: A Twenty-First Century Agenda for Teaching and Research' (2002) 55 *Current Legal Problems* 297; J Jackson and P Roberts, 'Beyond Common Law Evidence: Reimagining, and Reinvigorating, Evidence Law as Forensic Science' in DK Brown, J Iontcheva Turner and B Weisser (eds), *The Oxford Handbook of Criminal Process* (Oxford University Press, 2019).

International Criminal Justice were allowed to degenerate into narrow(er), doctrinally dominated, exclusionary conceptions of International Criminal Law. But I agree that preoccupations with taxonomy can become compulsive and an unhealthy distraction from more substantive work, and that a sensible division of academic labour will entrust theorists to take the labouring oar on theoretical tasks and inquiries.[92]

The advent of the first widely employed textbook is a pivotal moment in the formation of a new disciplinary specialism. A textbook is always, by implication if not design, an attempt to define the parameters, subject matter, central debates, research methods, and animating values and objectives of any juridical field. Textbook writers are the legislators of law curricula and the poets of the classroom. Antonio Cassese's *International Criminal Law*, published in 2003,[93] scooped that accolade in supplying the first course book to supplement our LLM handouts and reading lists. However, the work produced by Rob Cryer and co-authors four years later is a weightier, more considered contribution to research-led pedagogy, in my estimation. *An Introduction to International Criminal Law and Procedure*[94] is structured and written in an accessible style more obviously tailored to an upper-level student readership. Although the book concentrates on international criminal *law*, the opening chapters provide contextual scaffolding by ventilating questions of disciplinary taxonomy, normative jurisprudence and penal theory. The book's attention to highlighting procedural topics alongside substantive doctrinal analysis is another commendable feature and, hopefully, might serve to inoculate international criminal jurisprudence from the unfortunate aversion to procedural (including evidentiary) considerations, which too often infects domestic criminal law scholarship and teaching.[95] Above all, where Cassese was essentially a dyed-in-the-wool international lawyer to his core,[96] Cryer and colleagues made strenuous efforts to afford appropriate billing to the criminal law dimensions of their subject matter.

[92] P Roberts, 'Theorising Evidence Law' (2023) 43 *Oxford Journal of Legal Studies* 629.

[93] A Cassese, *International Criminal Law* (Oxford University Press, 2003). Now see A Cassese and P Gaeta, *Cassese's International Criminal Law*, 3rd edn (Oxford University Press, 2013).

[94] R Cryer, H Friman, D Robinson and E Wilmshurst, *An Introduction to International Criminal Law and Procedure* (Cambridge University Press, 2007). Now see R Cryer, D Robinson and S Vasiliev, *An Introduction to International Criminal Law and Procedure*, 4th edn (Cambridge University Press, 2019).

[95] A recurring overture with which I bent Rob's ear on more than one occasion. See also R Cryer, 'A Message from Elsewhere: Witnesses before International Criminal Tribunals' in P Roberts and M Redmayne (eds), *Innovations in Evidence and Proof: Integrating Theory, Research and Teaching* (Hart Publishing, 2007). But *cf* PM Wald, 'Rules of Evidence in the Yugoslav War Tribunal' (2003) 21 *Quinnipiac Law Review* 761, 763 ('scholars and commentators on the Tribunals appear to pay much more attention to substantive law developments than to procedure and process').

[96] As he would have it, '[i]nternational criminal law is a branch of *public international law*': Cassese (n 93) 16. See further '*In Memoriam*: Antonio Cassese (1937–2011)' (2011) 93 *International Review of the Red Cross* 1265; L Chand Vohrah, F Pocar, Y Featherstone, O Fourmy, MF Graham, J Hocking and N Robson (eds), *Man's Inhumanity to Man: Essays on International Law in Honour of Antonio Cassese* (Brill, 2003).

They insisted that '[i]nternational criminal law is double-structured, comprising both international law and criminal law. It should be appraised from the standpoints of both bodies of law'.[97] Rob rated this formative methodological commitment so significant that he enshrined it in the title of his personal chair at Birmingham, where he was 'Professor of International *and* Criminal Law' (his conjunction; my emphasis).

CONCLUSION: ANY DREAM WON'T DO

Rob Cryer's life and professional career were cruelly truncated, but this misfortune will not be readily apparent to future generations of scholars and students, who will reasonably assume that his extensive library of influential publications could have been produced only by an author active long into retirement. Though cheated in duration, Rob's timing was charmed. From *Tadic* and the signing of the Rome Statute, via the completion strategies of the ad hoc UN tribunals, to the institutionalised casework of a permanent ICC (and the sense of deflation that almost inevitably accompanies the practical frustrations of routine criminal proceedings),[98] the progression of Rob's academic career uncannily mirrored the arc of international criminal justice itself in the decades on either side of the millennium. As a new field crystallised, Rob was on hand to populate it with his prodigious generation of articles, notes and reviews. Subsequently, as the lead author of a market-leading textbook, he exerted a major influence on the shape and content of the disciplinary field of International Criminal Law as we know it today.

Whilst Rob's professorial stage was Birmingham Law School, his academic debut and early career were spent at Nottingham (aside from a brief loan spell in Manchester).[99] Besides the enduring influence of his masters year and doctoral apprenticeship, a positive experience of committed expert supervision common – one would hope – to all PhD graduates, Rob's involvement in co-teaching and developing the LLM in International Criminal Justice and Armed Conflict evidently continued to inspire his pedagogical practice and maturing scholarship

[97] Cryer et al (2007) (n 94) 12.

[98] D Luban, 'After the Honeymoon: Reflections on the Current State of International Criminal Justice' (2013) 11 *Journal of International Criminal Justice* 505; EH Ballin, 'The Value of International Criminal Justice: How Much International Criminal Justice Can the World Afford?' (2019) 19 *International Criminal Law Review* 201 (sounding 'a wake-up call for younger generations to avoid a situation in which growing cynicism about the international rule of law and international human rights, and diminishing support for multilateralism, undermine the project of international criminal justice').

[99] Tempting though it is to dismiss this interlude as more about music and football than scholarship, historical candour compels me to record Rob's avowed lifelong debt to Neil Duxbury, John Murphy and other Manchester colleagues for generous mentorship during his first lecturing post.

throughout his blossoming career. As the old Jesuit motto proclaims,[100] character and commitment are forged in the educationally formative years. But Rob would not have wanted this reflection to be maudlin or self-indulgently solipsistic: we have real ale and Joy Division for those moods. The creation story recounted in this memoir will have been worth retelling if it serves, incidentally, to inspire and inform reinvigorated cycles of creativity, ambition, social responsiveness and global vision in legal education. And there is one final twist in this tale.[101]

Ideas supply the vital creative spark driving innovation, but material conditions – as Marx taught – are equally important and often fatefully decisive. Effective vision must be *embodied*, and for disciplinary formation and development, this implies anchoring in nurturing, collegial, institutional environments. In a curious twist of fate, this tribute to Rob's life's work may now also serve as an epitaph to the specialist LLM, which I recently discovered is being offered for the last time in the 2024–25 academic year. It is inevitable and appropriate that degree programmes will come and go, in tune with current staff interests and the rhythm of global events. The euphoria surrounding international criminal justice in 1998 is long dissipated; the excitement of cutting-edge innovation in legal education now belongs to 'AI and the Law', climate change and culture wars.

Meanwhile, actual wars rage in Ukraine and Palestine,[102] a resurgence of authoritarian populism stalks European and North American politics, and an epidemic of weak, corrupt governance and failing (or, frankly speaking, failed) states, especially in the Global South, poses tangible risks of systematic human rights violations (including torture and gender-based violence), war crimes, crimes against humanity and even genocide. It is barely credible that international criminal justice is any less relevant in today's fragile world than it was in the 1990s, when it was possible to believe that the fall of the Berlin Wall and the dissolution of the USSR heralded universal assent to liberal democracy at 'the end of history'.[103] In fact, the arguments I have heard for cancelling the LLM in International Criminal Justice and Armed Conflict seem either muddled or spurious. A cursory internet trawl confirms that more than

[100] Though Loyola, apparently, never said 'give me the boy at seven …', which has been described as 'a bromide which has been fathered on us': P Andrews, 'The Jesuits and Education' (1991) 80 *Studies: An Irish Quarterly Review* 22, 28.

[101] One additional, slightly facetious observation: if you have the good fortune to collaborate in teaching with talented and able colleagues, be sure to have a Plan B ready for when they jump ship to become Head of School!.

[102] As well as in other places with less media attention: *cf* R Marsden, 'Sudan's Forgotten War: A New Diplomatic Push is Needed', Chatham House, 14 March 2024, available at: www.chathamhouse.org/2024/03/sudans-forgotten-war-new-diplomatic-push-needed; S Al-Atrush, R Spencer and G Weiniger, 'Saudis Back West in Strikes Against Red Sea Rebels', *The Times*, 9 January 2024; R Assheton, 'The World's Forgotten War: A Rare Journey beyond Boko Haram Lines', *Sunday Times*, 31 December 2023.

[103] F Fukuyama, *The End of History and the Last Man* (Free Press, 1992).

a dozen UK universities currently offer comparable or related programmes,[104] and many more similarly focused masters degrees are taught in English overseas,[105] refuting any impression of market exhaustion. International criminal justice's popularity may have receded from its spectacular zenith, but it remains a prominent specialism in masters level legal education in the UK and farther afield.

Twenty-seven years is a decent run for any degree programme, and the legacy of Nottingham's LLM in International Criminal Justice and Armed Conflict is assured, not least through Rob Cryer's direct missionary work in conveying its material and intellectual DNA from the East to the West Midlands. In addition to the scores of LLM graduates with this qualification on their CVs in perpetuity, there will be ten times as many students who participated in some of the individual modules comprising the degree. As well as the LLM graduates who went on to teach international criminal justice in their own academic careers,[106] there are countless PhD students who attended occasional seminars or were otherwise indirectly influenced by the programme (if only through

[104] See, eg, Bangor (LLM in International Criminal Law and International Human Rights Law); Birmingham (LLM in International Criminal Law and Justice); BPP (LLM in Transnational Criminal Justice); Cardiff (MSc in International Criminology and Criminal Justice); Essex (LLM in International Criminal Law); Huddersfield (LLM in International Criminal Law); Hull (LLM in International Law: Conflict, Security and Human Rights); Kent (LLM in International Criminal Justice); London (LLM in International Criminal Justice); Northampton (LLM in International Criminal Law and Security); Northumbria (LLM in International Criminal Law and Practice); Portsmouth (MSc in International Criminal Justice and Intelligence); Sheffield (LLM in International Law and Global Justice); and University of Law (LLM in International Criminal Law).

[105] The list includes: UVA Amsterdam Law School in partnership with Columbia Law School (LLM in International Criminal Law); UVA Amsterdam Law School (LLM in International and Transnational Criminal Law); Case Western Reserve University (LLM in International Criminal Law); Galway (LLM in international Criminal Law); Groningen (LLM in Global Criminal Law); Limerick (LLM in Law, Human Rights and Criminal Justice); University of New Hampshire Franklin Pierce School of Law (LLM in International Criminal Law and Justice); University of the Western Cape (LLM in Transnational Criminal Justice); and Utrecht (LLM in European Criminal Justice in a Global Context).

[106] See n 66 above. Published work includes: A Jones, 'Measuring Performance and Shaping Identity: Performance Indicators and the International Criminal Court' (2021) 18 *Journal of International Criminal Justice* 825; Y Brunger, *Investigations and Prosecutions of Sexual and Gender-Based Violence by the International Criminal Court* (Institute for Justice and Reconciliation, 2017); H Mistry, 'The Significance of Institutional Culture in Enhancing the Validity of International Criminal Tribunals' (2017) 17 *International Criminal Law Review* 703; H Mistry, 'The Paradox of Dissent: Judicial Dissent and the Projects of International Criminal Justice' (2015) 13 *Journal of International Criminal Justice* 449; JD Jackson and YM Brunger, 'Fragmentation and Harmonisation in the Development of Evidentiary Practices in International Criminal Tribunals' in E van Sliedregt and S Vasiliev (eds), *Pluralism in International Criminal Law* (Oxford University Press, 2014); R Mulgrew, *Towards the Development of the International Penal System* (Cambridge University Press, 2013); J Jackson and Y M'Boge, 'Integrating a Socio-legal Approach to Evidence in the International Criminal Tribunals' (2013) 26 *Leiden Journal of International Law* 933 and (2014) 27 *Leiden Journal of International Law* 189; M Bergsmo, O Bekou and A Jones, 'New Technologies in Criminal Justice for Core International Crimes: The ICC Legal Tools Project' (2010) 10 *Human Rights Law Review* 715.

their supervisors), including many who would become prominent and productive scholars in the field: Neil Boister,[107] Olympia Bekou,[108] Tom Obokata,[109] Ademola Abass,[110] Mashood Baderin,[111] Christy Shucksmith-Wesley[112] and Giovanna Frisso,[113] to name-drop only those I can vividly recall. Most of the individual option choices currently comprising the degree, including its international criminal law centrepiece and those modules on humanitarian law and collective security which actually pre-date the specialist LLM, will continue to be offered under the umbrella of an LLM in International Law. What will be lost is the specialist focus, which has both outward-facing and internal structural dimensions. For external audiences, we will no longer advertise International Criminal Justice as a dedicated masters-level specialism, and this omission is likely to harm student recruitment and constrict the career pipeline supplying talented doctoral researchers and early career scholars.[114] More tangibly and immediately, loss of an intentionally interdisciplinary degree pathway will make it more difficult to offer new modules blending topics in international criminal law, human rights law, criminal justice, criminology and penology – an opportunity for research-led teaching that dozens of Nottingham colleagues, past and present, have exploited in developing their own bespoke additions to the degree programme since 1998. In curriculum design and structure, as in much else, innovation begets innovation. Conversely, when the entire programme was presented and organised as the 'LLM in International Law', it was difficult to get a hearing for anything relating to criminal justice, and some students were even resistant to domestic (as opposed to *international*) human rights law. Relocating

[107] N Boister, '"Transnational Criminal Law"?' (2003) 14 *European Journal of International Law* 953; N Boister and RJ Currie (eds), *Routledge Handbook of Transnational Criminal Law* (Routledge, 2015); N Boister, *An Introduction to Transnational Criminal Law*, 2nd edn (Oxford University Press, 2018); N Boister, S Gless, and F Jeßberger (eds), *Histories of Transnational Criminal Law* (Oxford University Press, 2021).

[108] O Bekou and R Cryer (eds), *The International Criminal Court* (Ashgate, 2004); O Bekou and D Birkett (eds), *Cooperation and the International Criminal Court: Perspectives from Theory and Practice* (Brill, 2016); A Zidar and O Bekou (eds), *Contemporary Challenges for the International Criminal Court* (British Institute of International and Comparative Law, 2022).

[109] T Obokata, *Transnational Organised Crime in International Law* (Hart Publishing, 2010); T Obokata, *Transnational Organised Crime: A Comparative Analysis* (Routledge, 2016).

[110] A Abass (ed), *Protecting Human Security in Africa* (Oxford University Press, 2010); A Abass, 'Prosecuting International Crimes in Africa: Rationale, Prospects and Challenges' (2013) 24 *European Journal of International Law* 933.

[111] M Baderin, *International Human Rights and Islamic Law* (Oxford University Press, 2003).

[112] C Shucksmith-Wesley, *The International Committee of the Red Cross and its Mandate to Protect and Assist: Law and Practice* (Hart Publishing, 2017).

[113] GM Frisso, 'The Winding Down of the ICTY: The Impact of the Completion Strategy and the Residual Mechanism on Victims' (2011) 3 *Goettingen Journal of International Law* 1093.

[114] In 2023–24, enrolment for the 'International Criminal Law' module stood at 61, making it easily, by some distance, the most popular option on the entire LLM programme, with more takers than even the commercial and business law options. Time will tell how much of this popularity is the legacy of a dedicated LLM in International Criminal Justice and Armed Conflict and its halo effect for the reputation of the institution, and how much of it can be sustained within the framework of a generalist LLM in International Law. I predict numbers will plummet by half.

International Criminal Law within a PIL conceptual framework risks reinstating the pedagogic and intellectual silos that the LLM in International Criminal Justice and Armed Conflict was designed to break down.

Although arguably more an exercise in rebranding than a substantive curriculum overhaul, it remains a shame in my eyes to see the specialist degree culled, butchered on the altar of bureaucratic centralisation and administrative convenience[115] – with the impeccable logic of the man who decapitated himself to cure a toothache.[116] Under this *dirigiste* model of university management,[117] the LLM in International Criminal Justice and Armed Conflict would hardly have been viable and most likely would never have existed. The idea would have arrived stillborn and many academic careers, together with the education of hundreds of postgraduate[118] students and a chunk of disciplinary literature, would have been reduced and impoverished. This depressing denouement comes too late to get Rob's take on the demise of the specialist LLM, but I can venture an educated guess as to what he might have said. Knowing him as a passionate believer in pedagogical ideals and one of our foremost imagineers of international criminal justice, he would not have been favourably impressed.

[115] Nowadays embedded into the technological infrastructure. International Criminal Justice? Computer says, 'No!' See www.youtube.com/watch?v=x0YGZPycMEU.

[116] I don't deny the reality of prevailing exigencies but question the intelligence and agility of institutional responses. (*cf* R Adams, 'Three in Four England Universities Expected to Be in the Red Next Year', *The Guardian*, 15 November 2024; A Rahaman Sarkar, 'Universities Consider Firing Staff and Cutting Courses as Foreign Student Enrolments Plummet', *The Independent*, 16 March 2024).

[117] Pervasive across the sector, and driven in part by government policies and commercial pressures for which universities themselves are not responsible but are forced to navigate in order to stay afloat. For constructive critique, see S Collini, *What are Universities For?* (Penguin, 2012); S Haack, 'Out of Step: Academic Ethics in a Preposterous Environment' in Haack, *Putting Philosophy to Work* (Prometheus Books, 2013); S Haack, 'Universities' Research Imperative: Paying the Price for Perverse Incentives' (2022), available at: www.againstprofphil.org/2022/09/25/a-guest-essay-by-susan-haack-universities-research-imperative-paying-the-price-for-perverse-incentives. At the more doom-laden end of the market, see P Fleming, *Dark Academia: How Universities Die* (Pluto Press, 2021).

[118] In addition to paving the way for Rob and Olympia's undergraduate 'International Criminal Law' option, as discussed, Dino reminds me that the thinking we put into devising the LLM degree also percolated into the first-year undergraduate curriculum, not least by injecting 'a good dose of the Pinochet saga' into the introductory 'Understanding Law' module.

7

Rob Cryer and the Art of Teaching (International) Law

RAPHAEL OIDTMANN

INTRODUCTION

As PROFESSORS AND lecturers of law, as academic teachers, mentors and supervisors, we assume distinct roles.[1] With that, we also seize certain responsibilities that we owe not only towards our colleagues, departments and universities, and not only towards our respective academic communities or towards society at large, but first and foremost: to our students. A duty we owe to those who have decided to pursue a (legal) academic education and to embark on a challenging, sometimes frustrating and disenchanting, but eventually enriching and stimulating intellectual rollercoaster ride, in which we as academic teachers – to a greater or lesser extent – may take part and become intellectual companions. However, once we assume these roles and thereby accept these responsibilities, we are also confronted with a series of fundamental questions that are anything but trivial: what kind of academic teachers do we want to be (or to become)? How and to what extent do we appreciate and even cherish the privilege that is instructing the next generation of legal professionals? What is it that we want to convey, also beyond the topical confines of a textbook? And, moreover, how do we become 'successful' in this endeavour, whatever that may mean?

This chapter is in no way suggesting that there exists only one 'royal road' to becoming a good, let alone an inspiring and encouraging academic teacher. Rather than some form of attainable state, it is argued that evolving into a formative legal educator resembles a perpetual endeavour, comprising a constant and recurring pattern of reflection, adaption and improvement. Within this process, academic role models play a crucial role. Thus, when reflecting on our

[1] In the following, I will stick to the term '(academic) teacher', thereby comprising all professional stages of instructors in higher (legal) education.

own studies or our early steps as academic teachers of international law,[2] we may agree that our own understanding, our own philosophies of teaching have lastingly been shaped by personal experiences and encounters with such role models: by this one particular professor, who succeeded in invigorating even the most boring topic, hence turning lectures into memorable experiences, or this one remarkable lecturer, who engendered lasting interest even in the most niche-like subject. More often than not, these academic role models have had a lasting and formative impact on our intellectual development and growth both as students and – oftentimes with many years in between – as (emerging) academic teachers of law.

Professor Robert Cryer was such a role model.[3] An esteemed and beloved colleague, an inspiring and activating academic teacher, a caring and compassionate mentor to whom myriads of students, research assistants, early-career researchers and (most) senior scholars likewise looked up to. As Gerry Simpson so tenderly put it, his passing left 'a Rob Cryer-shaped hole at the heart of our field'.[4] For me personally, Rob Cryer was an academic paragon, even though this mainly accrued 'from a distance': as elaborated by Sergey Vasiliev, '[t]here are friends who knew Robert better than I did and will be able to tell fuller stories of him in celebrating his life and doing justice to his life's work'.[5] Hence, unlike many of these close friends and longstanding colleagues – many of whom also contribute to the present 'Festschrift' and disclose their very intimate and personal experiences and encounters with Rob throughout the years – I encountered Rob Cryer mainly through his scholarship, most importantly through his (still) unrivalled textbook *An Introduction to International Criminal Law and Procedure*,[6] which 'for many, many students is [and will remain] *the* introduction to the field'.[7] Beyond any doubt, '[t]o several generations of students around the world, the name of Cryer is synonymous with the textbook which provides an engaging and effective entry point into the fascinating field of international criminal law and procedure'.[8]

As a student coming from an interdisciplinary background and taking his first and tentative steps into the realm that was international criminal law, as

[2] For the purposes of this chapter, the focus predominately rests on Rob Cryer's oeuvre in the area of international law broadly conceived, while eventually spotlighting his extensive writings in the areas of international criminal law and international humanitarian law.

[3] Amongst the scores of scholarly obituaries honouring Rob Cryer, see N Boister et al, 'In Memoriam: Robert Cryer' (2021) 19 *Journal of International Criminal Justice* 235; E Myjer and N White, 'In Memory of Professor Rob Cryer' (2021) 26 *Journal of Conflict & Security Law* 1; G Simpson, 'Robert Cryer' (2023) *British Yearbook of International Law* 1.

[4] Simpson (n 3) 1.

[5] Boister (n 3) 239.

[6] R Cryer, D Robinson and S Vasiliev, *An Introduction to International Criminal Law and Procedure*, 7th edn (Cambridge University Press, 2019). Previous editions of this eminent international criminal law textbook also included contributions by Håkan Friman and Elizabeth Wilmshurst.

[7] Simpson (n 3) 6.

[8] Boister (n 3) 239.

well as during my early days as a (junior) lecturer tasked with preparing my first lecture on the topic, this magnum opus[9] became a steady companion that has not only facilitated my initial orientation in the field or guided the conceptualisation of my lectures, but has also remained an indispensable intellectual asset to the present day. Boiled down to the essence of it, I thus wholeheartedly agree with Gerry Simpson on this one: 'What a pleasure it is to teach with a textbook rather than against it.'[10]

Thus, even from a distance, Rob's work has had a formative impact on my own process of 'intellectually maturing' and for growing as an academic teacher: although I never studied under Rob, did not have the opportunity to closely collaborate with him on a research project, nor cooperated with him on any other (legal) endeavour, I have lastingly benefited from what could be characterised as his 'legal education by proxy'. In other words, my own development as a scholar and teacher of international law was vitally influenced and, at least in part, determined by effects caused through the act of conveying (legal) knowledge through intermediaries – such as the above-mentioned textbook – thereby accruing an increasing level of expertise in respective fields.

Rob's formative influence on generations of legal scholars, in fact, exceeds the conveyance of information and knowledge that contributes towards the accruement of personal expertise: to engage with his scholarship, for me, implies to likewise engage with the 'educator extraordinaire' that was Rob Cryer. Hence, at the very heart of Rob's impact on me – and surely on many other companions in similar ways – lies his extraordinary talent as an (legal) educator. Therefore, when we celebrate Rob Cryer's intellectual and personal legacy, we should particularly celebrate what could be summarised as his 'art of teaching (international) law' in such a way that only very few people mastered like Rob Cryer did. For us as academic teachers, I believe, Rob's intellectual legacy and in particular his legacy of how (international) law can be taught therefore establishes both a yardstick and a perpetual mandate.

Based on these considerations, in the following, I attempt to spotlight what I deem to be three constitutive dimensions that have led Robert Cryer to become the superb legal educator that he was and will be remembered as beyond his prolific scholarship. These dimensions comprise Rob in three different roles: as an academic teacher and educator, as a mentor and supervisor, and as an intellectual guardian and role model.

By expounding on Rob's excellence in the classroom (and beyond), it is thus intended to shed some light on a set of qualities that – unfortunately – is not always sufficiently appreciated in today's academic business; illustrating Rob Cryer's intellectual legacy through his mastery of teaching hence focuses

[9] As Sergey Vasiliev noted: 'Rob cared profoundly about this book and how it might impact the thinking of young members of the 'invisible college' of international criminal lawyers and, hence, the future of the field.' See Boister (n 3) 240.

[10] ibid.

on criteria that are not always perceived as the lynchpins of academic success: rather than focusing (more or less exclusively) on extensive publication records, on acquired external grants and funding, or on high-level consultancy work, it is in particular through disseminating and passing on knowledge and engaging in comprehensive mentorship that an intellectual legacy unfolds and role models are construed. Most obviously, this was the case with Rob Cryer and his formative and lasting impact on generations of students, colleagues and fellow peers.

However, in this context, two clarifications or disclaimers need to be made. First, it is not suggested that the above-mentioned skills and capabilities are in any way mutually exclusive by default. Rather, it is self-evident – not least from Rob's archetypical example – that inspiring academic teachers can be likewise prolific and cutting-edge scholars.

Second, in no way is this meant to 'degrade' the importance, relevance or value of top-notch research, which logically is also a constitutive component of an academic portfolio of excellence. Thus, rather than 'degrading' the significance of cutting-edge research, applying such a focus aims at 'upgrading' the weight and relevance of excellent teaching in assessing scholars' intellectual legacies.[11]

ROB CRYER AS AN ACADEMIC TEACHER AND EDUCATOR

Teaching is often referred to as a somewhat noble profession – one that requires dedication, empathy and a genuine commitment to the growth and personal development of others. Hence, at the heart of this vocation lies a profound sense of passion – an unwavering enthusiasm and love for the process that is imparting knowledge, nurturing curiosity and empowering learners to unlock and reach their full respective potentials.[12] As such, this understanding of academic teaching transcends the mere transmission of information. Rather, it embodies a deep-seated dedication to inspiring, motivating and uplifting others through the transformative process of educating. Becoming a fine teacher of (international) law is thus not confined to subject-matter expertise or pedagogical proficiency; rather, it emanates from a profound sense for purpose – a deeply anchored belief in the inherent value of education and its capacity to not only empower individuals, but also to catalyse positive change. In simple(r) terms, truly passionate academic teachers view teaching not primarily as a job, but as a calling – an opportunity to make a meaningful contribution and difference in the lives of

[11] In essence, this reciprocal appreciation of teaching and research as two sides of the same token is emblematic of the *Humboldtian* model of higher education as a distinct blend of both teaching and research.

[12] As Darryl Robinson so gallantly put it, this 'mosaic of Rob Cryer [was] in fact harmoniously unified by one glue: *enthusiasm*. Rob was infused with a life-affirming, curiosity-driven and *playful* enthusiasm – whether about international law, academic, teaching, friendships or any of his hobbies'. See Boister (n 3) 238.

their students, while leaving a lasting impact on them that extends far beyond the classroom walls.

Such difference-making teachers will serve as catalysts for intellectual curiosity, kindling in their students a, possibly, lifelong love of learning and a thirst for knowledge that extends beyond the confines of formal education. Through that, they inspire creativity, critical thinking and innovation while nurturing the next generation of leaders, thinkers and change makers who will play their part in shaping tomorrow. However, at the same time, such academic teachers will foster a keen sense of belonging, empowerment and self-confidence in the students entrusted to them, especially those who may face barriers or challenges on their educational journey. By believing in their students' individual potentials, celebrating their achievements, and providing directed support and encouragement, these teachers know how to guide their students, empowering them to overcome obstacles, embrace their individual strengths and pursue their objectives with determination.

As was so vividly recalled in many of the reminiscences and tales that were published or also shared at the conference in Rob's memory that has preceded this volume,[13] his natural habitat and intellectual safe harbour was the classroom. As his students, colleagues and peers would agree, acting and moving within the seeming confinement of a lecture theatre, immersing into his respective audiences and absorbing the atmosphere across the hall yielded Rob's sheer boundless intellectual curiosity and brilliance, which – almost contagiously – spilled over into the crowd. His characteristic enthusiasm, his deep-rooted love for arguing and engaging hence left marks with students just as they did with colleagues and peers. While, personally, I solely encountered Rob in this role once or twice at academic conferences[14] and thus as part of what would rather count as an expert audience, both his classroom presence and excellence instantly became tangible – a characterisation that was also substantiated through many of the recollections in his memory, as Darryl Robinson charmingly expounded:

> At academic conferences, Rob Cryer could rouse any audience back to life. Even if all the previous speakers had exceeded their time and drained the audience of its will to live, he could still resuscitate the flatlining crowd. Rob was loud. His voice easily boomed to the back of the room. His delivery was upbeat, humorous, and engaging. He was genuinely enthusiastic, and yet he spoke at a casual, conversational pace. He

[13] For an overview, see 'Robert Cryer Memorial Conference: A Life in Law and a Law unto Himself', Birmingham Law School, 29–30 June 2023. The programme as well as the tableau of speakers may be accessed through the website created in memoriam of Rob Cryer at www.rob-cryer-scholarship.com/conference/#program.

[14] It put a bright smile on my face to read Sergey Vasiliev's recollection of Rob's enthusiasm for electric guitars – a fascination we shared and to which our conversation quickly traversed upon our first encounter over post-conference drinks. Likewise, '[o]ur conversation changed course once Rob mentioned and walked me through his impressive electric guitar collection. As we both are music aficionados and semi-amateur musicians, we quickly bonded over this shared hobby'. See Boister (n 3) 239.

was talking *with*, not *at*, us: he engaged in the room as fellow humans and shared his inquisitive thought process. The effect was like a cool, refreshing breeze in an oxygen-starved room.[15]

Rob Cryer's mesmerising classroom presence thus emerged as a recurring leitmotif in many of the other chapters in the present volume. What these accounts substantiate and what surfaced as a common denominator from all kinds of discursive fora with which Rob engaged was his profound passion for intellectual exchange, constructive dialogue, fine legal reasoning and – most importantly – for his opposite and his or her opinions. Rob's self-understanding as an academic teacher was thus not only guided by a genuine and formative interest to convey knowledge to others, but likewise to learn from his counterparts, whom he regarded as creative, knowledgeable and intellectually challenging equals in and outside the classroom. His attitude of sincerely valuing others' opinions – probably even more so in the case of apparent disagreements – therefore emerged as yet another characteristic facet of Rob's art of teaching (international) law.

At the core of being this outstanding teacher of international law, Rob Cryer also held a deep-seated mastery of the subject matter with which he so passionately engaged. Almost self-evidently, excellent teachers of international law possess a comprehensive and versatile understanding of the foundational principles, theoretical frameworks, relevant jurisprudence and practical applications that underpin international legal regimes. With Rob, however, the degree of mastery left a lasting impression with everyone who encountered him within a lecture hall.

But there is something else that distinguished Rob's teaching, that made it both memorable and inspiring, that established this 'very distinctive Robism':[16] a pedagogical approach which was lastingly characterised by an interdisciplinary orientation and a focus on real-world applicability. Through inserting innovative teaching methodologies into his educational formats – even before this emerged as a new form of 'instructive avantgarde' – such as moot court simulations and extensive case studies, as well as other experimental learning exercises, Rob excelled in providing his students with a truly holistic understanding of the complexities, interdependencies, and eventual deficits and shortcomings of (international) law. Thus, by encouraging them to look beyond the rim of the (legal) teacup, by integrating theoretical knowledge with practically relevant capabilities, Rob succeeded in equipping his students with the necessary tools to navigate the intricacies of contemporary international law and politics.

In a nutshell, an academic teacher's overall intellectual legacy finds its way into and resides in the minds of students who emerge from their educational journey equipped with the intellectual tools for navigating the complexities of the (international) legal landscape. It is thus these students who go on to become legal practitioners, policy makers, scholars, advocates and judges who leverage

[15] ibid 238.
[16] Simpson (n 3) 4.

their knowledge and skills so as to address pressing societal, legal and political challenges, thereby advancing the cause of justice and promoting the rule of law. Undoubtedly, Rob Cryer has left an indelible impression on many of them.

ROB CRYER AS A MENTOR AND SUPERVISOR

Similarly to becoming an outstanding academic teacher, there is no default route for becoming a likewise outstanding mentor and supervisor, either in the realm of (international) law or any other academic discipline. Likewise, it appears that there exists a range of capabilities and skills that are characteristic of formidable mentors and supervisors, including, for example, topical expertise, empathy and communication skills, as well as deep commitment in fostering the academic and personal growth and development of mentees, students and 'non-formal fosterings'.[17]

When we thus contemplate the qualities that contribute towards excellence in mentoring and supervision, we encounter many traits that were also characteristic of Rob's interaction with his protégées. Therefore, reflecting on Rob's self-understanding and acting as a mentor and supervisor, we might arrive at this tentative but by no means conclusive enumeration of skills and capabilities.[18]

To start with, an outstanding mentor and supervisor in (international) law should likewise be an outstanding teacher and researcher, possessing a deep understanding of the (international) legal field, including targeted and extensive knowledge in their respective areas of expertise.[19] Ideally, such a person is able to combine a strong academic background with practical understanding and hands-on experience across the legal profession. Thus, broad competence across those different dimensions forms the foundation upon which effective and meaningful mentorship and supervision is built.

From the perspective of mentees and supervisees, accessibility and approachability of their counterparts is of crucial relevance for their individual advancement. Therefore, in their daily work, mentors and supervisors should ideally be available for and responsive to the respective needs of mentees and supervisees, including by facilitating an open, supportive and collegiate environment in which they find guidance, may ask questions and share their concerns. But how can such an environment be created? Obviously, as a core component for building the required trust between both sides, mentors and supervisors are

[17] By 'non-formal fosterings', I refer to a distinct, yet rather informal kind of mentor/mentee relationship, which exists outside formal study programmes and in which the mentor takes the mentee 'under its wings'.

[18] Boister (n 3) 237.

[19] As Darryl Robinson pointed out, Rob 'was a generalist international lawyer, who really knew the foundations of the field: he was versed in theory, legal history, and the classic authors. In a rare combination, he was excellent at both the fine-grained doctrinal details and at the big picture theory and implications. That is probably why his work is so strong and enduring'. See Boister (n 3) 238.

called upon to demonstrate empathy towards their mentees and supervisees by being active listeners, trying to understand their individual perspectives and needs, and sympathising with their respective challenges. By showing genuine concern and compassion, mentors and supervisors may thus establish a truly supportive and profound relationship that may have a positive effect on their protégées' overall mental and physical well-being, particularly during challenging periods when drafting theses or studying for major examinations.

Creating such a trustful relationship, in turn, requires mentors and supervisors to engage in clear and open communication, including by transparently articulating expectations, providing constructive feedback and offering guidance in an understandable manner. Especially in this context, it is characteristic of outstanding mentors and supervisors to collaboratively work together with their mentees and supervisees in working out clear and realistic goals and expectations – including correspondent time allowances – for their respective projects and endeavours. Therefore, by jointly identifying individually applicable objectives, milestones and timelines, mentors and supervisors may directly support their mentees and supervisees in focusing their efforts, track their progress and remain motivated throughout their respective projects.

Even beyond single (research) projects, a good mentor and supervisor may provide continuous and steady support and encouragement once mentees and supervisees leave the university context and embark on their (legal) careers. Hence, to partake in their individual successes, to offer encouragement during challenging times as professional newcomers or to provide reassurance in the event of inevitable setbacks as a natural part of the overall process of growing are facets that – at least in some cases – may also form part of the overall capability set characterising outstanding mentors and supervisors. In addition, at least in some mentoring relationships, mentors and supervisors may also assist in promoting their protégées' growth and advancement through making available other resources, such as their professional networks.

An outstanding mentor and supervisor is, finally, characterised by at least one additional trait: an honest commitment to continuous learning and improvement. Rather than engaging in some form of 'one-way mentorship and supervision', those individuals actively seek feedback from mentees and supervisees, reflect on their own mentoring practices and critically engage in professional development activities so as to enhance their overall skills and effectiveness.

Hence, by embracing a growth mindset and a willingness to learn, mentors and supervisors can thus adapt to the evolving needs of their mentees and supervisees, and foster a culture of continuous professional and personal improvement. As Gerry Simpson rightly put it: 'Rob, himself never ceased to be a student (in the strongest sense of that word) of the discipline and at the same time he was committed to it as a pedagogical practice.'[20]

[20] Simpson (n 3) 6.

All these qualities and capabilities, these desirable faculties and convictions epitomised in the mentor and supervisor that Rob Cryer was to so many students, from undergraduate freshmen to successful PhD candidates.[21] I invite you to embark on a short thought experiment: try to think of your 27-year-old self, intending to embark on a dissertation project in international criminal law at the University of Birmingham. Put yourself in the shoes of someone pitching his research project to Rob Cryer, sitting in this bibliophiles' office, intimidatingly packed with books. Now try to imagine the conversation unfolding with Rob, your envisaged mentor and supervisor – and you will immediately start to tick all the above-mentioned boxes.

ROB CRYER AS AN INTELLECTUAL GUARDIAN AND ROLE MODEL

While the two previously expounded dimensions are constitutive of an outstanding academic teacher, we may argue that they resemble necessary rather than sufficient conditions: teaching (international) law is thus not merely about imparting legal knowledge or holding a position as a supervisor, but also about instilling ethical consciousness and moral integrity in the next generation of legal professionals. Hence, outstanding legal educators also serve as exemplars of ethical conduct, embodying principles including integrity, honesty and accountability, both in their academic and professional practice. By modelling decent behaviour and encouraging students to uphold the highest standards of legal ethics, they imbue their legacy with a deep commitment to justice and fairness.

Thus, when reflecting on the role model that Robert Cryer embodied, we may also contemplate that his art of teaching (international) law was also about fostering ethical leadership of students, later to emerge from their educational experience with a firm sense of duty to serve and act in the interest of the public good; students who would later embrace their roles as stewards of (international) justice, advocates for the marginalised, and guardians of the rule of law, using their legal expertise to effect positive change in their communities and beyond. One of the most profound powers of academic teachers such as Rob Cryer is therefore their capacity to empower individuals to become effective agents of change who are well equipped to act as advocates for social justice, to inspire students to recognise the powers of their voices as well as the importance of using the law as a tool for societal transformation – both domestically and internationally.

Beyond conveying his scholarship in the classroom or through his mentoring and supervision, Rob Cryer's influence across the legal domain and, most importantly, in the realm of international criminal law reverberates across global academia and beyond, as Rob was an intellectual guardian not only within but

[21] See also Boister (n 3) 240.

also outside academia. Thus, through his extra-university engagement with international organisations, his exchange with legal practitioners or representation of civil society institutions, Rob also exhibited the qualities distinguishing him as an academic teacher as well as a mentor and supervisor to the outside world.[22] Having excelled as a sought-after expert and adviser, most importantly on notions of international criminal justice, Rob also played a pivotal role in crafting the contemporary international legal landscape through shaping international legal norms and institutions, through advocating for the protection of human rights and promotion of the rule of law, as well as fighting impunity for mass atrocities.

Central to Rob's approach in all these contexts was his unwavering commitment to upholding the principles of justice and accountability in the face of impunity and injustice. Whether through his involvement in landmark cases before international (criminal) courts and tribunals, his participation in diplomatic negotiations or his role as a legal-political consultant to both governmental and non-governmental entities, Rob adhered to the principles and convictions that were likewise emblematic of his scholarship, teaching, as well as mentoring and supervising.[23] Key towards becoming what Robert Cryer effectively resembled – namely an intellectual guardian and role model for so many of us – what characterised his scholarly activities as much as him as a loving human being was his firm commitment towards ethical conduct, social responsibility and the promotion of justice and human rights. In passing on this intellectual legacy, Rob also cultivated in his students and peers a global perspective that transcended national boundaries and cultural differences.

CONCLUSION AND FINAL REFLECTIONS

Professor Robert Cryer was an intellectual giant and academic vanguard who stood – and will continue to stand – as a beacon in the field of international law. Ioannis Kalpouzos found the perfectly right words, writing that Rob 'lived and breathed the institutional, social, and conceptual world of the international law academic, not uncritically, but with modesty and respect for the doctrine, the discipline, the job. And he never fancied himself above the field'.[24] I would dare to add that Rob's groundbreaking scholarship and contributions to the field transcended disciplinary boundaries,[25] just as his teaching shaped the minds and careers of future generations of international legal scholars and practitioners.

[22] See the discussion of Rob's wider impact in Bartels, ch 3 in this volume.

[23] Rob's participation in the negotiation of the Rome Statute establishing the International Criminal Court as a member of the British delegation is only one amongst countless examples.

[24] Boister (n 3) 244.

[25] As one example amongst many, 'Rob's major monograph – on selectivity (drawn from his doctoral thesis) – was a rather masterful piece of work for someone so inexperienced and young. In fact, it is full of that rarest of qualities: youthful wisdom'. See Simpson (n 3) 4. The book was later

As the example of Rob Cryer teaches us, teaching (international) law is not merely a noble vocation – indeed, it is part of a bigger legacy: a legacy of intellectual growth, ethical leadership and social advocacy. Through his unparalleled dedication, his passion and his overall commitment to academic excellence, Rob will be remembered for having shaped the minds and hearts of his students, colleagues and friends, hence instilling in them the values, skills and vision to become principled leaders and agents of change. Thus, as we reflect on Rob's intellectual legacy in this volume, let us not forget to recognise his transformative power to inspire, empower and shape the future of generations of legal students to come.

I concur with Sergey Vasiliev in that:

> I think it is people like Rob who make academia worth staying in, despite all its problems: its toxic competitiveness, creeping commercialisation and bureaucratisation, inattention to mental health issues and persistent lack of diversity across the board. Rob was the embodiment of human decency, integrity, and solidarity – the principles and values that, if pursued more doggedly and uncompromisingly, would make academia a better place.[26]

Rob leaves an indelible mark on the study and practice of international law. As his scholarly descendants, we thus not only mourn his loss and reflect on his myriad achievements, but also celebrate his 'life in law'. Contemplating on Rob's life in all its dimensions therefore confers a responsibility, an enduring task upon us: to heed the lessons taught by his intellectual legacy, including his mastery in the art of teaching (international) law. Therefore, let us follow his example and strive to uphold the principles of justice, accountability and human rights in our collective pursuit for a more just and peaceful world governed by the rule of law – and let us continue to engage in this endeavour by following in the footsteps of the role model that was Robert Cryer.

published as R Cryer, *Prosecuting International Crimes: Selectivity and the International Criminal Law Regime* (Cambridge University Press, 2009).

[26] Boister (n 3) 240.

8

Principle or Pragmatism? Misogyny as Genocide

MARIANNE L WADE

INTRODUCTION

THE MONTHS AFTER Rob's untimely death were marked by many things. Amongst the most painful were the moments during which I found myself deep in thought at work, phone in hand intending to dial his number to ask a quick question. Those moments forced me to recognise that I had in no way understood he was gone and also how deeply our lives were intertwined in a variety of contexts. There was no escaping how much I would miss him.

The spring after his death was the one for which UK universities sought 'COVID resilience'. In Birmingham this led to the rolling together of modules to ensure we would be able to offer something to our students. As a result, I was faced with the prospect of delivering the 'Issues in International Criminal Law and Justice' module on which Rob had signed off in the summer.

PRINCIPLED PLANNING

It was a far cry from the work Rob and I had undertaken several years before as we considered what we, together, wanted to offer our masters students. My arrival in Birmingham had signalled an intent to broaden teaching to feature EU criminal law and justice as well as more criminological approaches to cross-border penal justice cooperation. As a result, Rob declared himself willing to make a new effort to develop a module on transnational criminal law. He was pleased we would be one of very few law schools offering courses reflecting the world as we saw it – namely, with an independent international criminal law and justice module which was flanked by transnational criminal law, EU criminal law and justice and even a criminological look via my 'global crime problems' invention. Our LLM modules correctly reflected the substantive order of internationalised criminal law, something Rob certainly considered important as a matter of principle. He noted happily that his work on the transnational criminal law front would soon become easier as his 'mate' Neil Boister was working on a relevant textbook at the time.[1]

As much as Rob was a substantive lawyer and a proper, more traditional scholar who valued all things academic, he was not immune to pressures around us. He might not engage in such discussions readily, but he was clearly aware that our combined offering placed the teaching he loved in a setting facilitating talk of USPs,[2] pathways to specialised careers and other odious matters melodious to the ears of university management. Ignoring the vocabulary to which he was less partial, Rob happily reflected on how we might communicate the utility of the learning we offered. As a matter of principle, he certainly wanted to help excellent lawyers populate international organisations and criminal justice institutions. Indeed, he was fiercely proud of his contribution to forming the workforce that toils at the coalface of international criminal justice. His commitment to pedagogy is also set out in this volume by: Jamie Lee, who writes on Rob's view of the importance of textbooks and what they mean; Raphael Oidtmann, who unwraps Rob's role as academic educator; and Paul Roberts, who sets out how Rob helped create a new programme for Nottingham Law School and explores his innovations in teaching and practice development.

Rob and I spent significant hours moaning about the compromises we were forced to make as well as the pragmatism that too often disrupts the principled approach we considered we would prefer to take to work matters or the time we had to give to procedures we regarded as less necessary. Those conversations inevitably ended with one of us looking guilty, caught red-handed in a self-indulgent rant. The dialogue ended with a shared recognition that we still spent the majority of our time engaged with topics we found interesting, teaching and discussing them to and with people we respected. For all his ferocious intellect, Rob also relished his place in the chain transmitting knowledge. Although he was not sufficiently pragmatic to respond to emails he considered misdirected to an academic, Rob remained a deeply committed teacher. Anyone who saw the files he prepared for that first year teaching transnational criminal law could not fail to recognise commitment of the firmest kind. Rob the teacher was also the rigorous perfectionist we encountered on the page.

[1] *An Introduction to Transnational Criminal Law* (Oxford University Press) (now in its second edition (2018)) and to be found on several Birmingham Law School resource lists. Professor Boister has also contributed a chapter to this volume: see ch 9.

[2] Unique Selling Points for anyone lucky enough to have avoided this kind of marketisation diction thus far.

REALITY

However, it was a pragmatic Rob who was called upon to review our 'COVID-resilient' offering and who sentenced us to deliver a module lumping all our endeavours together. It was therefore an apologetic Rob who engaged with me how on I could deliver it. Mirroring what had become a bad UK habit, the EU had been dropped altogether and I was tasked with delivering international, criminal and (criminological) global criminal law and justice to our students. I wondered whether the issue upon which I could hang sufficient teaching of the substance and institutions of international criminal law was sexual violence in conflict. Rob – relatively fresh back from hearing Nadja Murad speaking to a parliamentary committee – reflected that it was a topic that brought even seasoned policy makers to tears. He therefore endorsed it as one that would doubtless connect with plenty of our students. Knowing that my expertise in no way extended far enough to teach this topic, I told Rob he would have to help me prepare for these sessions, even if he was not formally part of the module team. 'Course', he blustered nonchalantly. Such was Rob as a colleague: casually – endlessly – generous, as a matter of principle.

Of course, it was not to be. By the time I entered that classroom, Rob was ash. It was the time of COVID-19; weirdness was ubiquitous. As the mother of two small children and the teacher of teenagers and young adults, I had been shielding him from the walking contagion I felt myself to be. It therefore took us all some time to realise that the corridors really were devoid of his booming presence for that most awful reason, and to recognise we would never again have a head or deputy head of school who decried working (outside of the Bratby bar) after 6:30 pm and who physically enforced this policy going from room to lit room to propagate it evening after evening: unfailingly a man of principle in this regard too!

However, even if physically not present – and he had often not been insofar as he was a much sought-after teacher, speaker and examiner, so frequently to be found in a far-flung corner of the world – Rob was always reachable. One needed not to be within viewing or hearing range of Rob in order to be connected to him. That seems a silly statement for such a prolific writer, of course. However, friends had the privilege of speaking with a man who pretty much always answered his phone. This fact did not make that year easier. I found myself often, phone in hand, brutally confronted by the reality that he would never be again. The realisation of loss was a crushing, multi-weekly habit. Where Rob had been, there was now the opposite.

THE QUESTIONS RAISED

So at this coalface of Rob's making, I first toiled alone and missed him all the way. In the end, the teaching timetable dictated that it was not to be me delivering the sessions we discussed. And fortunately, I did not carry the burden of preparation alone. Janine Clarke kindly shared her expertise with me. Colleagues rallied to teach as Rob and I had planned.

Rob nonetheless loomed large. Our student body naturally featured members who had expected to be taught by him. Those of us unable to hide his loss as personal drew gentle questions at unexpected points. Birmingham Law School had lost a significant *characterful* presence: Rob the teacher, office-hour sounding board, potential dissertation or even PhD supervisor was irreplaceable. He had been an enormous presence – as busy in person as he was on the page.

But the topic we had settled on lived! Our students began discussing the topic as soon as their syllabus was published. Other colleagues delivered the sessions, but my inbox swelled and office hours were soon alive with reflections on the theory and reality of international criminal law and justice.

Both were found to be wanting. Pandemic lockdowns, of course, highlighted the need to discuss violence against women and girls with dire urgency.[3] The need for engagement around misogyny for which the Sarah Everard murder would tragically provide a lightning rod of the worst kind[4] was already alive in these students. Rob was needed to discuss these things with them. I could not match his command of the principles of international (criminal) law in any way.

And, of course, the students following the path we had cobbled together honed in on the substantive aspects of international criminal law. However, they did so from a standpoint I designated, and so adopted a phenomenological or problem-based perspective. Taking this approach to examining the weaponisation of sexual violence in conflict, this area of what should have been Rob's teaching became the subject for feminist ire.

The sheer scale of violence horrified. The regularity with which women and girls are subject to violence of the most personal, depraved nature quickly marked the class. The structure I had devised with Rob facilitated this.

Discussions spilled out of the classroom and into office hours and dissertation preparation sessions with student concerns centred around the destructive nature of rape and sexual violence itself. Set out as Rob and I had combined our perspectives, the criminological evidence led students to consider more closely the damage being inflicted. Rape and sexual violence was certainly very much in the minds of students, highlighted by the headlines surrounding pandemic domestic violence, the everyday nature of rape and female victimisation, as well as the woeful lack of prosecutions. Our students looked at the phenomenon and located information including that rape victims overwhelmingly suffer

[3] See, eg, House of Commons Library, 'Domestic Abuse and Covid-19: A Year into the Pandemic', 11 May 2021.

[4] For an overview, see Baroness Casey of Blackstock, 'Final Report: An Independent Review into the Standards of Behaviour and Internal Culture of the Metropolitan Police Service' (Metropolitan Police, March 2023), www.met.police.uk/SysSiteAssets/media/downloads/met/about-us/baroness-casey-review/update-march-2023/baroness-casey-review-march-2023a.pdf, 6–8.

post-traumatic responses[5] in non-conflict settings. In comparison, 17 per cent of soldiers deployed to combat roles in Iraq and Afghanistan are reported to suffer post-traumatic stress disorder (PTSD).[6] So our students asked why is it that so much of international law is concerned with soldiers and so little with the victims of rape and sexual assault? Rob would have answered the technical part of that question with ease, but I suspect have adopted a different tone in acknowledging the realities of power reflected in international law. This teaching was not comfortable and I often wondered what Rob would have made of it. He had an ability to surprise when he was treading lightly, and I wish I knew what he would have said.

Descriptions of rape in peacetime are harrowing. Stories of rape in conflict feature regular accounts of women subject to savagery in front of family and children they seek to protect, accompanied by othering, humiliating, dehumanising, debasing and indeed annihilating treatment. Descriptions range from taunts concerning the paternity of their expected pregnancy to unfathomable, unbearable cruelty. The variety of nightmares already lived is endless. If women raped in peacetime speak of being destroyed,[7] one can only imagine the effect upon those deliberately targeted in a context devoted to destruction.

THE LAW AS IT STANDS

International criminal law, of course, speaks to sexual violence in conflict. 'Rape, sexual slavery, enforced prostitution, forced pregnancy, enforced sterilization, or any other form of sexual violence of comparable gravity' is declared a crime against humanity 'when committed as part of a widespread or systematic attack directed against any civilian population, with knowledge of the attack' by Article 7(1)(g) of the Rome Statute. This is, of course, a basis for considerable punishment of perpetrators by the international order.

However, the overt drafting of the 'intent to destroy' as the key characteristic of genocide naturally draws the eye of lawyers after discussion of rape in zemiological terms. The fact that sexual violence as a means of perpetration

[5] BO Rothbaum, EB Foa, DS Riggs, T Murdock and W Walsh, 'A Prospective Examination of Post-Traumatic Stress Disorder in Rape Victims' (1992) 5(3) *Journal of Traumatic Stress* 455 (94 per cent within weeks of the assault and close to 50 per cent chronically). See also A Elklit and DM Christiansen, 'ASD and PTSD in Rape Victims' (2010) 25(8) *Journal of Interpersonal Violence* 1480.

[6] SAM Stevelink, M Jones, L Hull, D Pernet, S MacCrimmon, L Goodwin, D MacManus, D Murphy, N Jones, N Greenberg, RJ Rona, N. Fear and S Wessely, 'Mental Health Outcomes at the End of the British Involvement in the Iraq and Afghanistan Conflicts: A Cohort Study' (2018) 213(6) *British Journal of Psychiatry* 690.

[7] Now prominently under discussion after Gisèle Pelicot expressed precisely this sentiment. See C Lamb, 'Gisèle Pelicot Said the Most Powerful Four Words I've Heard This Year', *Sunday Times*, 21 December 2024.

apparently goes unrecognised and only the reproductive function of women[8] hints at the potential to destroy human groups via female bodies clearly indicates unacceptable gender (never mind racial) assumptions in the law to the modern reader in Birmingham Law School.

The jurisprudence and more recent discussions of international criminal law appear to offer more hope. Our students pursued these lines of study in their writing. The watershed *Akayesu* judgment recognised that the infliction of serious bodily and mental harm on Tutsi women intended to destroy the Tutsi group as a whole, thereby leading to genocide.[9] But our students remained dissatisfied. As feminist scholars have highlighted, any apparent recognition is deeply problematic due to the de-gendering price paid. Sexual violence is only recognised when it affects both men and women equally because it seems to recognise that what is destroyed is the function women have within communities as opposed to the female experience itself.

Considerations going forward thus focused on calling for women to be recognised in their own right and for the severity of what was being inflicted upon them to be appropriately acknowledged. Work was therefore directed to the need to reform the law of genocide in order to reflect that the destruction of females via rape and sexual violence in and of itself fulfils this weighty norm. Whether this requires recognition of gender as a group or securing female members of a group as integral and not only via their reproductive function was not entirely clear. But a highly symbolic change was demanded.

THE CONTEXT IN WHICH LAW IS BEING LEARNT

The urgency of this call has, of course, been lent fuel since Rob's death, not least by Sarah Everard's horrific victimisation, and the traumatising nature of official[10] and police[11] responses as women expressed their fears, as well as the reporting of increased domestic violence during lockdowns and indeed discussion of the prevalence of sexual offending by male students.[12] The reminders

[8] In a negative form only, namely 'imposing measures intended to prevent births within the group', as provided for in Article 6(d) of the Rome Statute of the International Criminal Court.

[9] *Prosecutor v Jean-Paul Akayesu*, ICTR 96-04, 1998, International Criminal Tribunal for Rwanda, Arusha 731-33 (as now captured by Article 6(b) of the Rome Statute of the International Criminal Court).

[10] Particularly the British government's suggestion of providing more police officers to protect women after a woman was murdered by a serving police officer (later found to have abused his position as an officer to trap her): see 'Sarah Everard: New Safety Measures after Killing', *BBC News*, 16 March 2021, available at: www.bbc.co.uk/news/uk-56410943.

[11] See, eg, A Topping and V Dodd, 'Met Police Pay Damages to Women Arrested at Sarah Everard Vigil', *The Guardian*, 14 September 2023, available at: https://www.theguardian.com/uk-news/2023/sep/14/met-police-pays-damages-to-women-arrested-at-sarah-everard-vigil.

[12] ST Hales and TA Gannon, 'Understanding Sexual Aggression in UK Male University Students: An Empirical Assessment of Prevalence and Psychological Risk Factors' (2022) 34(6) *Sexual Abuse* 744.

of vulnerability and insufficient criminal justice action were omnipresent. Why would a diverse group of law students not turn to the international legal order to seek a corrective voice? Hillary Rodham Clinton's call from 1995 that 'women's rights are human rights' was surely so antiquated that protection can be expected there, no? The international community and international law as the cradle of human rights appears the logical destination for a group seeking protection.

Our students were not naïve in their discussions of this topic, but, as lawyers, standards were certainly being set that envisaged international law as the best it can be. As women witness the miserable failure of their domestic criminal justice systems to protect their right to sexual self-determination, they can hardly be blamed for turning to human rights organisations for a response. When they read of women systematically targeted in the most brutal of ways during conflict, how can they but call upon the law – at the very least – to be improved as a focal point to affect change?

The particular context of this class was as follows: in 2020, the UK's Victim's Commissioner had decried the 'effective decriminalisation of rape' in her first annual report and highlighted the plummeting number of prosecutions as victims had become the targets of intrusive police investigation tactics and only five per cent of cases were even being charged.[13] So students were understandably looking for higher standards in international law, especially when confronted with the harrowing phenomena international criminal justice institutions are faced with.

THE NEED FOR ROB

At this point, a Rob intervention was badly needed. His insight into the law, its evolution and what it could potentially become would have provided a different grounding for our reflections. A discussion of international – also criminal – law as something requiring consensus would have been enlightening. This was a topic on Rob's mind. We had been considering how he could realise his desire to examine it more deeply, believing – as he did – that the so-called universal principles in play were strongly selected by Anglocentric law makers. Rob's incisive expertise distilling this context into digestible form for our students to explain the realities of this man-made construct in progress would have been helpful, even if it provided more of what our students did not want to hear. But Rob would have made sure the arguments they planned to carry into their future careers were the best they could possibly be.

Rob would have brought his encyclopaedic understanding to impart knowledge, but our discussions would still have been drawn to what must be.

[13] V Bird QC, '2020/21 Annual Report' (Victims Commissioner, 2021), https://victimscommissioner.org.uk/document/annual-report-of-the-victims-commissioner-2020-to-2021, 17–20.

Our classroom was in Birmingham Law School after all and, typically, it therefore contained representatives of most larger world religions. On this topic, females were most vociferous, but there were a diversity of perspectives that were represented. Furthermore, our studies left our students well able to articulate the moral force of their arguments and the need for international law to be what it should be, to wit, a symbolic start rather than what can politically be agreed in the now.

It should also be noted that recognition of male victimisation was not absent. Seminar readings included literature highlighting the distressing brutality faced by men who were raped, sexually assaulted and humiliated as a systemic feature of conflict. One assessment paper tackled this issue graphically, highlighting the literature associating sexual penetration and subjugation as treatment associated with females and thus convincingly arguing that this suffering too is grounded in misogyny. To be penetrated is the weaker, less human part[14] and the one to be scorned as expressed in language The very purpose of this violence perpetrated against men is to emasculate and humiliate ('making women out of men'), which further underscores the urgency with which the international community should tackle the scourge of misogyny that facilitates such endless cruelty. In the midst of marking, one student had me reaching for the phone to summon Rob for a discussion to marvel over how far his idea for this module had brought us. I would have wanted to meet him for a beer on that occasion, also to watch him squirm at the graphic arguments the student made. Rob would doubtlessly have quipped his way back to more comfortable territory.

Rob's voice is missing. The invasion of Ukraine, the Hamas attack of 7 October and indeed the Israeli ground offensive in Gaza see Birmingham Law School classrooms seeking international law authority and critique all the more, not least in relation to sexual violence in conflict. Precisely because of our diversity, discussions of what is, could and should be expected of international law and international criminal justice rage all the more strongly. And though we have other important voices, Rob's is sorely missed.

WHAT WOULD ROB HAVE SAID?

Having concluded all that belonged to this module, I was convinced that international criminal law remains deeply marked by a view of women as valuable within their groups, but not in and of themselves as a formatively constitutive part of it. Whilst the law doubtlessly captures some of what is taken from women – and can be interpreted constructively to a limited extent – feminist critiques retain their validity. Those harms protected by crimes against humanity, forced

[14] On this, see MM Dempsey and J Herring, 'Why Sexual Penetration Requires Justification' (2007) 27(3) *Oxford Journal of Legal Studies* 467 (specifically examining the language involved and what it expresses socially).

pregnancy and sterilisation are things also taken from men. This is law that can be mobilised to seek justice when women are brutally stripped of their ability to make choices that should be theirs, but it, painfully, appears to recognise them as community benefits, not personal decisions to be made. Perhaps 'Your body, my choice'[15] is also echoing in international law?

One can only speculate on how far Rob might have reflected on these issues as a scholar, but as a teacher and one of those of us who would inevitably face these questions in the classroom and office hours, they certainly would have been on his mind. I wish to have had the opportunity to reflect on them with him. A corner of the Bratby bar would thus undoubtedly have been dedicated to work after hours.

There would have been a dialogue about principle. I would have reflected upon discussions – also with our students – of the destruction of rape itself, the deeply personal invasion of a body designed to subjugate, humiliate, injure or indeed kill; destruction up close and personal.

Rob had relevant stories to tell and I wonder how public he would have made them. His recounting of the impression made by Nadja Murad was of dialogue changing the world. His personal experience of supporting friends as they became rape survivors he also remembered in terms of outrage at what women had to endure in even the very first steps of seeking justice. He would have understood perfectly why women also seek specific recognition of weaponised misogyny via the strongest norm of international criminal law.

Whether he would have agreed with the results desired by our students, I am more doubtful. Rob was always very clear that the law of genocide retains its power because it can only be used sparingly.[16] I cannot imagine him being comfortable with a line remaining drawn to systematically disadvantage women. He would doubtlessly acknowledge the destructive nature of rape and sexual violence in and of itself. But he also always mounted an unassailable argument that genocide must be reserved for the very worst of the worst. How enlightening it would have been to test him on this in light of what I learnt in discussion with our students, teaching the compromise offering we had found ourselves having to design.

I wonder what would have led Rob on this front. Pragmatism or principle? Would his work on universal principles have convinced him that a lacking consensus amongst states (ie, the prevalence of misogyny) prevents the prohibition of genocide as feminist analysis demands as a matter of principle? Or would a more pragmatic numbers game have prevailed?

[15] The dreadful jubilation of some Trump supporters intended to wound pro-choice feminists after his recent electoral victory.

[16] Note Sara Meger's criticism of the 'selective securitization of wartime sexual violence … the association of sexual- and gender-based violence with "genocide" enabled its politicization in international law, but not on the basis of the perpetration of gender-based violence itself'. See S Meger, *Rape Loot Pillage: The Political Economy of Sexual Violence in Armed Conflict* (Oxford University Press, 2016) 116.

There is an enormous problem relating to that as highlighted by MacKinnon[17] – namely, all the sexual atrocities that become genocidal are inflicted on women every day under conditions of sex inequality and are inflicted upon them as women because they are women.[18] Sexual violence perpetrated in conflict is the destruction wrought upon women in the everyday horrifically magnified by conflict contexts, some of which are overtly genocidal.

Rob's principle would have needed to hold fast in the face of this vehement argument, highlighting the plight of women targeted all too commonly for destruction. I am certain he would – perhaps pragmatically – have stuck to his principle that genocide must remain an exceptionally applied legal norm to retain its power. However, I imagine that he would have been extremely uncomfortable drawing a line seemingly subsuming so much female suffering, knowing that women so desperately require the symbolic protection of international law. But I have neither the right nor the ability to speak for him and he should have had decades to think on this, had he chosen to (or found himself unable to) avoid my reflections. He would not have been able to avoid the topic. University campuses are criminogenic spaces of rape and sexual assault.

CONCLUSION

Who knows what Rob might have said, thought and written? At his memorial conference, we already identified debates on Ukraine and the desire on different sides to cite Rob's as a voice that would agree with them. A part of Rob would doubtlessly have been pleased by that (in his – as Isobel Roele so brilliantly phrased it – 'humble, not humble' way). And he might have been baffled. But he would also have been pleased by the (always) passionate rantings elicited by the final module he framed. He would have been inspired by our students' determination to take their arguments for progress forward. How we miss his voice in the legal debates that unfold.

[17] C MacKinnon, *Are Women Human? And Other International Dialogues* (Harvard University Press, 2007), 15, 16, 93.

[18] As analysed by Meger (n 16) 120. For discussion of sexual violence in the Pacific Rim, see Drumbl and Mouthaan, ch 16 in this volume.

9

Remaking the Tokyo Tribunal

Robert Cryer and the Revival of Scholarship on the Tokyo Trial

NEIL BOISTER*

INTRODUCTION

THE AIM OF this chapter is to set out the general themes of the scholarship on the International Military Tribunal for the Far East (hereinafter 'Tokyo trial'), which sat in judgment on Japan's wartime leaders in Tokyo from 1946 to 1948.[1] I highlight the role that Rob Cryer played in reviving legal interest in the trial. This chapter is one among others in this volume to focus on the salience of Rob's scholarship on the Tokyo trial.[2]

Rob initiated a number of works on the Tokyo trial, particularly two we published in 2008. The first was *The Tokyo International Military Tribunal: A Reappraisal*,[3] an attempt to revisit the trial's contribution to international criminal law, which John O Haley called 'the most complete and objective account of the Tokyo Trials to date.'[4] This was followed by *Documents on the Tokyo International Military Tribunal: Charter, Indictment and Judgments*, a

* I must express my gratitude to Yuma Totani and Sandra Wilson for their comments. A version of this chapter was given at the 4th Asian Legal History Conference, Hue University of Law, Vietnam, 25 July 2024. Many thanks also to participants in the Rob Cryer Commemorative Conference, University of Birmingham, June 2023.

[1] Literature surveys include Fujita Hisakazu's 'The Tokyo Trial: Humanity's Justice v Victors' Justice' in Y Tanaka, T McCormack and G Simpson (eds), *Beyond Victor's Justice? The Tokyo War Crimes Trial Revisited* (Nijhoff, 2011) 3, 16 et seq; G Simpson, 'Writing the Tokyo Trial' in Y Tanaka, T McCormack and G Simpson (eds), *Beyond Victor's Justice? The Tokyo War Crimes Trial Revisited* (Nijhoff, 2011) 23; K von Lingen, 'Introduction' in K von Lingen (ed), *Transcultural Justice at the Tokyo Tribunal: The Allied Struggle for Justice, 1946–1948* (Brill, 2018) 1, 6.

[2] See Drumbl and Mouthaan, ch 16 in this volume; and Vasiliev, ch 19 in this volume.

[3] N Boister and R Cryer, *The Tokyo International Military Tribunal: A Reappraisal* (Oxford University Press, 2008) (Japanese translation, Kodansha, 2012, edited by K Awaya, F Hisakazu and Y Takatori) (Chinese translation, Shanghai Jiao Tong University Press, 2021, translated by H Mei).

[4] 'Review [Untitled]' (2009) 35(2) *Journal of Japanese Studies* 445, 447.

collection of key documents and the judgments that Rob pushed for in order to make the trial more accessible to researchers.[5] This chapter sheds light on the bewildering diversity of research on the trial both before and after Rob's intervention, in order to give some inkling of the singularity and good timing of Rob's scholarly advancement of research on the trial.

Richard Minear asks whether it is possible to be neutral in approaching the Tokyo trial.[6] While some scholars may aspire to neutrality, the historiography of the trial suggests that no one studies the trial entirely without an agenda. These goals tend to be set up in opposition to the goals of others, the most obvious dispute being between supporters of the trial who see it as the 'judgment of civilization' on Japan's leaders, and those who thought it thinly disguised 'victor's justice' dealt out by the victorious Allies to their defeated enemy, Japan.[7] Another binary is between those who denied Japan's leaders responsibility for aggression and atrocities, and those who felt they were responsible. Rob was among those who sought to look past these disputes. In his view, they meant the trial never got the treatment it warranted. What follows is a brief taxonomy of work on the trial in order to allow the reader to decide whether scholarship on the trial has escaped these binaries.

JUDGMENT BY CIVILISATION OR BY THE VICTORS?

Three immediate post-trial accounts published in the 1950s showed that the Tokyo trial was a terrain of scholarly contest, particularly regarding the prosecution of Japanese leaders for crimes against peace. In 1950, Joseph Keenan, who in his opening as Chief Prosecutor at Tokyo had claimed that the trial was the 'judgment of civilization', joined with the natural lawyer Brendan Brown and argued that its legitimacy arose from its application of positive law reflecting natural law precepts.[8] Also in 1950, former prosecutor Sol Horwitz thought that the trial reinforced the Nuremberg precedent in positive law.[9] However, in 1955,[10] the Indian Justice at Tokyo, Radhabinod Pal, revisited the argument he made in his dissenting opinion attacking the trial's legal validity in international law. He emphasised that prosecuting the vanquished power's leaders for a

[5] N Boister and R Cryer (eds), *Documents on the Tokyo International Military Tribunal: Charter, Indictment and Judgments* (Oxford University Press, 2008) xxxiiii. Detailed research was not easy to access until the Tokyo judgments were published by Röling and Rüter in 1977: B Röling and CF Rüter (eds), *The Tokyo Judgment: The International Military Tribunal for the Far East (IMTFE), 29 April 1946–12 November 1948* (Amsterdam University Press, 1977). The efforts in the 1980s of Pritchard to collect the trial materials and produce a workable index were of enormous value: see RJ Pritchard, SZ Pritchard and DC Watt, *The Tokyo War Crimes Trial* (Garland, 1981).

[6] R Minear, *Victor's Justice: The Tokyo War Crimes Trial* (Princeton: University Press, 1971) xiii.

[7] See further below.

[8] J Keenan and B Brown, *Crimes against International Law* (Public Affairs Press, 1950) 56.

[9] S Horwitz, 'The Tokyo Trial' (1950) 465 *International Conciliation* 475, 486.

[10] See generally R Pal, *Crimes in International Relations* (University of Calcutta, 1958).

war of aggression could not be just, because international relations themselves were fundamentally unjust. Rather than acting on the basis of law, the Allies had pursued national advantage.

In 1971, as Western claims to project justice abroad grew shaky during the wars of national liberation in Vietnam and elsewhere, in a searing indictment Richard Minear challenged the view that the trial 'corroborated our convictions about the dastardly and criminal nature of Japan's wartime leadership and policies' and set out to 'demolish the credibility of the Tokyo Trial and its verdict'.[11] Following Pal, Minear rejected the legal validity of individual criminal responsibility for aggression and recharacterised the trial as 'victor's justice'.[12]

In 2001, Tim Maga[13] tried to supply an antidote to denunciations of 'victor's justice [and] Allied racist agendas' by emphasising the trial's complexity and the firm commitment to justice of its participants.[14] Nonetheless, the 'victor's justice' critique stuck. In 2013, Kirsten Sellars used a positivist scalpel to expose the crimes against peace charges as a confluence of US moralism and legalism with the same goal – namely, US dominance in Asia.[15] In 2007, Gerry Simpson argued that the Japanese leaders' political project to expand Japanese and Asian power had been tried at Tokyo[16] and, expanding on this idea, in 2018 Damien Rogers argued that the Tokyo trial was a new form of politics in the conflict between Western powers and Japan over control of modernity itself.[17] In a more conventional analysis written in 2023, Gary Bass styled the trial as a site of conflict between imperial orders – those of the US, Russia, Europe, Japan and China – in which it was not always clear who was on whose side.[18]

A rich vein of this 'victor's justice' critique has been the impact of Pal's dissent on international law. In 1991, Elizabeth Kopelman[19] argued that Pal, incensed by the way that the US had collapsed the *ius ad bellum* into the *ius in bello* through the prosecution of crimes against peace, responded with arch-positivism, underpinned by a radical ideological position that accepted Japan's claim of self-defence because of his anti-imperialistic and Pan-Asian rhetoric.

[11] Minear (n 6) ix.

[12] ibid 134.

[13] T Maga, *Judgment at Tokyo: The Japanese War Crimes Trials* (University Press of Kentucky, 2001).

[14] ibid ix–x.

[15] K Sellars, *'Crimes against Peace' and International law* (Cambridge University Press, 2015).

[16] G Simpson, *Law, War and Crime: War Crimes Trials and the Reinvention of International Criminal law* (Cambridge University Press, 2007) 13.

[17] D Rogers, *Law, Politics and the Limits of Prosecuting Mass Atrocity* (Palgrave Macmillan, 2018) 48, 85.

[18] G Bass, *Judgement at Tokyo: World War II on Trial and the Making of Modern Asia* (Alfred A Knopf, 2023), 17 et seq.

[19] E Kopelman, 'Ideology and International Law: The Dissent of the Indian Justice at the Tokyo War Crimes Trial' (1991) 23 *New York University Journal of International Law and Politics* 373.

However, in 2014, following the lead of Ashis Nandy,[20] Milinda Bannerjee[21] countered more subtly that Pal's judgment was not a positivist tract designed to uphold Asian sovereigntist claims against those of the West; rather, it was an attack on sovereignty as the *grundnorm* of international society.[22] Bannerjee argued that Pal's Pan-Asianism led him to make a strategic decision to support Japanese sovereignty against a Western assertion of political and moral authority through the trial, even though he was suspicious of sovereign power as a precursor to state violence, racism and colonialism.[23] Pal, he argued, subscribed to a supra-national natural legal order, but not the contingent, imperialistic, Western-dominated naturalism of Keenan and Webb projected through the Tokyo trial.[24]

In 2018, David Cohen (writing with Yuma Totani)[25] reverted to a strict analysis of whether the judgments constituted a rational justification for their findings and conclusions. He attacked the majority judgment as an unbalanced recital of facts and findings, caused by reliance on the unproved prosecution case that the Japanese actions had amounted to a conspiracy, thereby making a weak basis for individual convictions. He criticised Röling's separate judgment as paradoxical and lacking in objectivity[26] and Pal's judgment as tending towards a 'political tract' and academic thesis on the state of international law.[27] He found President Webb's draft judgments better at establishing individual guilt.[28] As early as 1950, Lord Hankey had identified a tension between a legalistic analysis of the trial and one based on broader notions of justice:

> Anyone who can conceive that the judgements, however fair they may be in fact, will go down in history as an expression of justice and will be accepted in Japan as such may be something more than blind.[29]

His reference to reception in Japan was prescient. One contest in the scholarship, mainly in Japan, is between those who argue that the trial created an unfair

[20] A Nandy, 'The Other within: The Strange Case of Radhabinod Pal's Judgment on Culpability' (1992) 23(1) *New Literary History* 63.

[21] M Bannerjee, 'Does International Criminal Justice Require a Sovereign? Historicising Radhabinod Pal's Tokyo Judgment in Light of His "Indian" Legal Philosophy' in M Bergsmo, C Wui Ling and Y Ping (eds), *Historical Origins of International Criminal Law: Volume 2* (Torkel Opsahl Academic EPublisher, 2014) 67.

[22] ibid 70.

[23] ibid 76, 89.

[24] ibid 102.

[25] D Cohen and Y Totani, *The Tokyo War Crimes Tribunal: Law, History, and Jurisprudence* (Cambridge University Press, 2018).

[26] ibid 414 et seq.

[27] ibid 431 et seq.

[28] ibid 305 et seq.

[29] L Hankey, *Politics, Trials and Errors* (Pen-in-Hand, 1950) 89.

'Tokyo trial view of history'[30] and those who note how alleged unfairness has been used as a shield behind which to deny war responsibility.[31] In 2008, Yuma Totani[32] revealed the change in Japanese attitudes to the trial from the generally positive attitude to the trial while it was being held to a negative view as the victor's justice critique coalesced around Pal's visits to Japan in the 1950s. In 2003, Ushimura Kei[33] recast the trial as an exercise in Western 'orientalism' because it blamed the Japanese military for all that had gone wrong.[34] In 2008, Yoshinobu Higurashi[35] (in a book published in English only in 2022) revealed how support for the 1975 enshrinement at Yasukuni Shrine of war criminals convicted at the Tokyo trial was justified in part because not doing so would have meant affirming the trial's results.[36] Madoka Futamura's[37] 2008 study of Japanese reactions to the trial revealed that Japanese people were either ignorant of it or had negative feelings towards it. In 2014, Nakajima Takeshi recorded that Japanese nationalists continued to use Justice Pal's judgment to justify Japan's wartime invasion of Asia.[38] The rest of Asia has watched this debate within Japan with interest, albeit with some criticism.[39] As Bing Bing Jia pointed out in 2014,[40] the trial proceedings store the lessons of the past atrocities, whether or not they are open to criticism as victor's justice. In 2014, O-Gon Kwon[41] pointed out the neglect by the trial of the vicious nature of Japan's colonial occupation of Korea, again exposing the double standards of its imperial architects, while in 2017, Deokykyo Choi noted that leaving Korea out of the Tokyo trial undermined its claim to constitute the 'judgement of civilization' on Japan's leaders.[42] It appears that while the trial was inadequate, it is viewed by the victims of Japan's wars in Asia and the Pacific as an important measure of reckoning for Japan's invasions.

[30] K Noboru, *Tōkyō Saiban* (Chukoshinso, 1971).

[31] MH Chang and RP Barker, 'Victor's Justice and Japan's Amnesia: The Tokyo War Crimes Trial Reconsidered' (2001) 19(4) *East Asia: An International Quarterly* 55, 60.

[32] Y Totani, *The Tokyo War Crimes Trial: The Pursuit of Justice in the Wake of World War II* (Harvard University Asia Centre, 2008).

[33] U Kei, *Beyond the Judgment of Civilization* (LTCB Trust, 2003).

[34] ibid 166.

[35] Y Higurashi, *The Tokyo Trial: War Criminals and Japan's Postwar Relations* (JPIC, 2022).

[36] ibid 18 and the sources cited therein.

[37] M Futamura, *War Crimes Tribunals and Transitional Justice: The Tokyo Trial and the Nuremberg Legacy* (Routledge, 2008).

[38] N Takeshi, 'Justice Pal (India)' in Tanaka et al (n 1) 127.

[39] Centres like the Centre for Tokyo Trial Studies at Shanghai Jiao Tong University have received official support: see history.sjtu.edu.cn/En/Content/19.

[40] BB Jia, 'The Legacy of the Tokyo Trial in China' in Tanaka et al (n 1) 207, 224.

[41] H O-Gon Kwon, 'Forgotten Victims, Forgotten Defendants' in Tanaka et al (n 1) 227.

[42] D Choi, 'Defining Colonial "War Crimes": Korean Debates on Collaboration, War Reparations, and the International Military Tribunal for the Far East' in K von Lingen (ed), *Debating Collaboration and Complicity in War Crimes Trials in Asia, 1945–1956* (Palgrave Macmillan, 2017) 41, 54.

RESPONSIBILITY OF LEADERS FOR ATROCITIES OR WANT OF CULPABILITY?

Lord Russell, writing in 1958, was not concerned with the crime of aggression. His task was to justify the Tokyo trial's 'retribution' as justice for the:

> [U]nspeakable cruelties and merciless tortures … inflicted on Allied prisoners of war and innocent civilians by all ranks of the Japanese armed forces, without any compunction and, for the most part, without any feelings of compassion whatsoever.[43]

However, in 1975, Minear argued that holding Japanese leaders personally responsible for these crimes had been legally invalid by drawing on Pal's dissenting argument that they lacked culpability for the crimes of their subordinates.[44] In 1979, Piccigallo[45] took the contrary position, noting that the question of responsibility could not be reduced to a conflict between Western and Eastern judges. He pointed out, for example, that Filipino Justice Delfin Jaranilla had called for greater severity of punishment for the convicted. Minear insinuated that Jaranilla was biased, dismissing him as a 'survivor of the Bataan Death March' who had taken the 'hardest line'.[46]

One of Rob's motivations for a re-appraisal of the Tokyo Trial in 2008 was the need to look past the 'victor's justice' debate and instead towards the trial's contribution to international criminal law.[47] Rob was interested in examining what it had to say about legal doctrines like command responsibility. To this end, Rob was particularly taken with a draft discussion by Justice Röling, entitled 'Conventional War Crimes'.[48] Although war crimes were well established by the 1940s, they had not been subject to extensive judicial scrutiny, and Röling's discussion provides a rare view of the state of the law. In contrast, Rob thought Pal's judgment on responsibility for war crimes against prisoners of war (POWs) and civilians was 'not … his best'.[49] Rob was not alone in this. In 2008, Totani, also interested in transcending the victor's justice debate, devoted much of her book to the war crimes counts and command responsibility, and in the process debunked the view that the prosecution was more concerned with European POW deaths than those of Asian civilians.[50] In 2018, Cohen (with Totani) criticised the majority argument that the scale of the atrocities meant they must have been carried out under a guiding hand, but chided Pal on war crimes, particularly

[43] Lord Russell of Liverpool, *The Knights of Bushido: A Short History of Japanese War Crimes* (Cassell, 1958) 309–10.

[44] Minear (n 6) 134.

[45] PR Piccigallo, *The Japanese on Trial: Allied War Crimes Operations in the East, 1945–1951* (University of Texas Press, 1979).

[46] Minear (n 6) 160.

[47] Boister and Cryer (n 3).

[48] Memorandum: Conventional War Crimes; To: Sir William Webb; From: Justice BVA Röling, Northcroft Archive, Macmillan Brown Library, University of Canterbury, Acc No 1549, Box No 331. See Boister and Cryer (n 3) 175.

[49] Boister and Cryer (n 3) 96.

[50] Totani (n 32) 6, 162.

with regard to the illogicality of accepting that war crimes had occurred but that the accused should be exonerated on the grounds that they were not responsible because of their seniority.[51] He preferred Webb's position based on the inference that the leaders on trial were liable for omitting to stop the war crimes because they were in charge and must have known what was happening because of the scale of atrocities.[52] In 2014, Bannerjee explained Pal's refusal to accept that Japan's leaders were to blame as a measure to protect Japan from Allied sovereignty claims.[53] This 'sovereign immunity' (if one can call it that) had an elitist element because, as Maga pointed out in 2001, Pal had been happy for national military trials of lower ranks to continue, even though they were conducted by Western powers.[54]

The 'victor's justice' critique was also used to deny responsibility for war crimes in Japan, although in 1986 Yasuaki Ōnuma attempted to correct nationalist assumptions that Pal had asserted that no crimes had been committed rather than that the leadership were not responsible.[55] Japanese scholarship continued to veer between positions like Nasao Nishikawa's 1997 attack on the trial as a racist revenge for early war time defeats[56] and Yuki Tanaka's 1996 acceptance of Japanese commission of atrocities (while pointing out the Allies had also committed atrocities).[57] Unfortunately, Japanese scholars pointing out the culpability of the US or Europeans does not wash with Japan's neighbours. In 1986, Ōnuma acknowledged that 'it is obvious that the United States' atomic bombing of Japan in no way evens out the account between Japan and the peoples of Asia'.[58] Xiang Longwan and Marquise Lee Houle[59] noted in 2014 that from a Chinese perspective, the leaders on trial were clearly to blame for atrocities committed in China by the Japanese military from 1928 to 1945.[60]

LOOKING INTO AND BEYOND THE TOKYO TRIAL

Scholars have recognised that debates about the validity of the charges of crimes against peace have inhibited interest in the many hidden facets of the

[51] See Cohen and Totani (n 25) 349 et seq, 459 et seq.
[52] ibid 370 et seq.
[53] Bannerjee (n 21) 97.
[54] Maga (n 13) 67.
[55] Y Ōnuma, 'Beyond Victor's Justice' (1984) XI *Japan Echo* 63, 72.
[56] N Nishikawa, 'Japanese History in the Dock: Victory for a Viewpoint' (1997) 35(8) *Perspectives: The American Historical Association Newsletter* 5, 8.
[57] Y Tanaka, *Hidden Horrors: Japanese War Crimes in World War II* (Westview Press, 1996).
[58] Ōnuma (n 55) 69. See also Drumbl and Mouthaan, ch 16 in this volume.
[59] L Xiang and ML Houle, 'In Search of Justice for China: The Contributions of Judge Hsiang Che-chun to the Prosecution of Japanese War Criminals at the Tokyo Trial' in Bergsmo et al (n 21) 143. See also L Xiang, *Journey to Justice: The Inside Story of the Chinese Prosecutor Hsiang Che-chun and His Team at the Tokyo Trial* (Natural Logic, 2023).
[60] Xiang and Houle (n 59) 145.

Tokyo trial. In 1995, for example, Pritchard noted that the legal difficulties of the trial hindered appreciation of the richness and variety of its evidence.[61]

One field of scholarship on the trial has focused on its provenance and operation. In 1985, Kentarō Awaya explored the historical record to expose many of the wrinkles in its preparation and the balance of political forces in mid-1940s Japan either arrayed against the trial or intent upon using it to substantiate their favoured version of history.[62] In 1989, Arnold Brackman, who had covered the trial as a journalist, endeavoured in a chronological account to clear up misinformation and ignorance.[63] The Dutch Judge Bert Röling's reminiscences, published in 1994,[64] set about correcting the historical record on, inter alia, the US blocking of the indictment of Japanese who had experimented on Chinese POWs with biological weapons, and the defendant Kōki Hirota's innocence, while setting out Röling's view that the atomic bombings were war crimes. In 2014, a collection of essays on the trial investigated hitherto untouched subject matter, including biographical sketches of five of the key judges.[65] Lord Bonomy's[66] presentation of the Scottish Justice Lord Patrick, for example, reveals Patrick's scorn for US defence counsel and frustration with Justice Pal, but also portrays someone whose life was the law and who had personal experience of war as a fighter ace and POW in the First World War.[67] Other pieces in the collection explored an array of other topics. Tsuneishi Kei-ichi painted US attempts to lay its hand on Japan's wartime biowarfare research as morally compromised and inept.[68] Tina Dolgopol exposed a deliberate ignorance in regard to the treatment of comfort women.[69] Yuki Tanaka examined the contradiction of laying charges for murder when those who dropped the atom bomb were open to the same charges.[70]

A related area of research uncovered the attitudes of the various nations which participated in the trial. In 1979, Piccigallo was among the first to examine each participating Allied nation's policies towards Japanese suspects and

[61] J Pritchard, 'The International Military Tribunal for the Far East and its Contemporary Resonances' (1995) 149 *Military Law Review* 25.

[62] K Awaya, 'Tokyo Saiban eno Michi (The Road to the Tokyo Trials),' published in multiple parts in *Asahi Shimbun*, 1985. See also K Awaya, 'In the Shadows of the Tokyo Tribunal' in C Hosoya et al (eds), *The Tokyo War Crimes Trial: An International Symposium* (Kodansha America, 1986) 79.

[63] AC Brackman, *The Other Nuremberg: The Untold Story of the Tokyo War Crimes Trials* (Collins, 1989) 11, 31.

[64] B Röling and A Cassese, *The Tokyo Trial and beyond: Reflections of a Peacemonger* (Polity Press, 1998).

[65] Tanaka et al (n 1).

[66] L Bonomy, 'Justice Patrick (United Kingdom)' in Tanaka et al (n 1) 103.

[67] ibid 107.

[68] Tsi Kei-ichi, 'Reasons for the Failure to Prosecute Unite 731 and its Significance' in Tanaka et al (n 1) 177.

[69] U Dolgopol, 'Knowledge and Responsibility: The Ongoing Consequences of Failing to Give Sufficient Attention to the Crimes against the Comfort Women in the Tokyo Trial' in Tanaka et al (n 1) 243.

[70] Y Tanaka, 'The Atomic Bombing and the Shimoda Case': Lessons for Anti-nuclear Legal Movements' in Tanaka et al (n 1) 293. See also Drumbl and Mouthaan, ch 16 in this volume.

towards one another.[71] In 2014, Ann-Sophie Schoepfel explored how, on the one hand, France was concerned with the fairness of the trial, while, on the other hand, it pursued the political goal of establishing that in Indochina, France had been the victim of Japan rather than collaborating with Japan.[72] In 2018, Kerstin von Lingen edited a collection of pieces that focused on the 'transcultural encounters' between the 'unjustly forgotten' men and women from the different participating states who ran the trial.[73] Details surfaced ranging from the compromise-making role of the Russian and Chinese judges at Tokyo[74] to the fact that the Dutch prosecutor strengthened the prosecution for crimes against peace while simultaneously ring-fencing Dutch imperialism in Indonesia.[75]

A spin-off from interest in national attitudes which has proved highly productive concerns research into trials held under national auspices in Asia and the Pacific. In 1979, Piccigallo tried to rescue these 'minor' trials from the shadow of Tokyo.[76] In 2014, Ling Yan examined the largely ignored prosecutions in China in 1956, which included prosecution of crimes against peace using the same wording as the Tokyo trial and applying the same principles of individual responsibility; these prosecutions received input from the Chinese judge at Tokyo, Ju-ao Mei.[77] Other pieces in the collection dealt with trials in Singapore[78] and in Indonesia.[79] A 2014 collection again edited by Kerstin von Lingen[80] broadened the scope of inquiry, offering material on, for example, Soviet trials of Japanese defendants for Japan's wartime biological weapons programme.[81] In 2015, Yuma Totani[82] explored selected Allied war crimes prosecutions in Asia and the Pacific, and therein uncovered the evolution of general principles such as command responsibility. In 2016, Tim McCormack, Georgina Fitzpatrick

[71] Piccigallo (n 45) xiii.

[72] A Schoepfel, 'The War Court as a Form of State Building: The French Prosecution of Japanese War Crimes at the Saigon and Tokyo Trials' in Bergsmo et al (n 21) 119, 136.

[73] Von Lingen (ed) (n 1) vii.

[74] JB Sedgwick's, 'Building Blocks: Communities of Dissent, Manufactured Majorities and International Judgment at Tokyo' in von Lingen (ed) (n 1) 29, 32 et seq.

[75] L Schouten, 'In the Footsteps of Grotius: The Netherlands and its Representation at the International Military Tribunal for the Far East, 1945–1948' in von Lingen (ed) (n 1) 242, 255 et seq.

[76] Piccigallo (n 45) 32.

[77] L Yan, 'The 1956 Japanese War Crimes Trials in China' in Bergsmo et al (n 21) 215, 224. See also B Kushner, 'Chinese War Crimes Trials of Japanese, 1945–1956: A Historical Summary' in Bergsmo et al (n 21) 243.

[78] WL Cheah, 'Post-Second World War British Trials in Singapore: Lost in Translation at the Car Nicobar Spy Case' in Bergsmo et al (n 21) 301.

[79] NHB Jørgensen and D Friedmann, 'Enforced Prostitution in International Law through the Prism of the Dutch Temporary Courts Martial at Batavia' in Bergsmo et al (n 21) 331.

[80] K von Lingen (ed), *War Crimes Trials in the Wake of Decolonization and Cold War in Asia, 1945-1956: Justice in Time of Turmoil* (Palgrave Macmillan, 2014).

[81] V Polunina, 'From Tokyo to Khabarovsk: Soviet War Crimes Trials in Asia as Cold War Battlefields' in von Lingen (n 80) 214, 239.

[82] Y Totani, *Justice in Asia and the Pacific Region, 1945–1952: Allied War Crimes Prosecutions* (Cambridge University Press, 2015).

and Narrelle Morris began a comprehensive account of Australia's war crimes trial efforts.[83] In 2017, Sandra Wilson, Robert Cribb, Beatrice Trefalt and Dean Aszkielowicz[84] also examined trials across the region, pointing out that the broad legitimacy of these trials is more defensible than that of Tokyo because of the absence of crimes against peace.[85] However, in 2017, Aszkielowicz[86] detailed the slow shift of Allied policy from retribution to pragmatic accommodation of Japan as a new ally in the Cold War.

CONCLUSION

In the post-trial period, and particularly during decolonisation, scholarship on the Tokyo trial became fixated with different aspects of the trial as symbol of a watershed between, as Kirsten von Lingen and Robert Cribb put it:

> [T]he demise of an old political-legal international legal order defined by European hegemony and advent of a new, putatively anti-imperial one, based on contestations between the American and Soviet blocs and the rise of post-colonial nation states.[87]

It followed, as Fujita Hisakazu pointed out, that the trial can only be said to represent the interests of the international community 'in a sense'.[88] The value the trial purported to impose – universalism – was undermined by the fact that the trial was imposed by victorious states and was highly selective in its jurisdiction. The trial shrank from universalism as the national interests of its founders, particularly the US, were reasserted. In 2023,[89] Gary Bass grasped the hypocrisy inherent in many facets of the trial, while painting a broad and detailed picture of the trial 'in the round' and not retreating from its basic ideals of universalism.[90] However, it cannot be ignored that political elites in Japan were no fans of universalism either and did their part to frustrate it. For example the Japanese defence counsel Kenzō Takanyagi, who did much to shape the positivist critique of the trial, had been in the pre-war period a semi-official Japanese critic of the League of Nations, which he regarded as' the

[83] T McCormack, G Fitzpatrick and N Morris (eds), *Australia's War Crimes Trials, 1945–1951* (Brill, 2016).

[84] S Wilson et al, *Japanese War Criminals: The Politics of Justice after the Second World War* (Columbia University Press, 2017).

[85] ibid 369.

[86] D Aszkielowicz, *The Australian Pursuit of Japanese War Criminals, 1943–1958: From Foe to Friend* (Columbia University Press, 2017).

[87] K von Lingen and R Cribb, 'Justice in a Time of Turmoil: War Crimes Trials in Asia and the Context of Decolonization and Cold War' in von Lingen (n 80) 1, 3.

[88] F Hisakazu, 'The Tokyo Trial: Humanity's Justice v Victor's Justice' in Tanaka et al (n 1) 3. 4.

[89] Bass (n 18).

[90] ibid 6.

product of elevated sentiment' created by the First World War.[91] The victim-nation perspective appears to stand outside this debate about the authenticity of the trial's universalism. From a Chinese standpoint, for example, Xiang and Houle note that '[t]he historical lessons of the Tokyo Trial are profound'.[92] This reflects, I think, an underlying view that, lurking behind the hypocrisy of 'the judgment of civilization', the trial encapsulates an ideal of value, notably, criminal justice.

Moreover, in what Bannerjee calls 'the long scholarly aftermath'[93] of the Tokyo trial, it appears that commentators' views have become less entrenched, less concerned with its essence and more interested in its parts, as altitudinous expectations of international criminal courts have diminished.[94] Scholarship has moved past fixation with legal validity and has established the trial as a legitimate field of study. For one thing, the broad scope of the trial and the quantity of evidence heard makes it an historical repository of a highly unusual kind. In preference to a more particular view of the trial, I prefer the elemental description from our materials book, written by Rob in his characteristically careful tone:

> The Tokyo IMT [International Military Tribunal] can be viewed as a legal response, broadly, to the military expansionist phase of Japanese foreign relations in the nineteenth and twentieth centuries or more narrowly, 'to Japan's 'fifteen year war' in East Asia and the Pacific.[95]

Taking this broad view permits one to approach the trial without preconceptions and to dig deeper into the record, to reveal more, to understand the trial and its context better, and that is what more recent scholarship has tried to do. While not blind to its faults, Rob Cryer played an important part in that change of approach, primarily because he took the trial seriously as an exercise of law as well as of justice. By laying this groundwork, Rob made it easier for others to do so and forge ahead.

[91] Cited in UM Zachmann, 'Loser's Justice: The Tokyo Trial from the Perspective of the Japanese Defence Counsels and the Legal Community' in von Lingen (ed) (n 1) 284, 293.

[92] Xiang and Houle (n 59) 173.

[93] Bannerjee (n 21) 115.

[94] See, eg, M Damaška, 'What is the Point of International Criminal Justice?' (2008) 83 *Chicago-Kent Law Review* 329.

[95] Boister and Cryer (n 5) xxxiiii.

Act III

Violence and Reckoning

10

Tribute to Rob

Selectivity in International Criminal Law*

ELIES VAN SLIEDREGT

INTRODUCTION

I HAVE MANY fond memories of Rob, from meeting at conferences, at PhD ceremonies and most recently (at the end of 2017) at my 'inaugural address dinner' at Leeds University where he was one of a circle of international criminal law (ICL) friends and colleagues who attended that occasion. This is where the best ever picture of him was taken, together with Mark Drumbl. I regret not having seen him after that event; for not having met him in Birmingham, something we had talked about. The memories I have are warm and full of respect. This wonderful Festschrift now further shows how multifaceted Rob was as a legal scholar but also as a human being.

As a tribute, I want to dedicate this short intervention to a topic Rob wrote about in the early stages of his career: selectivity in international prosecutions. In his book *Prosecuting International Crimes: Selectivity and the International Criminal Law Regime* published in Cambridge's Studies in International and Comparative Law[1] and based on his PhD,[2] Rob explores and analyses the scope of selectivity in international criminal law. One of the insights his work on selectivity has brought is that it is not just selectivity in prosecution but also, and especially, the parameters of criminal responsibility that lead to selectivity. He calls this 'selectivity by stealth'.[3] These sneaky (and cruel) selectivities are

* This contribution is based on my tribute to Rob that was published as 'One Rule for Them: Selectivity in International Criminal Law' (2021) 34(2) *Leiden Journal of International Law* 283.

[1] R Cryer, *Prosecuting International Crimes. Selectivity and the International Criminal Law Regime* (Cambridge University Press, 2005).

[2] R Cryer, 'Towards an Integrated Regime for the Prosecution of International Crimes' (PhD thesis, Nottingham University, 2000), eprints.nottingham.ac.uk/11305/1/364444.pdf.

[3] R Cryer, 'The Boundaries of Liability in International Criminal Law, or "Selectivity by Stealth"' (2001) 6 *Journal of Conflict & Security Law* 3.

touched upon elsewhere in this Festschrift, for example, by Mark Drumbl and Solange Mouthaan in Chapter 16 on the Tokyo IMT.

FORMS OF SELECTIVITY

There are different forms of selectivity. We always talk about selectivity in the context of the Nuremberg and Tokyo trials; only crimes committed by the vanquished were prosecuted. The whiff of victor's justice forever surrounds these proceedings. One-sidedness was also part of the proceedings before the ad hoc tribunals in the 1990s. The International Criminal Tribunal for Rwanda (ICTR), established by the United Nations (UN) at the request of the Tutsi government of Rwanda, only conducted trials against Hutu defendants. While this was entirely appropriate when it came to prosecuting genocide, for war crimes this was at least debatable, since there was evidence of war crimes committed by both sides. Similarly, the decision by International Criminal Tribunal for the Former Yugoslavia (ICTY) Prosecutor Carla del Ponte[4] not to investigate the conduct of the North Atlantic Treaty Organization (NATO) in the conflict in Kosovo was controversial and fed accusations of selective prosecution.[5]

In his seminal piece 'Selective Reaction to Atrocity',[6] Tim McCormack goes back to ancient civilisations and European approaches in the Middle Ages to demonstrate that there is a red line running through the history of war crimes trials: states are reluctant to enforce the laws of war against nationals. Conversely, establishing structures and processes to try 'others' has been the engine behind developing a system of international criminal justice.

ROB'S SELECTIVITY FRAMEWORK

Selectivity *Ratione Personae*

Rob draws on McCormack's argument on selectivity and develops it by focusing on prosecutorial discretion. With regard to selective enforcement,[7] which Rob

[4] The decision was taken on the basis of the following internal report: *Final Report to the Prosecutor by the Committee Established to Review the NATO Bombing Campaign against the Federal Republic of Yugoslavia*, 8 June 2000, www.icty.org/en/press/final-report-prosecutor-committee-established-review-nato-bombing-campaign-against-federal. However, some risks of war crimes were raised – see, for example, P Rowe, 'Kosovo 1999: The Air Campaign – Have the Provisions of Additional Protocol I Withstood the Test?' (2000) 82 *International Review of the Red Cross* 137.

[5] See Cryer (n 1) 213–20.

[6] TLH McCormack, 'Selective Reaction to Atrocity: War Crimes and the Development of International Criminal Law' (1997) 60 *Albany Law Review* 681.

[7] Rob adopts Davis' definition of selective prosecution: 'When an enforcement agency or officer has discretionary power to do nothing about a case in which enforcement would be clearly justified

refers to as selectivity *ratione personae*, he notes that progress has been made since Nuremberg. The modern regime of international criminal law, culminating in the establishment of the International Criminal Court (ICC), is testament to 'the efforts of the "Like-Minded States" to at least accept international jurisdiction over their nationals.[8] At the same time, Rob is not blind to the reality of the ICC being hamstrung by its dependence on cooperation with member states.[9]

Selectivity *ratione personae* has two aspects: legality and legitimacy.[10] The former aspect concerns the independence of the prosecutor: whether they are instructed by outside sources or whether they act truly independently in selecting cases to prosecute. The latter implicates a more fundamental concern where selection of cases is motivated by power, patronage and/or political influence.[11] Rule of law adherence requires a coherent and consistent application of the law. This is at stake when prosecutors decide not to prosecute a certain class of crimes or a certain class of perpetrators.[12] The early practice of self-referrals at the ICC risked compromising both legality and legitimacy. The invitation to ICC Prosecutor Moreno Ocampo by the governments of Uganda and the Democratic Republic of the Congo (DRC) to investigate and prosecute crimes committed by armed opposition groups in these countries opened the ICC up to manipulation.[13]

Selectivity by Stealth

The other form of selectivity Rob discussed concerns limiting judicial discretion and the parameters of liability. Rob uses Michael Bothe's distinction of 'safe' and 'unsafe' law enforcement mechanisms[14] to discuss a state's approach to judicial discretion.[15] An international court or tribunal is considered 'unsafe' when it is likely to exert jurisdiction over a state's nationals. In such situations,

the result is a power of selective enforcement. Such power goes to selection of parties against who the law is enforced.' K Culp Davis, *Discretionary Justice: A Preliminary Inquiry* (Louisiana State University Press, 1969) 163.

[8] Cryer (n 1) 231.

[9] ibid 204–05.

[10] ibid 193.

[11] 'Political considerations, power and patronage will continue to determine who is tried for international crimes and who not': I Brownlie, *Principles of International Law*, 6th edn (Oxford University Press, 2003) 575.

[12] Cryer (n 1) 193–96.

[13] See WA Schabas, 'Complementarity in Practice: Creative Solutions or a Trap for the Court?' in M Politi and F Gioia (eds), *The International Criminal Court and National Jurisdictions* (Routledge, 2008) 25–48; WA Schabas, '"Complementarity in Practice": Some Uncomplimentary Thoughts' (2009) 19 *Criminal Law Forum* 5, 16.

[14] M Bothe, 'International Humanitarian Law and War Crimes Tribunals: Recent Developments and Perspectives' in K Wellens (ed), *International Law: Theory and Practice* (Brill, 1998) 581, 593.

[15] Cryer (n 3) 4; Cryer (n 1) 232–38.

Rob argues, there is a keen interest on the part of states to limit judicial discretion. Having been part of negotiations and drafting processes in establishing the ICC, Rob would have been acutely aware of the desire of state delegations to clarify and detail legal provisions. Indeed, the Rome Statute contains elaborate crime definitions, an addendum detailing the Elements of Crimes,[16] and comprehensive provisions on criminal responsibility, including a catalogue of defences. The drive for a comprehensive codification was criticised by former ICTY Judge David Hunt as reducing ICC judges to a 'mechanical function'.[17] Statute drafters, he argued, had displayed 'mistrust' in the independence of international criminal courts.[18] Detailed codification at the ICC stands in stark contrast to the loosely drafted statutes of the ad hoc tribunals for the former Yugoslavia and Rwanda. These tribunals – for a number of reasons – were considered 'safe'; it was very unlikely that nationals of those states creating the ICTY and the ICTR would be subjected to their jurisdiction.

Indeed, the creators of the ICC have taken a narrow approach towards liability in drafting the crime definitions and the general principles (modes of liability and intent). Where the creators were required to craft 'new' law, as in crimes against humanity, the definitions are restrictive.[19] With regard to war crimes, the distinction between the protections available in international and non-international armed conflicts remained in place, stifling the progressive development of international humanitarian law.[20] Article 30 spells out the different degrees of the mental element, the lowest degree of which is stricter than mens rea/intent in most domestic criminal law statutes.[21] Similarly, Article 25(3) lists a number of (partially overlapping) forms of liability that are more circumscribed than domestic equivalents. One probative example is the high subjective threshold of aiding and abetting liability under section 3(c).[22] The Rome Statute for the first time contains a catalogue of defences in Articles 31–33. What is noteworthy is the inclusion of superior orders, which had been explicitly excluded as

[16] ICC, 'Elements of Crimes' (2013), www.icc-cpi.int/sites/default/files/Publications/Elements-of-Crimes.pdf.

[17] Hon D Hunt, 'The International Criminal Court. High Hopes, "Creative Ambiguity" and an Unfortunate Mistrust in International Judges' (2004) 2 *Journal of International Criminal Justice* 61.

[18] ibid.

[19] LN Sadat and SR Carden, 'The New International Criminal Court: An Uneasy Revolution' (2000) 88 *Georgetown Law Journal* 381, in particular 426–34.

[20] J Stewart, 'Towards a Single Definition of Armed Conflict in International Humanitarian Law: A Critique of Internationalized Armed Conflict' (2003) 85 *International Review of the Red Cross* 313.

[21] Excluding the lowest degree of intent: *dolus eventualis* and advertent recklessness. See G Werle and F Jessberger, 'Unless Otherwise Provided: Article 30 of the ICC Statute and the Mental Element of Crimes under International Criminal Law' (2005) 3 *Journal of International Criminal Justice* 41.

[22] See K Ambos, 'Art 25 Individual Criminal Responsibility' in K Ambos and O Triffterer (eds), *Commentary on the Rome Statute of the International Criminal Court: Article by Article Commentary*, 2nd edn (Beck/Hart, 2008) para 23.

a full defence in the statutes of the Nuremberg and Tokyo tribunals and in the law of the ad hoc tribunals for the former Yugoslavia and Rwanda.[23]

Criminal law principles such as *nullum crimen sine lege* (Article 22), *nulla poena sine lege* (Article 23) and non-retroactivity (Article 24) guarantee definitional precision and fairness to the defendant. This is welcome and aligns with modern criminal law codes and human rights provisions. Yet, it stands in stark contrast to the law and practice of the post-Second World War Tribunals of Nuremberg and Tokyo. The contrast could not be greater than when the codification of the definition of aggression for the ICC is compared to the application of the crime against peace by the International Military Tribunal for the Far East (IMTFE). The dissenting opinions of Indian Judge Pal and Dutch Judge Röling to the IMTFE's judgment are testament to the controversy over crimes against peace. Pal and Röling argued that, at the time, there was no rule in international law *criminalising* the waging of war.[24] The crime of aggression was defined at the ICC years after the court started its operation, after a lengthy, careful and considered process of defining the crime and its jurisdiction. However, the development remains challenging, as Stoyan Panov reflects in Chapter 12 in this volume.

Rob concludes that the world has moved on from 'victor's justice'. However, he is not blind to the selectivity critique in ICL and, through the safe/unsafe argument, demonstrates that there still is selectivity albeit in a subtle, 'stealthy' way.

CONCLUDING THOUGHTS

I am grateful for Rob's scholarship and insights. His work has been a huge inspiration; I developed the selectivity argument in the context of the domestic prosecution of international crimes, discussing the interplay between international refugee law and ICL, and analysing prosecuting the 'other', often the foreigner, which led to the European Research Council (advanced grant) project that I am currently leading on *Joined Up Justice*.[25] It would have been so much fun to work with him on this project. Alas, it was not to be.

[23] Rob discusses the ambiguity over the (alleged) customary international law status of the superior orders defence: Cryer (n 1) 292–301. See also P Gaeta, 'The Defence of Superior Orders: The Statute of the International Criminal Court versus Customary International Law' (1999) 10 *European Journal of International Law* 172.

[24] Judge Pal further accused the Allied powers of double standards, arguing that colonial wars and the atomic bombs were at least as reprehensible as what the Japanese did. See BA Roling and A Cassese, *The Tokyo Trial and beyond: Reflections of a Peacemonger* (Polity, 1992) 60–78. See also Boister, ch 9 in this volume and Vasiliev, ch 19 in this volume.

[25] For more information, see: www.joinedupjustice.com.

11

Envisioning Targeted Killings and the Crime of Aggression in the Age of Autonomous Weaponry

SHAGUFTA SEN

INTRODUCTION

THE REVOLUTION IN military affairs (RMA) has transformed the military sector over the years paving the way for a Fourth Industrial Revolution where the primary focus has become emerging and disruptive technologies. Among these emerging and disruptive technologies is the transformative technology of lethal autonomous weapon systems (AWS), which aim to change the future of warfare. AWS do not have a concrete definition, but are interpreted in various contexts that highlight their multiple constitutive features. When defined in a more precise manner these are:

> A weapon system which, once activated, can select and engage targets without further human intervention and usually without any human pre-selecting those specific targets; and, in the process, to exercise discretion and self-direction to operate in a potentially complex and unstructured environment.[1]

As per the definition, artificial intelligence (AI), the foundation of autonomous functions, enables machines to replace some human judgement in warfare. It has, in turn, been defined as 'the capability of a computer system to perform tasks that normally require human intelligence'.[2]

[1] M Homayounnejad, 'Regarding Lethal Autonomous Weapon Systems I: Assessing the Sense and Scope of "Autonomy" in Emerging Military Weapon Systems' (2017) *TLI Think! Paper 76/2017* 22–23.

[2] See N Sharkey, 'Staying in the Loop: Human Supervisory Control of Weapons' in N Bhuta et al (eds) *Autonomous Weapon Systems: Law, Ethics, Policy* (Cambridge University Press, 2016), focusing on how this might be used to optimise *human-machine collaboration* specifically for designing systems with greater *humanitarian impact*; ML Cummings, 'Artificial Intelligence and the Future of Warfare' (2017) *Chatham House: The Royal Institute of International Affairs* 2; M Homayounnejad, 'The Lawful Use of Autonomous Weapon Systems for Targeted Strikes (Part 1): Concepts, Advantages and Technologies' (2018) *TLI Think! Paper 11/2018* 3, 30.

Autonomy is the functional and technical construct operationalising the weapon system. Autonomy defines the level of machine independence, considers the level of human control required at each stage, and is associated with intelligence, self-governance and the ability to learn and adapt. According to Boulanin,[3] autonomy is not the general characteristic of a system as a whole – what matters is decisions completed autonomously by a machine. Given the importance of AI and autonomy within the functioning of AWS, these characteristics define the limits or the threshold where the crime of aggression may occur when AWS is deployed in the field, autonomy being:

> The level of independence that humans grant a system to execute a given task. It is the condition or the quality of self-governing to achieve an assigned task based on the system's situational awareness, planning and decision-making. Autonomy refers to a spectrum of automation in which independent decision-making can be tailored for a specific mission, level of risk and degree of human-machine teaming.[4]

In the context of the above definition, there are three basic dimensions of autonomy within which the 'autonomy' of the machine can be augmented along the spectrum. The three dimensions are the type of task the machine is performing, the relationship of the human to the machine performing that task, and the sophistication of the machine decision making when performing the task.[5]

The importance of analysis of the crime of aggression within the context of autonomous weapons through the lens of international criminal law stems from the continued accountability and responsibility gaps these weapon systems pose. In this analysis, Professor Cryer's scholarship on international criminal law, especially his wide examination of aggression and command responsibility, finds relevance in placing the crime of aggression in the broader context of modern weapon technologies.[6]

THE CRIME OF AGGRESSION

Aggression has been considered a collective act of the state as it tends to be a 'use of armed force' against the sovereignty, territorial integrity and political independence of a state, which highlights that it is the violation of the prohibited use of force as entailed within Article 2(4) of the United Nations (UN)

[3] V Boulanin, 'Mapping the Development of Autonomy in Weapon Systems: A Primer on Autonomy' (2017) *Stockholm International Peace Research Institute*, www.sipri.org/publications/2017/policy-reports/mapping-development-autonomy-weapon-systems.

[4] A Feickert et al, *US Ground Forces Robotics and Autonomous Systems (RAS) and Artificial Intelligence (AI): Considerations for Congress.* (CRS Report No R45392, 20 November 2018).

[5] P Scharre, *Army of None: Autonomous Weapons and the Future of War* (WW & Norton Company, 2018) 27–28; J Cherry and D Johnson, 'Maintaining Command and Control (C2) of Lethal Autonomous Weapon Systems: Legal and Policy Considerations' 27 *Southwestern Journal of International Law* 4.

[6] For more on this, see Panov, ch 12 in this volume.

Charter.[7] The definition under Article 8bis[8] of the Rome Statute lists acts that would be construed as manifest violations of the Charter. Article 8bis adopts a large portion of the definition set out in General Assembly Resolution 3314 (XXIX) of 1974.[9]

Cryer highlighted in his work on the Tokyo International Military Tribunal (IMT) how the legacy of those trials has contributed to the recognition of aggression as a crime in international law, stating:

> Even though aggression was largely forgotten as a crime in the Cold War, slowly a series of actions taken by a broader international community have occurred which serve to link the Tokyo IMT with efforts to enforce its basic principles today. Nearly sixty years later, the Rome Statute provides a way of achieving the universalism and the legitimacy the Tokyo Tribunal pretended to have.[10]

The basis of the evolution of aggression within the Nuremberg and Tokyo IMTs remains. As Cryer points out, the Nuremberg and Tokyo IMTs enacted the crime within their Charters without providing a concise or detailed definition.[11] However, it was necessary to include the definition of aggression in the Rome Statute. The IMTs did not lay down fixed parameters based on which aggression could be prosecuted, leaving it open to interpretation.[12] The Rome Statute provided a clearer conceptualisation of circumstances in which the crime could be prosecuted.[13]

The definitional dilemma of the crime has remained controversial over time, making it difficult to prosecute. Though the crime of aggression attracts leadership crime because of its nature, the Kampala definition certainly extends to individual criminal responsibility from the traditional concept of 'war of aggression' to 'acts of aggression' under Resolution 3314.[14]

The intention of the International Criminal Court's (ICC) definition of the crime of aggression was to exclude grey areas of international law on the use of force, such as humanitarian intervention, self-defence against terrorist groups in the states and anticipatory self-defence.[15] This exclusion may be contradictory to the core objective of the chapter; it is worth noting that with the development of new weapon technology, these grey areas have begun to blur because of

[7] Scharre (n 5).

[8] Rome Statute of the International Criminal Court (Rome Statute), Article 8bis.

[9] UNGA 3314 (XXIX) (14 December 1974).

[10] N Boister and R Cryer, *The Tokyo International Military Tribunals: A Reappraisal* (Oxford University Press, 2008).

[11] R Cryer, *Prosecuting International Crimes: Selectivity and International Law Regime* (Cambridge University Press, 2005) 245.

[12] ibid.

[13] ibid.

[14] Boister and Cryer (n 10); C Stahn, *A Critical Introduction to International Criminal Law* (Cambridge University Press, 2018).

[15] C Kress, 'The Crime of Aggression before the First Review of the ICC Statute' (2007) 20 *Leiden Journal of International Law* 851, 855–56; E Wilmshurst, 'Aggression' in R Cryer et al, *An Introduction to International Criminal Law and Procedure*, 2nd edn (Cambridge University Press, 2010) 327–28.

increased global conflict and continuous assertion of the right to self-defence when the act constitutes an act of aggression or unlawful use of force within the constraints of Article 2(4).

A necessary part of the crime of aggression is the aggressive aim or the intention of the leader. The act of aggression is also known as a 'leadership crime'. This highlights that intention or mens rea is the foremost consideration as to when the crime of aggression occurs. In the Rome Statute, two element requirements operate to establish a crime of aggression. These are Elements 4 and 6.[16] Element 4 requires that the perpetrator is aware of the factual circumstances establishing the inconsistency of the use of armed force by the state with the UN Charter. In contrast, Element 6 requires that the perpetrator is aware that the use of armed force would result in a 'manifest' violation of the UN Charter.[17] To prosecute the crime of aggression, establishing 'intent' is primary. In the context of autonomous weapons, 'intent' would be attributed to the human operator. The reason for this is found in the Guiding Principles, which were affirmed by the Group of Governmental Experts (GGE) on Emerging Technologies in the Area of Lethal Autonomous Weapons System in 2019. The principles established that the accountability and responsibility of acts committed by the AI-driven system would continue to vest in the human operator.[18]

Stahn[19] stated that there remain ambiguities in the law regarding the legality of force, including how the crime of aggression is not a state sovereignty crime, but a global crime. He further states that aggression can take multidimensional forms as it can constitute a full-fledged war as well as surgical strikes, with a broad range of victims thereby affected.

Considering this opinion, imagining targeted killings as part of the crime of aggression is not far from reality. Targeted killings are considered a threat of force and a violation of sovereignty, countering the argument of targeted killings falling within the 'grey area' of international law regarding the use of force. Furthermore, how drone strikes have been used in the past for executing either state or non-state actors highlights that developing autonomous drones or integrating autonomous functionalities within drones would make target identification precise for execution.

Sari and Celik[20] emphasise that for an act of aggression to occur, certain requirements need to be met so that the act can be prosecuted, ie, violation

[16] E Wilmshurst, 'Aggression' in Cryer et al (n 15) 327–28.

[17] ibid.

[18] Group of Governmental Experts on Emerging Technologies in the Area of Lethal Autonomous Weapons Systems, Principles (b) and (c), 'Guiding Principles' (Meeting of the High Contracting Parties to the Convention on Prohibitions or Restrictions on the Use of Certain Conventional Weapons Which May Be Deemed to Be Excessively Injurious or to Have Indiscriminate Effects, CCW/MSP/2019/9, 13 December 2019).

[19] Stahn (n 14).

[20] See generally O Sari and S Celik, 'Legal Evaluation of the Attacks Caused by Artificial Intelligence-Based Lethal Weapon Systems within the Context of Rome Statute' (2021) 42 *Computer Law & Security Review* 36.

of the Charter and manifestation of this violation.[21] They reiterate that whenever the use of force is authorised by the UN Security Council within Article 51 of the Charter, it would hardly constitute a crime of aggression, emphasising the two requirements to make the crime prosecutable:[22] first, a crime will not occur unless there has been a manifest violation of the Charter; and, second, the prohibition on the use of force may be widely interpreted to include exceptions of 'pre-emptive' and 'preventive self-defence'.

The scope and extent of the crime of aggression emphasises the need to address how targeted killings, which may be conducted by AWS, would be placed within its ambit, highlighting the need to assess whether such killings would constitute themselves as a manifest violation of the use of force.

TARGETED KILLINGS: A NEW ACT OF AGGRESSION?

According to Melzer, targeted killings are 'the use of lethal force by a State or its agents with intent, premeditation and deliberation to kill individually selected persons who are not in the physical custody of those targeting them'.[23]

Targeted killings have routinely been labelled as 'inhumane' or 'cruel' as they result in violation of the fundamental right to life and human dignity. The human rights argument runs at the forefront of the targeted killings debate. According to the above-cited definition, the use of lethal force becomes essential, thus highlighting that it may be construed as an act of aggression as there exists the element of intent, which has been dubbed crucial for prosecuting such acts.

Aggression has constantly been emphasised as a leadership crime from which 'command responsibility' may emanate and would be accorded to state actors in the position of authority. Since the evolution of drones, targeted killings have been conducted against non-state actors under the guise of anticipation or a so-called 'imminent threat', which is adjudged only in accordance with the circumstances surrounding the strike so conducted. The assassination of Qassem Soleimaini by a US drone strike in 2020 stirred up a controversial debate over the concept of anticipatory self-defence and what constitutes an imminent threat, while also changing the scope of targeted killing in international law.

The drone strike is a unique case as it involved the targeting of a 'state actor', thereby changing how the strike is viewed in the context of not just unlawful use of force or its justification, but also as a targeted killing. Targeted killings would have to be assessed within the spectrum of autonomy to place them within the scope of the crime of aggression. The spectrum of autonomy, as already

[21] ibid; MJ Glennon, 'The Blank-Prose Crime of Aggression' (2010) 35 *Yale Journal of International Law* 72, 100.
[22] Glennon (n 21) 100.
[23] N Melzer, *Targeted Killing in International Law* (Oxford University Press, 2008).

highlighted, determines the level of machine independence and the level of human control, meaning whether a 'human-on-the-loop' is required.

It is the moral and ethical debate that calls for analysing this aspect within the ambit of the crime of aggression and how responsibility for the same may be assessed. Many scholars emphasise that a necessary connection exists between humans and morality and the ethical use of lethal force. Amoroso claims that: 'In order to be non-arbitrary, the act of killing must be grounded on human judgement for only human decision-making guarantees full appreciation of the value of individual life and the significance of its loss.'[24] The 'moral judgement' objection to machine killing necessarily assumes that an autonomous weapon 'decides' to take human life in a manner akin to human decision making. According to Krishnan, 'what remains dangerous about killer robots is how they can make life-and-death decisions in the place of a human'.[25] This argument, where a machine is given the right to kill or elevated to the position of a killing machine, would certainly anthropomorphise it.

Keeping the above premise in mind, it should be understood that AI-enabled weapons are not the ones that decide the target. In the opinion of Heller, they do not 'decide' and thereby execute the targeting rules that have been programmed into them before their activation.[26] This point is further emphasised by McFarland that AWS:

> [M]ay not be programmed with precise predetermined responses to every situation they encounter, they are programmed with some system for developing a response and are thereby operating according to their programming regardless of whether or not the specific behaviours they in fact adopt were or could have been foreseen during development or at the time of deployment.[27]

The human element remains in targeting decisions, even if it is concerned with executing or conducting targeting killing within the justification of self-defence. According to McFarland, AWS would remain 'an instrument of the will of the developer' and cannot be characterised as an 'independent decision maker'.[28] Crootof maintains that autonomous weapons would not simply be deployed or directed to 'eliminate the enemy'.[29] This highlights that a degree of 'effective human control' would continue to be exercised within the decision-making

[24] D Amoroso, '*Jus in Bello* and *jus ad Bellum* Arguments against Autonomy in Weapons Systems: A Re-appraisal' (2017) 43 *Questions of International Law* 5, 23.

[25] A Krishnan, *Killer Robots: Legality and Ethicality of Autonomous Weapons* (Routledge, 2010).

[26] KJ Heller, 'The Concept of "The Human" in the Critique of Autonomous Weapons' (2024) 14 *Harvard National Security Journal* 4.

[27] T McFarland, 'Factor Shaping the Legal Implications of Increasingly Autonomous Military Systems' (2015) 97 *International Review of the Red Cross* 1313, 1328.

[28] T McFarland, *Autonomous Weapon Systems and the Law of Armed Conflict: Compatibility with International Humanitarian Law* (Cambridge University Press, 2020) 1328.

[29] R Crootof, 'The Killer Robots are Here: Legal and Policy Implications' (2015) 36 *Cardozo Law Review* 1837, 1849.

process of whether targeted killing should be conducted or not.[30] However, the execution of a targeted killing by an AWS certainly reduces the human target into an object that is eligible for mechanised targeting.

In the words of Heller, the aspect of 'mechanised targeting', wherein the human target is reduced to 'a data point in an automated killing machinery', becomes the defining characteristic of modern forms of remote warfare.[31]

Furthermore, whenever an AWS is deployed, the operator's intent would have to be inferred as to the target attack – ie, whether the operator was already aware of the target to be identified. However, the International Committee of the Red Cross (ICRC) argued that the user 'may' not be aware of the target to be attacked and only be an agent in pressing the button to execute the decision automatically made by the machine. In this respect, it would further become relevant to infer whether any amount of 'lethal force' was used when the AWS executed the pre-programmed operation, irrespective of the fact that the human agent was only pressing a button.[32]

Deciding the threshold of lethal force is crucial to determine if all the elements of the crime of aggression have been fulfilled, as a violation of the prohibition on the use of force embodied in Article 2(4) of the UN Charter is a crucial ingredient. The threshold of force can be determined through a 'sensor-analysis-force' (SAF) process and encoded 'target profiles', wherein the SAF process is gathering information via sensors, calculating whether this matches a predetermined 'target profile' and applying force if so.[33] 'Target profiles' in this context are 'encoded representations that serve to approximate human concepts for the purpose of applying force'.[34] In its evidence to the UK House of Lords Special Inquiry Committee on AI in Weapons Systems, the non-profit organisation Article 36 suggests that these target profiles are conditions translated into 'intent', meaning that this process involves a reduction of the human concept of a target into a pattern of sensor signals.[35] It may identify human targets on the basis of human biometrics, and it would become important for a human commander to understand what would fall within the target profile so that they can evaluate the likely outcomes from the use of that system in a specific context, while recognising that 'what falls within' includes both intended and unintended objects of attack.[36] The concept of 'target profile' may reiterate the point of humans being reduced to

[30] ibid.

[31] Heller (n 26).

[32] ICRC, 'Ethics and Autonomous Weapon Systems: An Ethical Basis for Human Control?' (3April2018),https://www.icrc.org/sites/default/files/document/file_list/icrc_ethics_and_autonomous_weapon_systems_report_3_april_2018.pdf.

[33] E Minor, 'Written Evidence from Article 36', *Report on the Use of Artificial Intelligence in Weapon Systems*, 2023, committees.parliament.uk/writtenevidence/120190/html.

[34] ibid.

[35] ibid.

[36] ibid.

data points, though what it aims to do remains complex in certain contexts like conferring responsibility.

A target profile in the SAF process may prove itself to be beneficial in construing whether a 'crime of aggression' or targeted killing has been committed by AWS or not, as the 'target profile' encoded would be analysed and translated into intent later when the force is applied. The 'intent' and 'knowledge' would continue to vest in the human commander, as they would be aware of the decisions as to 'what' and 'where and when' should the force be applied.

The inference of 'intention' is key to establishing whether a crime of aggression has been committed; as per the general principles of liability in criminal law, intention is essential to ascertain whether a certain crime has been committed.

IMMINENCE OR IMMINENT THREAT

According to Dworkin, 'the self-defence justification is based on the logic of individual threat ... that a strike is necessary to avoid an imminent threat to life that cannot be prevented in any other way'.[37]

The aspect of imminence is a crucial determiner of when the right to self-defence is to be employed by a state. Imminence is the 'immediacy' or the 'urgency' of the threat that assesses whether self-defence is necessary to be exercised within the limitations of Article 51 of the Charter. Imminence is not only a determiner of the exercise of exception under Article 51, but also a decisive factor in assessing the justiciability of anticipatory self-defence by states.

The criterion of imminence may further the legality of exercising that particular state's right to self-defence.[38] The term has come to be used by commentators in very different ways, such as a term for justification or review of the use of a putatively defensive force. Imminence has been interpreted by the International Court of Justice (ICJ) in the context of necessity as a circumstance precluding wrongfulness, especially eliminating any independent requirement of temporal proximity.[39]

Coupled with the concept of imminence, threat also plays a major role in assessing the threshold of force that enables a state to use self-defence. A threat is a situation where the causal chain can lead from the status quo to an undesired future. The essential components of threat are type; likelihood of an attack; gravity, or the severity of the attack; and the timing, or when the attack occurs.[40] The requirements of likelihood and gravity of a threat determine the threshold

[37] A Dworkin, 'Drones and the Target Killing: Defining a European Position' (2013) *European Council on Foreign Relations* 5, https://ecfr.eu/wp-content/uploads/ECFR84_DRONES_BRIEF.pdf.

[38] N Lubell, 'The Problem of Imminence in an Uncertain World' in M Weller (ed), *The Oxford Handbook on the Use of Force in International Law* (Oxford University Press, 2015).

[39] *Gabčikovo-Nagymaros Project* (*Hungary v Slovakia*) [1997] ICJ 7.

[40] D Akande and T Liefländer, 'Clarifying Necessity, Imminence, and Proportionality in the Law of Self-Defense' (2013) 107 *American Journal of International Law* 563, 564.

of an attack, thereby further increasing the justification and availability of anticipatory self-defence. The elements of likelihood and gravity are connected to another aspect highlighted by Bethlehem in his principles about imminence 'whether the anticipated attack is part of a concerted pattern of continuing armed activity'.[41]

So where do the criteria of 'imminence' rest in the framework of the *jus ad bellum*, which governs the threshold of use of force that states may employ? When attempting to understand what constitutes 'imminence' or an 'imminent threat' within the ambit of the use of force or its exceptions, the concepts of anticipatory self-defence, pre-emptive self-defence and preventive self-defence call for an in-depth exposition.

The clear trend that existed before the 9/11 attacks was for states to bring their use of force within the ambit of Article 51 and claim the existence of an armed attack rather than expressly arguing for a wider right under customary international law. In a December 2004 Report, the UN Secretary-General proclaimed that 'long established customary international law makes it clear that States can take military action as long as the threatened attack is imminent, there are no means that would deflect it, and the action is proportionate'.[42] This statement established the existence of an imminent attack as a prerequisite for resorting to the justification of self-defence under Article 51.

However, when understanding imminence in a wider context, Bethlehem's Principle 8 highlights the following criteria for an attack to be construed as 'urgent' or 'imminent':

> Whether an armed attack may be regarded as 'imminent' will fail to be assessed by reference to all relevant circumstances, including a) the nature and immediacy of the threat, b) the probability of an attack.
>
> Whether the anticipated attack is a part of a concrete pattern of continuing armed activity
>
> The likely scale of the attack and the injury, loss, or damage likely to result therefrom in the absence of military action and
>
> There is a likelihood that there will be other opportunities to undertake effective action in self-defence that may be expected to accrue less serious collateral injury, loss, or damage.[43]

When taking into consideration the timing of an attack, the reference to the scale and effects of an armed attack might indicate a different threshold of violence compared to threatened armed attacks.

Principle 8 reflects the temporal element in the concept of imminence. The same can be seen in Bethlehem's references to the concept of 'immediacy of

[41] D Bethlehem, 'Self-Defense against an Imminent or Actual Armed Attack by Non-state Actors' (2012) 106 *American Journal of International Law* 769, 775.

[42] UNGA, 'Follow up to the Outcome of the Millennium Summit', A/59/565 (2004).

[43] Bethlehem (n 41).

threat' and 'other opportunities to undertake effective action'.[44] Imminence is derived from Daniel Webster's definition.[45] In the aftermath of *The Caroline* incident, Webster stated that the British government had to show 'the necessity of self-defence, instant, overwhelming, leaving no choice of means anon amount of deliberation in order for it to be a lawful act of self-defence'.[46] Webster's definition does not reference an armed attack, but the 'necessity of self-defence'. This definition was a reasonable place to start in terms of developing the conceptual meaning and was reiterated in the IMTs after the Second World War. However, the approach of the IMTs has subsequently been criticised, with the Tokyo IMT departing from the traditional view.[47]

Cryer's analysis of the Tokyo IMT highlights how an 'imminent' and 'instant' threat continues to remain controversial. Citing the example of the finding that Japan had committed aggression against the Netherlands and the opinion of the majority that the attack was 'imminent', highlights that the Netherlands had started a preventive war, which may have been an early example of informal collective self-defence.[48] Judge Röling, a dissenter in the Tokyo IMT judgment, stated that 'imminent threat' remained one of the specific cases of threats qualifying as armed attacks permitting self-defence which was in contrast to the view held in Nuremberg IMT, wherein it held the 'overwhelming and instant' nature of threat similar to *The Caroline* case.[49]

The UK's All-Party Parliamentary Group on Drones Inquiry Report of 2018 contended that the aspect of imminence should be understood along the lines of *The Caroline*[50] formula, as there is a need for a specific and identifiable threat that is being prepared at the time and about to be delivered.[51] The 'last window of opportunity' aspect is also implicated in the concept of imminence, which exists for a state to respond effectively to an anticipated armed attack.[52]

An armed attack can be an 'international intervention' in or against another state without that state's consent. It does not include mere economic damage, but involves the use of force. According to the ICJ in the *Oil Platforms* case,[53] an armed attack means any use of armed force and does not need require an intensity threshold be crossed. Intention on the part of the attacker to conduct

[44] ibid.

[45] ibid 769.

[46] *The Caroline v United States*, 11 US 496 (1813).

[47] ibid; Boister and Cryer (n 10).

[48] GK Walker, 'Anticipatory Collective Self-Defence in the Charter Era: What the Treaties Have Said' (1998) 31 *Cornell International Law Journal* 321, 358; Boister and Cryer (n 10).

[49] BVA Roling, 'On Aggression, on International Criminal Law, on International Criminal Jurisdiction' (1955) 1 *Netherlands International Law Review* 167, 175.

[50] *The Caroline* (n 46).

[51] All-Party Parliamentary Group on Drones, 'UK's Use of Armed Drone: Working with Party Partners' (2018).

[52] C O'Meara, 'Reconceptualising the Right of Self-Defence against "Imminent"' Armed Attacks' (2022) 9 *Journal on the Use of Force and International Law* 278, 281.

[53] *Oil Platforms (Iran v US)* [2003] ICJ 161.

an armed attack is required. Hence, when aggression crosses this threshold, it would amount to the use of force or threat of force.

Three factors assess if an imminent act has occurred or is about to occur, the gravity of the threatened attack; the capability of what is threatened; and the nature of the attack. Within the socio-technical context, these factors would play a crucial role in determining if any AWS deployed has committed an act of aggression, as an immediate threat would indeed emerge from the aggressive act so committed. In the past, there was no imperative to set clear standards because deciding what was 'excessive' was left to military commanders and was rarely second-guessed.[54] Therefore, determining what is excessive force within the crime of aggression becomes crucial, considering how the Rome Statute has defined the crime.

The aspect of imminence remains central to the debates on the determination of self-defence or anticipatory self-defence, and can be utilised as a criterion to assess whether a crime of aggression was called for. The idea has been to understand how this criterion of imminence will play a role in determining if the targeted killings can potentially be labelled as a crime of aggression. The brief analysis above has highlighted that an act of aggression can be construed under an 'imminent threat', as the threshold is such that it fulfils the ingredients of the crime. Furthermore, when talking about the liability that may be accrued or who is held responsible for the commission of the crime, command responsibility would be applied.

Professor Cryer highlights that command responsibility has been widely interpreted by the International Criminal Tribunal for the Former Yugoslavia, which asserted that, as per customary law, there are three requirements which infer the application of this responsibility: first, a superior/subordinate relationship; second, a 'mental element'; and, third, a failure to take reasonable measures to prevent or punish violations of international criminal law.[55] In addition to these requirements, the Rome Statute adds that the violations must occur as a result of a failure to exercise control over those subordinates, which requires the element of causation and remains controversial, as it has continued to be a subject of considerable debate.[56]

Given these elemental considerations involving the application of command responsibility, Chengeta argues that command responsibility is inapplicable to the relationship between AWS and those deploying them because such responsibility is applicable only between a human commander and their human

[54] AL Schuller, 'Artificial Intelligence Effecting Human Decisions to Kill: The Challenge of Linking Numerically Quantifiable Goals to IHL Compliance' (2019) 15 *Journal of Law and Policy for Information Society* 105, 109.

[55] *Prosecutor v Delalić et al*, Judgment, IT-96-21, para 344; R Cryer, 'War Crimes' in D Akande and B Saul (eds), *The Law of Armed Conflict* (Oxford University Press, 2018).

[56] R Cryer et al, *An Introduction to International Criminal Law and Procedure*, 2nd edn (Cambridge University Press, 2010).

subordinate.[57] A human commander can only be held responsible for the acts that are committed by the 'human subordinate' deploying it, as the AWS cannot be elevated to the status of a commander or the person actually deploying it.[58] This emphasises the role of 'effective control' that the human commander has over the actions of human subordinate deploying or programming the weapon system.[59]

Taking this argument into account, Cryer highlighted command responsibility and the elemental considerations. Cryer emphasises that the doctrine remains problematic, as it covers different forms of liability[60] from deliberate and knowledgeable failure to intervene despite a duty to act through to a negligent dereliction.[61]

Since the previous argument raises the concern about who may be held liable in the chain of command, identifying a particular individual may become difficult. Even when Cryer has emphasised that the doctrine is strongly linked to the duty of the superior to prevent international crimes over which the superior has control, a failure to prevent the same would be criminalised.[62] The point of view is indeed correct, but identifying the superior would become a very complex task, given the involvement of multiple stakeholders from the process of development to deployment. The level of control the superior has over the encoding of 'target profiles' may become a causation consideration. From the perspective of 'target profiles', it can be construed that the liability may fall on the commander executing the targeting decision, but that only raises the 'possibility' of holding an individual in the capacity of commander as responsible.

However, some argue that in cases where autonomous weapons are deployed, commanders are accountable for calibrating how AWS is deployed and 'express their autonomy' along with designating parameters that act as precautions for their operation.[63] Sehrawat underscores that due to the lack of human control and unpredictability of AWS, it becomes challenging to find individuals involved in programming and deployment as criminally liable for crimes, as they may not

[57] T Chengeta, 'Accountability Gap: Autonomous Weapon Systems and Modes of Responsibility in International Law' (2016) 45 *Denver Journal of International Law and Policy* 3.

[58] B Docherty, 'Losing Humanity: The Case against Killer Robots', *Human Rights Watch*, 19 November 2012, www.hrw.org/report/2012/11/19/losing-humanity/case-against-killer-robots; M Sassbli, 'Autonomous Weapons and International Humanitarian Law: Advantages, Open Technical Questions and Legal Issues to Be Clarified' (2014) 90 *International Law Studies* 308.

[59] Chengeta (n 57) 30.

[60] R Cryer, 'Prosecuting the Leaders: Promises, Policies and Practicalities' (2009) 1 *Gottingen Journal of International Law* 45, 59.

[61] ibid; M Damaška, 'The Shadow Side of Command Responsibility' (2001) 49 *American Journal of Comparative Law* 455, 460–71.

[62] R Cryer, 'General Principles of Liability in International Criminal Law', in D McGoldrick et al (eds), *The Permanent International Criminal Court: Legal and Policy Issues* (Bloomsbury, 2004).

[63] M Schulzke, 'Autonomous Weapons and Distributed Responsibility' (2013) 26 *Philosophy & Technology* 203, 210; J Kraska, 'Command Accountability for AI Weapon Systems in the Law of Armed Conflict' (2021) 97 *International Law Studies* 407, 446.

have the required knowledge or the intent for such acts, leading to a command responsibility gap.[64]

Even though there are settled principles in the Rome Statute as to the prosecution of aggression and the liability that may emanate from its commission, would targeted killing be prosecuted in a similar manner or treated merely as a violation of human rights? This question will continue to be debated in the coming years as AI advances in shaping the future of military technology, redefining warfare and its rules, and continually challenging established traditional frameworks of international law.

CONCLUSION

Looking towards the future of this weapon system for international criminal law, hypothetically a fully autonomous weapon system can exist, but in reality, it would not as human control would be retained irrespective of the level of autonomy of the weapon system. What remains doubtful is how criminal law would prosecute cases involving AI-driven weapons. Criminal responsibility and accountability have always focused on establishing intention and guilt in order to hold an individual or individuals responsible for the commission of a crime. According to observers, machines can never replicate human decision making.[65] The statement highlights the challenge of automation bias and complacency that may permeate AWS when deployed on the battlefield.

AWS has begun to come into shape with continuous development. The challenges that it poses will remain at the forefront as unresolved unless a regulation is developed before they enter the battlefield in real time. The technical intricacies in developing these weapon systems make them unique and make it difficult to determine the commission of a particular crime in international crimes and how to accord responsibility. According to Heller, AWS are tailor-made to engender automation complacency as they have high levels of autonomy and use 'time-critical' situations such as combat. Further, human operators are unlikely to challenge AWS targeting decisions even when incorrect.[66] However, this would not be the case if automation complacency is debased. Studies have shown that automation complacency 'is pernicious, and perhaps even intractable',[67] as it affects individuals and teams[68] and cannot be presented by warning operators

[64] V Sehrawat, 'Autonomous Weapon Systems and Command Responsibility' (2021) 31 *Florida Journal of International Law* 315, 330; B Docherty, 'Losing Humanity: The Case against Killer Robots', *Human Rights Watch*, 19 November 2012, www.hrw.org/report/2012/11/19/losing-humanity/case-against-killer-robots.

[65] Schuller (n 54).

[66] Heller (n 26).

[67] J Zerilli et al, 'Algorithmic Decision-Making and the Control Problem' (2019) 29 *Minds and Machines* 555, 556.

[68] ibid.

to verify machine decisions because they might be incorrect.[69] With the improvement of technology, complacency would also increase, as a human operator would rely more on the weapon system's decision, leading to the non-supervision of the executed decision by the weapon system due to over-reliance on machine functions.[70]

Furthermore, when considering automation bias and how automation complacency permeates the weapon system's usage, it becomes clear that both would impact how accountability and responsibility are meted out in international criminal law. According to Coco,[71] automation bias and complacency are different examples of the effects that trust in technology can engender on the attitude, alertness and attention levels of humans interacting with automated or autonomous machines,[72] and has been termed a 'control problem' in the ethics and psychological discourse of human-machine interaction within international law regime.[73] The foundational pronouncement in the Nuremberg Trials is noteworthy in the present context as it emphasised that:

> [C]rimes against international law are committed by men, not abstract entities, and only by punishing individuals who commit such crimes can provisions of international law be enforced … individuals have international duties which transcends the national obligations of obedience imposed by individual state.[74]

Highlighting automation bias and complacency as one of the consequences of utilising automated decision making in addition to the above-cited pronouncement clearly highlights that only 'humans' can be prosecuted for the crimes committed, and weapon systems are abstract entities driven by pre-programmed data and so cannot be prosecuted.

Therefore, the existing challenge of permeating automation bias and complacency would become a deciding factor in conferring criminal responsibility as well as adjudging the occurrence of the crime of aggression. Eventually, the crime of aggression will move out of the bubble of being a leadership crime as this kind of criminal violation within international law has a very wide scope, which will further evolve as military technologies progress in the next few years.

[69] R Parasuraman and DH Manzey, 'Complacency and Bias in Human Use of Automation: An Attentional Integration' (2010) 52 *Journal of the Human Factors and Ergonomics Society* 381, 391.

[70] EA Stanley and KL Larsen, 'Difficulties with Emotion Regulation in the Contemporary US Armed Forces: Structural Contributors and Potential Solutions' (2021) 47 *Armed Forces & Society* 77.

[71] A Coco, 'Exploring the Impact of Automation Bias and Complacency on Individual Criminal Responsibility for War Crimes' (2023) 21 *Journal of International Criminal Justice* 1077, 1082.

[72] Parasuraman and Manzey (n 69).

[73] Zerilli et al (n 67).

[74] Nuremberg IMT, 'Judgment and Sentence' (1947) 41 *American Journal of International Law* 172, 221, 223.

12

'Prosecuting the Leaders' Reflections on the Prohibition and Prosecution of the Crime of Aggression in International Law

STOYAN PANOV

INTRODUCTION

In comparison to war crimes, crimes against humanity and genocide, the crime of aggression has not been widely litigated before international or hybrid tribunals or domestic courts. This chapter offers an overview of developments with respect to the criminalisation of waging war as aggression and some of the pressing issues associated with the institutional approach to seeking accountability for the crime of aggression at the international level. This reflection is primarily anchored around Professor Robert Cryer's approach in his scholarship on prosecuting leaders for international crimes. The methodology in his contributions captures practical as well as political intricacies in international criminal justice in relation to so-called leadership crimes.[1] Such a method is particularly pertinent for addressing the contemporary example of the crime of aggression perpetrated in the context of the ongoing Russia-Ukraine war. Professor Cryer's take on the intertwined political and legal aspects of prosecuting international crimes is instructive as ever on the efforts to seek accountability for the crime of aggression.

As this chapter aims to reflect on possible avenues for investigation and prosecution of the crime of aggression, the role of the ICC is analysed along with the possibility for the creation of an international tribunal for the crime of aggression. Selected pertinent issues are also addressed, such as the possible invocation of immunities *ratione materiae* and *ratione personae* of the high-political-echelon

[1] R Cryer, 'Prosecuting the Leaders: Promises, Politics and Practicalities' (2009) 1 *Gottingen Journal of International Law* 45.

offenders and the scope of indictments for the crime of aggression. Ultimately, the scope of this chapter attempts to capture the complexity of prosecuting one of the most serious crimes of international law by utilising the guiding practicality and pragmatism of Professor Cryer's approach for international criminal justice.

DEFINITION OF THE CRIME OF AGGRESSION AND THE ACT OF AGGRESSION

The first efforts to criminalise war as aggression can be traced to the post-First World War period, specifically in the unratified 1924 Geneva Protocol on the Pacific Settlement of International Disputes.[2] The League of Nations Assembly subsequently proclaimed aggressive war as a crime in 1927.[3] After the Second World War, the most important development in the criminalisation process at the international level is the London Charter of the International Military Tribunal (IMT) of 1945, which included crimes against peace, war crimes, and crimes against humanity. Article 6(a) of the IMT Charter provided the definition of crimes against peace:

> [P]lanning, preparation, initiation or waging of a war of aggression, or a war in violation of international treaties, agreements or assurances, or participation in a common plan or conspiracy for the accomplishment of any of the foregoing.[4]

The article was replicated in Article 5(a) of the Charter of the International Military Tribunal for the Far East.[5] The war of aggression as a crime against peace was proclaimed by the Nuremberg International Military Tribunal as 'the supreme international crime' because 'it contains within itself the accumulated evil of the whole'.[6] Subsequently United Nations General Assembly (UNGA) Resolution 95 affirmed that 'the principles recognised by the Charter of the Nurnberg Tribunal and the Judgment of the Tribunal'.[7] Modern international law also places the war of aggression as the supreme international crime.[8]

In comparison to other core international crimes like war crimes, crimes against humanity and the crime of genocide, the crime of aggression has not been widely litigated before international or hybrid tribunals or domestic courts. The Nuremberg IMT judgment on the criminalisation of war of aggression was

[2] Geneva Protocol on the Pacific Settlement of International Disputes (1924) 2 Int Leg 1378, 1380.
[3] See R Cryer, *Prosecuting International Crimes* (Cambridge University Press, 2005) 241.
[4] Article 6(a) of the Charter of the International Military Tribunal, Annexed to the London Agreement for the Establishment of an International Military Tribunal (1945).
[5] Y Dinstein, *War, Aggression and Self-Defence* (Cambridge University Press, 2005) 118–19.
[6] *Nuremberg Trial*, Nuremberg International Military Tribunal, Judgment (1946) 1 IMT 171, 186.
[7] GA Resolution 95 (I) UN Doc A/64/Add.1.
[8] Dinstein (n 5) 121.

replicated in the reasoning and findings of the IMT for the Far East.[9] The crime was also litigated and upheld in other trials against Second World War criminals, but no indictments for crimes against peace or aggression have been known since the immediate post- Second World War period.[10] For example, the crime of aggressive war was not included in the United Nations Security Council (UNSC) resolutions establishing the International Criminal Tribunal for the Former Yugoslavia (ICTY) and the International Criminal Tribunal for Rwanda (ICTR).

Following the IMT definition of the criminalisation of aggression, multiple attempts have arisen to define or crystalise the definition of Article 6(a) of the IMT Charter, such as the Draft Code of Offences against the Peace and Security of Mankind in 1950, which replicates the IMT definition. The efforts of the International Law Commission culminated with the 1996 Draft Code of Crimes against the Peace and Security of Mankind, which largely followed the established definition and defined the crime of aggression as 'an individual who, as leader or organiser, actively participates in or orders the planning, preparation, initiation or waging of aggression committed by a State shall be responsible for a crime of aggression'.[11] The most contemporary definition of the crime of aggression is found in Article 8bis of the Rome Statute of the International Criminal Court (ICC) after the Kampala Review Conference:

> [T]he planning, preparation, initiation or execution, by a person in a position effectively to exercise control over or to direct the political or military action of a State, of an act of aggression which, by its character, gravity and scale, constitutes a manifest violation of the Charter of the United Nations.

As there is no jurisprudence relating to Article 8bis of the Rome Statute, it is worth analysing the elements of the definition. It is noticeable that the crime of aggression includes the planning, preparation, initiation or execution of the act of aggression. Planning includes the formation of a design or scheme for a specific act or war of aggression,[12] whilst the preparation may contain various steps in order to implement the plan before the actual use of armed force. Initiation is inherently linked to the moment of the start of the armed conflict, while execution is proximate to the waging of the aggression for the duration of the armed conflict.[13]

Article 8bis of the Rome Statute includes *ratione personae* jurisdiction and limits it to 'a person in a position effectively to exercise control over or to direct

[9] See *In re Hirota et al* (International Military Tribunal for the Far East, *Tokyo* trial, 1948) AD 356, 362–63. See also R Cryer, 'The Tokyo International Military Tribunal and Crimes against Peace (Aggression)' in L Sadat (ed), *Seeking Accountability for the Unlawful Use of Force* (Cambridge University Press, 2018) 88–89.

[10] Dinstein (n 5) 121.

[11] Draft Code of Crimes against the Peace and Security of Mankind, Report of the International Law Commission, 48th Session, 1996 II (2) *ILC Yearbook* 42–43.

[12] Dinstein (n 5) 132.

[13] ibid. See also Cryer (n 9) 84.

the political or military action of a State'. Such a requirement for political or military control incorporates the rationale of the various military tribunals after the Second World War. This qualification aims to attach criminal responsibility to particular persons from the political or military spheres without labelling the entire population of the aggressor state as being responsible for the act of aggression.[14] High-ranking military personnel and high-level state officials would fall within the requisite remit, classified in the Tokyo IMT as 'class "A" criminals' (for example, cabinet members, presidents or prime ministers, high-ranking generals or admirals) or leadership roles.[15] The purpose is to capture the role of the political and military leadership echelon as integral actors in the decision-making process of waging an act of aggression or aggressive war while the low- or mid-level officials and military personnel who act as instruments in the execution of the master plan may not fall within the definition.[16] Related to the issue is the formation of a plan to wage the aggressive war, which is reflected in the mens rea of *animus aggressionis*. Such an intent can be formed by high-ranking political leaders or a few high-ranking political or military officials with the knowledge to further the aggressive plan or scheme.[17]

Article 8bis of the Rome Statute includes the term 'act of aggression'. In UNGA Resolution 3314, aggression is defined as 'the use of armed force by a State against the sovereignty, territorial integrity or political independence of another State, or in any other manner inconsistent with the Charter of the United Nations, as set out in this Definition'.[18] The requirement for actual use of armed force is absolute. Article 3 of the same Resolution enumerates the specific acts of aggression such as the invasion or attack by the armed forces of a state of the territory of another state, or any military occupation, however temporary, resulting from such invasion or attack, or any annexation by the use of force of the territory of another state or part thereof; the blockade of the ports or coasts by the armed forces of another state; and the sending by or on behalf of a state of armed bands, groups, irregulars or mercenaries which carry out acts of armed force against another state of such gravity as to amount to the acts of aggression or its substantial involvement, among others. Specifically, UNGA Resolution 3314 reaffirms the individual criminal responsibility for aggressive war.[19]

[14] See *USA v Krauch et al* ('the IG Farben case') (1948) 8 NMT 1081.
[15] See 1996 Draft Code of Crimes against the Peace and Security of Mankind, 42–43. See also Dinstein (n 5) 134; Cryer (n 9) 83.
[16] Dinstein (n 5) 134. See also *USA v Von Leeb et al* ('the High Command case') (Nuremberg, 1948) 11 NMT 462, 489.
[17] Dinstein (n 5) 137.
[18] UNGA Res 3314 (XXIX), 29(1) RGA 142, 144 (1974).
[19] Cryer (n 3) 243.

AGGRESSION IN UKRAINE

In order to contextualise the listed definitions so far, the enumerated examples above firmly fit within the pattern of armed force used against the territory of Ukraine since at least 24 February 2022 by the Russian Federation.[20] The ongoing war in Ukraine that included an act of invasion by the armed forces of Russia on 24 February 2022 would squarely fit within the definition of an act of aggression. Moreover, the UNGA adopted a resolution 'Aggression against Ukraine' with 141 votes in favour, five votes against and 25 abstentions on 2 March 2022, deploring the aggression against Ukraine as a violation of the prohibition of the use of force under Article 2(4) of the UN Charter as well as recalling the definition of aggression under UN Resolution 3314 of 14 December 1974 and condemning in the strongest terms 'the aggression by the Russian Federation against Ukraine in violation of Article 2(4) of the Charter'.[21]

Special emphasis should be placed on the provision that no political, economic or military nature may serve as a justification for aggression per Article 5(1) of the Definition of Aggression UNGA Resolution 3314. Related to the non-applicability of the justification is Article 7, which outlines that the definition of aggression could not prejudice the right to self-determination, freedom and independence of peoples forcibly deprived of that right in accordance with the UN Charter, in particular peoples under colonial and racist regimes or other forms of alien domination. In the particular context of the situation in Ukraine, the provision is not applicable as there are no people under colonial or racist regimes or other forms of alien domination to be 'liberated' by Russia. Additionally, Russia has not invoked this provision in its official discourse, but has continued to use the incongruous terminology 'special military operation'. Such discourse may be linked to the distinction in Article 5(2) of the Definition, which differentiates between 'aggression' which gives rise to international responsibility and the war of aggression which is inherently a crime against international peace. In this manner, some observers believe that an act of aggression which is somehow short of war might not result in individual criminal responsibility, but would trigger the general applicability of state responsibility.[22] However, such a differentiation may be considered to go against the gravamen established by the IMT judgment, which clearly outlines that '[t]he principle of international law, which under certain circumstances protects the representatives of a state, cannot be applied to acts which are condemned as criminal by international law. The

[20] Another pertinent example may be the unlawful use of force against the territorial integrity of Ukraine and the subsequent illegal annexation of Crimea in 2014.

[21] UN General Assembly Resolution ES-11/1 of 2 March 2022, pt 2.

[22] See J Hogan-Doran and BT van Ginkel, 'Aggression as a Crime under International Law and the Prosecution of Individuals by the Proposed International Criminal Court' (1996) 43 *Netherlands International Law Review* 321, 335. See also Dinstein (n 5) 125.

authors of these acts cannot shelter themselves behind their official position in order to be freed from punishment in appropriate proceedings'.[23]

As illustrated above, the act of aggression incorporates the use of armed force against the territorial integrity and sovereignty of the target state. The crime of aggression can be classified as a *jus ad bellum* crime, since the material element of the crime may begin at the planning stage of waging an aggressive war, as shown above. The pattern of the crime of aggression is usually associated with the commission of the other core international crimes, such as war crimes and crimes against humanity, as is currently observed in the armed conflict in Ukraine, as seen in the continuous flagrant violations and grave breaches of international humanitarian law in Bucha, Mariupol and other localities across Ukraine. Once the illegal use of armed force under the act of aggression commences, other international crimes may take place in the same or subsequent operations.

INTERNATIONAL EFFORTS TO RESPOND TO THE CRIME OF AGGRESSION

After reviewing the elements of the crime of aggression, the next question is whether a possible recourse to promoting accountability for the crime exists. One potential avenue is the investigation and submission for the purpose of prosecution before an international criminal court vested with jurisdiction over the crime of aggression. Article 8bis of the Rome Statute is particularly relevant as it presents the most contemporary codification of the crime of aggression as a core international crime, as established above. In relation to the situation in Ukraine, although Ukraine has made two Article 12(3) of the Rome Statute declarations, granting jurisdiction of the ICC over crimes committed on its territory after 21 November 2012 until the present moment, the jurisdiction of the ICC over the crime of aggression is precluded. This is so because the ICC has no jurisdiction over the crime of aggression when committed by non-party nationals or on the territory of a state that is not party to the ICC according to Article 15bis(5) of the Rome Statute. This creates a jurisdictional problem for investigating the situation in Ukraine with recourse to the crime of aggression.[24] Moreover, in the likely absence of a UNSC referral of the situation in Ukraine to the ICC due to the veto power wielded by Russia at this moment, the ICC would not be able to exercise jurisdiction over the crime of aggression perpetrated by nationals of a non-state party such as Russia.

The ICC's Office of the Prosecutor has affirmed that 'the scope of the situation encompasses any past and present allegations of war crimes, crimes against humanity or genocide committed on any part of the territory of Ukraine by

[23] *Nuremberg Trial* (n 6) 223.

[24] See O Bekou and R Cryer, 'The International Criminal Court and Universal Jurisdiction: A Close Encounter?' (2007) 56 *ICLQ* 49, 51.

any person from 21 November 2013 onwards'.[25] On 17 March 2023, the ICC issued arrest warrants against the sitting head of state of Russia and the Russian Commissioner for Children's Rights for war crimes.[26] The charges focus on a limited set of crimes under Article 8(2) of the Rome Statute, namely war crime of unlawful deportation of population (children) under Article 8(2)(a)(vii) and that of unlawful transfer of population (children) from occupied areas of Ukraine to the Russian Federation under Article 8(2)(b)(viii) of the Rome Statute.[27] In addition, the ICC issued arrest warrants for the former Commander of the Long-Range Aviation of the Aerospace and the former Commander of the Black Sea Fleet of the Russian Federation in March 2024, and the former Minister of Defence and the Chief of the General Staff of the Armed Forces of the Russian Federation in June 2024 for the war crime of directing attacks at civilian objects, the war crime of causing excessive incidental harm to civilians or damage to civilian objects, and the crime against humanity of inhumane acts.[28] Although the indictments illustrate the limits of the applicability of Article 8bis of the Rome Statute to the situation in Ukraine at the ICC, the current list of indicted officials of the Russian Federation basically captures the essential leadership of the state to wage a war of aggression.

Is there another plausible pathway to activate the jurisdiction of the ICC with respect to the crime of aggression in the context of the situation in Ukraine? One alternative avenue would be to revise the ICC Statute with retroactive effect as of 17 July 2018, the date of activation of the ICC's jurisdiction over the crime of aggression. Such an amendment would concern the exercise of the jurisdiction of the ICC in a narrow sense as the crime of aggression has already been of customary character well before July 2018, as seen above.[29] In this manner, the jurisdiction would be 'activated' for an already criminalised act under international law by filling up the existing procedural gap of the Rome Statute. In substance, the crime of aggression has existed in international law. Moreover, the customary character of the crime of aggression is observed in the emphasis on the investigation and eventual prosecution of the crime of aggression in various reactions of supranational and international organisations: the European Council has stressed the EU's support for the investigations in Ukraine, performed by the ICC, and has accentuated its commitment to 'ways to secure accountability for the crime of aggression' as 'the prosecution of the

[25] ICC, 'Ukraine: Situation in Ukraine' ICC-01/22, www.icc-cpi.int/situations/ukraine.

[26] ibid.

[27] ICC, 'Situation in Ukraine: ICC Judges Issue Arrest Warrants against Vladimir Vladimirovich Putin and Maria Alekseyevna Lvova-Belova', www.icc-cpi.int/news/situation-ukraine-icc-judges-issue-arrest-warrants-against-vladimir-vladimirovich-putin-and.

[28] ICC (n 25).

[29] C Kress, S Hobe and A Nussberger, 'The Ukraine War and the Crime of Aggression: How to Fill the Gaps in the International Legal System', *justsecurity.org*, 23 January 2023, www.justsecurity.org/84783/the-ukraine-war-and-the-crime-of-aggression-how-to-fill-the-gaps-in-the-international-legal-system.

crime of aggression is of concern to the international community as a whole'.[30] This innovative approach to addressing the jurisdictional gap in the Rome Statute with respect to the crime of aggression aims to overcome the jurisdictional conundrum that the ICC's Chief Prosecutor currently faces with respect to the crime of aggression in the situation of Ukraine. That said, this approach primarily situates itself within current academic discussions.[31]

The involvement of the ICC with respect to the crime of aggression in the situation of Ukraine is more theoretical than practical, as seen above. This creates a paradox, since the ICC was created with the ultimate aim to offer a permanent international court for international crimes. A similar tenet is observed in Professor Cryer's scholarship in his interpretation of the inactivity on part of the UNSC to trigger its 'delegated jurisdiction' to refer the situation to the ICC.[32] The inherent deficiency in 'the jurisdictional regime of the Statute means that some offences may go unpunished' when the UNSC is blocked from exercising its function to maintain international peace and security.[33] One needs to search for alternative pathways for the creation of an ad hoc tribunal for the crime of aggression. In this manner, the lacuna in international level with respect to the crime of aggression and the (non-)involvement of the ICC with respect to the situation in Ukraine can be addressed.

An ad hoc international tribunal for the crime of aggression would not fully replicate the ICTY/ICTR establishment via a resolution of the UNSC due to the veto power of Russia. A possible solution to the roadblock of the UNSC veto is the active engagement of the UNGA. The UNGA noted in its 23 February 2023 resolution that 'the need to ensure accountability for the most serious crimes under international law committed on the territory of Ukraine through appropriate, fair and independent investigations and prosecutions at the national or international level'.[34] One possibility for the involvement of the UNGA in the formation of an ad hoc international tribunal for the crime of aggression is through a recommendation by the UNGA to the UN Secretary-General to negotiate an international agreement between the UN and Ukraine for a special international tribunal for the crime of aggression.[35] Such an act would also be in congruence with Article 1 of the UN Charter, which outlines the purposes of the UN to maintain international peace and security, including the suppression of acts of aggression or other breaches of international peace.

The resolution for the creation of the ad hoc tribunal can be passed by the UNGA under Article 10 of the UN Charter as it provides the UNGA with the

[30] European Council, Conclusions (15 December 2022), EUCO 34/22 CO EUR 29 CONCL 7.

[31] Kress, Hobe and Nussberger (n 29).

[32] Bekou and Cryer (n 24) 51–52.

[33] ibid 52.

[34] UNGA Resolution ES-11/6 of 23 February 2023, pt 9.

[35] See UNGA Resolution 57/228 of 27 February 2001, where the UNGA requested the UN Secretary-General to negotiate with Cambodia an agreement to create the Extraordinary Chambers in the Courts of Cambodia (ECCC).

competence to discuss any matters within the scope of the Charter and to make recommendations to the UNSC and the UNGA. This is the so-called *Uniting for Peace Resolution* legal authority as 'if the Security Council, because of lack of unanimity of the permanent members, fails to exercise its primary responsibility for the maintenance of international peace and security in any case where there appears to be a threat to the peace, breach of the peace, or act of aggression, the General Assembly shall consider the matter immediately with a view to making appropriate recommendations to Members for collective measures'.[36] As the ad hoc tribunal would not strictly amount to a coercive or enforcement action, the UNGA may have residual competence within the object and purpose of the Charter. In this 'residual insurer' role, a UNGA resolution may serve as the legal authority for the attempt to establish an ad hoc international tribunal.[37]

The request for the establishment of the ad hoc tribunal would not contain a jurisdictional defect for several reasons. First, the consent of the territorial state where the crime of aggression has taken place would be obtained as in all previous occasions with similar tribunals, such as the Special Court for Sierra Leone (SCSL) or the Extraordinary Chambers in the Courts of Cambodia (ECCC).[38] Second, as the crime of aggression is of a customary law character and as the prohibition of aggression is of a *jus cogens* nature, the existing international jurisdiction can be activated through a specific legal instrument in the form of an agreement to establish the ad hoc tribunal.[39] Although no exact precedent like the situation in Ukraine exists, since this is the first time where an ad hoc tribunal for the crime of aggression has been deliberated, the jurisdictional title for the crime exists either by consent of the territorial state or international criminal jurisdiction over the crime of aggression. In this manner, jurisdiction exists and it is not strictly created by the UNGA.

In addition, international tribunals can be created through the UN. Such a pathway represents 'an expression of the will of the international community' to create a truly international tribunal.[40] An international tribunal would have the legitimacy of the international community to investigate and prosecute the crime of aggression. In this way, the mechanism would guarantee respect for the core prohibition of the use of force and provide accountability for gross violations of the UN Charter. Moreover, international tribunals may be perceived

[36] UNGA Resolution 377 (V) Uniting for Peace of 3 November 1950.

[37] O Hathaway, M Mills and H Zimmermann, 'The Legal Authority to Create a Special Tribunal to Try the Crime of Aggression upon the Request of the UN General Assembly', *justsecurity.org*, 5 May 2023, www.justsecurity.org/86450/the-legal-authority-to-create-a-special-tribunal-to-try-the-crime-of-aggression-upon-the-request-of-the-un-general-assembly.

[38] The SCSL was created pursuant to a UNSC Resolution under Chapter VI (not Chapter VII) as the UN Secretary-General was mandated to negotiate with the Sierra Leonean government the establishment of an independent special court. Consent of the territorial state was acquired and a tribunal with an international character was created. See https://rscsl.org.

[39] ibid.

[40] *Prosecutor v Charles Ghankay Taylor*, SCSL Appeals Chamber, Decision on Immunity from Jurisdiction, SCSL-2003-01-I (31 May 2004) para 38.

as impartial, independent and competent by the international community and states to prosecute the crime of aggression, especially when the prosecution might include the highest political and military echelon of a state.

The added legitimacy at a regional level might be seen in the reaction of regional organisations such as the Council of Europe. The Parliamentary Assembly of the Council of Europe reiterated its support for the creation of a special international criminal tribunal for the crime of aggression.[41] Such regional reactions add legitimacy to the push for accountability, protection of human rights, the rule of law and peace through justice and international cooperation as regional organisations are in close proximity to the conflict. In light of the inactivity of the UNSC or eventual difficulties with passing the requisite resolutions at the UNGA, a possible solution is a special criminal tribunal for the crime of aggression against Ukraine with regional focus or cross-regional support.[42] It may be modelled on the structure of the internationalised Extraordinary African Chambers (EAC), created by an agreement between the African Union, a regional organisation, Senegal and Chad to apply international criminal law in the case against Hissène Habré. The EAC has navigated the difficult circumstances of putting to trial a former head of state, demanding essential contextualisation of 'these kinds of trials in the broader international political arenas'.[43] A similar international tribunal with close connection with the Council of Europe could offer a viable alternative for the prosecution of the crime of aggression in the context of the Russian invasion in Ukraine.

The benefit of an international tribunal for the crime of aggression would also address the jurisdictional gap of putting conflicts beyond the reach of the ICC by exempting the crime of aggression for non-state parties to the Rome Statute.[44] Such an international tribunal would remedy the existing gap of international criminal justice system in a similar role as the previous ad hoc tribunals, namely, the IMT, the ICTY and the ICTR, since it has been challenging to reduce the nature of aggression to purely legal aspects.[45] In this manner, the effort would be seen as a stepping stone to address impunity for the crime of aggression. The ad hoc attempt to establish a tribunal for the purpose of prosecution of the crime of aggression fits well within Professor Cryer's metaphor of the oscillation pattern observed in international law. Accountability at the international level ebbs and flows, and the low moments such as aggression may create a reaction, which manifests itself in establishing a specific judicial mechanism to

[41] Parliamentary Assembly of the Council of Europe Resolution 2842 (2023) of 26 January 2023.

[42] Declaration of the Ministers of Justice of the Council of Europe, 'Towards Accountability for International Crimes Committed in Ukraine' (Vilnius, 5 September 2024), https://rm.coe.int/final-vilnius-declaration-en-eu-note/1680b17523.

[43] S Weil, K Seelinger and KB Carlson, 'Theorizing Empirical Court Research: The Test Case of the Trial of Hissène Habré' (2021) 103 *International Review of the Red Cross* 1073, 1080. See also J Burke, 'Hissène Habré Trial Provides Model for International Justice', *The Guardian*, 30 May 2016, www.theguardian.com/world/2016/may/30/hissene-habre-trial-provides-model-for-international-justice.

[44] Bekou and Cryer (n 24) 52.

[45] Cryer (n 9) 99.

address the crime at the international level. As seen above, pitfalls such as the veto at the UNSC or the jurisdictional issue at the ICC with respect to the crime of aggression may exist, but what is essential is the response to impunity by not allowing serious offences to go unpunished.[46] Any effective prosecution of the crime of aggression in light of the UNSC veto blockage will be based on cooperation with the judicial body.[47] In this sense, even efforts to establish a special tribunal, based on a treaty between interested states, for the crime of aggression of states willing to collect evidence, protect witnesses and ensure effective and genuine prosecution would be preferable to having no avenue for international or regional accountability for aggression.[48]

DOMESTIC PROSECUTION

As the ICC cannot establish jurisdiction for the crime of aggression, and an international alternative is still to materialise, recourse to investigations and prosecution of the crime of aggression on the domestic level via domestic, hybrid or special internationalised criminal courts offers yet another accountability avenue.[49] For example, Ukraine as the *locus delicti* jurisdiction has the competence to prosecute the planning, preparation and waging of an aggressive war according to Article 437 of the Criminal Code of Ukraine. A potential hurdle is Article 125(5) of the Constitution of Ukraine, which prohibits the establishment of extraordinary courts that may need to be set up with the specific purpose for prosecuting the crime of aggression.[50] Another recurring dilemma with national proceedings against the high political and military echelon of the aggressor state is alleged impartiality. Can such a domestic-based tribunal dispel the cloud of lack of impartiality? As the nature of the act of aggression affects core political and military decisions undertaken at the highest level of the aggressor state, domestic prosecution may give the impression of 'victor's justice'.[51] Moreover, hybrid tribunals may also water down or put aside the duty to prosecute the crime of aggression at an international level, which would be of concern to the international community. To dispel such potential bias, the *locus delicti* state may opt to create specialised chambers which may include third-state judges in order to prevent bias against the offenders. Nevertheless, such a domestic court may have a counter-effect as the problem with the applicability of immunities

[46] See Bekou and Cryer (n 24) 52.

[47] See ibid 60–61.

[48] House of Commons, *Conflict in Ukraine: A Special Tribunal on the Crime of Aggression*, Research Briefing (27 August 2024) 12–13.

[49] For hybrid tribunals, see M Kersten, 'As the Pendulum Swings: The Revival of the Hybrid Tribunal' in MJ Christensen and R Levi (eds), *International Practices of Criminal Justice* (Routledge, 2017) 251–73.

[50] There are some exceptions, such as the High Court against Corruption in Ukraine. Nonetheless, another pertinent issue is whether the Ukrainian Constitution can be amended while martial law applies.

[51] See Dinstein (n 5) 145.

would not be resolved. While it is true that immunities would not be applicable to Members of Parliament, the Minister of Defence or the Chiefs of the General Staff of the aggressor state, the most responsible political leaders for the act of aggression may enjoy immunities before domestic or hybrid courts. Overall, it may be concluded that domestic prosecution efforts for the international crime of aggression may hold a different authoritative weight in comparison to an international tribunal vested with jurisdiction for the same crime.[52]

The investigation of one of the most complex criminal designs associated with the act of aggression uncovers one recurring theme of the inherent political effect of investigating and eventually prosecuting the highest political and military echelon of the aggressor state. Nonetheless, states must be reminded that there is an obligation to investigate and prosecute core international crimes, including the crime of aggression, in order to close the impunity gap at the international level. As the number of victims of the armed conflict in Ukraine in multiple European states is high, it is to be expected that even third-party states that have the crime of aggression or the crime against peace in their national legal orders should open an investigation, gather valuable evidence from victims of international crimes and even submit the cases for prosecution. An unwillingness to do so would be tantamount to shirking the responsibility to close the impunity gap for core international crimes. There is no doubt that all trials should incorporate the highest international standard of the right to a fair trial in the forum state.[53]

PROCEDURAL ISSUES WITH LITIGATING THE CRIME OF AGGRESSION

Procedural issues relating to the crime of aggression need to be thoroughly examined as well. One pertinent procedural aspect concerns the possible invocation of immunities *ratione materiae* and *ratione personae* of the offender. If a serving head of state is prosecuted in national courts, they would most likely enjoy jurisdictional immunity *ratione personae* in a similar manner to diplomatic immunity.[54] The more intricate aspect relates to the applicability of immunity *ratione materiae* once the head of state is no longer in office. Immunity *ratione materiae* would be applicable to acts performed in the official capacity of a head of state.[55] The crux is whether the functional immunity would cover all official

[52] J Trahan, 'Why a "Hybrid" Ukrainian Tribunal on the Crime of Aggression is Not the Answer', *justsecurity.org*, 6 February 2023), www.justsecurity.org/85019/why-hybrid-ukrainian-tribunal-on-crime-of-aggression-is-not-the-answer.

[53] Related to the issue of investigations and eventual prosecutability of the crime of aggression is the human rights question of the possibility for in absentia trials when the accused cannot be apprehended and/or extradited.

[54] R Jennings and A Watts (eds), *Oppenheim's International Law*, 9th edn (Oxford University Press, 2008) 1038.

[55] See *Ex parte Pinochet Ugarte (No 3)* [1999] 2 All ER 97, 172.

acts or whether there are certain exceptions in relation to war crimes, crimes against humanity and other international crimes, including the crime of aggression. State practice indicates that the exception of functional immunity can be invoked for international crimes.[56] On the other hand, the International Court of Justice (ICJ) in the *Arrest Warrant* judgment did not make explicit reference to exceptions for international crimes of former heads of state before domestic courts.[57] Other high-ranking officials such as ministers of foreign affairs would also benefit from jurisdictional immunities. The ICJ affirmed that the procedural nature of the jurisdictional immunity does not affect the criminal responsibility of the offender, as there are circumstances in which no bar to prosecution exists for a minister of foreign affairs or the heads of state: (1) when the prosecution is conducted in the home state of the foreign minister; (2) when there is a waiver of immunity; (3) when the person ceases to serve as a foreign minister and is prosecuted in the domestic courts of another state in relation to acts committed in the private capacity during their time in office; and (4) when the foreign minister is prosecuted before an international criminal court with jurisdiction (such as Article 27(2) of the Rome Statute).[58]

A pertinent issue is the interpretation of the acts committed in private capacity, as it could hardly be envisaged that the planning and execution of the act of aggression could be done in a private capacity. As mentioned above, the planning and waging of aggressive war is inherently linked to the highest-level decision making apparatus of the state. Moreover, it should be noted that the prohibition of aggression is of a *jus cogens* character in international law.[59] Contemporary practice also indicates that international tribunals or hybrid tribunals established by international treaties could set aside immunities for international crimes, as reflected in the jurisprudence of the SCSL.[60] The ICC has declared in a similar vein that 'there is neither State practice nor *opinio juris* that would support the existence of Head of State immunity under customary international law vis-à-vis an *international court*' (emphasis added).[61] The non-applicability of immunities would concern the Big Three: the head of state, the head of government and the minister of foreign affairs.

As seen above, the crime of aggression is a leadership crime. Along these lines, the non-applicability of immunities would match the ultimate responsibility of the top political echelon to prevent large-scale crimes.[62] In this way, the

[56] ibid 152 (Lord Hope).

[57] *Case Concerning the Arrest Warrant of 11 April 2000* (2002) ICJ Rep 3, 20–21.

[58] ibid 25–26.

[59] ILC, 'Peremptory Norms of General International Law' (2019) A/72/10, 205, https://legal.un.org/ilc/reports/2019/english/chp5.pdf.

[60] See *Prosecutor v Charles Ghankay Taylor*, SCSL Appeals Chamber, Decision on Immunity from Jurisdiction, SCSL-2003-01-I, 31 May 2004, paras 43–58.

[61] *Judgment in the Jordan Referral re Al-Bashir Appeal*, ICC Appeals Chamber ICC-02/05-01/09 OA2 (6 May 2019) para 113.

[62] Cryer (n 1) 54.

principle that no one is above the law is affirmed. An additional political angle is the focus on top-level officials. Professor Cryer raises in his scholarship the importance of the incapacitation and deterrence effect of eventual prosecution of the highest-level perpetrators and the inability to hide behind the procedural immunity veil: if the highest-level perpetrators are removed from office, then their ability to instigate renewed conflict(s) would drop significantly, as such perpetrators will be removed from public and political life.[63]

Another possibility would be to investigate the top political and military echelon: not all political officials and cabinet members or military officials would have the same type of functional and personal immunity as the foreign minister or the head of state. The planning and preparation of the act of aggression would include a high number of political and military appointees and, unless they enjoy any type of immunity, they would be liable for investigation and prosecution in the domestic courts of the forum state. Hence, it would not be surprising if initial efforts are focused on mid-level political and military officials in order to circumvent the immunity procedural bar, as well as to gather evidence against the highest echelon of the aggressor state. Nonetheless, the overall accountability focus of international prosecutions against the crime of aggression should be on those who bear the greatest responsibility for that international crime – namely, the top political and military echelon of the aggressor state. This does not mean under any circumstances that low-level perpetrators should avoid investigation and prosecution for international crimes, especially if they have committed particularly egregious international crimes in the context of the act of aggression. Such a pragmatic approach to international criminal law aligns with the purpose of international justice. A balance may need to be struck between prosecuting at all levels of responsibility, as low-level perpetrators may be positioned closer to the victims and may increase the legitimacy notion of the work of international tribunals. On the other hand, as Professor Cryer noted, international criminal law should aim at the apex of responsibility as international crimes do not happen in a vacuum and are rarely perpetrated in a non-systematic manner.[64]

The prosecutorial strategies and scope of indictments are also pertinent. Broad indictments such as those implemented as early as the Nuremberg and Tokyo IMTs provide the chance to weave an extensive narrative. Professor Cryer remarked that the narrative is collected as a result of testimonies as well as elaborate fact finding missions through forensic scrutiny.[65] It is important to note that the ongoing armed conflict in Ukraine has been well documented and forensically assessed.[66] It is essential to obtain the cooperation of the *locus*

[63] ibid.
[64] ibid 55.
[65] ibid 72.
[66] See, eg, EUAM Ukraine, 'Documenting War Crimes While under Attack: Steps Forward towards Deserved Justice', 28 November 2023, www.euam-ukraine.eu/news/documenting-war-crimes-while-under-attack-steps-forward-towards-deserved-justice/.

delicti state in order for the proper collection of direct evidence.[67] In contrast, indictments that are smaller in scope are simple, less time-consuming and relatively easy to run. The defence may also use tactics to slow the process, based on the sheer scope of the indictment. In any case, the proceedings must enshrine, respect and implement the principles and rights of international human rights law with 'particular emphasis … on the right to a fair trial by an independent and impartial court, access to a lawyer, the timely examination of cases, and the enforcement of final and binding judicial decisions without undue delay'.[68] In complex litigation, involving the crime of aggression, 'the fairness of the proceedings and its ability to render an accurate rendering of the facts' is of crucial importance.[69] Prosecuting the crime of aggression at an international forum would be a complex endeavour for the prosecutor. Professor Cryer captures the essence of the challenging task of the international prosecutor in terms of calibrating the scope of such complex indictments and associated difficulties by stating that '[a] prosecutor is offered a difficult choice, and is in some ways caught on the horns of an almost insoluble dilemma'.[70]

The crime of aggression concerns the perpetration by the highest political and military echelon. The added value of investigation and prosecuting aggression is reflected in the notion that everyone is equal before the law, respecting a culture of the rule of law, and even the political and military elite cannot hide behind their positions, elude accountability and enjoy impunity. In this sense, deterrence is relevant in the function of international criminal law and international prosecutions seem to have an effect on political actors.[71] Moreover, to ensure compliance, 'international law (and international courts) ought to step in to assist in preventing violations' of core international crimes.[72]

CONCLUSION

This chapter aims to provide an overview of the crime of aggression. It engages with the scholarship of Professor Cryer. As illustrated above, the ongoing war in Ukraine may qualify for the initiation of investigations and potential prosecution of the crime of aggression against high-ranking Russian officials. Nonetheless, legal obstacles arise for the domestic prosecution of the crime of aggression. These are primarily linked to the applicability of functional and

[67] See Bekou and Cryer (n 24) 66.

[68] Declaration of the Ministers of Justice of the Council of Europe, 'Towards Accountability for International Crimes Committed in Ukraine' (Vilnius, 5 September 2024) pt 6.

[69] Cryer (n 9) 100.

[70] Cryer (n 1) 74.

[71] R Cryer, 'The Role of International Criminal Prosecutions in Increasing Compliance with International Humanitarian Law' (2014) 44 Israel Yearbook on Human Rights 247, 250–251 and 258–265.

[72] ibid 270.

personal immunities of the highest political echelon of the aggressor state. The ICC currently lacks jurisdiction for the crime of aggression under the Rome Statute for the situation in Ukraine. Accordingly, one possible avenue might be recent developments such as the proposal for an ad hoc international tribunal for the crime of aggression.[73] The establishment of the ad hoc international tribunal would ultimately resolve the procedural immunity bar that domestic courts might face when hearing cases related to the crime of aggression. Moreover, an international ad hoc tribunal might offer the requisite expertise to collect evidence and conduct the complex accountability steps in a professional and independent manner in light of the considerable complexity of the crime of aggression, involving the highest political and military stratum of the aggressor state. Time is of essence, 'the longer the leader can avoid arrest, the less likely he is to be fit to face the type of justice that does not rely on the existence of a perfect metaphysical realm'.[74] Moreover, the international response to the crime of aggression may create a deterrence effect. This is particularly pertinent for the role of international justice as Professor Cryer reminds us that while 'criminal law can never eradicate crime … if fewer leaders succumb to this temptation, international criminal justice will have proved itself worthwhile'.[75]

[73] See PACE, Resolution 2436 (2022) 'The Russian Federation's Aggression against Ukraine: Ensuring Accountability for Serious Violations of International Humanitarian Law and Other International Crimes' (28 April 2022).

[74] Cryer (n 1) 65.

[75] ibid 75.

13

Robert Cryer and the Jus Post Bellum

JAVIER S ESKAURIATZA

INTRODUCTION

THESE ARE TROUBLED times, and it feels like Rob's voice is missing. It is impossible not to wonder what he would have had to say about many things.[1] A parsing of his scholarship might give us the confidence to make a guess, but it is impossible to be sure. Yet, what really matters is not *what* he would have said or thought about something; it is simply *that* we miss thinking and talking about it, whatever it was, with him. It was in a supervisor-supervisee context that I first came to know Rob. I was very lucky to be one of his doctoral students, and later one of his friends. I am grateful to the editors of this collection for the opportunity to contribute a few thoughts in honour of his memory. He is very much missed. I think Rob would not mind if I broke one of the unwritten rules of traditional legal writing and began with a personal memory or two. Indeed, this was a rule that Rob himself had to set aside, at least once.[2]

The first time I 'met' Rob was in an online interview. I was in a non-academic role in Puebla, Mexico, and I had applied to start a PhD at Birmingham Law School on an 'emerging' legal concept: the *jus post bellum*. When the time came for Rob to speak, he asked simply: 'Javier, what is the *jus post bellum*?' I began to rant about liberal constitutionalism, the fragmentation of international law, the invasion and 'reconstruction' of Iraq, neo-colonialism, capitalism and Afghanistan, and I think I even said something about Marxism. As I ranted, Rob smiled. He would look down and then look up again, still smiling. He listened and waited patiently. Eventually, I stopped, and he said: 'Yes, but what *is* the *jus post bellum*?' I remember feeling quite stumped. In truth, I had not actually answered *that* question. It was not just pedantry (though Rob could play the

[1] This was something of a 'running joke' at his memorial conference at Birmingham Law School in 2023.

[2] R Cryer, 'Superior Orders and the International Criminal Court' in Burchill, ND White and J Morris (eds) *International Conflict and Security Law: Essays in Memory of Hilaire McCoubrey* (Cambridge University Press, 2005) 49–67, 49.

pedant as well as anyone); it was about accuracy.[3] Machine-gun tactics would not work on him. I suppose that was the first lesson.

Years later, towards the end of my doctoral studies, I charged into his office in one of those (rare) moments of 'PhD euphoria'. I shot out: 'Rob, have you got anything good on the exhumation of mass graves?' He leant back in his chair and hollered (that is the only word for the sound he made) and he began to chuckle gleefully. Then, as ever, he got up and began to shuffle back and forth around his room, surveying his bookshelves, craning his neck upwards, mumbling at himself and scratching at his wrist. That is how I will remember Rob, typing away in his office, surrounded by his books, radiating an unbridled enthusiasm for academic research – a playfulness which he brought to the most serious matters.

In what remains of this short chapter, I want to honour Rob's legacy by focusing on his scholarship. As is well known, he published a huge amount on a variety of topics in international and criminal law. So, rather than attempt a general overview, I will go the other way and engage in a close reading of a specific piece, namely, a chapter that he contributed to an edited collection on the *jus post bellum*.[4] The topic is fitting for many reasons. In the first place, it was the topic of my doctoral thesis, and so it formed the basis of countless hours of discussions between us.[5] Second, it is one of my favourite Rob pieces. It is rich and edifying, and it covers a lot of ground.[6] After a brief section on definitional matters, I will focus on a few salient themes that emerge, themes which are echoes of our discussions and give rise to memories, and themes which may illuminate something of Rob's scholarship as a whole.

THE *JUS POST BELLUM*: DEFINITIONAL MATTERS

Rob was a very careful scholar. In his contribution to the *jus post bellum* topic, he was at great pains to say that it was not his intention 'to implacably oppose *jus post bellum* as a concept'.[7] In fact, modern ideas about *jus post bellum* were varied and the concept was used in at least two different ways.

[3] As Neil Boister has remarked, Rob had a 'zeal' for accuracy: N Boister, 'In Memoriam: Robert Cryer, b. 2 August 1974 – d. 3 January 2021' (2021) 19(2) *Journal of International Criminal Justice* 235, 237.

[4] R Cryer, 'Law and the *Jus Post Bellum*: Counselling Caution' in L May and AT Forcehimes (eds), *Morality, Jus Post Bellum and International Law* (New York, Cambridge University Press, 2012) 223–49.

[5] Although it was very much the case that there were three of us, and I remain immensely indebted to Gavin Byrne.

[6] Although a close reading of any of Rob's pieces is likely to be very instructive. I would argue his entire oeuvre (and not just the textbook) could form the basis of a course in international (criminal) law.

[7] Cryer (n 4) 223.

In the first wave of scholarship, Brian Orend, Michael J Schuck, Michael Walzer and others defined the concept as 'post-war justice' or 'justice after war'.[8] These scholars argued, in essence, that contemporary just war theory distinguished between the *jus ad bellum* (the justice in resorting to armed force) and the *jus in bello* (just conduct during armed conflict), but that the *jus post bellum* had (wrongly) been ignored.[9] Thus, for these scholars, the *jus post bellum* was about the theoretical and practical application of just war theory to the post-conflict phase. For just war theorists, the *jus post bellum* appeared necessary as a matter of disciplinary coherence and completeness.

Orend and others found justification for the (re-)emergence of *jus post bellum* in classical European philosophy on war and peace (ie, in St. Augustine, Vitoria, Suárez, Grotius, Vattel or Kant).[10] Many of these classical writers, of course, did say things about post-war justice. The question is whether and how their ideas should provide the foundation for a new law that applies to the post-conflict phase in contemporary international relations. For Rob, the answer was a resounding 'no'.[11] Nevertheless, insofar as these kinds of discussions were confined to the *morality* of the post-war phase, he was not opposed.

It was the second wave of *jus post bellum* scholarship which had implications for the law of armed conflict. This second wave began with Kristen Boon and Jean Cohen, who were the first to discuss the *jus post bellum* as a legal concept.[12] Subsequently, the project of the *jus post bellum* as 'post-conflict *law*' gathered momentum under the auspices of the '*Jus Post Bellum* Project' at the University of Leiden in the Netherlands.[13]

[8] MJ Schuck, 'When the Shooting Stops: Missing Elements in Just War Theory' (1994) *The Christian Century* 982; B Orend, 'Kant's Just War Theory' (1999) 37(2) *Journal of the History of Philosophy* 323; B Orend, 'Justice after War' (2002) 16 *Ethics and International Affairs* 43; B Orend, '*Jus Post Bellum*: A Just War Theory Perspective' in C Stahn and JK Kleffner (eds), *Jus Post Bellum: Towards a Law of Transition from Conflict to Peace* (TMC Asser Press, 2008) 31; M Walzer, *Arguing about War* (Yale University Press, 2004); L May and AT Forcehimes (eds), *Morality, Jus Post Bellum and International Law* (Cambridge University Press, 2012); M May, *After War Ends* (Cambridge University Press, 2012).

[9] For a historical review of the central figures in just war theory and their contributions, see JT Johnson, *Ideology, Reason and the Limitation of War: Religious and Secular Concepts 1200–1740* (Princeton University Press, 1975); see also M Walzer, *Just and Unjust Wars* (Basic Books, 2006). See SK Sharma, 'Reconsidering the *Jus Ad Bellum*/*Jus in Bello* Distinction' in Stahn and Kleffner (n 8) 9 for an argument that the distinction is too easily assumed.

[10] On the historical tripartite conception of the law of armed force, see C Stahn, '"*Jus Ad Bellum*", "*Jus in Bello*" … "*Jus Post Bellum*"? Rethinking the Conception of the Law of Armed Force' (2006) 17(5) *European Journal of International Law* 921.

[11] Cryer (n 4) 232: 'history is not necessarily an argument for or against a concept'.

[12] K Boon, 'Legislative Reform in Post-conflict Zones: *Jus Post Bellum* and the Contemporary Occupant's Law-Making Powers' (2005) 50 *McGill Law Journal* 285; JL Cohen, 'The Role of International Law in Post-conflict Constitution-Making: Towards a *Jus Post Bellum* for "Interim Occupations"' (2006–07) 51 *New York Law School Law Review* 497.

[13] See two edited collections: Stahn and Kleffner (n 8); and C Stahn, J Easterday and J Iverson (eds) *Jus Post Bellum: Mapping the Normative Foundations* (Oxford University Press, 2014). For information on the '*Jus Post Bellum* Project', see juspostbellum.com.

Even here, there were different things going on and Rob's chapter does not necessarily reject the idea of *jus post bellum* as 'post-conflict law'. For example, some legal scholars were using the term in a purely descriptive sense, ie, as an umbrella term for the law that applied. Rob thought there was no problem in doing so and that it might even 'focus the mind on the various areas of law that need to be brought together'.[14] However, it should be noted that this is a very complicated mixture. Briefly, it would include several areas of national law, international law, any relevant peace agreement(s), United Nations (UN) Security Council Resolutions etc, so even if only *describing* the law that is already there, the phrase '*jus post bellum*' may be challenged as implying a level of coherence that is hard to justify.[15]

However, Rob's chapter is really directed at those who relied on just war theory approaches to the *jus post bellum* to argue that certain 'deficiencies' in the current legal framework, and especially the law of occupation, had to be remedied.[16] There was a particular normative strain of the *jus post bellum* propounded by Brian Orend and (to a certain extent) by Carsten Stahn which drew on Kantian ideas of democratic peace to call for a new legal regime which would deal *in toto* with post-conflict legal issues – ie, a new Additional Protocol to the Geneva Conventions.[17]

Now, of course, Rob was interested in (new) ideas. In supervisions and in his writing, he would often say that 'ideas mattered' and he meant this in the sense that the power and influence of ideas ought to be taken seriously in any international relations theory. He would regularly cite the constructivists (Wendt, Fiss and Kratochwil) in his work.[18] Even so, as Gerry Simpson and others have recalled, Rob had a soft spot for a certain *Schwarzenbergian* sensibility which might be described as: 'positivist, dubious of grandiose claims, and … somewhat (perhaps rightly) fearful of change'.[19] Thus, he was sceptical of those who

[14] Cryer (n 4) 225.

[15] JS Eskauriatza, 'The *Jus Post Bellum* as "Integrity": Transitional Criminal Justice, the ICC, and the Colombian Amnesty Law' (2020) 33(1) *Leiden Journal of International Law* 189; J Gallen, 'The *Jus Post Bellum*: An Interpretive Framework' in Stahn, Easterday and Iverson (n 13) 58; C Bell, 'Of *Jus Post Bellum* and *Lex Pacificatoria*: What's in a Name?' in Stahn, Easterday and Iverson (n 13) 181.

[16] Proponents of a new *jus post bellum* focused on the law of occupation: see Articles 27–34 and 47–78 of the fourth Geneva Convention – Geneva Convention Relative to the Protection of Civilian Persons in Time of War (GC IV) 75 UNTS 287 (all four Conventions were adopted on 12 August 1949 and entered into force on 21 October 1950).

[17] Orend, '*Jus Post Bellum* (n 8) 31; C Stahn, '*Jus Post Bellum*: Mapping the Discipline(s)' in Stahn and Kleffner (n 8) 93.

[18] After he passed, I said to myself that I would read A Wendt's *Social Theory of International Relations* (Cambridge University Press, 2009). I did not own the book, so I ordered it from a well-known online book retailer. When it arrived, I opened it, and a makeshift bookmark fell out. It was an airline ticket in the name of Dr Robert Cryer, and it is printed at the end of this chapter; for Rob's constructivism, see R Cryer, 'The Limits of Objective Interests' (2006), 82(1) *International Affairs* 183.

[19] R Cryer, 'International Law and the Illusion of Novelty: Georg Schwarzenberger' in R McCorquodale and JP Gauci (eds), *British Influences on International Law (1915–2015)* (Brill, 2016) 458–83; see also G Simpson, 'Robert Cryer' (2023) *British Yearbook of International Law*, doi.org/10.1093/bybil/brad012.

claimed, without sufficient justification, that things were now very different, that the world had changed and that therefore the law had to change. Schwarzenberger called this the 'over-emphasis and over-valuation of the dynamic aspects of current events'.[20] In this respect, Rob wrote:

> Since the attacks on the US on 11 September 2001 there has been a repeated refrain that the world has changed and that this justifies redescriptions and new approaches to the law. Maybe the world has changed, maybe not, but it is necessary to inquire into two things before reaching judgement. First, why someone is suggesting the world has fundamentally altered; and second, whether the purported changes require that the law must change or give way to the critique that it is simply utopian, and as such barely relevant.[21]

For Rob, the *jus post bellum* as identified by Orend and others was a product of this 'repeated refrain' that the world had changed and that the law, and particularly the law of armed conflict, had to change. It is no surprise that Orend's contribution and those of many others were focused on the US-led invasion of Iraq in 2003 and the subsequent calamities of the 'post-conflict' phase. They are exclusively focused on 'post-intervention' issues and they had almost nothing to say about non-international armed conflict (which remains the most common type of armed conflict). To my mind, Rob's contribution to the *jus post bellum* topic most clearly identified that theirs was really an idea for a new 'post-*intervention* law', a law designed to circumvent certain aspects of the law of occupation which restricted what occupiers wanted to do.

METHOD: HISTORY, MORALS, LAW

However, before getting to the issues of applicability and content, I want to focus on the fact that Rob's critique of the *jus post bellum* (as post-intervention law)[22] begins with the title of his piece: 'Law and the *Jus Post Bellum*'. This allows us to consider Rob's methodological leanings. Lest anyone think I am reading too much into this, Rob cared a lot about titles.[23] Therefore, it is clear that the decision to separate and juxtapose these concepts is part of the work.

[20] G Schwarzenberger, *International Law and Totalitarian Lawlessness* (Jonathan Cape, 1943); see the reviews by K.L. in (1943) 8(2) *Cambridge Law Journal* 230 and by Oppenheimer in (1943) 37(3) *American Journal of International Law* 552.

[21] Cryer (n 19) 479.

[22] From now on, unless the contrary is made clear, the *jus post bellum* refers to this pro-intervention version of the *jus post bellum* as propounded by Orend et al.

[23] Some of the titles he chose contained obvious allusions to The Beatles and (maybe his favourite) Bob Mould, ie, 'Come Together: Civil and Criminal Jurisdiction in *Kiobel* from an International Law Perspective' (2014) 12 *Journal of International Criminal Justice* 579–92; 'The International Committee of the Red Cross' Interpretive Guidance on the Notion of Direct Participation in Hostilities: See a Little Light' in R Geiss, A Zimmerman and S Haumer (eds), *Humanizing the Laws of War. Part II: The International Committee of the Red Cross and the Development of International Humanitarian Law beyond Treaty Regimes* (Cambridge University Press, 2017) 113–38.

It reflects, frankly, Rob's view that whatever the relevant authors thought it was, the *jus post bellum* was not 'law'. An academic exploration of what a particular version of just war theory meant in respect of today's post-conflict dilemmas may be useful in some respects, but it was not necessarily useful in terms of what the law is or should be. This is not least because Vitoria, Suárez and others were 'working in a very different tradition' and that 'similarities may turn out to be what translators call "false friends"'.[24] This is true. In relation to Orend's reliance on Kant, for example, what to do about the fact that in *Perpetual Peace*, Kant says that his book provides 'abstract ideas' that ought not to trouble the 'worldly – wise Statesman'?[25]

Rob has been called the 'leading British intellectual positivist of his generation', and it is true that he was sceptical and wary about reliance on natural law (though not aimlessly dismissive).[26] His preference was positivism and inductive reasoning.[27] It is for this reason that Rob preferred Christine Bell's attempt to conceptualise post-conflict law as a *lex pacificatoria*.[28] Consider Rob's review of Bell's classic *Peace Agreements and Human Rights*, which ends: 'well researched, well argued, well written, and shows consistent good judgement. Not only is it a welcome addition to this reviewer's library, it deserves to be studied closely by all persons interested in the area of international law and conflict. Those who do read it will come away glad that they did'.[29] The crucial difference between these two Latin-monikered concepts is that, for Bell, the *lex pacificatoria* 'does not signal a fully-fledged regime as a possible, or desirable, end point … it signals that the indeterminacy of post-conflict law may indeed be a "good thing"'.[30]

To my mind, for Rob to prefer Bell's approach to the theorising of post-conflict law also reflects a common law sensibility. For common lawyers, it is the *experience* of law (and not only logic) that produces identifiable legal rules.[31] Rob wrote:

> [W]hat matters more to many common criminal lawyers is not intellectual purity, but outcomes. It is not clear that this is the worst way of proceeding. Incompletely theorized agreements are not necessarily bad practice … Common law thinking may

[24] Cryer (n 4) 223, 226.

[25] H Reiss, *Kant: Political Writings*, HB Nisbet (ed and trans) (Cambridge University Press, 2001) 93.

[26] In the pub, talking about positivism, Rob intimated that there was something to Lon Fuller's version of natural law: Simpson (n 19).

[27] In the pub, I once put him on the spot, and he said: 'Benthamite positivism'.

[28] On the *lex pacificatoria*, see C Bell, *Peace Agreements and Human Rights* (Oxford University Press, 2000); C Bell, *On the Law of Peace: Peace Agreements and the Lex Pacificatoria* (Oxford University Press, 2008); Bell (n 15) 181.

[29] R Cryer, 'Review of Christine Bell, *Peace Agreements and Human Rights* (Oxford, OUP, 2000)' (2001) 1(1) *Human Rights Law Review* 169.

[30] Bell (n 15) 181, 205. Some scholars have said there is no difference between the concepts and that *jus post bellum* should be preferred: C Rojas-Orozco, *International Law and the Transition to Peace in Colombia: Assessing Jus Post Bellum in Practice* (Brill, 2021) 41. It is submitted that Professor Bell's is the better view.

[31] R Cryer, 'Imputation and Complicity in Common Law States: A (Partial) View from England and Wales' (2014) 12 *Journal of International Criminal Justice* 267, 269.

> often be experiential rather than transcendental/idealist, but that does not mean that it is necessarily less wise on that basis.[32]

Thus, in response to calls for a new Kantian-inspired Protocol from academics, he wrote:

> Whatever the merits of *jus post bellum* as a moral system of evaluation it must be doubted whether states would take the naturalist bait offered. In the end, if a new form of international law is to be created, states, not academics, have to be convinced by the argument in its favour.[33]

But this brings us to consider the content of the *jus post bellum* as discussed by Orend and others. What was the argument in its favour? Why exactly was Rob opposed to this new form of post-intervention law? Owing to the space limitations in this chapter, I will focus on two simple ideas: the first is that the law of occupation was inadequate, out of date and obsolete; and the second is that decisions about when the *jus post bellum* should apply should be left to the 'war winner'.

THE *JUS POST BELLUM* AND THE LAW OF OCCUPATION

As mentioned above, a great deal of *jus post bellum* scholarship was about fixing perceived problems with the legal framework that applied in post-intervention situations, ie, the law of occupation. Many scholars and practitioners were happy to point to several instances where the law seemed inadequate to deal with the issues that arose for occupiers in, inter alia, post-conflict Iraq. Examples included the law on the use of force, the issue of 'transformative occupations', post-conflict detention and transitional criminal justice.[34]

Needless to say, Rob was unimpressed by these pro-intervention arguments. In the first place, it was not clear that the law was broken beyond repair. There was not only the law of occupation but also human rights law and, in his view, most of the issues could be worked out by a careful interpretation of the law that was already available. For Rob, if and when things became very difficult, it fell to the UN Security Council to step in and regulate matters in an ad hoc manner. Further, insofar as the legal framework was 'too conservative' – well, that was the entire point of the law. As Eric de Brabandere argued, 'the very reason the laws of occupation are inadequate to deal with comprehensive post-conflict reconstruction missions … is precisely the reason for their existence, namely to limit the occupier's powers in a territory for which the occupier has no title'.[35] Or as Adam

[32] ibid.

[33] Cryer (n 4) 223, 240.

[34] For a general review, see C Garraway, 'The Relevance of *Jus Post Bellum*: A Practitioner's Perspective' in Stahn and Kleffner (n 8) 153 (though Garraway did not say a new post-intervention law was necessary).

[35] E Brabandere, 'The Responsibility for Post-conflict Reforms: A Critical Assessment of *Jus Post Bellum* as a Legal Concept' (2010) 53 *Vanderbilt Journal of International Law* 119.

Roberts put it, it was a law designed to regulate 'a temporary set of affairs pending a peace agreement'.[36] Equally, Rob was entirely unconvinced that the Iraq experience should form the template of a new post-invasion regime. As he wrote:

> That something did not work in Iraq, against the entire backdrop of that conflict, does not mean that the law is fundamentally flawed. Never mind hard cases, bad cases often make bad law.[37]

For Rob, even taking the *jus post bellum* 'at its very best', it was obvious that any new post-intervention legal regime, which was designed to be more permissive than the law of occupation, could only have one result: to grant more authority to militarily powerful states to carry out interventions in weaker states likely to be subject to the new law.

THE *JUS POST BELLUM*, NEO-COLONIALISM AND REGIME CHANGE

The most controversial aspect of the Orend-inspired notion of the *jus post bellum* is that it would allow 'forcible regime-change' in certain contexts, including when: (i) the *jus in bello* was adhered to, (ii) the 'target' regime was illegitimate; (iii) the goal of the new regime is 'minimally just'; and (iv) respect for the *jus in bello* and human rights is integral to the transformation process.[38] Further, when it came to deciding when the new and permissive *jus post bellum* should apply, in the accounts of just war theory (upon which Orend and others relied), it is the *just war winner* that is to decide.[39]

It is impossible to do justice to Rob's reply to this proposal[40] other than to say that it represents a kind of *Cryeresque* 'gentle-fury' which permeates much of his writing. Rob takes Orend and Stahn's *jus post bellum* 'at its very best'[41] and then demonstrates that even then, it is a bad idea which is likely to make things far worse.[42] He begins by equating the proposal with James Lorimer's nineteenth-century scholarship which divided nations into 'levels of development', and he ends with a reaffirmation of the principle of sovereign equality:

> It appears practically impossible to imagine that many states would accept such a normatively tinged form of law that could only serve to increase the power of the

[36] A Roberts, 'Transformative Military Occupation: Applying the Laws of War and Human Rights' (2006) 100 *American Journal of International Law* 580, 582.

[37] Cryer (n 4) 237.

[38] Orend, '*Jus Post Bellum*' (n 8) 31, 48.

[39] ibid 31, 50.

[40] Cryer (n 4) 241–48.

[41] ibid 237.

[42] Rob is careful to make the point that he did not think that Orend and others were arguing in bad faith. In essence, Rob was helping them to see the very controversial and undesirable implications of their argument.

> already powerful, and leave decisions to judgment calls of those who win wars and will naturally consider themselves to have acted justly.[43]

Rob ends the piece by citing one of his favourite articles: Benedict Kingsbury's 'Sovereignty and Inequality'.[44] The point is that sovereign equality is not perfect, but that the alternatives may be far worse. Anyone who spends any time with Rob's scholarship will immediately recognise this as a cornerstone of his approach to international law and international relations.

CONCLUDING THOUGHTS

It is interesting that, in legal circles, the phrase '*jus post bellum*' has been (relatively) conspicuous in recent times by its absence.[45] Where it is referred to, it tends to be used as an umbrella term for all the law that applies (ie, changing nothing) or as a synonym for some of the other post-conflict law terms that are routinely used, ie, transitional justice (that is, changing nothing).[46] I think Rob would be pleased with this result. Looking back at some of the earlier *jus post bellum* scholarship today, it is remarkable that some of the more aggressive pro-intervention proposals could be taken seriously by international lawyers. How would scholars today react to the view that Russia (which evidently considers itself to have acted *justly*) should be left to decide: (a) when a new post-intervention law applies in Ukraine; and (b) what that law requires? Of course, for Rob, this was entirely unacceptable, no matter who was invading whom.

A final thought – when he knew he was not well, Rob and I talked about his *in memoriam* volume. I said I would not know what to write. It is still immensely saddening. The *Cambridge English Dictionary* says that kindness is 'the quality of being generous, helpful, and caring about other people'. Rob was all these things, as a person and as a scholar. But as a scholar, he managed to balance that kindness with a fierce and honest critique. He had a unique academic sensibility,

[43] Cryer (n 4) 248.

[44] In the pub, in serious playfulness, we used to chat about our 'Top 5s', eg, name a top 5 article in the *European Journal*. One that he would come back to would be Benedict Kingsbury, 'Sovereignty and Inequality' (1998) 9(4) *European Journal of International Law* 599.

[45] See, for example, contributions to the *Ukraine Peace Settlement Project* (University of Cambridge Lauterpacht Centre for International Law, 2022), cambridgepeace.org/projects/ukraine. However, it continues to attract attention; see S Sayapin and E Tsybulenko, *The Use of Force against Ukraine and International Law: Jus ad Bellum, Jus in Bello, Jus Post Bellum* (TMC Asser Press, 2018). However, the *jus post bellum* is used as either a purely descriptive 'umbrella term' (encompassing a range of other subfields including transitional justice) or as a synonym for one of these fields; see G Kemp and I Lyubashenko, 'The Conflict in Ukranian Donbas: International, Regional, and Comparative Perspectives on the *Jus Post Bellum* Options' in S Sayapin and E Tsybulenko (eds), *The Use of Force against Ukraine and International Law* (TMC Asser Press, 2018) 330–52.

[46] Kemp and Lyubashenko (n 44); CR Orozco, *International Law and the Transition to Peace in Colombia: Assessing Jus Post Bellum in Practice* (Brill, 2021).

a concern for his work and a concern for other people. That, for me, is the enduring lesson of Robert Cryer, from whom we can all continue to learn so much.

Figure 3 A Passage to Cryer's Library (cf n 18)

Act IV

Acoustics and Storytelling

14

'Diving into Noise and Bringing Clear Melody'*

AGNIESZKA JACHEC-NEALE

INTRODUCTION

EVERYONE WHO WAS close to Rob knew that music was immensely important in his life. Even those who didn't know him too well would, at some point, get a sense of its importance. Some of his colleagues recall how, every now and then, Rob would play metal music full blast in the office. He claimed that it helped him concentrate on his writing and research.[1] No doubt, this would serve as a deterrent to any visitors, students and colleagues alike, who might have been tempted to disturb the creative process. Indeed, his former PhD students fondly recall his office littered with big tubs of sweets and – amongst the stacks of books, journals, papers and notes – a scattering of CDs. These visual signs of music's omnipresence in Rob's life complemented the audible clues from the loud music often preceding, and initially hindering, entry to his personal, academic and creative space. Many of his friends and family would know that Rob played the guitar with passion and talent that amazed others. He had a sophisticated guitar collection. And he was reputed to be able to replicate a tune instantly after hearing it for the first time.[2] I have even heard his friends say that he was so good he would have probably succeeded in playing music as a professional if he had not ended up in academia.

Rob also had a remarkable memory and encyclopaedic knowledge of music, buoyed by his studious mind and research skills. He loved thinking and analysing music with his friends. Karaoke nights with Rob were legendary and many can still hear his powerful voice carrying the lyrics of his favourite tracks with

* I Kalpouzos, 'Rob, *in Memoriam*' (2022) 19 *Journal of International Criminal Justice* 2, 235, 246.

[1] From the personal recollections of Rob's colleagues at the University of Birmingham during a conference dedicated to Rob's life and scholarship: 'Robert Cryer: A Life in Law and a Law unto Himself' (29–30 June 2023, Birmingham, UK).

[2] ibid; *cf* Drumbl and Mouthaan, ch 16 in this volume.

such strength that it would stop chatter in the pub or bar. He would lose himself in the track and give you little choice but to join him in doing so.

Music was such a prominent feature in Rob's life that I wondered if it also slipped into his scholarly work. Therefore, I have undertaken a review of a significant selection of Rob's scholarly publications: over 80 pieces, spanning nearly 25 years of his academic career. I examined a variety of his monographs, co-edited books, chapters in books, articles, published reviews and case reports. I was fascinated by my findings for two reasons. First, I was rather surprised to see barely any references to music: I found two, and one more was brought to my attention during the conference. Second, notwithstanding the rigour of the doctrinal content, I found myself totally gripped by the mastery of Rob's writing technique. As much as his scholarship lacked explicit or implied mentions of music, I found a wealth of beauty in his writing, so much so that I started noticing some patterns and characteristics of his own style. Thus, I felt compelled to reflect on the aesthetics of Rob's writing in greater detail.

This short chapter is divided into two sections of unequal length. The first section recalls the scarce references to music that I encountered. The second, much longer section offers reflections on what I have aesthetically discovered alongside my inquiry, featuring what I count among Rob's lasting contribution to scholarship.

THE LANGUAGE OF MUSIC

My initial research of Rob's musical references returned only one. Then, while writing this chapter, one more reference made its appearance in my survey of Rob's writing. Moreover, during the 2023 conference dedicated to Rob's life and work, where I had a pleasure to share the outcome of my investigation, colleagues present at the conference alerted me to a third source where a passing music-related reference had been made. There is a possibility that another skilled reader may encounter further references in Rob's writings that I missed; hence, I would very much welcome it if any such reader considered sharing their findings with me. That said, there is no doubt in my mind that additional discoveries would be rare. Rob did not make music references in his scholarship and, if there were any, they were in his early writings. In fact, the two identified mentions both appear to have been published in 1998. I have asked some of his close friends and work colleagues if Rob ever reflected on matters of music in his writings, and it does not appear that he did. However, some of his former doctoral students, now legal experts and academics in their own right, did recall Rob using 'language of music' in his PhD supervisions sometimes.[3] It could be

[3] More personal recollections of Rob's PhD students and colleagues (thank you, J Eskauriatza and S Vasiliev).

because they shared a passion for music and guitars and therefore extending this commonality into the realm of a doctoral project was just a natural extension of kindred interests. And it could be easier and clearer to explain issues during PhD supervision if you use the 'language of music', knowing that the other person would understand.

Now, on to the musical unicorns in Rob's writing. The first reference comes from a piece Rob wrote following his attendance, as an observer, at an historical conference leading up to adoption of the Rome Statute of the International Criminal Court (ICC).[4] The reference to music appears in the title as 'cadenza of the song of those who died in vain'. This phrase emerges only once in his entire piece; no other references appear to have been made. Here, Rob uses the word 'cadenza' (meaning a virtuoso solo passage inserted into a movement in a concerto or other musical work, usually at the end) in relation to the newly established ICC. In his commentary, he went on to analyse the outcome of the 1998 Rome Conference as a culmination of decades of effort in bringing the ICC to life as a part of the global criminal justice project.

In this very title, Rob touches upon a larger moral question too – and he does so poetically. He asks if the ICC or the Rome Statute constitutes a 'song for those who died in vain'. The latter phrase is taken from the title of a poem written by Primo Levi. Rob cites a passage from Levi in his first footnote:

> Sit down and bargain, all you like grizzled old foxes. We'll wall you up in a splendid palace … Provided that you discuss, negotiate, for our and our children's lives … But outside in the cold we will be waiting for you, the army of those who died in vain … Heaven help you if you come out disagreeing, You'll be clutched tight in our embrace … Sit down and bargain, until your tongues are dry. If the havoc and shame continue, we'll drown you in our putrefaction.[5]

It would be hard to find a more appropriate quote to refer to the high-level negotiations involved in the agreement that has changed the landscape not only of international law or international justice, but also of perceptions on accountability globally. This is not an isolated occurrence of Rob's referral to poetry in his writing, but, in my view, one of the most powerful ones.[6]

[4] R Cryer, 'Commentary on the Rome Statute for an International Criminal Court: A Cadenza for the Song of Those Who Died in Vain?' (1998) 3 *Journal of Armed Conflict Law* 271.

[5] P Levi, 'Song of Those Who Died in Vain' in *Collected Poems*, R Feldman (trans) (Faber & Faber, 1992). As Emma Breeze reminded me (thank you!), this poem also featured on the back cover of the 1993 Manic Street Preachers' album *Gold Against Soul*. There is a theoretical possibility, though I have no evidence to support it, that Rob's reference to the same poem might be related to the mention of it on the album cover, which Rob likely had in his collection.

[6] Early in his writings, Rob appeared to have been inspired by poetry. Another example of the use of poetry can be found in a later piece that examines Operation Enduring Freedom in Afghanistan. Rob challenges the metaphorical 'friendship' of allies. Along this journey, he quoted, among others, William Butler Yeats. The quote comes from seventh stanza of Yeats's poem 'The Municipal Gallery Revisited' and is found in fn 2 of the text.

The second reference is to be found in a 2009 article on the interplay among three branches of international law: international human rights law, international criminal law and international humanitarian law. Rob specifically indicates that human rights law and humanitarian law 'can end up playing in harmony if not unity'.[7] This passage, which is also discussed later in this chapter, makes an almost-passing comment on the interrelationship between these two branches of law. Of course, harmony and unity are distinct methods by which the elements of a musical piece work together. Unity refers to the overall cohesion of all elements within a musical composition, whereas harmony implies unity between chords and melodies and, thereby, complementing lyrics. In other words, harmony concerns how elements relate to one another, while unity concerns how they relate to the entire piece. Rob clearly thought that the two branches of law could complement rather than exclude each other.

The third reference related to music comes from a book review, mentioned in a presentation by Professors James Lee and Martin George during the conference in memoriam of Rob.[8] In the introductory part of the review, Rob forewarned:

> As this review began with an attempt to clear up any misunderstanding, so it shall end with one … it may be thought that the criticisms raised herein either stem from, or evidence a dislike for this book. This would not be correct, this book is amongst the best currently available and certainly merits inclusion in any library, the criticisms noted are no more than *scratches on a much enjoyed album*. The authors are to be congratulated for a serious analysis of the law and practice of international criminal law. (Emphasis added)[9]

Rob plainly used the metaphor of 'album' here, undoubtedly a vinyl one that could possibly be 'scratched', given that a physical 'scratch' on an album (which still plays) does not detract from the fact that such album is still 'much enjoyed'. Whilst this phrase may appear a little outdated among a younger generation of listeners who access music digitally, it would nonetheless ring true to committed vinyl record collectors.

HIGH NOTES IN ROB'S WRITING

Though Rob was regarded and saw himself as an international lawyer more broadly, one of his key areas of expertise was international criminal law. The majority of his writings pertain to this branch of international law, joined by

[7] R Cryer, 'The Interplay of Human Rights and Humanitarian Law: The Approach of the ICTY' (2009) 14(3) *Journal of Conflict and Security Law* 527.

[8] M George and J Lee, '*Cryer, et seq*: Reflections on Scholarship and Collegiality' (2023); see n 2 above.

[9] R Cryer, 'Book Review: SR Ratner and JS Abrams, *Accountability for Human Rights Atrocities in International Law: Beyond the Nuremberg Legacy*' (1998) 3(2) *Journal of Conflict and Security Law* 291.

scholarship in laws of armed conflicts or international humanitarian law. Rob's lifetime dedication to international justice and criminal law seems to have been intertwined with moral and ethical questions of the human condition. A particular passage from one of Joy Division's tracks, 'Atrocity Exhibition', seems to capture, in my opinion, the existential undertones of Rob's lifelong scholarship, starting with: 'You'll see the horrors of a faraway place, Meet the architects of law face to face, See mass murder on a scale you've never seen, And all the ones who try hard to succeed …'[10] These same words read in different contexts can give us entirely different meanings. The lyrics are said to be inspired by JG Ballard's book of the same title and reflect upon the lyricist's own existential angst and personal troubles. Yet, the same words read in relation to Rob's work and convictions can be interpreted to signify similar themes to those found in Primo Levi's poem, cited by Rob. Among the 'mass murders' and 'horrors', the lyricist, Curtis, would guide us on 'what was and will be'.

Joy Division's haunting music, along with the band's name and themes in particular, draws a chilling connection to the horrors of genocide. The band was named after a disturbing aspect of Nazi concentration camps, where Jewish women were forced into sexual slavery in so-called 'Joy Divisions' during the Second World War. This link to Nazi atrocities resonates with the raw, existential anguish found in Primo Levi's poetry, which confronts the dehumanization and suffering of the Holocaust. Both Joy Division's work and Levi's poetry evoke a profound reflection on human suffering and survival, and the profound human impact of atrocities. By confronting the horrors of genocide and crimes against humanity, international criminal law seeks to ensure accountability, thereby offering a legal response to the moral and existential questions raised by such historical atrocities.

During my research, I found myself transfixed not so much on the expert substance of Rob's writings as on their admirable form. He clearly developed his own expressive style over the years, particularly when it came to word use. I shall focus on Rob's mastery of words in the first part of my observations. Furthermore, I shall also reflect on Rob's skilful way of delivering criticism. In the second section, I shall touch upon on an interesting use of reflective 'braces' when beginning and ending a writing. Finally, I want to reflect on some of the pertinent messages Rob incorporated into his writings.

WORDSMITH

Rob loved reading. He read voluminously. Words were immensely important to him. His early writings especially showed his creative thinking; namely, his use of sensory words portraying images and metaphors. Rob thought that the

[10] Joy Division, 'Atrocity Exhibition' (Factory Records, 1980).

Rome Statute was characterised by 'Byzantine complexity', implying excessiveness and needlessness. He also indicated that the ICC got 'caught on the horns of dilemma' at times.[11] Going further, he repeatedly used the phrase 'the stone in the shoe of this view' to describe the small but irritating crux of the opinion or issue.[12]

Occasionally, Rob's visual narrative depicted vivid parables and symbolism. In his aforementioned commentary on the Rome Statute, he stated that 'after years in the *desert* of academic insignificance International Criminal Law is finally receiving the attention it deserves' (emphasis added).[13] When embarking on an analysis of the challenges surrounding criminal prosecution and state sovereignty, Rob would get the reader's attention by personifying sovereignty as death:

> When sovereignty appears in international criminal law scholarship, it commonly comes clothed in hat and cape. A whiff of sulphur permeates the air. Generally, international criminal law scholars see sovereignty as the enemy. It is seen as the sibling of realpolitik, thwarting international criminal justice at every turn.[14]

Themes of travelling and taking a certain road surface in some of Rob's writing. Again, within his piece on the Rome Statute, Rob characterised himself as a 'fellow traveller', offering his reflections as 'more a tourist guide or a map than a monograph'. In a 2002 review of Martti Koskenniemi's book, *The Gentle Civilizer of Nations*, Rob uses 'road' as a metaphor for writing, the creative process, and the end product (namely, the book):

> In part, the book is a response to criticisms of *From Apology to Utopia*. That book had been criticised as having failed to show why international lawyers choose or have chosen certain positions if international legal discourse was as indeterminate as he claimed … Still, his ambitions are higher. Koskenniemi's road onwards, or backwards, is a surprising one: formalism. For a writer who has been critical of rule-based reasoning in the past, this cannot be a smooth road. So how does Koskenniemi travel it?[15]

Over the years, Rob's words became more elegant, complex and even old-fashioned. He did write to a specialist audience, but he did so with relative concession to the reader. He smuggled words like *factotums*, *shibboleth*, *transmogrify* and *fissiparous*[16] into his writing without the unbearable heaviness of

[11] R Cryer, 'Royalism and the King: Article 21 of the Rome Statute and the Politics of Sources' (2009) 12 *New Criminal Law Review* 390, 404.

[12] ibid 400.

[13] Cryer (n 4).

[14] R Cryer, 'International Criminal Law vs State Sovereignty: Another Round?' (2005) 16(5) *European Journal of International Law* 979.

[15] R Cryer, 'Déjà vu in International Law', Review of: *The Gentle Civilizer of Nations: The Rise and Fall of International Law 1870–1960* by Martti Koskenniemi' (2002) 65(6) *MLR* 932.

[16] See, eg, R Cryer, 'The Definitions of International Crimes in the Al Bashir Arrest Warrant Decision' (2009) 7 *Journal of International Criminal Justice* 296.

gratuitous (or deliberate) impenetrability. Here is an example from a 2005 article on 'art of defence (aggression)':[17]

> The question of Security Council (or other body) involvement in determining aggression, which is correctly identified as a proposed precondition for ICC (not national court) action in the third quoted sentence, is *transmogrified*, by the final sentence, into an 'essential element of the crime'. (Emphasis added)[18]

One can see that Rob favoured some words and phrases, as they feature frequently in several of his publications; some of the regulars included: Delphic, apposite, all that said, or human justice. And he absolutely loved using Latin in his writing; one would struggle to find a piece written by Rob where none of the following phrases was used: whether more common legalese, such as *in absentia*, *obiter*, *jus cogens*, *nullem crimen*, *mala fide* and *ultra vires*,[19] or less common phrases, including *forum propagatum*, *lex mitior*, *rebus sic stantibus*, *non bis in idem*, *rule esjudem generis*, *fons et origio*, *in dubio pro reo*, *caveat lectorem*, *magnum opus* and *ceteris paribus*.[20]

From time to time, Rob would create his own clever formulations. For instance, in a 2002 review of Lindsay Moir's seminal monograph on non-international armed conflicts, Rob mentioned 'return to *ad hocery*'.[21] In a 2009 article on the interplay of the three branches of international law, he stated that:

> [E]ven though international human rights law, international criminal law and international humanitarian law are not identical, they can be '*fuzzier*' sets than is sometimes thought, and are certainly not *autopoietic* systems. Therefore, they ought not to be treated as such, but like many things, with due respect for context, human rights law and humanitarian law can end up playing in harmony if not unity. (Emphases added)[22]

It was not clear what the 'fuzziness' was, or how it was supposed to be measured. This phrase also stood in a stark contrast to the more eloquent 'autopoietic' used to reflect the complex nature of the relationships among the three branches of law.

Finally, one cannot help but notice that Rob was a notoriously prolific reviewer of books he read and, as mentioned above, he certainly read a lot of books. He published numerous reviews and, as reviews go, some were more appreciative

[17] Rob used the term 'art of defence (aggression)' in his article. To understand what he means, one must consult his writing: R Cryer, 'Aggression at the Court of Appeal' (2005) 10(2) *Journal of Conflict and Security Law* 228.

[18] ibid.

[19] See, eg, R Cryer, 'The Security Council and Article 39: A Threat to Coherence' (1996) 1 *Journal of Armed Conflict Law* 165.

[20] See, eg, R Cryer and AP Simester, 'Iraq and the Use of Force: Do the Side-Effects Justify the Means?' (2006) 7 *Theoretical Inquiries in Law* 34.

[21] R Cryer, 'Review of: *The Law of Internal Armed Conflict* by Lindsay Moir' (2002) 7(1) *Journal of Conflict and Security Law* 144.

[22] Cryer (n 7) 527.

of the reviewed material than others. Yet, even in his most damning critiques, he managed to retain a positive tone. This is most apparent in his previously mentioned review of Steven Ratner and Jason Abrams' book, where he warns the reader of his ensuing critical observations, yet frames his criticism positively overall. In another example, he concludes his highly critical assessment of Jack Goldsmith and Eric Posner's book *Limits of International Law* as follows:

> By excluding at the start the possibility of states wanting to act in accordance with international law on the basis that they genuinely perceive it to be in their interests to fulfil legal obligations per se, the authors guarantee their conclusion but they ensure that their case cannot be considered proven.[23]

When pointing out the scholarship's crucial shortcoming – a lack of scientific rigour – Rob carefully isolates the most fundamental flaw of the authors' argument in a single sentence.

EMBRACING STRUCTURE

In addition, Rob used words masterfully to frame an entire piece of writing. One can see how using connected comments on the same topic serves almost as a 'brace' to convey important messages amidst often-dense analytical commentary. In his 2002 piece on Operation Enduring Freedom, he began and ended with friendship-themed reflections, which sandwiched nearly 50 pages of comprehensive factual and legal analysis.[24] Rob's article begins with the following text:

> There are at least two ways in which our friendships provide others with evidence upon which to judge us. The first way that we are judged in relation to our friends is how we treat them … We have all made adverse comments about those who mistreat their friends, or leave them in their hour of need. The company we keep is also considered to reflect upon us. Many claim the confidence of celebrities, of friendships with felons. It is the purpose of this piece to evaluate the conduct of operation 'Enduring Freedom' through these lenses.[25]

Ultimately, his article concludes with the following two sentences:

> [Reminder] … that not only should we treat our friends well, but also remind them of their obligations when they appear to overstep the boundaries of what is acceptable. The ways our friends act also reflects upon us, and thus it is important to take care when choosing friends and allies, and appraise the actions of both friend and foe by reference to the same law.[26]

[23] R Cryer, 'The Limits of Objective Interests', Review of: *The Limits of International Law* by Jack L. Goldsmith and Eric A. Posner' (2006) 82(1) *International Affairs: Perspectives on Emerging Would-Be Great Powers* 188.

[24] Breeze and Turns reflect on this article in more depth in ch 17 of this volume.

[25] R Cryer, 'The Fine Art of Friendship: "Jus in Bello" in Afghanistan' (2002) 7(1) *Journal of Conflict and Security Law* 37.

[26] ibid 83.

Not only did Rob convey the same argument in both passages, but he even used comparable words and phrases such as 'reflect[s] upon us', strengthening the message he sent; however, this is not the only example of his application of this particular technique.

MESSENGER

Rob's scholarship was not just focused on the pure letter of the law; it also contained philosophical and ethical reflections and messages on the nature of international law, as well as the contributions of states and lawyers to the development and reshaping of law. In a 2006 article about an International Committee of the Red Cross (ICRC) study of Customary International Humanitarian Law, Rob illustrated – with brilliant simplicity – the inherent paradox of customary international law and state practice as evidence of this source of international law:

> Turning back to later evidence, one frequently resorted to piece of evidence is the number of states that have ratified the relevant treaty. In some ways this is paradoxical, given that the greater the number of parties, the more practice can be referred to the treaty. Similarly, the greater the claim of a treaty to customary status at the time of its adoption, the lesser the impetus for states to bother to ratify the convention, as it will not alter their obligations. Still, a very widely ratified treaty has a considerable 'pull' towards acceptance, as there is a feeling that if a treaty is very broadly ratified, it represents the general expectations of those states.[27]

Providing another example of sophisticated critique in the same article, Rob compared the ICRC study to an impressionist painting:

> The Study had been described as a photograph but it can be seen in a different manner, namely as a great impressionist painting. From a broad view, in its general conception and in many ways, it is a masterpiece, but the closer the look taken into the way it approaches custom, the less beautiful it can seem.[28]

Rob's analogy underscores the nuanced complexity of his analysis. While the ICRC study may appear cohesive and masterful at a macro-level, a closer examination reveals imperfections in its treatment of custom, suggesting that its depth may diminish under detailed scrutiny.

Reflecting on the role of lawyers in his review of Koskenniemi's monograph, Rob commented in the following two passages:

> Despite their sincere humanitarian concern for the colonised, the lawyers still made use of the logic of inclusion/exclusion, emphasising the difference of non-Europeans

[27] R Cryer, 'Of Custom, Treaties, Scholars and the Gavel: The Influence of the International Criminal Tribunals on ICRC Customary Law Study' (2006) 11(2) *Journal of Conflict and Security Law* 241, 244.

[28] ibid.

> but tempering the refusal to apply international law in full by a naturalistic universalism in relation to human rights.[29]
>
> Nonetheless, after a time spent staring into the abyss, one of international law's most trenchant, albeit sympathetic critics, by the end of this extraordinarily thought-provoking and well written work, appears to have accepted that there is, after all, utility in what international lawyers do. By doing this, Koskenniemi seems to have pulled the teeth of his own theoretical critique. He denies its relevance to practical international law and accepts that an approach to international affairs integrating international legal discourse is, like democracy for Churchill, 'the worst form of government except all those other forms that have been tried from time to time'. Most international lawyers can be expected to agree.[30]

Rob presents his critique of Koskenniemi's contracting approach to assessing the role and impact of international legal practice and discourse with his signature Rob flair. In the first passage, Rob highlights the paradox faced by lawyers who, despite genuine humanitarian intentions, perpetuate the logic of inclusion and exclusion. This duality underscores a tension within international law: a universalistic approach to human rights is tempered by a reluctance to fully apply the same standards to non-European peoples. Rob's analysis exposes how this selective application undermines the purported universality of international law.

In the second passage, Rob observes Koskenniemi's re-evaluation of his own critical stance. By the conclusion of his work, Koskenniemi appears to reconcile his theoretical critique with the practical utility of international legal practice, likening it to Churchill's infamous defence of democracy. Rob deftly captures this shift, noting that Koskenniemi's acknowledgement of the practical value of legal discourse effectively blunts his earlier, more trenchant critiques. This concession, Rob argues, resonates with the broader community of international lawyers who recognise flaws in the system, but acknowledge its relative effectiveness compared to other frameworks. Rob's critique not only dissects Koskenniemi's theoretical journey but also emphasises the enduring tension between critical theory and pragmatic practice in international law.

CONCLUSION

I have unabashedly borrowed the title of my presentation at the conference, as well as this ensuing chapter, from a sentence that Ioannis Kalpouzos wrote in his memorial to Rob.[31] I couldn't find better words that so succinctly epitomised my observations regarding the beauty of Rob's scholarship, expressed in the language of music. While Rob's writings brought lasting clarity and understanding of both normative and doctrinal law, they also offered critical insight on the

[29] Cryer (n 15) 937.
[30] ibid 949.
[31] Kalpouzos (n 1).

philosophical and ethical direction of those involved in creating and shaping international law and global affairs.[32]

Rob celebrated words. He used them in a purposeful and meaningful way. He did not shy away from critique, but delivered it in a fair and respectful manner. Rob, as Kalpouzos recalls, did not see himself as a critical scholar.[33] Most surprising to me was the discovery that, given the significance of music in Rob's life, he did not incorporate more language of music references into his rich record of publications.

To close my thoughts on Rob's masterful scholarship and his passion for music, I chose a song to be played at the end of my talk – a song to celebrate Rob's larger-than-life personality and his *joie de vivre*. In the process, I spent quite some time considering some of Rob's favourite bands: Hüsker Dü, Big Star, The Replacements and Joy Division, among others. Eventually, I settled on Motörhead and its track, 'Ace of Spades', which I know was one of Rob's Karaoke-night staples.[34] So, raise a glass and join me in listening to this track. Imagine Rob's mighty voice gregariously singing that 'the pleasure' was 'to play' as we assure you that, whilst you 'walk away in silence' from our lives, you 'don't walk away in silence' from our memories.[35]

[32] Many of these have been reflected in this volume – see, for example, Simpson, ch 2, Bartels, ch 3, Roberts, ch 6, van Sliedregt, ch 10 and Lee, ch 18 in this volume.

[33] ibid.

[34] ibid 246.

[35] Motörhead, 'Ace of Spades' (Bronze Records, 1980).

15

Music and War
The Themes from Anti-war Music and the Impact they have

EOIN CAMPBELL

INTRODUCTION

I SADLY NEVER had the opportunity to meet Rob personally, but I was fortunate enough to be briefly taught by him during the second year of my LLB. I was in the International Law degree programme, which meant that I took public international law before I otherwise would have had the opportunity to do so. Pandemic restrictions in the UK meant that, by the time of his classes, lectures were pre-recorded and uploaded online, so my interactions with Rob were solely from the bedroom of my accommodation in Selly Oak. However, he left a significant impression on me that continues to this day.

Rob's lectures were on the use of force in international law. Before I even began my studies in law, I knew that the use of force was going to capture my attention due to my prior interest in conflict. Rob effectively served as my introduction to this topic, alongside Javier Eskauriatza and Alexander Orakhelashvili, the remaining members of our teaching team that year. The use of force, and how law and conflict are related, continued to be my main area of interest after Rob's passing. In my final year of my undergraduate studies, I wrote my dissertation under Javier's supervision on the crime of aggression, on which I conducted a critique of the International Criminal Court's (ICC) definition of the crime through the lens of Third World approaches to international law. While including aggression in the Rome Statute may indeed amount to little more than pure symbolism,[1] a line from Rob's textbook on international criminal law has

[1] W Schabas, 'The Unfinished Work of Defining Aggression: How Many Times Must the Cannonballs Fly, before They are Forever Banned?' in D McGoldrick, P Rowe and E Donnelly (eds), *The Permanent International Criminal Court: Legal and Policy Issues* (Bloomsbury, 2004) 123, 141.

remained in my mind since the first time I read it.[2] The chapter on aggression ends with the lines:

> If one prediction may be safely made, it is that there will not be many prosecutions for aggression before the Court. However, if the existence of ICC jurisdiction acts as a deterrent to even a few war-mongering presidents and prime ministers, it has the potential thereby to save many lives.[3]

With war raging across the continents, this quote returns to me frequently. When it came time to pick a topic for this book, I knew that I had to do something that was personally meaningful and that had a connection to Rob and his teachings, as well as his great love of music. I decided to combine elements of my masters dissertation (supervised by Emma Breeze, another former student of Rob's), inspired by Rob's teachings and the teachings of many of his colleagues and former students, my interests in the use of force, and Rob's love of music.

In this chapter, I will look at how and why states use emotive language when asserting a state of necessity to justify using force. Following this, I will examine how music can do the opposite. By looking at a number of different themes from anti-war songs, I hope to show the impact that language can have in the other direction – to advocate for a world in which war disappears, or, at the very least, to try to advocate for such a world.

A STATE OF NECESSITY TO JUSTIFY FORCE

The theme of necessity appears in numerous different conflicts globally. Necessity in this context will refer to the requirement to pursue essential security interests. In other words, states argue that when their very survival is at stake, the use of force is necessary.

The theory of preventive self-defence present in the argument advanced by the Bush administration – 'we cannot afford to stand idly by as grave dangers materialise' – clearly alludes to a justification of necessity without explicitly using the word.[4] The US exports its counterterrorism focus abroad through a policy of using force. From October 2010 to July 2021, prosecutors charged 1,584 defendants in federal district courts with crimes relating to domestic terrorism.[5] In contrast, an estimated 288,923 to 295,998 opposition fighters have been directly killed as a result of post-9/11 wars in Afghanistan, Pakistan, Iraq, Syria

[2] For further reflections and analysis of the impact of textbooks and learning 'by proxy', see Oidtmann, ch 7 and Lee, ch 18 in this volume.

[3] R Cryer, D Robinson and S Vasiliev, *An Introduction to International Criminal Law and Procedure*, 4th edn (Cambridge University Press, 2019) 317.

[4] National Security Strategy.

[5] US Government Accountability Office, 'Domestic Terrorism: Further Actions Needed to Strengthen FBI and DHS Collaboration to Counter Threats' (Report to the Ranking Member, Committee on Homeland Security, House of Representatives, February 2023) 46.

and Yemen.[6] This disparity between the former and latter numbers demonstrates that the US is primarily interested in stopping terrorist threats outside of its territory and, considering the difficulties of enforcing any accountability for illegal uses of force,[7] it serves as an apparently viable and effective mechanism, keeping the destructive nature of terrorism and military force far from its borders. Airstrikes are believed to have a strong deterrent effect as terrorist attacks in Pakistan tend to decrease in an area for a number of days following a strike, regardless of its success.[8] From a utilitarianist perspective rooted in a US-centric viewpoint, using force is a justified method of combatting terrorism, as it poses essentially no risk to US citizens, but has the potential to eradicate its enemies and secure geopolitical interests.

The UK, too, stated that its use of force against the Syrian government was based on an 'overwhelming humanitarian necessity' and that 'deterring further chemical weapons attacks was necessary and proportionate and therefore legally justifiable'.[9] France offered a similar argument for attacking potential chemical weapons development sites in Syria, with the presidential office stating that 'we cannot tolerate the recurring use of chemical weapons, which is an immediate danger for the Syrian people and our collective security'.[10] Again, whilst not referring to necessity directly, the language is clear – if we do not act, these weapons will be used and the survival of the state will be at risk.

States are appearing to, if not outwardly endorse, increasingly tolerate necessity as a justification to employ the use of force; states at least refrain from openly condemning it, or they take a tepid stance and defend it as not necessarily legal, but morally justifiable. A discernible pattern emerged in United Nations (UN) General Assembly's resolutions and Security Council discussions regarding states' attitudes towards the use of force. The Security Council condemned the Osirak bombing by Israel in 1981,[11] and the US invasion of Grenada in 1983, which the government justified as 'necessity to protect American citizens in the country',[12] was condemned by the General Assembly.[13] However, the events

[6] Watson Institute, 'Human Costs of Post-9/11 Wars', Brown University, March 2023, www.watson.brown.edu/costsofwar/figures/2021/WarDeathToll.

[7] J Trahan, 'The Crime of Aggression and the International Criminal Court' in LN Sadat (ed), *Seeking Accountability for the Unlawful Use of Force* (Cambridge University Press, 2018) 331–32.

[8] D Jaeger and Z Siddique, 'Are Drone Strikes Effective in Afghanistan and Pakistan? On the Dynamics of Violence between the United States and the Taliban' (December 2011) *Institute for the Study of Labour*, IZA DP No 6262, 13.

[9] Prime Minister's Office, 'Syria Action – UK Government's Legal Position' (Policy Paper, 14 April 2018), www.gov.uk/government/publications/syria-action-uk-government-legal-position/syria-action-uk-government-legal-position.

[10] J Borger and P Beaumont, 'Syria: US, UK and France Launch Strikes in Response to Chemical Attack', *The Guardian*, 14 April 2018, www.theguardian.com/world/2018/apr/14/syria-air-strikes-us-uk-and-france-launch-attack-on-assad-regime.

[11] UNSC Res 487 (19 June 1981) UN Doc S/RES/487.

[12] RA Pastor, 'The Invasion of Grenada: A Pre- and Post-mortem' in S McDonald, H Sandstrom and P Goodwin Jr (eds), *The Caribbean after Grenada: Revolution, Conflict and Democracy* (Bloomsbury, 1988) 89.

[13] UNGA Res 38/7 (2 November 1983) UN Doc A/Res 38/7.

of 9/11 spawned a trend towards states being more relaxed about the use of force. In the words of former Director of Intelligence George Tenet and British Prime Minister Tony Blair: 'All the rules have changed.'[14] Despite the fact that the invasion of Afghanistan appeared more a reprisal than a genuine act of self-defence,[15] it still received significant support from the international community as a whole.[16] The invasion of Iraq also garnered support from a wide range of states.[17] This thread continued with regard to the 2018 attacks on Syria aimed at destroying chemical weapons facilities. This time, a significant number of states offered political support for the strikes, although they did not argue for their legality. For instance, Lithuania explicitly referenced necessity in its own approval of the strikes, with the Minister of Foreign Affairs expressing that 'the targeted airstrikes on chemical weapons facilities of 14 April were necessary steps for encouraging the Syrian regime and its supporters to seek a political solution to the conflict'.[18] Whilst a significant number of states still condemned the strikes,[19] it is striking to note that over half (54 per cent) that released statements about the strikes made no explicit claim about the legality of the strikes, while another 27 per cent made no explicit legal claim about the strikes, despite referencing either international law or the UN Charter.[20] Indeed, only 15 per cent of states made an explicit statement that the strikes were illegal. When considering political reactions to the strikes, the African Group was the only one that had a majority actually condemn the strikes.[21] Across the Western Europe and Others Group and the Eastern European Group, most states lent their political support to the strikes; in the Asia-Pacific Group and the Latin America Group, the vast majority of states either offered no view on their political stance or explicitly gave it a political endorsement.[22] In considering the entirety of states

[14] G Tenet, *At the Centre of the Storm: The CIA during America's Time of Crisis* (Harper Perennial, 2008) 179; P Wintour, 'Blair Vows to Root out Extremism', *The Guardian*, 6 August 2005, www.theguardian.com/politics/2005/aug/06/terrorism.july7.

[15] J Quigley, 'The Afghanistan War and Self-Defence' (2003) 37 *Valparaiso Law Review* 541, 562.

[16] UNSC Res 1368 (12 September 2001) UN Doc S/RES/1368.

[17] For example: J Lubecki, 'Poland in Iraq: The Politics of the Decision' (2005) 50 *Polish Review* 69, 73; J Watts, 'End of an Era as Japan Enters Iraq', *The Guardian*, 26 July 2003, www.theguardian.com/world/2003/jul/26/iraq.japan; G Geunwook Lee, 'South Korea's Faustian Attitude: The Republic of Korea's Decision to Send Troops to Iraq Revisited' (2006) 10 *Cambridge Review of International Affairs* 481, 486.

[18] Ministry of Foreign Affairs of the Republic of Lithuania, 'Linkevičius: Attack on Syria's Chemical Weapons Facilities was a Necessary Step towards a Peaceful Political Solution', 16 April 2018, www.urm.lt/default/en/news/linkevicius-attack-on-syrias-chemical-weapons-facilities-was-a-necessary-step-towards-a-peaceful-political-solution.

[19] For example, 'Foreign Ministry Spokesperson Hua Chunying's Regular Press Conference on April 16, 2018', om.china-embassy.gov.cn/eng/fyrth/201804/t20180416_1296362.htm.

[20] For a complete list and the compiled statistics, see A Gurmendi Dunkelberg, R Ingber, P Pillai and E Pothel, 'Mapping States' Reactions to the US Strikes against Syria of April 2018: A Comprehensive Guide', *Just Security*, 7 May 2018, www.justsecurity.org/55835/mapping-states-reactions-syria-strikes-april-2018-a-comprehensive-guide.

[21] ibid.

[22] ibid.

that presented statements regarding the strikes, just under half (49 per cent) expressed approval, whilst only 22 per cent offered a condemnation.[23]

Evidently, states are review the use of force through a lens reflecting moral rather than legal judgement. When the language of necessity is invoked and states justify their use of force under a mantra that 'there was no other option', other states appear more willing to accept the use of force, particularly when it aligns with their own political agenda. In a post-9/11 world, states appear more ready to approve these uses of force from a political standpoint than they were during the Cold War. Indeed, reactions indicate that while the law and the rules remain unchanged, states are willing to accept that there are circumstances in which they should disregard rules hindering their security interests. Indeed, perhaps this is a reason why the ICC's jurisdiction over aggression has been watered down relative to the other core crimes, leading to Rob's conclusion that there will be few prosecutions.

THE LANGUAGE OF MUSIC

States are not the only ones with the power of language. Music has always served as a way to convey messages.[24] Next, I will seek to identify themes across anti-war songs. I aim to use a variety of sources, across the world and relating to different times, to demonstrate why these themes are effective and so frequently used. The list of songs considered may seem random, but all are among my favourite songs by my favourite artists, which I simply wished to include due to their personal impact.

FRUSTRATION AND ANGER

Unsurprisingly, the first theme that jumped to mind was anger at war, and the two songs that immediately followed were 'Born in the U.S.A.' by Bruce Springsteen and 'Fortunate Son' by Creedence Clearwater Revival. (Coincidentally, in the midst of writing this chapter, I attended a Springsteen concert in Cork. Emma mentioned that Rob had also previously attended one of his shows and they had discussed it during a PhD supervision meeting. As far as I'm aware, Rob was not a particularly huge fan, but he greatly admired Springsteen's performance.)

The above songs effectively push an idea that the circumstances of birth play a significant role in the outcome of life, particularly when it comes to how people are impacted by war. However, they choose to approach the issue from opposite perspectives. Springsteen's focus is on how he is personally affected: he is 'born

[23] ibid.
[24] For more on this, see Jachec-Neale, ch 14 in this volume.

down in a dead man's town', he is kicked around from the moment of his birth, he ends up in Vietnam because of his little hometown jam, and when he gets back, he is left to suffer alone. He endures the loss of his brother in Vietnam, and even 10 years after the end of the war, he has 'nowhere to run … nowhere to go'.[25] Due to the consequences of his birth, he is forced into war and mistreated when he returns. He is left to rot; his country has forgotten him. In contrast, 'Fortunate Son' looks at those lucky enough to be born into a well-connected family, where they are largely unaffected by the Vietnam War. While most men in the US were worrying about being drafted, the 'senator's son', 'millionaire's son' and the 'military son' all happen to avoid being sent to the front lines.[26] The people who make the decision to go to war, those who are privileged and wealthy, and those benefiting from the military-industrial complex are all free to make decisions on foreign policy that will change the lives of millions of people at home and abroad, but which sustain no impact to themselves and their own family. The images that these songs convey – of someone 'born in the U.S.A', and someone 'born made to wave the flag' – paint what initially appears to be a pro-war picture and, naturally, have often been misinterpreted as pro-American anthems.[27] Instead, the language used throughout both songs expresses anger at being forced to go to war – namely, anger at those who made the decisions, anger at the inequality of their respective situations and anger that they are expected to sacrifice their lives for a worthless cause. The heavy-hitting vocals and instruments on both songs symbolise the anger and frustration of people needlessly dying, and the combination of all of these wrongs inspired two iconic songs that, unfortunately, continue to be relevant, particularly with regard to the war in Ukraine.[28]

More calm in melody than the two songs above, and yet fiercer in words, is Bob Dylan's 'Masters of War'. Dylan encapsulates the rage and frustration he feels with those who start and perpetuate war – the weapons manufacturers and the politicians. Directing the entire song at these people, he decries that all they do is 'build to destroy' and he laments that those who decide to go to war, who 'put a gun in [his] mind', 'turn and run farther when the fast bullets fly'.[29] There is anger at the lack of accountability for their actions. They decide who goes to war and they live without fear of death or of war's horrors. The anger at this continues throughout the song and, indeed, becomes more intense. The fourth verse contains the most realistic images of war from any of the songs I have chosen for this piece; it accuses the politicians and weapons manufacturers of 'sit[ting] back and watch[ing] while the death count gets higher', as 'young

[25] Bruce Springsteen, 'Born in the U.S.A.' (Columbia, 1984).

[26] Creedence Clearwater Revival, 'Fortunate Son' (Fantasy, 1969).

[27] J Terry, 'Politicians Have Always Misunderstood Springsteen's "Born in the U.S.A.", *Vice News*, 5 October 2020; K Grow, John Fogerty Addresses "Fortunate Son" Concert for Valour Controversy, *Rolling Stone*, 13 November 2014.

[28] O Ivshina, 'Russia Conscription Laws Change, Leaving Some Fearful of Ukraine War Call-up', *BBC News*, 5 August 2023, www.bbc.co.uk/news/world-europe-66388422.

[29] Bob Dylan, 'Masters of War' (Columbia, 1963).

people's blood flows out of their bodies and is buried in the mud'.[30] War is no longer an abstract idea; it is deadly, it is violent and it is ugly. Those who start it and profit from it are unaffected by the bloodshed and the destruction, and ordinary people suffer indescribably. Dylan's anger continues to grow until it peaks in the final stanza, with some of the most intense language used in any anti-war song. Unlike many of the others, which long for a better future or stick with mere frustration, Dylan's anger turns to hatred. The final verse starts off harsh, blunt and honest: 'And I hope that you die, and your death will come soon.'[31] While it may seem brutal, it still is nothing compared to the pain suffered by those who fight in war. In fact, he is simply hoping that the perpetrators meet the same fate into which they led so many others. His anger is so palpable that he is not satisfied with the bare knowledge of their deaths: 'and I'll stand over your grave' [t]il I'm sure that you're dead'.[32] Ultimately, Dylan suggests that the whole system is so broken that the only way for it to heal and for a better future to emerge is for all the participants of the pro-war system to be extinguished. This scathing song demonstrates the anger of needless death and suffering in a way that so few others can match.

The last song I will mention in this category is Edwin Starr's 'War'. Starr sets the tone immediately, declaring that war is good for 'absolutely nothing', then delving into the consequences of war in his first verse.[33] Again, building on the themes above, he focuses on the 'destruction of innocent lives' caused by war. War eventually destroys all those who come into contact with it – from soldiers on the front lines to civilians and families affected by loss – even when they had no part to play in the reason for the conflict. Consequently, the effects of war are so widespread that it 'is the enemy of all mankind'. The concept of wanting to cause destruction, death and chaos is so alien to Starr that the very 'thought of war blows [his] mind'. Even when war is over, the survivors are left 'disabled, bitter and mean'. The destruction that war causes is summed up by the line that 'war can't give life, it can only take it away'. War never ends in a perfect way for anyone; the only ones who benefit are those who can enrich themselves from geopolitical or economic power.

HUMOUR

A more lighted way of demonstrating the horrific conditions of war can be found in 'The Recruiting Sergeant'.[34] Composed by Seamus O'Farrell in 1915, the song tells a story of a recruiting sergeant trying to convince the singer to enlist into

[30] ibid.
[31] ibid.
[32] ibid.
[33] Edwin Starr, 'War' (Motown, 1970).
[34] Seamus O'Farrell, 'The Recruiting Sergeant' (1915).

the British Army during the First World War – a more humorous way of revealing an anti-war message. The sergeant repeatedly tries to sell the image of war as a great adventure, telling the singer that 'you'd look fine in khaki' and that 'a life in Flanders … would be a fine vacation'. Rather than being enamoured by the prospect of a life of adventure, opting to fight because 'the King, he is in need of men' as so many men did, the singer retorts by asking the sergeant 'if I had a pack stuck up on my back, would I look fine and cheery?' He knows the conditions he will face: 'It may be warm in Flanders, but it's draughty in the trenches.' The sergeant and the singer continue this battle of wits throughout their meeting, until the singer ends the meeting with the line: 'Let your sergeants and your commanders go.' The singer humorously deflates the sergeant's promises of glory with the real conditions that he will face on the Western Front. Humour can be an essential means for countering propaganda and forming grassroots resistance that seek to question the official line of the state.[35] Of course, Rob was also a great purveyor of humour in his classes – I think, when dealing with a subject that can be as harrowing as international criminal law, dark humour can serve to help compartmentalise some of the horrors being discussed. The fact that Rob's conference in Birmingham contained a presentation on the use of memes in legal education just goes to show the importance Rob placed on humour!

Additional examples of the use of humour in anti-war music can be seen in the works of the satirist/mathematician Tom Lehrer. His song 'So Long, Mom' seeks to make light of what seemed like inevitable nuclear destruction during the Cold War.[36] Similar to 'The Recruiting Sergeant', he parodies a number of pro-war slogans throughout his song. He contrasts the future World War III with the previous world wars, demonstrating in his cheery voice and happy tune that the destruction seen in those previous conflicts will be nothing compared to the 'agonising nuclear holocaust'. One of the most powerful contrasts used is the verse that describes how their armies will 'attack frontally', and while they are engaged with enemy forces, those back home can watch the newscasters 'describing contrapuntally the cities we have lost'. While the army may be making progress securing territory, it comes at the cost of so many cities that the newscasters can read them out on a list. This message is emphasised again, where Lehrer describes a soldier who will 'come back … home, although [he] may be a pile of debris'. His lyrics paint a picture of an apocalypse and of the realities of nuclear war, and they are delivered in such a way that can only make people laugh, which ideally helps to weaken pro-war narratives. Through humour, people realise how ridiculous the whole thing is – is going 'off to get a commie' worth the death and destruction that will entail? Does human life really come so cheaply? And should the fact that the war will be over 'an hour and a half from

[35] D Chernobrov, 'Strategic Humour: Public Diplomacy and Comic Framing of Foreign Policy Issues' (2022) 24 *British Journal of Politics and International Relations* 277, 278.

[36] Tom Lehrer, 'So Long, Mom (A Song for World War III)' (Reprise/Warner Bros, 1965).

now', yet cause more destruction than the human mind can fathom, give cause for concern? The absurdity is plain to see: technology has developed so fast and so far that we can watch the entire human race be wiped out live on television – a dark image that will make you cry if you don't laugh instead.

LOSS AND SUFFERING

While the lyrics and themes of the above songs are apt for the frustration and anger section, others have a more forlorn melody, echoing a feeling not of anger, but of grief. A song that perfectly encapsulates this sentiment is 'The Green Fields of France'.[37] In it, the singer visits a First World War graveyard in France and talks to Willie McBride, the soldier buried under the tombstone by which he rests. According to the tombstone's engraving, McBride died in 1916 at the young age of 19. The singer wonders about the circumstances of McBride's life and death: whether he left a lover behind when he went to war or whether he is 'a stranger without even a name'. In the third verse, the singer briefly turns to his present surroundings, and contrasts them to how they appeared during the war. The vibrant description of the sun on green fields and the red poppies dancing in the warm summer breeze paint a stark contrast to the gas, barbed wires and gunfire from years past. The end of the stanza brings up those feelings of frustration at 'man's blind indifference to his fellow man' and 'a whole generation that were butchered and damned'. The mournful feeling returns for the final verse; as in Starr's song, the singer contemplates the pointlessness of war and the deaths of so many people. Were they so naïve that they 'really believe[d] that this war would end wars?' The culmination comes as the singer informs McBride that his death, and the deaths of millions of others – 'the sorrow, the suffering, the glory, the pain' – were 'all done in vain'. Wars continued, and people continued to kill each other by the thousands and the millions. By structuring this song as a conversation with someone killed in war, it allows for a much more personal feeling of grief than the previous songs did. The listener becomes personally invested in the life and death of McBride, faceless and unknown as he may be. The melody further provokes the feelings of a personal loss, as the slow tune forces the listener to engage with each word spoken, and to process the true horror of the scale and suffering that those in war experience.

The final song I wish to highlight that evokes a similar feeling of mournfulness is 'Scarborough Fair/Canticle' by Simon & Garfunkel.[38] This song is a mix of two older ones: a folk song called 'Scarborough Fair' and an original composition by Paul Simon by the name of 'The Side of a Hill'. It contains exquisite harmonies that tell two tales at once: one of a lost love, and one of suffering and

[37] Eric Bogle, 'The Green Fields of France' (Plant Life, 1981).
[38] Simon & Garfunkel, 'Scarborough Fair/Canticle' (Columbia, 1966).

pain from war. It is the backing in the canticle that is particularly poignant, as the airily light tones sing of a collection of metaphors hidden through poetry. The imagery contained within 'Canticle' is hidden and speaks of the impact of war on children: 'Snow-crested ground blankets and bedclothes the child of the mountain', and the child 'sleeps unaware of the clarion call.' They are buried under the ground, unaware that the conflict that ended their life continues to rage above. The only way they have found peace from war is through death. This implication is further evidenced in the next verse, as 'a sprinkling of leaves washes the grave with silvery tears' and 'a soldier cleans and polishes a gun'. The soldier does not care that he stands by the graveside of a young child; the only mourning comes from nature, as if the earth itself is affected by the death of children in war. The war itself is described with vivid imagery – it 'bellows blazing in scarlet battalions'; the sound of gunfire, of planes, of artillery, and the sight of fire and scarlet blood dominate the battlefield, bringing ruin to all war touches. And while '[g]enerals order their soldiers to kill', the soldiers are fighting 'for a cause they've long ago forgotten'. This line is particularly reminiscent of 'The Green Fields of France'. Indeed, the imagery of the child killed in the war is particularly pertinent now, with horrific numbers of innocent children being slaughtered in Gaza. It is a reminder that in war, even the most innocent humans are not safe. War is a scourge upon the Earth.

CONCLUSION

Just as states use emotive language to advocate for war, so too can individuals use language to demonstrate war's horrific effects and advocate for an anti-war stance. Frustration and anger, humour, and loss and suffering are all identifiable themes from anti-war songs. Perhaps we may be able to use some of the lessons from these songs – whether it's to point out the hypocrisy that those who decide to go to war are never threatened, highlight the anger at a military-industrial complex that actively encourages war or depict vivid imagery describing the pain and suffering loss on an individual level.

That is not to say that people are not doing this; rather, perhaps it is something to consider. From my own experience, a single line in a book, such as Rob's at the start of this chapter, can have a profound impact on readers and influence the course of their studies and their career. Writers, even of academic pieces, can stay with a person for years if they are bold enough to make these statements. Rob had that impact on me. I am grateful for his teachings and guidance, brief as it was, and to have been taught by so many of his former students. His impact lives on through them.

16

The Tokyo International Military Tribunal

Another Sequel to a Prequel

MARK A DRUMBL AND SOLANGE MOUTHAAN*

THIS CHAPTER AIMS to recognise the love the authors felt for Rob Cryer. This was a bold love, not cowed, and always respectful and affectionate. We both – together twice, and on one occasion joined by Barbora Holá – went to visit Rob in the midst of the COVID-19 pandemic in the autumn of 2020. We talked law and drank beer while sitting in the backyard of his flat in between his treatments.

This chapter nods in the direction of nudging international criminal law (ICL) writing and imagining out of well-worn venues (law journals), spaces (languid United Nations (UN) and formal international institutions), judgments that are often incomprehensible to the public, bureaucratic ossification and language (technical and echo chamber) that we believe – many decades into this costly ICL 'project' – help explain its entropy and, in what is increasingly a red flag, a disillusionment that folks express towards it. Rob welcomed all of these kinds of nods.

This chapter gives rise to a double imaginary. We imagine a trial that never happened, and then present that trial not in trial proceedings, but, rather, in a conversation between a trial observer inhabiting the empire of law with a listener who inhabits a different world. Hence, there is a double transposition. Separateness, along with melding, arises. This, in a sense, reflects the outreach challenge of international criminal law.

* The authors thank Maria Elander, Rachel Killean, Gerry Simpson, Emma Breeze, Irit Dekel, Carla Apel, Shannon Fyfe, Elena Maculan, Carlyn Kirk and Barbora Holá for wonderful comments and suggestions on early drafts, and recognise the stellar research assistance of Will Vardy. The input of participants in a discussion group at LaTrobe University (Melbourne, Australia) Faculty of Law in May 2024 is heartily acknowledged and deeply valued; so too is feedback from participants at the ICC Scholars Workshop (June 2024, The Hague), notably Colleen Murphy and Jocelyn Getgen. The authors also acknowledge input from participants in the deeply moving Symposium on Rob Cryer at the University of Birmingham Faculty of Law in June 2023.

Just as this chapter was finalised, past connected to present under the *chapeau* of recognition in that Japan's Nihon Hidankyo – a grassroots movement of atomic bomb survivors – won the 2024 Nobel Peace Prize for their efforts to achieve a nuclear-free world.

OVERVIEW

The International Military Tribunal for the Far East (Tokyo IMT) welcomes an additional trial. Proceedings are ongoing against US officials for dropping the atomic bomb on Nagasaki. Tokyo IMT prosecutors claim this is a war crime (indiscriminate, inhumane and excessive). The US defence is that atomic weapons are not illegal and, even if their use were presumptively illegal, then in this instance the defence of necessity (justification) applies[1] – specifically, dropping atomic weapons was necessary to compel a Japanese surrender and thereby save millions of what would otherwise have been lost lives. Americans place considerable reliance on the Battle of Okinawa, the last and among the bloodiest Second World War battles (April–June 1945).

Okinawa is a distant part of the Japanese archipelago. Casualties were staggering, so much so that US President Truman became convinced that atomic weapons had to be dropped on Japan, otherwise the human costs of a land invasion of Japan would result in a million American service member deaths, plus even higher numbers of Japanese military and civilian deaths. Atomic weapons were indeed dropped at the start of August 1945: first at Hiroshima, on 6 August, and then three days later on Nagasaki. A total of 210,000 people, mostly civilians, are estimated to have died from the twin bombings by the end of 1945. Approximately 75,000 deaths occurred at Nagasaki. The USSR, following the Nazi German surrender, broke its non-aggression pact with Japan, declared war and invaded Manchuria. Japanese settlers in the region suffered terribly. The Soviets threatened to invade Japan from the north. The Emperor surrendered on 15 August.

The imagined Tokyo IMT prosecution, led by Joseph Keenan, retorts that any defence of necessity could perhaps have applied to Hiroshima, but certainly not to the dropping of 'Fat Man' on Nagasaki on 9 August.

Mark attends the trial as a law clerk to the Canadian Tokyo IMT judge. Both sides (prosecution and defence) extensively invoke the scholarship and expert testimony of Rob Cryer in their submissions.

Mark discusses the trial with Solange, while Solange shares her views in response to Mark's sharing of the trial and adds her own life experiences. Throughout, Rob's work on selectivity, colonialism, necessity and war crimes undergirds the conversation just as it undergirds the trial.

Tokyo IMT: Another Sequel to a Prequel is critical fabulation that unfurls the ability of political arguments regarding the use of atomic weapons to be

[1] *cf* Campbell, ch 15 in this volume.

translated into law, and also how pointlessly fighting could be a war crime or, as a minimum, a justification for the use of totalising force, and what this means for the beauty of resistance and the power of futility. *Tokyo IMT: Another Sequel to a Prequel* explores the interface between law peoples and lay peoples. The loneliness of law's selectivity is a key thread.

The journey also continues through a dual epilogue in which a descendant comes to wander through Japan in 2023, and again in 2024, on the trail of the trial. These dual epilogues peer through the lens of imagery of war remnants in 2023 and 2024 Japan: Tokyo, Nagasaki, Okinawa – museums and memory, commemoration and colour. Time further flattens the lines between the earthly and the spiritual. Both merge as do divides among generations and between life and death, all while affirming the closeness of friendship and the aesthetics of loss.

TALKING DIFFERENTLY ABOUT ICL'S SILENCES AND OVERSIGHTS

How to situate this work? Perhaps situating does not matter. The project just is. But perhaps situating can serve as a roadmap for the reader. Perhaps it can responsively foretell likely questions. Many of these questions relate to time. For example, Rob did not live in 1945. How can his work be relied upon? The authors, too, were not yet born – far from it. How can they speak? Moreover, Rob's work on law reflects a law whose content did not exist in 1945. So how does this make any sense? How can Rob's work on the law written during his life apply to events well before then? How can fact dangle and fiction entangle in a dialectic?

One tradition in which to ground this project, then, is 'historical fiction', that is, imagining people in places in the past. But historical fiction generally hews tightly to how law, and life, were *at the time*. It values precision. In this case, historical fiction might imagine a trial of Americans that never happened, but apply to it the law of the time, along with the politics. This is not what this project does. This project applies the politics of the time, and the facts of the time, yet applies law, and one individual's characterful perspectives on the law, that came 70 years later. And then this project pivots into the present, 80 years later, which becomes the future in a story about the past rather than the present. Moreover, dotted throughout are photographs taken in the present that share remnants of the past, and commemorations of before-times, and that are included in the present. The temporalities are too jumbled so as to square with even the pretext of historical fiction.

What, then? We are drawn to Maria Elander's suggestion to look through the lens of 'critical fabulation', as coined by cultural historian Saudyia Hartman in 'Venus in Two Acts'.[2] What is meant by 'critical fabulation'? Hartman notes

[2] S Hartman, 'Venus in Two Acts' (2008) 12(2) *Small Axe* 1, https://warwick.ac.uk/fac/arts/history/research/centres/blackstudies/venus_in_two_acts.pdf. Hartman engaged in this practice in both of her previously published full-length books, *Scenes of Subjection* and *Lose Your Mother*.

that historical records and archives are filled with many gaps and omissions and elisions, specifically in the case of her work as it concerns the lives of enslaved peoples. In light of the pervasiveness of these omissions, Hartman uses storytelling to imagine what *was* through what was never recorded or recognised as recordable. Hartman enlivens time and space, toggles and juxtaposes; she mixes media and form.[3] She does so to document how knowledge is registered through absences and silences, which obliterate lives, and therefore challenge the composition and dependability of what it is that 'we' actually 'know'. 'Critical fabulation' signifies a writing methodology that combines historical and archival research with theory and fictional narrative. Hartman turns to critical fabulation in her scholarship to excavate, and then fill, gaps and silences in the archive of transatlantic slavery that absent the voices of enslaved women. Favouring elasticity over linearity, Hartman turns to fabulation to provide voice. Fabulation is not confabulation; rather, it is a way to pursue redress through the imaginary. In this context, the linearity of time and precedent dissolves. Experience becomes rescued from the strictures of colonialism and conquest, the violence of what was actually judged, how it was judged, by a Tokyo IMT that is a product of its time and itself trapped by history. In a sense, critical fabulation aims to liberate 'us' from our 'own' histories that subjugate how 'we' imagine epistemology.

The shattering of the linearity of time, and the idea of precedent as 'good', is further assailed by indigenous approaches to law in Canada and Australia that posit that time and history are authorially problematic. Hence, to argue that precedent of any sort, in any case, is somehow desirable is deeply gerontocratic and controlling. Another methodological angle that could be tapped further involves the relationship between 'critical fabulation' and the most conservative and traditional tools of legal pedagogy; for example, the 'hypothetical' and the argument by analogy – the spin-offication of *Palsgraf* and *Hadley*, common law chestnuts – all of which dabble in how law might apply to imaginaries. While not self-identifying as 'critical fabulation', there is lengthy history even in legal scholarship – for example, in the US – of fabulously innovative and anti-chrononormative writing. We are thinking in this space of the work of American critical race theorists such as Derrick Bell, Richard Delgado and Kimberlé Crenshaw; as well as Canadian feminist author Ruth Buchanan.

We build upon critical fabulation to work within a trial that did not happen and a Rob Cryer who was not yet born. Our storytelling mixes different timelines rather than focusing only on filling gaps and silences.

What should also be noted in all this is that, despite any now faltering upturn in interest in international criminal law beginning in the 1990s, the fact remains that the vast majority of 'accountabilities' that had been undertaken following the Second World War, including in the Pacific, remain under-discussed. So many proceedings, notably those not conducted in English (which has emerged

[3] See, eg, www.moma.org/audio/playlist/298/4088.

as the *lingua franca* of international criminal law (ICL)) or through liberal legalist modalities, fall outside of the transnational gaze. Tellingly, this was a project with which Rob himself had already become engaged a decade before his passing.[4] Rob was keen to give voice to, and unearth, trials outside the liberal Anglosphere so as to diversify and enrich the epistemology of ICL. His goal was to put the marginalised and unrealised *international* back into international law. The need to excavate these overlooked stories gives further value to devices such as critical fabulation that accept that so much of what 'happened' has been ignored, that the 'official' is deeply distorted, and that the entire process of contemporaneous corroboration is woefully political.

SETTING: A BAR IN ICHIGAYA, TOKYO

Time period: 1947, during a fictional Tokyo IMT trial of US General Leslie Groves for developing and dropping the atomic bomb on Nagasaki

A bartender gently goes about her business of cleaning glasses and meticulously restocking shelves and fridges. It is quiet. The bar is empty. The bartender's name is Solange. She is not Japanese. It is difficult to situate where she might be from: the Philippines, Indonesia or maybe the Dutch East Indies?

Mark walks in. Briskly. It's early. He is the first. He's new. He sits at the bar. He clutches a thin book.

'Three days isn't a lot of time, is it?'

Solange half shakes her head, pours Mark a beer and replies: 'You need to give me more than that. It depends, no? Three days can feel like forever. Depends on what you're doing. Or what is being done to you.'

'Well, in this case, you're giving up. Surrendering. I think it might take more than three days to surrender. Especially when you don't want to and have to get word out. And you can't fully figure out what really happened in the first place. Or absorb it.'

'Not sure. You can surrender on the spot and just say so.'

'Well, that's not what the prosecutors are saying.'

'Yeah, I heard … You work at the tribunal?' Solange is prepared to be bored, and avoidant, yet again, the tribunal is just next door, the pitter-patter of all these lawyers pours like concrete shitter-shatter.

'Sort of', Mark replies. 'I help a judge. The Canadian one. Kinda like a student assistant.'

[4] Thank you to Marianne Wade for informing us of this attempt on Rob's part.

Solange looks nonplussed. But the bar is empty, as is her gaze, and all the glasses are clean, so she's stuck, and so she adds, in monotone: 'I heard that they say the Americans should have waited longer after Hiroshima before dropping an even more powerful bomb on Nagasaki and killing all those civilians in a second go-around. Communication out of Hiroshima was totally cut off. But I don't understand why that even matters, I mean Hiroshima, Nagasaki, so much death … ?'

'Prosecutors seem to think Hiroshima was OK but Nagasaki was too soon and not necessary', Mark adds. 'And Nagasaki anyway was just an ill-fated second choice because of a break in the clouds. The Americans went for Kokura first. Cloud cover was dense. Visual sighting wasn't possible. The B-29 plane circled three times, to no avail, and then went to Nagasaki instead. Here, too, it was cloudy, so the pilots decide to leave, they're running out of fuel, and then suddenly the clouds break, the bombardier glimpses the arms factory through a crack in the cloud cover, so they drop the bomb, which explodes at 11:02 am.'

Solange is thinking 'Oh, here, yet another know-it-all who gets-nothing-whatsoever', and then she looks at Mark: 'So Hiroshima was OK? Seriously? We now live in a world in which we accept the use of atomic bombs? C'mon, that's messed up.'

'Well, they didn't actually say that Hiroshima was OK, after all, they made the point that dropping a weapon of mass destruction was a war crime. They talked a lot about this British professor, Robert Cryer, and his understanding of war crimes. Cryer testified. He said that military tactics and weapons that are indiscriminate, inhumane and disproportionate to any military advantage are war crimes. But they aren't charging anyone with Hiroshima. Instead, the prosecutors argue that, whatever was the case for Hiroshima, this was all the more so in Nagasaki since the Americans never gave the Japanese enough time to surrender. And that's the accusation.'

'The Japanese did surrender a few days after Nagasaki so perhaps the Americans were right?'

'You believe that?', Mark asks.

Solange laughs. 'Not really. But trials are all about making stuff up and faking it, no? For whose benefit is this trial anyway? It's not for mine so it doesn't matter if I believe in it or not. But I suspect you take this seriously?'

'Seriously enough, I suppose.'

Solange adds: 'Well the Soviets declaring war on Japan and invading from the North surely also had an effect. And, you know, I wonder whether the dropping of the bombs was intended by the Americans also to flex American military might to the Russians. This is the next fight, in case you haven't noticed.'

'Sure, yeah, but the trial doesn't care about all that. It only cares about the fact that, had the Americans waited longer than three days, maybe there would have been a Japanese surrender. This is the prosecution's main argument at trial. And the fake it 'til you make it of a trial is only about whatever is charged. It's a stage.'

'The trial seems like it's your world. That's a pretty small world.'

'I guess, maybe, but it brought me here, now, into your world, your big bar-world.'

Solange chortles and switches gears: 'There is something so cruel in the atomic bomb. It's a fast death for some, and a slow wretched death by poison for others, death can last for years, it's like being on death row.' She looks at her feet, and goes on: 'In Nagasaki nearly everyone within a kilometre radius from the bomb drop died, and more people will keep on dying just from exposure, and people four kilometres away got exposure burns.' She pauses, and the void of her gaze returns.

There's a lull.

Solange keeps the conversation going: 'What do the Americans say in return?'

'Well, they first say that the Tokyo Tribunal should follow what was said in a case in Germany called the *Einsatzgruppen* trial. These were about the mobile killing squads who exterminated so many Jews in Eastern Europe. In that case, and in another called the *Hostages* case, the defence lawyers argued that the Germans could not be prosecuted for these crimes because the Americans had committed a war crime in dropping the atomic bombs on Japan. They raised a defence called *tu quoque* – this means 'you too'. So if you did something terrible, you can't accuse me; if you didn't get punished for such bad behaviour, well, nor can I. However, the judges in Germany rejected this outright. First they said you can't raise a wrongdoing as a defence for another wrongdoing. But then they went out of their way to say that the dropping of the atomic bombs was just not illegal. Indeed, they said that atomic bombs were not any special kind of weapon. They were aerial bombs made and used for military targets and to prompt a surrender. They were what was called "morale bombing". Professor Cryer testified at length about all this today. But he also said that that the Tokyo Tribunal was different, that what the judges in Germany said was *obiter dicta*, which means just an opinion not a decision, and that no American was charged anyway in that case so they had no facts in front of them.'

Mark stops. Solange looks at him blankly. Mark goes on: 'I really liked this Cryer guy. He was funny and smart. And he had such beautiful eyes. Blue eyes can be so icy sometimes, but his shone like stars when he spoke. And he was moving his hands a lot. So much so that his shirt became untucked. He didn't even notice. You should come to the court tomorrow. He is speaking again. He's a real character. I heard he moonlights as a guitarist. You could invite him here to play.'

Solange thinks: 'Well, this is a first … none of these droning lawyers ever said something like this while sitting at the bar.' But she lets that thread drop, along with this stuff about glittering eyes and strumming guitars, and responds: 'OK, but from what you say it does seem these Allied judges in Germany were nervous about the possibility that such charges could be brought. And "morale bombing" just sounds like gaslighting to me. So insensitive to the victims of the atomic bombs.'

'I dunno. Part of it makes sense to me. But anyway, the Americans say that this is totally unlike the Holocaust of Jewish civilians, which had nothing to do with any war effort. Here, at Nagasaki, the story is that the Americans had to drop the bomb twice because the other alternative, a land invasion, would have cost millions of lives. So in a sense by dropping the bomb they hurt fewer people. They call it the defence of necessity, other times they call it the defence of justification, in other words, bringing into play the lesser of two evils. Cryer spoke about this too. He says these defences exist under international criminal law. The Americans also added that their intelligence reported that, after Hiroshima, the Japanese leadership denied that anything had happened, and the only way to impress upon Tokyo to surrender was to create the belief that the Americans had enough bombs to annihilate all of Japan. Which they didn't. They just had one more, which ended up at Nagasaki. But now that they knew how, certainly, I guess they could have built more in upcoming months.'

'Come on, that's crazy', Solange exclaims. 'They were just worried about saving American lives. And they also wanted revenge. Else in a show of strength they could have dropped the second bomb over the ocean and let the Japanese know that. It has been revenge for a long time. Sooooo much of Tokyo was totally obliterated in the firebombing. Look around! In some areas all that is left is a stray building or two. More people died on one night in Tokyo in March 1945 in firebombing than in Nagasaki. Prosecutors glommed onto this atomic bomb, maybe because it was so exceptional, and just ignored the so-called ordinary stuff that killed so many more people. I mean, the atomic bomb is terrible, but there's a lot more going on that what you lawyers see.'

Mark jumps in: 'In my world, lawyers for the American defendants also say over and again that millions of Japanese lives would have been lost in a land invasion. They mentioned several times their experiences in Okinawa in 1945. The Americans invaded the island in something called Operation Iceberg.'

Solange now looks intent: 'Yes, that is closer to my neck of the ocean. The Japanese really resisted there, down to the last soldier, ordinary people in the streets with mops and brooms and pipes. Two thousand child soldiers – high school boys under 18, called the Blood and Iron Student Corps – were recruited by Japanese authorities. Half of them died. Surrender was not much of an option, really, the fighting went on to the bitter end. Commanders told the Okinawans they would be raped and tortured if captured by the Americans. There were so many mass suicides. Other civilians were murdered because they were accused of being spies or of having stolen food.'

'Yes, the Americans brought into evidence all of these details. Fighting started in earnest in early April 1945. At first there was no resistance, but this is because the Japanese strategy was to lure the Americans inland and then wage a war of attrition from defensive positions embedded in the mountains. The US 10th

Figure 4 Captured Japanese child soldiers, Okinawa, Motobu Regional Museum, August 2024, photo taken by one of the authors

Army suffered extensive kamikaze attacks. Fighting officially ended on 22 June 1945. This was a bloody battle – 12,000 Americans were killed, and many tens of thousands more were injured; 110,000 Japanese combatants died and deaths among Okinawan civilians, many of whom slipped into combat roles, including as you say children, was as high as 150,000. That's staggering. On the topic of child soldiers, in March 1945 the Japanese authorities, in desperation, adopted a national policy permitting boys aged 15 and girls aged 17 to serve as a home defence force. They were armed with the most pitiful weapons, sticks and stuff like that. But since Japan was never invaded – because of the surrender triggered by the atomic bombs – the Americans say they protected the rights of the child, the rights of Japanese children, as abused by their own Japanese government. Seeing how fiercely the 2,000 boys on Okinawa fought was among the factors that led the US, so they say, to scrap the general land invasion. The Americans brought some photos into evidence. The boys were so young, scrawny and small.'

Figure 5 Another captured Japanese child soldier, Okinawa, Motobu Regional Museum, August 2024

'You have so many words. I have three, once again: so much death.'

'The Americans say that resistance was so fierce on Okinawa – a distant part of the Japanese archipelago – that it would be even more so if Honshu had to be invaded. So Truman authorised the bomb drop.'

'Actually', Solange chimes in, 'I am not so sure. On Okinawa a lot of the resisters were indigenous Japanese who were forced by the Japanese government to resist. The Japanese government ordered them to kill themselves rather than surrender to the Americans. Abuses have been going on there for a very long time. The imperial Japanese felt themselves ethnically superior to the native Okinawans. They did not see Okinawans as Japanese. Okinawa was annexed into Japan in 1879. This was one of the first steps of imperial Japanese expansion, a precursor to the Second World War. Okinawa previously had its own indigenous governance, royalty and palaces for many centuries. Okinawa was its own kingdom, united in the fifteenth century from three earlier kingdoms. The imperial Japanese felt the Ryukuyans – indigenous Okinawans – were expendable. Did the Americans bring any of this into evidence? I guess not. It fits a lot of storylines but likely not the one that says the dropping of "Fat Man" was truly necessary because of what happened at Okinawa.'

Mark pauses, listens and drinks. Solange picks up the thread again: 'Let's get back to this idea of resistance. Let's put the abuse of the indigenous Okinawans to the side for now. Do you think there can be such a thing as resisting too much? I mean, do you think that there should be a duty to surrender.'

'This is really interesting. It didn't come up straight on in the trial, but kind of roundabout. The defence lawyers said that fighting on hopelessly and needlessly down to the last person in a situation of inevitable defeat itself should be seen as criminal. And they say this is what Japan was doing. I find this an intriguing idea, because it suggests that it can be unethical to resist, in a sense, that fighting to the last person is to be condemned. Instead you should give up and just stop. The defence invoked – in reverse fashion – Cryer's work on disproportionate attacks as a war crime to argue that deliberately inflicting harm on one's own people in resisting, when such harm was utterly disproportionate to securing any tangible military advantage since defeat was inevitable, is no different and should be a war crime too.'

'Yeah, all that is fine. But isn't it weird to blame the Japanese for the fact that two atomic bombs were dropped on Japan? For me, though, more important is that I also wish that there would be other trials. Against the Japanese and the Americans. For what the Okinawans went through from their side and from the other side. The indigenous Okinawans were abandoned by all sides. And the other day I heard chatter about the fact that Japanese conducted medical experiments in Manchuria that were like the kind of experiments that the Nazi Mengele conducted. Some Dutch guys were in here talking about that and never thought I would be able to understand. They always look right through me. But I speak Dutch. Fluently in fact. And what about all the sexual violence, the sex slaves and forced prostitutes? I think it is awful that no lawyers or judges or officials are even speaking about this. At all. People really suffered.'

Mark is listening intently.

'You want another pint?'

Mark nods.

Solange looks at him, he seems to be listening, all the time, to her, as she speaks more and more. He strangely listens even while he talks, and she listens while she does not talk, so she talks, flatly, because she is weary of listening, and he seems a mediocre talker but an interesting listener, so she ploughs ahead.

'Let me tell you something. I am here in Tokyo, and I don't even know why I ended up here of all places, but my home and family are no longer familiar. This war, like for so many, cost me dearly. I am 'Eurasian', from Java – and a survivor of *jugun ianfu*. In your law words, that is military sexual slavery. I was taken by the Japanese military from my home in Ungaran in central Java at the same time as my father was taken to be interned in a camp. I don't know if he has returned or ever will. At the time, I was 17 years old.'

'You say law words, label them my law words, and yes I know what military sexual slavery is, but this is the first time that I have heard of this happening. There's no mention of it in the trial', Mark bounces in.

'Your trial isn't my life … Well, at least you're honest about your ignorance.'

'Why lie to you?'

After all the discussions Solange has overheard by law people, parachuted in for the trial, arrogant dumbfucks most of them, she wants to be able to say her piece. As if she forgot where she was. As if she forgot her learned bartender role to listen and gild the conversation on, not pick fights or reveal too much. Yet this is the closest she has ever actually wanted to get to the judicial space, for some reason. So she rolls the ball forward, once again.

'Isn't it odd how life works out: that I come to work in a bar which is next to where a bunch of law people discuss crimes committed by the Japanese and Americans in this awful bloody war? Instead of providing solace, I feel disconnected. I can't be alone feeling like this. Those who felt the war's impact most acutely were the people from this region. There are people who were hurt by both sides to this war. They have no side, They are in a bottomless well. Yet the trial has sidelined us and instead what is on trial is Japan's territorial expansion in stark opposition to the wishes of European colonial powers. And now the atomic bomb. But lots more happened.'

Mark nods, says nothing, lights up a cigarette and looks at Solange.

Solange puts her elbows on the bar, faces Mark and gets nearer to him: 'The more I hear law people discuss what is happening inside that building, the closer I get to people like you, the further the building moves away from me, because nothing in that building relates to me and my experience as a woman who was … as a person who grew up in this part of the world. I hear Tribunal talk about civilisation and humanity demanding that this trial be held, yet … the harms I have suffered are not important enough to be acknowledged, as if they remain nothing more than an afterthought: I and the other women, we are "just women" and in many cases also "just colonials". We don't display the characteristics of perfect victims. For sure we are not allied white people. I had no say, yet somehow my brutal experience stained me (or at least so I am told) and most certainly brought shame to my family who cannot forgive me and prefer me not to return for fear of the neighbours finding out. And here on the fringes of judicial activity, slopping you all up drinks, I still have no say.'

Mark replies: 'Yeah, you're right; there's no interest here in prosecuting sexual crimes. They are recognised in international law, somewhat at least. I read about them in Cryer's book. But the prosecutors won't bother investigating them. And I think the Japanese and the Europeans share this dismissiveness. To look into Japanese sexual crimes would mean looking into European colonial sexual crimes. There's a Dutch judge on the Tokyo IMT.[5] He's kind of pro-defence, actually, the Anglo judges tend to avoid him, and he has some musician girlfriend here, so he seems somewhat different. But there's no way even he would have any stomach for looking into Dutch imperialism and colonialism in Java.[6] No way. There is an Indian judge on the Tokyo IMT, Judge Pal, he seems game to have a far broader conversation. But beyond him, there's no appetite for this. After all, it is time to punish the Japanese for the same violent colonialism that the West did for centuries previous. Prosecuting Nagasaki just slipped in there somehow. I think that's the most anyone, even the Indian judge, could hope for.'

There's a long silence. Words are digested. It is a productive silence, not a dreary one. Solange turns away. She feels strange. Good strange. That felt good.

The place has filled up, quickly – it's going to be a busy evening. Solange tends to other customers who have arrived. Mark remains, smoking, sitting and reading.

[5] *cf* Vasiliev, ch 19 in this volume.

[6] See Vasiliev, ch 19 in this volume for a somewhat more nuanced view on the Dutch judge Bert Röling on the subject of critically engaging with the theme of Dutch colonialism. Looking beyond Röling, see also Boister, ch 9 in this volume, who notes that 'the Dutch prosecutor … ring-fenc[ed] Dutch imperialism in Indonesia'.

Eventually Solange passes by. Mark opens the book in his hands and points at a page and says: 'Isn't this is beautiful line: *Ah! Comme la neige a neigé!*, in English, "O how the snow has snowed!", it's by Émile Nelligan, from Québec, where I am from, it is from 1898, he was so young when he wrote it, and right after he was locked up in an asylum, forgotten, in loneliness, for 43 years until his death, and there is just so much snow where I am from, constant snowing.'

'I've never seen snow,' responds Solange, 'or heard snowing.'

'I know. And snowing is very quiet. You really have to hold your breath and listen. Patiently. Come tomorrow with me to the Tribunal? I know you feel law is ugly, and dead, and it probably is, but have you really seen law or heard lawing? Maybe start with seeing and hearing this Cryer guy? He's simply so alive, I think he will make you smile. I'm serious. I'll wait for you at the visitor's entrance there at 10. No worries if not, totally fine, I have to be there anyway. Maybe another day you can tell me more about your father, what you miss the most about him. I'd love to learn.'

The bar is noisy, crowded, stinky. Patrons, thirsty and demanding, are gesturing towards Solange. Mark slides off his seat and slips out the door.

NEARLY 80 YEARS LATER

6 August 2023
From: mt3@specialdimension.org
To: secretalphabet@aol.com

Hi PB, So I made it. Well, not to Okinawa. There was a typhoon. So I couldn't go. I ended up in Nagasaki as a second choice. Just like it was on that fateful day in 1945.

Nagasaki used to be one of Japan's gateways to the world. A huge port. I learned about that, in Tokyo, at the Sumida Hokusai museum. He's the famous Japanese artist from the late 1700s. He did the waves and expressive faces and Mt Fuji. Totoya Hokkei was one of Hokusai's students. Hokkei was enamoured with Nagasaki's harbour, thronged with Dutch and Portuguese ships, on their colonial missions, starting in the sixteenth century, from Indonesia and Goa, bubbles of smoke and steam, and the overseeing mountain, Inasa. I really love the style of these artists. It is called *ukiyo-e*. That means pictures of the daily life of ordinary people. *Ukiyo-e* artists made woodcut prints as well as brush-drawn paintings.

One of Hokusai's finest works is 'Watching Fireworks'. I saw it in Tokyo. I was thinking about it here in Nagasaki in the Peace Museum. How fireworks just turned to fury. And the daily life. The ships, the harbour, the port – hey, that's also why Nagasaki made the bombing short list. It has always been a centre for shipbuilding, including for warships during the Second World War. It was General Leslie Groves who added Nagasaki to the list of four places, joining Hiroshima, Kokura and Niigata.

Figure 6 Totoya Hokkei, Mount Inasa

Figure 7 Sumida Hokusai, 'Watching Fireworks', August 2023, Yamatame Museum of Art, Tokyo, photo taken by one of the authors

Anyway, here I am sitting at Nagasaki's old stone bridges. They survived. The river is small. The Peace Garden is huge. Folks were ringing the Peace Bell, as they do on certain days at 11:02 am. The group that gathered today is called the Nagasaki Bell for Peace Association. They gave me one of their pamphlets. A bombing veteran was out in the heat that morning as part of the ceremony. It was really hot and humid. So he got heatstroke. He was 92. A veteran not of fighting but of the bombing. Anyway, he was tilted out by these activists to make a point. But then he totally wilted and fainted in his chair.

I wonder if my great-uncle, who worked for the Tokyo Tribunal, had ever come to Nagasaki? Back then, it would have been mostly obliterated. I know they went to Okinawa, when the prosecutors and the defence lawyers went to interview folks as part of the American failure to surrender claim.

Nagasaki is all about peace. Peace here, peace there, peace everywhere. There is a huge Peace Statute in the Peace Park of this super-jacked-up gym bro. A plaque next to it pompously says it represents divine omnipotence embodied

Figure 8 Nagasaki, August 2023, photograph taken by one of the authors

in a sturdy physique, with a folded right leg symbolising quiet meditation and a left leg poised in action to assist humanity. 'Peace begins in Nagasaki' is the city's slogan. But who knows what peace actually means? Or if people actually are at peace with themselves even?

The Atomic Bomb Museum is pretty sobering. It's near the hypocentre, where the bomb fell, which is just next to the Peace Park. As for the Museum: there is so much about the explosion, the desperate thirst, the searing pain from all these awful fireworks and then the languid radiation sickness. I attach a pic, it kind of says it all.

I found a book by Rob Cryer along the trail at the Peace Museum in the library. It's called *Selectivity in International Criminal Law*. After all, I remember my great-uncle telling me that it was Cryer's testimony that really grounded that judgment in which the court found both sides at fault, found that bombing Nagasaki was a war crime, and that the failure to surrender could be a war crime though no Japanese official was actually accused of that. Groves was convicted as being a 'principal leader' with 'primary responsibility for acts committed' as part of a 'common plan or conspiracy' to drop the atomic bomb on Nagasaki, this being a war crime. Groves was the only person convicted. He only spent two years in prison for it, but many of the Japanese also spent little time in prison, though two years is pretty short still.

I was thinking a lot about Cryer's idea that international criminal trials have a selectivity problem,[7] by which he means that it is generally only the losers who are prosecuted while the powerful go scot-free. There were so many more trials of Japanese at the Tokyo IMT than of Americans. Can you imagine had there been no trials of the Americans at all??? That would have really been wretched. But Cryer's idea of selectivity is bigger than *who* is prosecuted. It is also *what* is prosecuted. So many crimes, including all the forced prostitution and gender-based violence, well, none of them were prosecuted at all against anyone. There wasn't even a charge that involved all those abuses in Manchuria, Indonesia, Korea. I see that as a different kind of selectivity, no? As Cryer pointed out in *Selectivity in International Criminal Law*, states are much more willing to create 'safe' international tribunals whose rules apply only to others than 'unsafe' ones whose rules also apply to them. The bottom line is that there were bigger losers at the Tokyo IMT than the Japanese. Those were the people that both warring sides hurt and then that neither side bothered to defend or support. So, as Cryer wrote in his textbook, which I read, if criminal procedures and punishment are designed to make the offender 'understand what was wrong with what they have done, whilst also reaffirming the [violated] norm in the community and educating society

[7] *cf* van Sliedregt, ch 10 in this volume. For specific discussion of contradictions at the Tokyo IMT, see also Y Tanaka, 'The Atomic Bombing and the Shimoda Case: Lessons for Anti-nuclear Legal Movements' in Y Tanaka et al (eds), *Beyond Victor's Justice* (Martinus Nijhoff, 2011).

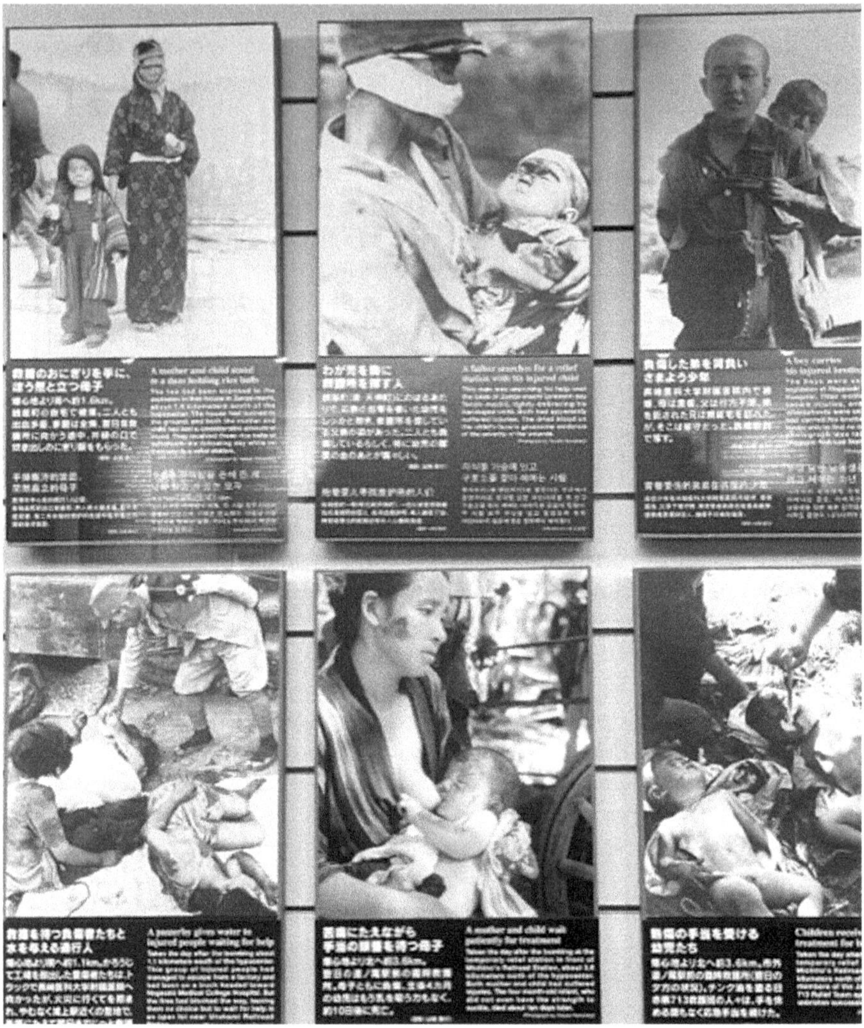

Figure 9 Atomic Bomb Museum, Nagasaki, August 2023, photo taken by one of the authors

about the unacceptable nature of the conduct condemned',[8] well, then, the Tokyo IMT hurt a lot of already pained folks by making them invisible.

Well, enough about law and loss and life. CG says hi. CG says some things are timeless. Like a magic kiss. Like friendship. And concrete and stone. They revolve around each other, unconditionally, just because and whatever is, through

[8] R Cryer, H Friman, D Robinson and E Wilmshurst, *An Introduction to International Criminal Law and Procedure* (Cambridge University Press, 2007) 23.

time, they endure even with cracks, sometimes, it depends, but sometimes, just like the bridges over Nagasaki's little trickle of a river, they continue to dazzle rather than drizzle, they take new forms, they burst like a garden rather than linger like languor. But other kisses aren't so magical. You ever listen to that techno British band OMD? They're from the early 1980s. They have a zippy anti-war dance song, about Hiroshima, and the Enola Gay, the bomb-dropping plane there, named after its pilot's mom: 'Ah-ha, Enola Gay / This kiss you give / It's never ever gonna fade away'.

But some things that don't fade away begin to glow and grow wonderfully. Like those photos of Cryer in that narrow crammed Tokyo bar, helping cook *sate*, playing the guitar, eating all that scrumptious Indonesian food, those photos are priceless, along with the letters he wrote to Solange at the bar for many years after, the requests he filed in Japanese court to investigate sexual crimes against women committed by the Japanese army, and his testimony in other national proceedings in other national courts for crimes that were overlooked at the Tokyo IMT, and the music scores he posted, how those experiences prompted him to write a book with some New Zealander that 're-appraised' the Tokyo IMT,[9] to get word out about what was done well and badly and what was crummily overlooked, and Cryer blasted the US for hiding the Japanese medical torture experiments evidence from the Tribunal because the US wanted to retain the data: he insisted that biological and medical experiments are war crimes[10] … well, all this is really beautiful, it amounts to some gorgeousness in those gaunt times. Sorry for the palavering! But as you can tell, I am so glad that all these documents are in the archives, here: these archives are so alive.

Je t'embrasse

ALMOST EXACTLY ONE YEAR LATER THAN NEARLY 80 YEARS LATER

4 August 2024
From: mt3@specialdimension.org
To: secretalphabet@aol.com

Hi there PB. No typhoon this year, so I made it to Okinawa. I landed yesterday in the capital, Naha. I've been driving on narrow roads through woods and staring at beaches. The Tokyo IMT prosecutors had come here to investigate the failure to resist for that 1947 trial. I'm staying in a cottage near Motobu, a town in the northern part of the island. The cabin is so joyfully isolated. Last night a bat came to visit me, perched in the tree off the balcony, stretching out one wing at a time, unfurling like a flag in the wind.

[9] *cf* Boister, ch 9 in this volume.
[10] Cryer et al (n 8) 243.

I've been reading this book by Benjamin Labatut a friend recommended. It is called *When We Cease to Understand the World*. Labatut talks a lot about scientists and their world. So, get this, there is a German, Heisenberg, who was a total genius in quantum mechanics. He won the Nobel Prize in 1932. In 1939 the Nazis ordered him to see whether it was feasible to develop a nuclear bomb. He investigated and two years later said that such a weapon lay beyond the capacities of Germany or of its enemies. Heisenberg decided that it was a no go.[11] When he later heard the Americans dropped such a bomb on Hiroshima he was totally dumbfounded. So, you know, that *Oppenheimer* film was a bit on to something when it emphasised the ingenuity, intrepidness and secrecy of this entire operation, this idea of nuclear fission exploding while imploding on a core of plutonium.

Oppenheimer as a film has a totally ignored sibling. It's from 2023. It's called *Richland*. This film looks at a town (called Richland) in the US built only for folks who supplied the plutonium for the two dropped atomic bombs (and thereafter too, for nuclear power). Get this: the Richland high school's symbol is a mushroom cloud and the school's nickname is 'The Bombers'. I had no idea. So weird. The film's not very good. I saw it in Tokyo, in a tiny film house, but the storyline is gripping and almost surreal.

The amount of money spent on the Manhattan Project was more than the sum total of the Japanese economy at the time. Japan's physical infrastructure was puny. Get this: near the end of the war, in 1944, the Japanese built hangars out of concrete at the airfield in Chofu, outside of Tokyo; they built 30 of them to shelter their rapidly dwindling numbers of airplanes from the bombings. Thirty planes! They built clay shelters for 30 more. It is so desperate. Parrying the inevitable. Shadowboxing the end. In 1944 the Americans could probably factory-build 60 new airplanes in a week. Junior high school students and gardening groups helped build the hangars by hand. Two hangars remain, now, in a park that buzzes with cicadas. I went to see them with K who sat in the shade close to dragonflies. It was so hot and sunny. The old adjacent airfield is used for private planes though it has weeds on the runway cracks. I attach a pic.

I've been thinking a lot about the role of scientists in the atomic bomb. The scientists were so keen to make the bomb, to feel important and validated and relevant, and then so many regretted it afterwards when the enormity of what they did to people finally hit them. Even Oppenheimer. Then they suddenly all became pacifists. They say they were just used by the politicians and military. Well, in the end Groves was convicted. He did supervise the whole Manhattan Project. He was military. Yet he died a free man in 1970. But I wonder if the scientists also should have been held accountable. Weren't they, too, part of this 'common plan'?

[11] B Labatut, *When We Cease to Understand the World* (New York Review Books, 2021) 170.

Figure 10 Bunker, Chofu, Tokyo, August 2024, photo taken by one of the authors

Figure 11 Atomic Bomb Museum, Nagasaki, August 2023, photograph taken by one of the authors

Anyway, back to now. Okinawa I mean. And another now: Okinawa's become super-touristy. Jammed and crammed, certainly outside of the interior mountains and the north. Beaches, muchly, nightlife. Okinawa is webbed with sinuous roads and bisected by one expressway. But the war footprints of 1945 – of what has been called the 'Typhoon of Steel' – are all around the island, discreetly, including in the woods a couple of minutes from where I stayed.

The residues of the war are so quiet, but remain very present. These are cenotaphs marked with names (like in the photo), memorials also marked with names, graves, and exhibits. The local museum in Motobu has a room on the war. There are other more high-profile sites, peace places and museums spaces, and Imperial Navy tunnels whose walls are scarred by suicide grenades, but I was happy to see sites where there was no one else visiting.

I also went to visit an ancient Ryukyuan castle, now in ruins. It's from before the 1400s when the Ryukyuan kingdom hadn't yet been consolidated but was still divided into three. This is way before Japan colonised Okinawa. The castle

Figure 12 Cenotaph, Okinawa Island, August 2024, photo taken by one of the authors

ruins sit in a prominent place in a town called Nakijin. The remaining walls trace lines to the mountains and then gesture towards the sea. One rock is engraved with a beautiful poem written five hundred years ago to a woman who through its words still lives today. There's a translated version in the local museum:

> Orange Fruit Out Of Season
>
> In The Castle Of Nakijin
>
> Pretty Shigema Utudaru Wears And Takes Off A Lei
>
> Again And Again
>
> Made From Passing Ivy Through Oranges

Isn't that last line something? So, you, be well, and try to pass at least one ivy through an orange before the summer ends!

Oh, something else. Something from Nagoya. From a shrine. Something weathered that reminds me of friendship, time, aging, and of a pair getting older while remaining colourful.

Figure 13 Shrine, Nagoya, August 2024, photo taken by one of the authors

Act V

Friendship and Kindness

17

A Fine Art of Friendship Revisited

EMMA J BREEZE AND DAVID TURNS

INTRODUCTION

ALTHOUGH INTERNATIONAL HUMANITARIAN law (IHL) was not the main focus of much of Rob Cryer's published research through most of his career, it is, in a sense, where he began; it also underpinned much of his subsequent specialisation in international criminal law, through the prism of criminal liabilities resulting from violations of IHL. This chapter reflects on selected aspects of IHL in a way that mirrors to some extent the consideration given by Rob to the armed conflict in Afghanistan in the very early stages of the 'Global War on Terror'.[1] In that piece, whilst using friendship as a core thread, Rob adopted a thematic approach to IHL, considering in turn the nature and legal classification of the armed conflict in Afghanistan, the conduct of the American-led Coalition's air campaign (including the selection of targets and the use of various types of weaponry) and the conduct of the ground campaign (including the practice of denial of quarter, the treatment of persons hors de combat and the status and treatment of prisoners and detainees). His piece in the *Journal of Conflict and Security Law* was quite long, at 47 pages, and his treatment of the issues was correspondingly extensive. This chapter is considerably shorter, with the result that a necessarily more selective approach has been adopted.

Whilst our concluding remarks will reflect on aspects of the conflict in Afghanistan, specifically considering the end of that conflict with the fall of Kabul to the Taliban in August 2021, we have chosen to focus on the currently ongoing phase of the Russo-Ukrainian War that commenced with the Russian offensive (termed a 'special military operation' by the Kremlin)[2] in February 2022. We consider some of the ways in which warfare and IHL have evolved in the 22 years

[1] R Cryer, 'The Fine Art of Friendship: *Jus in Bello* in Afghanistan' (2002) 7 *Journal of Conflict and Security Law* 37.

[2] The obscurantist descriptor applied by a party to an actual armed conflict, purporting to obfuscate the armed conflict paradigm and obviate the application of a particular body of international law, cannot affect the legal classification of the situation as one of armed conflict. Russia has been in a state of international armed conflict with Ukraine ever since the belligerent occupation of Crimea commenced in February 2014: see Organization for Security and Co-operation in Europe, 'The Legal Framework Applicable to the Armed Conflict in Ukraine', www.osce.org/files

since Rob published his piece about Afghanistan, and some of the ways in which IHL has been (and is being) applied in Ukraine, and include reflections on the nature and classification of armed conflict, the conduct of hostilities in targeting operations, and the protection of victims and status of participants in the armed conflict. In doing so, we pay tribute to Rob's scholarship in this area of international law, whilst also considering what has changed – and what has stayed the same – in IHL.

Tying all these topics together, and indeed many of the other chapters in this volume, is an underlying reflection on the implications of 'friendship'.[3] Rob's friendship influenced both of us as scholars, and discussions with him challenged, tasked and elevated our research interests in ways that are innumerable, for which we are both grateful. In this chapter we reflect on Rob's application of such valued friendship in the practical implementation of IHL when it comes to the involvement of non-belligerents in situations of armed conflict.

ON THE NATURE AND CLASSIFICATION OF ARMED CONFLICT

Twenty-two years ago, the overriding preoccupation of the IHL community – at least in so-called Western states – was with non-international armed conflicts (NIACs). The engagement of a US-led coalition against Al-Qaeda and the Taliban in Afghanistan from 2001, followed by the invasion of Iraq by a similar constellation of states in 2003 and the ensuing protracted counterinsurgency (COIN) operations there, generated a great deal of attention in the academic literature to the importance of using and developing IHL in NIACs,[4] with the subtext – often unspoken, but implied – that international armed conflicts (IACs) were, as a matter of legal interest, somewhat passé. The armed conflict with which Rob's article was concerned was, after the ejection of the Taliban from government in Kabul in December 2001, by common consent a NIAC inasmuch as it involved the intervention of foreign states on the side of the government against insurgent forces; the same was true of the armed conflict in Iraq following the end of belligerent occupation in June 2004. These two conflicts dominated the military thinking of the US and its allies until 2021 and 2017, respectively, in terms of both doctrine (COIN and expeditionary warfare operations)[5] and the application of law.[6]

/f/documents/d/4/548614.pdf. This chapter is concerned with IHL in situations of armed conflict (*jus in bello*), not the legality of the resort to armed force by states (*jus ad bellum*).

[3] See, for example, Bartels, ch 3, Eskauriatza, ch 13 and Lee, ch 18 in this volume.

[4] See, eg, S Sivakumaran, 'Re-envisaging the International Law of Internal Armed Conflict' (2011) 22 *European Journal of International Law* 219.

[5] See, eg, S Metz and R Millen, 'Insurgency and Counterinsurgency in the 21st Century: Reconceptualizing Threat and Response' (2004) US Army War College Strategic Studies Institute, www.jstor.org/stable/resrep11453?seq=1; 'TRADOC and the Release of FM 3-24, Counterinsurgency', 7 July 2023, www.army.mil/article/268197/tradoc_and_the_release_of_fm_3_24_counterinsurgency (wherein TRADOC stands for US Army Training Doctrine and Command, and FM stands for Field Manual).

[6] See W Banks (ed), *Counterinsurgency Law: New Directions in Asymmetric Warfare* (Oxford University Press, 2013).

In that context, the onset of full-scale battlefield hostilities between Russian and Ukrainian armed forces in 2022 has set the clock back by over two decades in respect of legal issues as much as military tactics and the art of warfare. The tactics used on the battlefield (notably on land), especially in the first two years of the conflict, have resembled nothing so much as the static trench warfare of the First World War, complete with long-range saturation artillery bombardments and mass infantry assaults on fortified-in-depth defensive positions, with relatively few changes to the battlelines; the result is now a pure war of attrition.[7] In parallel, the nature of the armed conflict as being fought between the (mostly) regular armed forces of two states has refocused legal minds on the rules of IHL applicable in traditional IACs.[8] Both Russia and Ukraine are parties to all the principal treaties governing such armed conflicts, and notably the four Geneva Conventions (GCs) of 1949 and their first Additional Protocol (AP I) of 1977.[9] The Hague Regulations of 1899/1907 were already binding on Ukraine as customary international law at the time of that state's independence in 1991, but in any case Ukraine acceded to them in 2015 – doubtless in reaction to Russia's annexation of Crimea and the start of the Donbas War the previous year. As a result, discussion of such topics as explicit classification of combatants and prisoner of war (POW) status once again become relevant, as do concepts of non-belligerency and neutrality, which is where we pick up the thread of friendship from Rob's article.

ON NON-BELLIGERENCY AND NEUTRALITY

The issues of friendship in Afghanistan two decades ago concerned the relationship between the Coalition states and their Afghan allies in the conflict against Al-Qaeda and the Taliban; as a NIAC, the law of neutrality was inapplicable. In the Russo-Ukrainian War, the parallel issues concern the connections in conflict between the belligerent states and other states that are de jure neutral powers under international law, whether they have formally declared their neutrality or not. The issue does not arise so much on the Russian side: although Russia is suspected of procuring arms and materiel from such sympathetic states as Iran and North Korea, by far the greater recipient of outside assistance in various forms is Ukraine.[10] European states aim to increase their support to Ukraine,

[7] See SG Jones, 'Russia's Ill-Fated Invasion of Ukraine: Lessons in Modern Warfare', Center for Strategic & International Studies, 2022, www.csis.org/analysis/russias-ill-fated-invasion-ukraine-lessons-modern-warfare.

[8] See S Watts, W Williams and R Alcala, 'Symposium Intro: Ukraine-Russia Armed Conflict', *Articles of War*, 18 February 2022, lieber.westpoint.edu/symposium-intro-ukraine-russia-armed-conflict.

[9] Ukraine, although not an independent state at the time of the adoption of these instruments, was one of two constituent Soviet Socialist Republics (the other being modern-day Belarus) that had a limited constitutional power to engage in foreign relations. As such, it was a founder member of the United Nations (UN) (separately from the USSR) and became a party to the GCs and AP I in its own right.

[10] In the first 11 months of the war, Ukraine received over €143 billion in commitments from other states: see Kiel Institute for the World Economy, 'The Ukraine Support Tracker: Which Countries Help Ukraine and How?' (Kiel Working Paper No 2218, February 2023), 2, www.ifw-kiel.de/

while the Ukrainian President constantly reiterates that his country's defence against Russian invasion constitutes a defence of all Europe.[11] Russian diplomats, on the other hand, have sought to justify massive attacks on Ukrainian civil infrastructure by reference to Western aid to their enemy,[12] and the Kremlin periodically threatens military – up to and including nuclear – retaliation if certain weapons or weapon systems are delivered to Ukraine[13] or authorised for use against targets on Russian territory (as opposed to Russian forces on Ukrainian territory). Behind the geopolitical concerns, the headlines throw into relief the legal implications of assistance provided by neutrals to a belligerent state.

The issue is given added topicality, at the time of writing, by the decision of an appellate court in the Netherlands to order the Dutch government to stop shipments of war materiel to Israel on the grounds that they violate international law obligations of the Netherlands and arms export regulations of the EU due to alleged IHL violations in the Israel-Hamas conflict in Gaza since October 2023.[14] Similar litigation is currently pending in the UK[15] and several other states,[16] as well as in the International Court of Justice.[17] Notwithstanding that the latter application (a request for provisional measures) was rejected by the Court, and that the situations of Israel and Ukraine are different inasmuch as there are serious allegations of criminality in respect of the Israeli conduct of hostilities, both states are widely acknowledged to be fighting in self-defence against terrorism (in the first instance) and against aggression (in the second).[18]

fileadmin/Dateiverwaltung/IfW-Publications/fis-import/87bb7b0f-ed26-4240-8979-5e6601aea9e8-KWP_2218_Trebesch_et_al_Ukraine_Support_Tracker.pdf.

[11] See, eg, A Brzozowski, 'If "Ukraine is Left Alone, Russia Will Destroy Us", Zelenskyy Tells Munich Security Conference', *Euractiv*, 2024, www.euractiv.com/section/europe-s-east/news/if-ukraine-is-left-alone-russia-will-destroy-us-zelenskyy-tells-munich-security-conference.

[12] United Nations Security Council, 9,202nd meeting (23 November 2022), S/PV.9202, 11–12 (Mr Nebenzia).

[13] See, eg, 'Russia Warns of Response as NATO Returns to Cold War "Schemes"', *Al Jazeera*, 13 July 2023 www.aljazeera.com/news/2023/7/13/russia-warns-of-response-as-nato-returns-to-cold-war-schemes.

[14] *Stichting Oxfam Novib et al v The State of the Netherlands (Ministry of Foreign Affairs)* [2024] The Hague Appeals Court, 12 February, uitspraken.rechtspraak.nl/details?id=ECLI:NL:GHDHA:2024:191 (in Dutch); for comment in English, see M Zwanenburg and J Voetelink, 'Appeals Judgment in Case Concerning the Shipment from the Netherlands of Parts for F-35 Fighter Aircraft to Israel', *EJIL:Talk!*, 2024, www.ejiltalk.org/appeals-judgment-in-case-concerning-the-shipment-from-the-netherlands-of-parts-for-f-35-fighter-aircraft-to-israel/?utm_source=mailpoet&utm_medium=email&utm_campaign=ejil-talk-newsletter-post-title_2.

[15] See Global Law Action Network Media, 'UK Arms Exports Challenge Revived, Expedited and Now Set for Full Hearing in October' (2024), www.glanlaw.org/single-post/uk-arms-exports-challenge-revived-expedited-and-now-set-for-full-hearing-in-october.

[16] See V Lanovoy, 'Arms Transfers to Israel: Knowledge and Risk of Violations of International Law' (2024) *Just Security*, www.justsecurity.org/94674/arms-transfers-israel/.

[17] *Case Concerning Alleged Breaches of Certain International Obligations in Respect of the Occupied Palestinian Territory (Nicaragua v Germany) [2024] (Provisional Measures)*, General List No 193, www.icj-cij.org/sites/default/files/case-related/193/193-20240430-ord-01-00-en.pdf.

[18] For a contrary view, specifically in respect of Israel, see Ralph Wilde, 'Israel's War in Gaza is Not a Valid Act of Self-Defence in International Law', *Opinio Juris*, 9 November 2023, https://opinio-juris.org/2023/11/09/israels-war-in-gaza-is-not-a-valid-act-of-self-defence-in-international-law.

The risk here for Ukraine's friends is not that their provision of support to embattled Ukrainians is illegal under general international law, but rather that it may at some point cross the line into co-belligerency for the purposes of IHL – with a consequent risk of escalation and widening of the conflict. Such worries were manifested, for example, in the reaction to German Chancellor Olaf Scholz's comments about British and French assistance to Ukrainian forces by way of 'target control and accompanying target control',[19] to say nothing of Russian Foreign Minister Sergei Lavrov's threat, in reaction to the news that French instructors may be sent to provide training to Ukrainian troops in Ukraine, that: 'Regardless of their status, [foreign] military officials or mercenaries represent a legitimate target for [Russian] forces.'[20]

States providing assistance to a belligerent technically infringe the *lex scripta* of neutrality in international law,[21] but are said to be non-belligerent; such states incur no legal responsibility for the actions of the assisted belligerent, unless they are actually exerting effective control over the latter[22] – something that would be hard to imagine in cases of IAC, assuming the assisted state is not a puppet of the assisting states.[23] Whilst undefined in international law, non-belligerency is understood as referring to the position of a state that more or less openly supports one side in a conflict, without itself directly participating in military operations.[24] While non-belligerent states are free to provide support to a party to the conflict, on the understanding that they are technically violating the traditional law of neutrality,[25] '[n]ationals of a neutral state who find themselves in

[19] A Rai, 'Germany Accused of "Flagrant Abuse of Intelligence" for Revealing British Help in Ukraine', *The Independent*, 29 February, www.independent.co.uk/news/world/europe/british-soldiers-in-ukraine-germany-b2504462.html.

[20] 'French Military Instructors in Ukraine Would Be "Legitimate Target", Russia Says', *The Guardian*, 4 June, www.theguardian.com/world/article/2024/jun/04/french-military-instructors-in-ukraine-a-legitimate-target-russia-says.

[21] The Hague Convention (XIII) Concerning the Rights and Duties of Neutral Powers in Naval War (1907), Article 6. Despite the absence of an analogous provision in the equivalent instrument for land warfare, namely The Hague Convention (V), the prohibition has been regarded as having attained the status of a customary norm of general applicability: see MN Schmitt, 'Providing Arms and Material to Ukraine: Neutrality, Co-belligerency and the Use of Force' (2022) *Articles of War*, lieber.westpoint.edu/ukraine-neutrality-co-belligerency-use-of-force. Schmitt notes that what is technically prohibited is *the provision of aid by the state itself on an inter-governmental basis*, but the provision of aid by the private sector is not prohibited. In any event, referring *in casu* to the Russo-Ukrainian War, Schmitt argues convincingly for an adaptive interpretation of the neutrality rules in light of the UN Charter, the right of self-defence against aggression and evolving state practice since 1945.

[22] By analogy with the principles enunciated by the European Court of Human Rights in *Ilaşcu and Others v Moldova and Russia* [2004] Application No 48787/99, ECHR 2004-VII, at paras 377–94.

[23] In practice, this would be most likely to occur in cases of belligerent occupation: see B Ivanel, 'Puppet States: A Growing Trend of Covert Occupation' (2015) 18 *Yearbook of International Humanitarian Law* 43.

[24] Examples are Spanish assistance to Germany and Irish assistance to the UK during the Second World War (although both Spain and Ireland formally declared neutrality in that conflict).

[25] It is suggested that this increasingly prevalent attitude among states is indicative of a shift in state practice, and therefore the customary law of neutrality: Hitoshi Nasu, 'The Future Law of Neutrality'(2022) *Articles of War*, ieber.westpoint.edu/future-law-of-neutrality. The practice had

the territory of a belligerent state … shall not be regarded as protected persons while the state of which they are nationals has normal diplomatic representation in the state in whose hands they are';[26] the immediate adverse consequences of non-belligerent friendship are therefore borne by individuals rather than the state itself. This will be discussed further in the section on combatants and their status after capture below.

At what point might non-belligerent support cross the line into co-belligerency and what (if any) might be the consequences in international law? As has been noted:

> 'Co-belligerent' is simply a fairly informal term of identification. It is a label for entities, historically states … that have joined an armed conflict on the side of one of the parties. It is similar in meaning to 'ally', though it lacks any requirement for the formal ties that label suggests. The label 'co-belligerent' has been used historically, though without great frequency … it is used today as a label for states that are partners in an armed conflict … But there is little to no international law content elaborating further on the meaning of the term 'co-belligerent' or on what precise conglomeration of activities would suffice to make an entity a 'co-belligerent'.[27]

The essential requirement for co-belligerency is that the assisting states participate directly in the armed conflict, thereby effectively becoming belligerents – in the case of Ukraine, this would involve Western states actively committing to hostilities against Russia, which evidently is not the case. There have been arms transfers, training of troops and intelligence sharing – all clear manifestations of friendship and a desire to help Ukraine prevail in the face of Russian aggression – but no direct participation in the planning or execution of combat operations, or provision of military facilities on the territories of those states for Ukrainian use.[28] On the other side, Belarus has been described as having co-belligerent status due to its willingness to allow Russian forces to use its territory and military bases as staging posts for the full-scale invasion of Ukraine in February 2022[29] – in violation of The Hague Convention (V), customary international law and the prohibition of aggression[30] – but has not permitted its own armed forces to be used in operations against Ukraine. What the positions

already shifted in this direction during the Second World War, notably in light of US assistance to the UK before the US declarations of war on Japan and Germany: see FR Coudert, 'Non-belligerency in International Law' (1942) 29 *Virginia LR* 143. See also Schmitt (n 21).

[26] Geneva Convention (IV) relative to the Protection of Civilian Persons in Time of War (1949), Article 4.

[27] R Ingber, 'Co-belligerency' (2016) 42 *Yale Journal of International Law* 67, 80–81.

[28] See J Grignon, '"Co-belligerency" or When Does a State Become a Party to an Armed Conflict?' (2022) *Institut de recherche stratégique de l'École Militaire*, Strategic Brief – 39, www.irsem.fr/media/sb-39-grignon-cobelligerency.pdf.

[29] R Bailey, K Stepanenko and FW Kagan, 'Russian Offensive Campaign Assessment, December 11', Institute for the Study of War, 2022, www.understandingwar.org/backgrounder/russian-offensive-campaign-assessment-december-11.

[30] UN General Assembly, *Definition of Aggression* (1974) A/RES/3314 (XXIX), Article 3(f).

of states vis-à-vis Russia and Ukraine in their conflict seem to be indicating is that as the world grows ever more polarised, friendship is increasingly a matter of choice that is impelled: neutrals feel a need to take sides, and the traditional rules of neutrality are increasingly being obviated in practice.

ON THE STATUS AND TREATMENT OF COMBATANTS

While the qualification under IHL of the regular armed forces of Ukraine and Russia as combatants entitled to POW status after capture is typically uncontroversial, the conflict has seen attention focused on other actors who have been present on the battlefield. In some cases this has led to a revival of interest in some IHL concepts that had been widely assumed to be of little relevance to contemporary armed conflict, as in the spontaneous self-mobilisation of civilians in the population of Kyiv to defend the city as the initial Russian invading columns approached. This corresponded to the category of persons known as the *levée en masse*: lawful combatants (subject to carrying their arms openly and respecting the laws and customs of war) entitled after capture to POW status.[31] However, in other cases, the theme of friendship surfaces again: Ukraine, in particular, has benefited from the physical support in combat of numerous volunteers from other countries who have travelled there to fight for the country against its much more numerous enemy.

In some instances, controversy has arisen over the legal status of citizens of neutral states who have 'gone to Ukraine to fight': what would their rights be if they had the misfortune to fall into enemy hands? In the UK a prominent feature of the discussion was whether their travel to Ukraine to participate in a war was lawful under domestic law: British legislation has long prohibited British nationals from 'engagement in the military or naval service of any foreign state at war with any foreign state at peace with Her Majesty'[32] and has for almost as long lacked enforcement (the last successful prosecution was in 1896 in connection with the Jameson Raid against the Transvaal Republic). In practice, the situation is not as alarming as might be imagined: provided that they join the regular armed forces, they are protected by combatant status and will be entitled to treatment as POWs if captured.[33]

[31] Geneva Convention (III) relative to the Treatment of Prisoners of War (1949), Article 4(A)(6). The last clear example prior to the present conflict is thought to have been the mobilisation of the Warsaw population to help fortify the city in the early days of the German invasion of Poland in September 1939. Notwithstanding that and some occasional judicial consideration since 1949, the conventional wisdom has been that the *levée en masse* had fallen into desuetude: see E Crawford, 'Tracing the Historical and Legal Development of the *Levée en Masse* in the Law of Armed Conflict' (2017) 19 *Journal of the History of International Law*, 329.

[32] Foreign Enlistment Act 1870, s 4.

[33] Regulations Concerning the Laws and Customs of War on Land, Annex to The Hague Convention (IV) (1907), Article 1; GC (III), Article 4(1).

The best-known manifestation of this phenomenon has been the International Legion of Territorial Defence of Ukraine (or Ukrainian Foreign Legion), established within three days of the full-scale Russian assault in February 2022, which fits into a long and distinguished military tradition of foreign service regiments in European armies;[34] there are also less well-known units with volunteers from specific countries, such as the Georgian Legion and the Belarusian Kastuś Kalinoŭski Regiment. The soldiers of these units, fully integrated as formations of the regular Ukrainian Armed Forces, are clearly combatants with entitlement to POW status upon capture. Some of them have benefited from that status by being included in POW exchanges, which have been a prominent feature of the conflict so far.[35] What is interesting about the POW exchanges in this conflict is that they have not been effected by the mechanism traditionally recognised in IHL – parole (as provided for in Article 21 of GC III) – but rather by ad hoc bilateral agreements for mass POW exchanges. Historically these agreements were often in the form of a 'cartel' for repeated use during the conflict, although this usage appears to have fallen into disuse since the First World War (it is noteworthy that cartels are not mentioned in the modern IHL treaties, but there is ample evidence of their use in customary international law since the early nineteenth century).[36]

Friendship in the Russo-Ukrainian War has also sometimes come in unexpected guises, as with raids in the Belgorod region of southern Russia in May–June 2023 that were attributed to various non-state actors for which Ukraine declined to claim responsibility.[37] The armed groups in question were two separate groups of dissident Russian citizens, who apparently decided on their own initiative to attack targets in Russia as a way of supporting Ukraine's operations: the Freedom of Russia Legion (FRL) and the Russian Volunteer Corps (RVC). However, there is a big difference between these two groups: whereas the FRL claims to be under the Ukrainian Armed Forces' command and control, which would make it a militia or volunteer corps forming part of the armed forces,[38] the RVC appears to consist of extremist Russian ethno-nationalists operating independently of Ukrainian military oversight. Therefore, it is odd that the

[34] Famous examples include the British Army's Brigade of Gurkhas, the Vatican's Pontifical Swiss Guards, and the French and Spanish Foreign Legions; the latter themselves built on a tradition of employing Swiss and Irish soldiers, originally as mercenaries but eventually as regular army regiments.

[35] See D Turns, 'Ukraine War: Prisoner Swaps Have Been Going on for Centuries – Here's How They Work', (2022) *The Conversation*, theconversation.com/ukraine-war-prisoner-swaps-have-been-going-on-for-centuries-heres-how-they-work-191880.

[36] See examples in HS Levie (ed), 'Documents on Prisoners of War' (1979) 60 *International Law Studies*; 'Practice Relating to Rule 128 (Release and Return of Persons Deprived of Their Liberty), Section C (Exchange of prisoners)', Customary IHL Database, ihl-databases.icrc.org/en/customary-ihl/v2/rule128#90ea6f64-77ca-48ee-aed3-8623edffac51.

[37] See D Turns, 'Ukraine War: What International Law Says about the Russians Fighting against Their Own Country' (2023) *The Conversation*, theconversation.com/ukraine-war-what-international-law-says-about-the-russians-fighting-against-their-own-country-207638.

[38] Therefore entitled to POW status under GC III, Article 4(A)(1).

authorities in Kyiv disclaim all responsibility for the actions of the FRL (they might well be thinking 'with friends like these, who needs enemies?'), but objectively, these fighters seem to satisfy the legal criteria for combatant status under IHL. Members of the RVC, on the other hand, run the risk of being treated as saboteurs or, worse, traitors under Russian law, and if captured are unlikely to benefit from any specific protections under IHL as they would not be in the hands of a party to the conflict of which they are not nationals. Although they might be considered 'other militia' not incorporated into the armed forces, they would not seem to satisfy the criterion of 'belonging to a Party to the conflict'[39] and therefore would fall outside the scope of entitlement to POW status.

ON METHODS AND DANGEROUS FORCES

Rob divided his analysis of the methods and means of warfare into air and ground campaigns, drawing parallels from Kosovo and considering some specific incidents to assess legal compliance at that early stage of the war in Afghanistan. The consideration of mistakes, the Red Cross Compound bombings of October 2001, and the use of highly destructive weapons such as 'daisy cutters' and cluster bombs could easily be reflected upon with numerous similar examples littering the history of the war and subsequent conflicts in Iraq and Syria. However, the Russo-Ukrainian War has some distinct characteristics which demonstrate how the obligations of friendship may be more far-reaching than before. In some respects it could be argued that, as this is a 'traditional' IAC, the treaty obligations are simpler to apply than Rob found was the case in Afghanistan. However, challenges of application remain and old problems recur. Notably, specific threats to the environment both within and without Ukraine through the release of 'dangerous forces' have become increasingly pertinent, both in terms of attacks on dams and against nuclear power plants.

The targeting of dams during armed conflict is hardly a new feature of warfare,[40] but the increasing awareness of environmental damage and the subsequent impact on civilian life has warranted greater consideration under IHL. The destruction of the Nova Kakhovka dam is one such example. The dam was the largest in the Dnipro River, being the final one of six along the watercourse in Ukraine. Completed in 1956, this dam held around 18 cubic kilometres of water which supplied more than 700,000 people in south Ukraine and Crimea.[41] The

[39] ibid Article 4(A)(2).

[40] Recall perhaps the Dambusters of the Second World War, 'The Incredible Story of the Dambusters Raid', *Imperial War Museum*, www.iwm.org.uk/history/the-incredible-story-of-the-dambusters-raid. More recently, see D Phillips, A Khan and E Schmitt, 'A Dam in Syria was on a No-Strike List. The US Bombed it Anyway', *New York Times*, 20 January 2022, www.nytimes.com/2022/01/20/us/airstrike-us-isis-dam.html.

[41] M Naddaf, 'Ukraine Dam Collapse: What Scientists are Watching' (2023) *Nature*, www.nature.com/articles/d41586-023-01928-8.

collapse of the dam on 6 June 2023 led to significant flooding, extensive damage, loss of civilian life and massive ongoing environmental impact.[42] Whilst it is clear that this is a severe consequence of the armed conflict, it is less clear if it amounts to a breach of IHL.

Dams are specifically protected by AP I, to which both Russia and Ukraine are parties, unusually allowing an application of a treaty rule without the need for detailed consideration of custom. Article 56 outlines the special protections for dams, detailing that they 'shall not be made the object of attack, even where these objects are military objectives, if such attack may cause the release of dangerous forces and consequent severe losses among the civilian population'. This goes further than the standard requirements of distinction, proportionality and precautions, such that even if a dam is considered a military objective, it cannot be the target of an attack if the consequences of such result in the release of dangerous forces or severe loss of life. In that manner, any attack on the Kakhovka dam could be considered a breach of IHL, presuming that the attack 'may cause' the release of dangerous forces, in this case water, and the consequent civilian losses. It is argued that this qualification is not the same as the proportionality assessment required under Article 52,[43] in that it is not balanced against the anticipated military advantage, but only requires that the attack 'may cause' severe losses. However, it is important to recall that these are losses among the civilian population rather than environmental or civilian objects and, in any event, 'severe' is a vague term. Moreover, it is unclear whether this relates to direct deaths and injuries or the reverberating effects of the attack – in this case, the loss of access to drinking water, health hazards due to chemical contamination and displacement of entire communities. The civilians affected by the dam collapse number in excess of 100,000 residents who had homes and livelihoods in the 80 settlements downstream of the dam.[44] Thus, it would be reasonable to suggest that it was foreseeable that any destruction of the dam would cause severe losses among the civilian population.

However, the main difficulty for IHL in this situation is in the need for there to be an 'attack'. This is a special term of art in IHL defined in Article 49 as 'acts of violence against the adversary, whether in offence or in defence'.[45] As such, the previous dams that had been destroyed by Ukraine during the conflict would not amount to a breach of IHL, as it would not be an attack against the adversary, Russia.[46] To establish any breach of Article 56, it is vital to understand the

[42] B Balachandran (ed), 'United Nations Ukraine: Post Disaster Needs Assessment, 2023 Kakhovka Dam Disaster, Ukraine' (2023) United Nations & Government of Ukraine, ukraine.un.org/sites/default/files/2023-10/PDNA%20Final%20and%20Cleared%20-%2016Oct.pdf.

[43] ibid.

[44] ibid 3.

[45] AP I, Article 49(1).

[46] See, for example, 'Ukraine Blew up a Dam to Stop the Russian Advance on Kyiv, Some Homes Remain Flooded', *Reuters*, 29 May 2022, www.reuters.com/world/europe/months-after-dam-destroyed-stop-russian-advance-parts-village-still-flooded-2022-05-29.

cause of the dam collapse. A prevailing feature of any conflict, perhaps more so in this conflict, is the desire of adversaries to manipulate the narrative.[47] The fog of war obscures clarity both during battle and in the aftermath to the extent that it can be difficult to determine the facts of any incident when an investigation is not conducted. In this case, it could be a deliberate attack by either side, with the Russians in control of the dam immediately prior to its collapse, but it being within Ukrainian territory and in a contested space. Each side has blamed the other,[48] with Ukraine previously stating that Russia was planning a 'false flag' operation to destroy it and requesting an international observation mission.[49] These false flag operations are a type of deception operation wherein a statement or act is deliberately falsified or misattributed to an adversary in order to gain an advantage in terms of public perception. Those are a form of *ruse de guerre* that is in no way illegal under IHL, provided that they do not violate any other rules of IHL and are not perfidious in nature.[50] AP I specifically mentions 'mock operations and misinformation' as examples of permitted uses; other suggestions (derived from the military manuals of various states and cited by the International Committee of the Red Cross (ICRC)) include 'transmitting misleading messages by radio or in the press; knowingly permitting the enemy to intercept … despatches or news items which actually bear no relation to reality'.[51] In today's world of 24-hour news coverage and social media, the impact of such operations in the international consumption of the conflict (in terms of public opinion, diplomatic relations etc) is hard to underestimate: one's friends may be as galvanised in support as one's enemies are in condemnation. In the Russo-Ukrainian War, as in other contemporary armed conflicts, both sides have resorted extensively to such operations.

In the specific instance of the Kakhovka Dam, the *New York Times* and others have claimed that Russia had placed explosives inside the dam at a known weak point,[52] but equally it could just have collapsed following the ravages of

[47] See for example, Organisation for Economic Co-operation and Development, 'Disinformation and Russia's War of Aggression against Ukraine' (2022) *OECD Policy Responses*, www.oecd.org/ukraine-hub/policy-responses/disinformation-and-russia-s-war-of-aggression-against-ukraine-37186bde; O Robinson, A Robinson and S Sardarizadeh, 'Ukraine War: How TikTok Fakes Pushed Russian Lies to Millions', *BBC News*, 15 December 2023, www.bbc.co.uk/news/world-europe-67687449; A Demus, K Holynska and K Marcinek, 'The Nightingale versus the Bear: What Persuasion Research Reveals about Ukraine's and Russia's Messaging on the War' (2023) *RAND Research Report*, www.rand.org/pubs/research_reports/RRA2032-1.html.

[48] P Wintour, 'Russian Floundering in "Mud of Lies" over Kakhovka Dam Destruction, Ukraine Tells UN', *The Guardian*, 7 June 2023, www.theguardian.com/world/2023/jun/07/russia-accused-of-floundering-in-lies-at-un-security-council-after-claiming-ukraine-behind-dam-destruction.

[49] D Bilefsky, 'Zelensky Says Russia Plans to Blow up a Major Dam in a "False Flag" Attack, Flooding Southern Ukraine', *New York Times*, 21 October 2022, www.nytimes.com/2022/10/21/world/europe/zelensky-putin-russia-ukraine-dam.html.

[50] The Hague Regulations Concerning the Laws and Customs of War on Land (1907), Article 24; AP I, Article 37(2).

[51] ICRC, *Commentary on Additional Protocol I* (1987), para 1521.

[52] J Glanz et al. 'Why the Evidence Suggests Russia Blew up the Kakhovka Dam', *New York Times*, 16 June 2023, www.nytimes.com/interactive/2023/06/16/world/europe/ukraine-kakhovka-

war. Satellite footage prior to the collapse showed damage to the roadway from Ukrainian strikes as well as from retreating Russian troops who had damaged another part. As such, the water had been flowing uncontrollably over the sluice gates for some time. In any event, it is less than clear that an 'attack' took place, and if it failed because of poor maintenance compounded by the ongoing conflict, then it is far from certain that this would amount to an attack.

However, the general IHL principles of distinction,[53] proportionality[54] and precautions[55] prevail, and it could be that the precautionary obligation to 'take the other necessary precautions to protect the civilian population, individual civilians and civilian objects under their control against the dangers resulting from military operations'[56] could be said to be applicable. This compels both parties to the conflict to minimise the impact of military operations on the civilian population. In the case of Kakhovka dam, territory occupied by Russia and Ukraine was affected, with civilian casualties in both areas. Thus, if either party had information relating to the dam collapse, they were, where feasible, required to take steps to mitigate the impact on the population, perhaps through evacuation or relocation.[57] However, without a full investigation into the cause of the collapse and, as Milanovic suggests, why it was destroyed,[58] we are unable to reach a definitive conclusion. Thus, we reach a similarly dissatisfying conclusion as Rob did earlier, in which he recalled[59] Kalshoven, who said:

> To the extent that this conclusion might lead to a feeling of frustration at the law of armed conflict, it may be useful to recall that like the rest of international law, the law of armed conflict is a reflection of, and finds its limits in, the perceived interests and political will of states, not the idealistic notions of kind souls.[60]

Despite this, the issue of the release of dangerous forces bears further scrutiny. Whilst in some respects the impact of the Kakhovka dam is limited to the territory surrounding the dam, this includes the supply of water to the Zaporizhzhia Nuclear Power Plant, the largest nuclear power plant in Europe, one that has been the focus of attention since Russia took control of it early on in the conflict, attacking the plant overnight on 4 March and launching projectiles that hit a

dam-collapse.html?campaign_id=190&emc=edit_ufn_20230623&instance_id=95846&nl=from-the-times&regi_id=202286374&segment_id=137341&te=1&user_id=7031166ada6cc6b7d3c1be370a89aa5b.

[53] AP I, Articles 48, 51(2) and 52(2).

[54] ibid Article 51(5)(b).

[55] ibid Article 57.

[56] ibid Article 58(c).

[57] JF Quéguiner, 'Precautions under the Law Governing the Conduct of Hostilities' (2006) 88 *International Review of the Red Cross* 793, 819.

[58] M Milanovic, 'The Destruction of the Nova Kakhovka Dam and International Humanitarian Law: Some Preliminary Thoughts' (2023) *EJIL:Talk!*, www.ejiltalk.org/the-destruction-of-the-nova-kakhovka-dam-and-international-humanitarian-law-some-preliminary-thoughts.

[59] Cryer (n 1) 60.

[60] F Kalshoven, 'Arms, Armaments and the Law' (1985) 191 *International Review of the Red Cross* 183, 288.

training building and caused a fire.[61] Whilst the International Atomic Energy Agency (IAEA) emphasised that the attack took place away from the six reactors, other sources suggest that multiple strikes took place, causing damage to reactor buildings and a high-voltage powerline outside the plant.[62] It is clear that damage to nuclear power plants is of considerable concern, with a potential radioactive leak contaminating areas far beyond the immediate location. Furthermore, the short- and long-term effects of radiation on human health and the environment can be devastating.[63]

In an IAC, such as in Ukraine, nuclear power plants are again protected by Article 56, as any attack risks the release of dangerous forces, in this case radioactive materials. However, unlike the parallel obligations in AP II[64] for NIACs, which are absolute, there are some limited and exceptional circumstances under which nuclear power plants may lose their protection. This is far more limited than the establishment of a military objective for the regular principles of IHL, with the protection lost 'only if it provides electric power in regular, significant and direct support of military operations and if such attack is the only feasible way to terminate such support'.[65] As such, the power generated must directly support the military operations themselves and not just infrastructure; additionally, it needs to be a sizeable contribution and not just a sporadic provision of power. It would appear difficult to reach those thresholds for the Zaporizhzhia Plant, given that it provided over 10 per cent of Ukraine's power prior to the invasion.[66] It would be particularly difficult to establish a 'direct' relationship to the military operation which was 'close and immediate'[67] rather than merely incidental. Even if that test could be met, the second part of the limitation also needs to be attained – to wit, that attacking the plant is the only 'feasible way to terminate' the support. Even if the Zaporizhzhia Plant had lost its special protections due to the manner in which it was being used prior to the attack on 4 March 2022, the general rules of IHL continue to apply, and parties must take all feasible precautions to protect civilians from the release of radiation.[68] This could involve the choice of appropriate weapons, avoiding the use of explosive munitions with wide area effects and targeting specific parts of the plant in a way that reduces risk to the reactors. Perhaps the attack on the training

[61] Nuclear Energy Agency, 'Ukraine: Current Status of Nuclear Power Installations' (2023) OECD NEA, www.oecd-nea.org/jcms/pl_66130/ukraine-current-status-of-nuclear-power-installations.

[62] G Brumfiel et al, 'Video Analysis Reveals Russian Attack on Ukrainian nuclear plant veered near disaster' (2022) www.npr.org/2022/03/11/1085427380/ukraine-nuclear-power-plant-zaporizhzhia.

[63] For a discussion of radiation sickness, see Drumbl and Mouthaan, ch 16 in this volume.

[64] Additional Protocol II to the Geneva Conventions, 1977 (AP II).

[65] ibid Article 56 (2)(b).

[66] A Prokip, 'Why the Zaporizhzhia Nuclear Power Plant Matters … for the Whole World' (2022) *Wilson Center*, www.wilsoncenter.org/blog-post/why-zaporizhzhia-nuclear-power-plant-mattersfor-whole-world.

[67] Y Sandoz et al (eds) 'Commentary on the Additional Protocols to the Geneva Conventions' (1987) (hereinafter ICRC Commentary) 2162, ihl-databases.icrc.org/en/ihl-treaties/api-1977/article-56/commentary/1987.

[68] Articles 57 and 56 (3); also see ICRC Commentary (n 67) 2.7 at 399.

building at Zaporizhzhia was part of this consideration; however, it remains unclear if the plant could be considered to have lost its special protections. Moreover, given the pattern of attacks on Ukraine's civilian infrastructure more widely, it becomes less likely that this obligation under IHL has been met.[69]

The concern over nuclear radiation during this conflict, unlike those before, is notable, with the IAEA placing permanent observers at all of Ukraine's nuclear power plants held by both parties to the conflict.[70] Additionally, the EU pre-emptively supplied five million potassium iodide tablets to Ukraine in mid-2022.[71] The significant support provided by various states in support of Ukraine during the conflict has been notable, and perhaps demonstrates an aspect of friendship akin to that envisaged by Rob.

ON INTELLIGENCE SHARING AND FRIENDSHIP

Throughout the conflict, the US, the UK and the North Atlantic Treaty Organization (NATO) have been unusually open about their intelligence sharing with Ukraine. This is one part of the package of measures discussed above in support of Ukraine that fail to reach a belligerency threshold, with the US saying: 'Ukraine combines information that we and others provide with intelligence they're gathering themselves … and then they make their own decisions.'[72] Whilst provision of intelligence to another state is relatively common practice and does not place IHL obligations on that state, it is important to consider what happens if that intelligence is incorrect and leads to a misstep.

The precautionary principle of IHL, established by Article 57, requires parties to take all feasible precautions in the methods and means of attack to avoid, or at least minimise, collateral damage to civilians. It is a continuing obligation covering initial target identification through the targeting cycle to the later battle damage assessment. It is here that the issues of intelligence sharing become apparent; when one state identifies a target that is then executed by another. Coalitions have been sharing intelligence for many years, both NATO[73]

[69] UN Human Rights Council, 'Report of the Independent International Commission of Inquiry on Ukraine' (2023) UNHRC A/HRC/52/62 40 et seq, www.ohchr.org/sites/default/files/documents/hrbodies/hrcouncil/coiukraine/A_HRC_52_62_AUV_EN.pdf.

[70] World Nuclear Association, 'Ukraine: Russia-Ukraine War and Nuclear Energy' (2023), world-nuclear.org/information-library/country-profiles/countries-t-z/ukraine-russia-war-and-nuclear-energy.aspx.

[71] Directorate General for European Civil Protection and Humanitarian Aid Operations, 'Ukraine: EU Donates 5 Million Potassium Iodide Tablets to Protect Ukrainians from Potential Radiation Exposure', 30 August 2022, civil-protection-humanitarian-aid.ec.europa.eu/news-stories/news/ukraine-eu-donates-5-million-potassium-iodide-tablets-protect-ukrainians-potential-radiation-2022-08-30_en#:~:text=The%20EU%20is%20pre%2Demptively,to%20high%20levels%20of%20radiation.

[72] S Harris et al, 'U.S. Intelligence Helped Kyiv Sink Russian Warship', *Washington Post*, 5 May 2022, www.washingtonpost.com/national-security/2022/05/05/us-intelligence-ukraine-moskva-sinking.

[73] NATO, 'Joint Intelligence, Surveillance and Reconnaissance' (2023), www.nato.int/cps/en/natohq/topics_111830.htm.

and the FIVE-EYES alliance[74] demonstrate this, but the details have always been rather harder to establish. However, there is past evidence of this and examples of mistakes caused in some part by intelligence sharing, notably the Vavarin Bridge case in 1999 following a NATO airstrike and more recently in airstrikes conducted near Deir ez-Zor in Syria in 2016.[75]

In the Vavarin Bridge case, the German Air Force provided the intelligence that added the bridge to the target list, which was later struck by US F-16 aircraft. In the final judgment, the Bundesverfassungsgericht established that German forces did not breach IHL. They asserted that the significant fact is that the addition of the bridge to a possible targets list 'did not reflect a final military decision by NATO to attack those targets but a temporary and abstract assessment that they might be marked for attack should circumstances occur that would allow such action in conformity with international law'.[76] Thus, on this basis, the supplying of intelligence to Ukraine on general topics such as troop movements, Russian preparedness and similar 'temporary and abstract' assessments does not appear to create liability for the donor state. That said, if a state is providing intelligence to Ukraine to further their military endeavours, then it would seem counter-intuitive to provide faulty intelligence. Moreover, if this is done under the guise of friendship, then one reflects that the quality of intelligence provided perhaps speaks to the quality of that friendship.

The situation in Syria was somewhat more complex as it related to several states and the collation of disparate intelligence. The airstrike involved aircraft from Denmark, Australia, the UK and the US, with the resulting investigation concluding that 'confirmation bias stemming from that first misidentification coloured subsequent decisions made by others involved in the strike'.[77] The planning process was said to take several days, with the summation that the use of multiple states' intelligence sources, the blurring of targeting procedures and the confirmation bias presented by the initial intelligence analyst resulted in an incorrect attack. Significantly, following this, the Royal Australian Air Force (RAAF) took steps to improve their information sharing with coalition partners.[78]

Therefore, whilst sharing intelligence with Ukraine may not create direct legal accountability for 'friendly' states, they would be wise to consider the responsibility to provide accurate and verifiable intelligence to their friends.

[74] JV Tossini, 'The Five Eyes: The Intelligence Alliance of the Anglosphere' (2020) *UK Defence Journal*, ukdefencejournal.org.uk/the-five-eyes-the-intelligence-alliance-of-the-anglosphere.

[75] See also EJ Marchant, 'Intelligence Sharing and Ukraine: The *Jus in Bello*' (2022) *OpinioJuris*, opiniojuris.org/2022/05/13/intelligence-sharing-and-ukraine-the-jus-in-bello.

[76] KF Garditz, 'Bridge of Varvarin' (2014) 108 *American Journal of International Law* 86.

[77] S Ackerman, 'US Military Admits it Mistakenly Targeted and Killed Loyalist Syrian Forces', *The Guardian*, 29 November 2016, www.theguardian.com/world/2016/nov/29/us-military-airstrikes-mistake-syria-assad-deir-ez-zor.

[78] A Greene, 'RAAF Fighters Dropped Six Bombs on Government Forces in Botched Air Strikes in Syria', *ABC News*, 30 November 2016, www.abc.net.au/news/2016-11-30/syria-botched-air-strikes-australian-hornets/8077588.

The targeting decisions, and thus obligations under IHL, remain Ukraine's, but in order for them to ensure they are complying with the precautionary principle, they need to be able to reach timely and accurate decisions. History shows us that it is all too often the initial information that can lead to confirmation bias and error.

A good example of this returns us to Afghanistan and the final days before the withdrawal of troops in late August 2021. On 29 August 2021, the US undertook a drone strike against a Toyota Corolla in Kabul, killing 10 people (including seven children).[79] The intended target was a suspected ISIS-K bomb maker who was thought to be planning an attack at Kabul Airport, where the evacuation of allied military and civilians was underway. The US operators had observed the vehicle leaving a suspected safehouse and tracked it for another eight hours before launching the attack. The driver was later identified as Zemari Ahmadi, who was an aid worker for Nutrition and Education International in Kabul.[80] The investigation into the mistake revealed that confirmation bias from intelligence in the very early stages of the tracking led to the error, with each additional action being viewed through the lens of a threat.[81] Whilst it is unlikely that this incident amounts to a war crime, due to it being a mistake of fact, it highlights the important role intelligence can play, and thus the sharing of such, in protecting civilians during armed conflict and the troubling final days of the war in Afghanistan.

The final withdrawal from Afghanistan has become characterised as a period of chaos, with thousands of Afghans trying to escape their country through Kabul Airport.[82] The collapse of the government and the takeover by the Taliban led many to fear for their lives, particularly those who had supported and provided services for the US-led forces. Both the US and the UK have processes in place to enable relocation for those who risked their lives to support troops,[83] but there are significant criticisms of the schemes, with the UK Ministry of Defence (MOD) having to apologise for telling Afghan interpreters that they required

[79] D Vergun, 'Air Force Official Briefs Media on Deadly Drone Strike in Kabul' (2021) *DOD News*, www.defense.gov/News/News-Stories/Article/Article/2831896/air-force-official-briefs-media-on-deadly-drone-strike-in-kabul; C Savage, E Schmitt, A Khan, E Hill and C Koetti, 'Newly Declassified Video Shows U.S. Killing of 10 Civilians in Drone Strike', *New York Times*, 19 January 2022, www.nytimes.com/2022/01/19/us/politics/afghanistan-drone-strike-video.html.

[80] A California-based aid organisation.

[81] For more on this, see US Department of Defense, 'Transcript: Pentagon Press Secretary John F. Kirby and Air Force Lt. Gen. Sami D. Said Hold Press Briefing' (2021), www.defense.gov/News/Transcripts/Transcript/Article/2832634/pentagon-press-secretary-john-f-kirby-and-air-force-lt-gen-sami-d-said-hold-a-p.

[82] 'Year after US Withdrawal from Afghanistan Many Afghans Who Helped the US Still Trapped and Living in Fear', *CBS News*, 30 August 2022, www.cbsnews.com/news/afghanistan-war-year-after-us-withdrawal-afghan-translators-trapped-fear-taliban.

[83] Ministry of Defence, 'Plans to Bring Vulnerable Afghan Interpreters to the UK Accelerated' (2021) *UK Government News*, www.gov.uk/government/news/plans-to-bring-vulnerable-afghan-interpreters-to-the-uk-accelerated; US Department of State, 'Afghan Arrivals under the U.S. Refugee Admissions Program', www.state.gov/afghan-arrivals-under-the-u-s-refugee-admissions-program/.

permission from the Taliban before they were eligible for the scheme.[84] It is unknown how many remain in Afghanistan, but there are potentially thousands of people who were treated as friends during the conflict, but who now face an uphill struggle to relocate.[85] Whilst not a legal matter under IHL, this illustrates the continuing impact of the conflict and perhaps calls us to reflect on friendship even after we return home.

CONCLUSION

It has been 22 years since Rob published his carefully crafted analysis of the early stages of the 'Global War on Terror'. His usage of friendship to call on states to consider their acts during conflict, and under international law, bears as great a relevance today as it did at that time. This chapter has taken that concept, and some of Rob's framework, to consider its application to a recent conflict, specifically the Russo-Ukraine War. The notable level of support provided to Ukraine during the conflict, under the guise of friendship, prompts reflection. Beyond merely holding our friends accountable for their conduct, we need to consider how our friends' actions reflect upon us. To that extent, we may wish to consider how liberal interpretations of international law can extend beyond our own borders and how actions of our friends need to be considered in the light of our former actions.

Beyond his characteristically balanced legal analysis, Rob provides much to reflect upon. The nature of the challenges within international humanitarian law has developed in the years since he wrote about the early days of the war in Afghanistan. There has been extensive academic ink spilled writing on the impact of technological developments, such as drone warfare, and altered strategic situations, such as COIN. Today, we even see legal arguments over the possibility of nuclear platforms in space.[86] Despite the changing details, Rob's article reveals some enduring challenges, both for law and for those attempting to analyse the legal landscape during armed conflict. The information relating to incidents is characteristically difficult to obtain, relying heavily on journalists to relay issues from the frontlines. This presents opportunities and challenges, but always risks

[84] J Perreira, 'MOD Apologies for Telling Afghan Interpreters to Get Taliban's Permission to Come to UK' (2023) *Forces Net*, www.forces.net/politics/mod-apologises-telling-afghan-interpreters-get-talibans-permission-come-uk.

[85] See, for example, HL Deb (2023) vol 833, cols 208 et seq, hansard.parliament.uk/Lords/2023-10-18/debates/AF79B43D-9D28-41AC-ABD3-9B39D62C3ED9/AfghanInterpreters; L Holland, 'Afghan Translators Left Behind and Fearing for Their Lives after Helping UK Forces to Sue British Government', *Sky News*, 8 August 2022, news.sky.com/story/afghan-translators-left-behind-and-fearing-for-their-lives-after-helping-uk-forces-sue-british-government-12668236; H Honderich and B Debusmann Jr, 'From Afghan Interpreter to US Homeless: The Long Road to the American Dream', *BBC News*, 2 August 2021, www.bbc.co.uk/news/world-us-canada-58020494.

[86] WH Boothby, 'Russian Nuclear Weapons in Space' (2024) *Articles of War*, https://lieber.westpoint.edu/russian-nuclear-weapons-space/.

incorrect legal conclusions lacking the full facts. More often than not, it results in a non-conclusion, caveated by the lack of information. However, in the intervening years, it has become increasingly relevant, not only for academics and commentators, but also for prosecutors, with the International Criminal Court (ICC) issuing arrest warrants for war crimes during the Russo-Ukraine conflict.[87] This rapid resort to criminal justice was not seen in Afghanistan, and maybe this marks a watershed moment for IHL, as well as international law more generally. But without care in legal analysis, evidence gathering and the wider aspects of criminal justice, this rapid resort to prosecution could pose novel challenges for IHL, which was arguably originally designed for the battlefield rather than the courtroom.[88]

Despite this, both international law and friendship can adapt and endure. Rob drew his fine art of friendship from Eisenhower, but the link between justice and friendship is far deeper.[89] The nature of these friendships has also adapted and adjusted over the intervening years, but they remain a touchstone of international law and the relations between states. The potential for increasingly 'obliged friendships' may cause us to pause, but we should recall Rob's declaration that 'not only should we treat our friends well, but also remind them of their obligations when they appear to overstep the boundaries of what is acceptable'.[90] We need to consider what kind of friends we want to be, and indeed to whom.

[87] ICC, 'Statement by Prosecutor Karim A.A. Khan KC on the Issuance of Arrest Warrants in the Situation in Ukraine' (2024), www.icc-cpi.int/news/statement-prosecutor-karim-aa-khan-kc-issuance-arrest-warrants-situation-ukraine.

[88] See Bartels, ch 3 in this volume.

[89] See Aristotle, *The Nicomachean Ethics of Aristotle,* FH Peters (translated) (1891, Kegan Paul, Trench, Trubner & Co. Ltd: London) 280 et seq. https://dbooks.bodleian.ox.ac.uk/books/PDFs/590030593.pdf, 137, 9.

[90] Cryer (n 1) 83.

18

Cryer, et seq The Collegial Character of Legal Scholarship

JAMES LEE*

INTRODUCTION

THIS CHAPTER ENGAGES with contemporary debates over the state of legal scholarship, as a way of reflecting upon Rob Cryer's key contributions to the legal academy.

I was lucky to work with Rob for six years, having been appointed as a lecturer at the University of Birmingham in 2008. He took an active interest in the integration and development of junior colleagues. I first met him at my interview and I recall him smiling benignly throughout, pausing only to ask a couple of searching questions about my research plans. He was a tremendous influence on me, as a friend and an individual colleague, but also in terms of what it means to be collegial.

Rob was always very, and rightly, proud of the textbook which he co-authored, *An Introduction to International Criminal Law and Procedure*.[1] For him, it was vital that leading scholars made a meaningful difference to shaping the discipline and pedagogy through textbooks, alongside articles and monographs.

* Much of the research for this chapter was undertaken while I was on sabbatical: I warmly acknowledge the support of the Lee Kong Chian Visiting Professorship at Singapore Management University; a Visiting Fellowship at All Souls College, Oxford; and the Beaufort Visiting Fellowship at Lady Margaret Hall, Oxford. I benefited from discussions with Martin George, who collaborated with me on the original conference presentation on which this chapter is based. I also thank Simon Lee, Jill Martin, Jamie Glister, all the participants at the Legacy conference and the editors, though any errors are mine alone. Most importantly, I am so very grateful to Rob.

[1] R Cryer, D Robinson and S Vasiliev, *An Introduction to International Criminal Law and Procedure*, 4th edn (Cambridge University Press, 2019), considered in section II below.

Drawing upon Rob's exemplary contributions, I shall examine the role of the textbook and doctrinal traditions,[2] including some personal reflections on their modern character. This theme also connects with wider discourse around different kinds of writing in legal academia,[3] and what Lord Burrows, once a leading law professor and now Justice of the United Kingdom Supreme Court, has described as 'practical legal scholarship'.[4] His Lordship has gained recent support for the utility of such work from Baroness Carr, the Lady Chief Justice of England and Wales.[5]

I have particularly valued two aspects of preparing to write this chapter: first, remembering so many conversations with Rob over the years; and, second, reading many of Rob's publications – especially his textbook and his book reviews in leading journals. His wit, generosity and insight permeate all his writing. Rob *loved* his subjects: he had a fierce enthusiasm for the imperativeness of international justice, but never to the exclusion of others' views or interests. A particularly striking quality was his enthusiastic willingness to discuss scholarship with academics of all traditions and legal subjects, providing mentorship with humour, insight and humility. I am therefore especially pleased, as a private lawyer, to contribute alongside eminent international law colleagues to this

[2] On the textbook tradition, see D Sugarman, 'Legal Theory, the Common Law Mind and the Making of the Textbook Tradition' in W Twining (ed), *Legal Theory and the Common Law* (Basil Blackwell, 1986); F Cownie, 'Are We Witnessing the Death of the Textbook Tradition in the UK?' (2006) 3 *European Journal of Legal Education* 79.

[3] B McDowell, 'The Audiences for Legal Scholarship' (1990) 40 *Journal of Legal Education* 261; F Cownie, *Legal Academics: Culture and Identities* (Hart Publishing, 2004); A Bradney, 'Law as a Parasitic Discipline' (1998) 25 *Journal of Law and Society* 71; S Bartie, 'The Lingering Core of Legal Scholarship' (2010) 30 *Legal Studies* 345; JM Smits, *The Mind and Method of the Legal Academic* (Edward Elgar, 2012); J Hojnik, 'What Shall I Compare Thee to? Legal Journals, Impact, Citation and Peer Rankings' (2021) 41 *Legal Studies* 252; W Lucy, 'Law School 2061' (2022) 85 *MLR* 539; S Manley, 'Chilling and Warming Effects on the Production of Legal Scholarship' (2023) 86 *MLR* 1077; J Conaghan, 'Legal Research and the Public Good: The Current Landscape' (2023) 43 *Legal Studies* 569.

[4] L Burrows, 'Professor Sir Guenter Treitel (1928-2019)' in J Goudkamp and D Nolan (eds), *Scholars of Contract Law* (Hart Publishing, 2022); L Burrows, 'Judges and Academics, and the Endless Road to Unattainable Perfection' (2022) 55 *Israel Law Review* 50. In the context of tort, Professor Stapleton has similarly championed 'reflexive tort scholarship': J Stapleton, *Three Essays on Torts* (Oxford University Press, 2021). Lady Arden has described such work as 'beneficial': *Prickly Bay Waterside Ltd v British American Insurance Company Ltd (Grenada)* [2022] UKPC 8, [2022] 1 WLR 2087, 33. See also M Dixon, 'Real Property, Licences and the Slippery Idea of Possession' (2023) 139 *Law Quarterly Review* 552, 553–54, 560–61. *cf* G Samuel, 'What is the Role of a Legal Academic? A Response to Lord Burrows' (2022) 3 *Amicus Curiae* 305. For a more theoretical perspective on doctrinal scholarship, see N Simmonds, 'Protestant Jurisprudence and Modern Doctrinal Scholarship' (2001) 60 *Cambridge Law Journal* 271.

[5] LJ Carr, '"Delicate Plants", "Loose Cannons", or "a Marriage of True Minds"? The Role of Academic Literature in Judicial Decision-Making' (2023) 23 *Oxford University Commonwealth Law Journal* 1, 11: 'Without traditional scholarship, it is more difficult for judges to understand the law and apply it to a particular case'; and 16: 'Academic scholarship is vital – helping us to reach law that is conceptually, morally, and legally sound'; and N Underhill, 'Book Review: *Three Essays on Torts* by Jane Stapleton' (2022) 138 *LQR* 154, 154: 'Academics who take this approach have the chance to make a fundamental impact on the way that the law develops.'

collection in memory of Rob. This intellectual collegiality, I argue, is what we should look for in scholarship and in the academy.

TEXTBOOK TRADITION(S)

My title, 'Cryer, et seq', is inspired by a fond memory of Rob that illustrates his collegiality and commitment to collaboration. In 2007, Cambridge University Press published *An Introduction to International Criminal Law and Procedure*,[6] written by Robert Cryer, Håkan Friman, Darryl Robinson and Elizabeth Wilmshurst. It was conceived by the authors as 'a manageable and useful introduction to the field'.[7] Described by Heller as a 'seminal textbook',[8] its fourth edition was published in 2019,[9] with Sergey Vasiliev having joined the team. The first edition of the book was reviewed by Roger O'Keefe in the *International and Comparative Law Quarterly*,[10] who hailed it as:

> [T]he best general text on international criminal law so far. It has the great merit of combining inclusiveness of coverage, a detailed but discerningly exhibited knowledge of those areas it chooses to tackle and, for by far and away the most part, reliability with a pithy and accessible writing style and presentation.[11]

Rob came first alphabetically by surname, but he always emphasised that it was a team effort. His insistence extended to taking on journal house styles. Sometimes, for references to multi-author publications in the footnotes, house style may require that it is only the first author who should be named, with the rest covered by 'et al', short for 'et alii', which is Latin for 'and others'. If he ever found that his co-authors had been 'othered' during the copy-editing or typesetting stage, Rob would always change it back. He was keen on ensuring this equal recognition generally, but also conscious that if 'et al' appeared in one of his own pieces, it would look self-aggrandising in a way that Rob was definitely not. 'Et al'-ing is a practice that saves words, and perhaps reflects scientific conventions where the first named author is the lead author, both on the page and on the project. But it risks diminishing the contributions of each individual and Rob did not think that was right. And if Rob did not think something was the right thing to do, he would not do it.

Since Rob did not like the use of 'et al', here I use 'et seq', which can be short for either 'et sequentia' or 'et sequentes' – either 'and what follows' or 'and

[6] R Cryer, H Friman, D Robinson and E Wilmshurst, *An Introduction to International Criminal Law and Procedure* (Cambridge University Press, 2007).

[7] ibid xi.

[8] KJ Heller, 'Vale, Rob Cryer' (2021) *OpinioJuris*, available at: www.opiniojuris.org/2021/01/04/vale-rob-cryer.

[9] Cryer, Robinson and Vasiliev (n 1).

[10] (2009) 58 *ICLQ* 485.

[11] ibid 485.

those who follow'. I do so because I still think of myself as following in Rob's footsteps, both in this chapter and in my career.

With Jamie Glister, I now write *Hanbury and Martin's Modern Equity*, first published in 1935 and now in its 23rd edition.[12] When we were first asked to take on joint responsibility for the book, the invitation was humbling and daunting, given the standing of the book and our celebrated predecessors Harold Hanbury, Ronald Maudsley and Jill Martin. It was also momentous because I myself had used the 16th edition of the work as an undergraduate student learning the subject of equity and trusts in the first place. I consulted Rob, who said 'First of all, you should definitely do it', and then took me for a pint and offered sage advice from his own experience on why it would be worth it.

In 1929, Hanbury published an article in the *Law Quarterly Review*, entitled 'The Field of Modern Equity',[13] arguing for the potential value of the book that would become *Modern Equity*. For Hanbury, the 'Modern' in 'Modern Equity' was to offer a thorough, fresh analysis of the state of English equity after the significant reforms in conveyancing, property and trusts in the then-recent legislation of 1925.[14] His approach would be grounded in history but not beholden to it.[15] Hanbury anticipated that practitioners might instead prefer incremental updates, but he made the case for a book based 'on the principles of our imaginary alternative school of thought'.[16] Writing such a book was central to his vision of what the academic can contribute to the development of the law. Rather than the practitioner, who must focus on one case at a time, Hanbury claimed that:

> [I]t is for the jurist, in the seclusion of his own study, to enter the case in his commonplace book and use it as a link in the long chain of cases that go to make up the great scheme which it is his life's work to elaborate, thinking about it, writing about it, treating it in all its bearings.[17]

Having taken Rob's advice, I agreed to take on the book with Jamie Glister. In the decade since, and across four editions, it has been a privilege to elaborate, think and write, as Hanbury said, and as Rob predicted. In working on a textbook, one gets to know a subject, and the evolution of the law, so much more deeply than one might otherwise think possible. It has taught me discipline, in reading widely and then trying to synthesise the material into a great scheme, which is for the benefit, one hopes, of fellow teachers of law, students, practitioners, judges and law reformers. Taking on an existing title also means that we are endeavouring to curate the legacy of the book, which is intended to

[12] Sweet & Maxwell, 2024. For the legacy of the book, see A Phang, 'Equitable Fraud: Some Personal Reminiscences and Reflections' (2019) 13 *Journal of Equity* 114, 115.

[13] H Hanbury, 'The Field of Modern Equity' (1929) 45 *LQR* 196.

[14] Chiefly, the Law of Property Act 1925, the Land Registration Act 1925 and the Trustee Act 1925.

[15] ibid 201–02.

[16] ibid 202.

[17] ibid 203; see also L Goff, 'Judge, Jurist and Legislature' (1987) 2 *Denning Law Journal* 79.

be 'authoritative'. In our case, by 'authoritative', we mean to present what the current state of law is generally thought to be, and to address ongoing controversies, but then always make clear when we are offering our own view.

Importantly, in supporting the idea that textbooks can continue to make a contribution, I am not claiming that textbooks need be conservative in approach.[18] On the contrary, as Leyland and Woods have argued, 'it would be making a serious mistake to suggest that there is an unbridgeable chasm between the black letter textbook tradition and more recent attempts to set the law in context'.[19] The Law in Context series, for example, has situated the law in a wider perspective.[20] And the market is able to welcome books offering critical perspectives, which can enhance student understanding.[21] In the case of *Modern Equity*, over the course of our four editions, we have deliberately included greater reference to literature adopting different perspectives, as well as further and fuller coverage of relevant authority from other common law jurisdictions.

SCHOLARSHIP AND RESEARCH

A theme of Rob's own scholarly project was the blending of perspectives and traditions: his publications included book reviews, case comments, responses to recent developments, foundational theory, critique, doctrinal work, historical studies and the joint textbook. Rob wrote in *An Introduction to International Criminal Law and Procedure* that 'law, legal theory and practice exist in synergistic fashion in modern international criminal law'.[22] He considered the difficult work in producing a critical, normative survey of an area of law as being just as valuable as other forms of academic writing.[23] He would always emphasise the 'and' in his chair title – he was an international criminal lawyer who insisted on being 'Professor of International AND Criminal Law'.[24]

I thus turn to discuss ongoing debates about the types of legal scholarship which are promoted in the contemporary academy. My main claim is that the

[18] For analysis, see, eg, M Doupe and M Salter, 'Concealing the Past? Questioning Textbook Interpretations of the History of Equity and Trusts' (2000) 22 *Liverpool Law Review* 253; J Hackney, 'The Politics of the Chancery' (1981) 34 *Current Legal Problems* 113; S Anderson, 'Land Law Texts and the Explanation of 1925' (1984) 37 *Current Legal Problems* 63; M Thompson, 'The Textbook Approach to Modern Land Law' (1989) *Conveyancer and Property Lawyer* 268.

[19] P Leyland and T Woods, 'From Homogeneity to Pluralism: The Textbook Tradition Revisited' (1999) 33 *The Law Teacher* 18, 29.

[20] For the history of pioneering series, see, eg, W Twining, *Law in Context: Enlarging a Discipline* (Clarendon Press, 1997); W Twining, *Jurist in Context: A Memoir* (Cambridge University Press, 2019).

[21] See, eg, K Horsey (ed), *Diverse Voices in Tort Law* (Bristol University Press, 2024); D Cowan, L Fox, O'Mahony and N Cobb, *Great Debates in Land Law*, 3rd edn (Hart Publishing, 2023).

[22] Cryer, Robinson and Vasiliev (n 1) 26: 'Therefore, theoretical approaches ought to be seen as part and parcel of international criminal law rather than a distraction from its study.'

[23] R Cryer, 'Review of International Criminal Evidence' (2003) 7 *International Journal of Evidence and Proof* 216, 219.

[24] On the importance of this distinction to Rob, see also Hunt, ch 4 in this volume.

problem is not with particular methodologies or perspectives, but of narrowness and dismissiveness in terms of how other approaches can be treated. We should instead be optimistic and open-minded in the production of legal scholarship: an approach of intellectual collegiality.

A focus of recent debate has been on the role of doctrinal or 'practical legal scholarship' and how it compares – or is thought to compare – with more theoretical, critical or interdisciplinary approaches.[25] Doctrinal analysis comes in several forms: it may comprise close analysis of case law to reveal the current picture, and/or an element of normative argument about how the law should respond or develop in response to particular solutions.[26] Yet it is the sort of scholarship that can appear to be institutionally de-prioritised in law schools, whether in reality or at least in perception, in the eras of the Research Assessment Exercise (RAE) or the Research Excellence Framework (REF), for not being sufficiently original, rigorous or significant.

In discussing this problem of perception and the kind of work that emerging scholars in particular are incentivised to pursue, John Gardner once asked:

> Why should the great works of the best legal commentators, such as Smith and Hogan or Treitel, now be sidelined as 'student textbooks'? This is not law schools becoming more intellectual. It is law schools becoming less intellectual, as often first-rate academic law is marginalized in favour of often second-rate interdisciplinarity.[27]

In the 2021 Lionel Cohen Lecture, Lord Burrows picked up this theme, worrying that the UK legal academy risked 'giving the impression that what goes on in the courts, as a matter of legal reasoning and argument, is rather too dull and straightforward for high academic minds',[28] which he considered were more interested in 'deep theory'. His Lordship pointed to the critical role that academic writing plays in assisting judges and the development of the law, and made the case for doctrinal scholarship:

> [I]n my view, the pursuit of theory should not be at the expense of traditional doctrinal scholarship which can assist the law in action in its most direct form in the courts. The courts want the academic analysis of the law in language and at a level which they can understand and use in their judgments. They want legal reasoning – designed to produce practical justice – and not reasoning from another discipline.[29]

[25] I focus here on written work, but similar themes of course also appear in our approaches to legal education, at a time of disruption and diversification in the UK university sector.

[26] C McCrudden, 'Legal Research and the Social Sciences' (2006) 122 *LQR* 632, 634.

[27] J Gardner, 'Putting Legal Philosophy in its Place' (2012) *Rivista di filosofia del diritto* 253, available at: www.johngardnerathome.info/pdfs/whatisphilosophyoflaw.pdf. References are to pages in the open access version: p 11. See also the analysis of another colleague of Rob's, Alan Bogg: A Bogg, 'Doctrinal Method in Labour Law: Potential, Problems, Prospects' in A Blackham and S Cooney (eds), *Research Methods in Labour Law: A Handbook* (Cheltenham, Edward Elgar, 2023).

[28] Burrows, 'Judges and Academics, and the Endless Road' (n 4) 56.

[29] ibid 55. See also Goff (n 17) 92. With Gareth Jones, Robert Goff first wrote *The Law of Restitution* (London, Sweet & Maxwell) in 1966, and it continues today in its 10th edition (as

His Lordship noted that it is also for judges to play their part in maintaining the standing of practical legal scholarship by expressly citing such work: 'the trade-off for the help given by practical legal scholars is the judicial public acknowledgement of that help'.[30]

In his own judgments, Lord Burrows has himself regularly given credit where academic work has influenced his thinking.[31] In a recent concurring judgment, his Lordship emphasised the symbiotic relationship of judges, practitioners and academics in the evolution of the common law:

> The epithet 'judge-made' is a bit of a misnomer. In reality these step by step developments in the common law are the result, not merely of judicial decision, but also of academic analysis, coupled with the imaginativeness and wisdom of counsel's submissions.[32]

AV Dicey, who wrote textbooks on both constitutional law and private international law,[33] once observed that 'wherever Courts have power to form the law, there writers of textbooks will also have influence'.[34]

It can be contested whether the primary audience of legal scholarship should be judges, or the primary motive that of assisting the courts.[35] And practical utility, influence or 'impact' are not the only measures of the success of research. However, if as legal scholars we are interested in the law and making a difference with our work, we may think that it is worthwhile framing at least some contributions in a way that can contribute to or effect the relevant change.

Insofar as 'doctrinal' is sometimes interpreted as a judgemental epithet, it is likely thought to stand as a shorthand for dull, descriptive work that is merely narrating recent events.[36] Narrow work lacking rigour is not to be commended if it is the full extent of one's writing. Much legal scholarship is inherently 'reactive and involved'[37] – being responsive to recent developments – but practical

C Mitchell, P Mitchell and S Watterson, *Goff & Jones on Unjust Enrichment* (London, Sweet & Maxwell, 2022)).

[30] Burrows, 'Judges and Academics, and the Endless Road' (n 4) 57. On citation practices, see K Stanton, 'Use of Scholarship by the House of Lords in Tort Cases' in J Lee (ed), *From House of Lords to Supreme Court: Judges, Jurists and the Process of Judging* (Hart Publishing, 2011).

[31] See, eg, *Trustees of the Barry Congregation of Jehovah's Witnesses v BXB* [2023] UKSC 15, [2023] 2 WLR 953, para 7; *Byers v Saudi National Bank* [2023] UKSC 51, [2024] 2 WLR 237, paras 103–04; and *Paul v Royal Wolverhampton NHS Trust* [2024] UKSC 1, [2024] 2 WLR 417, 245 (dissenting).

[32] *Armstead v Royal & Sun Alliance Insurance Co Ltd* [2024] UKSC 6, [2024] 2 WLR 632, para 78.

[33] On Dicey's continuing influence in this respect, see BC Jones, 'The Rule of Law in UK Public Law Textbooks: From Critique to Acceptance?' [2018] *Public Law* 594; A Dickinson, T Endicott and W Ernst (eds), *Albert Venn Dicey: A Centennial Commemoration* (Intersentia, 2024).

[34] AV Dicey, 'Droit Administratif in Modern French Law' (1901) 17 *LQR* 302, 312.

[35] Samuel (n 4) 307 ff.

[36] For a riposte to such a critique, see DW Vick, 'Interdisciplinarity and the Discipline of Law' (2004) 31 *Journal of Law and Society* 163; MM Siems and D Mac Sithigh, 'Mapping Legal Research' (2012) 71 *Cambridge Law Journal* 651.

[37] EL Rubin, 'Law and and [sic] the Methodology of Law' (1997) *Wisconsin Law Review* 521, 550.

legal scholarship need not be unimaginative. High-quality doctrinal research can be interesting, exciting and important.

Furthermore, as Conaghan has noted,[38] 'practical legal scholarship' can include things that may not fall within the REF's idea of research, but can still occupy a valuable place in the academy – such as case comments, writing for practitioner-focused journals or books and, indeed, some textbooks. Such work can provide a valuable service for fellow academics, students and those in practice.

Also, it may be said that doctrinal scholars must themselves recognise that a close-minded, unduly defensive approach towards other kinds of legal scholarship, as may have been the case when insurgent new methodologies were first developing, is not helpful either. But even the more strident critics of the classic textbook/doctrinal traditions in legal scholarship have emphasised that it is narrowness, rigidity of thought and lack of imagination that have been their main targets. To that end, William Twining, pioneer of 'Law in Context' as an approach, has argued that there is a need for assumptions and orthodoxies to be interrogated, but not for the tradition to be entirely dismissed.[39] For Twining, 'rules and doctrine are a central part of understanding law; that doctrine and context are complementary; rather, one of my main concerns has been to build bridges between two traditions that have strayed apart'.[40] We should build, maintain and repaint those bridges, recognising the contribution that dialogue can make.

Joanne Conaghan, the Chair of the Law Sub-Panel for the last REF exercise, has thoughtfully reflected upon the influence of the REF and has disavowed the idea that doctrinal scholarship is not valued; rather, 'doctrinal scholarship is a necessary, indeed fundamental, part of the legal academic portfolio'.[41] She stirringly argues that we should 'critique legal research on its own merits and in accordance with the norms and standards of research peers. Do not invest labels with the power to silence or diminish particular types of legal scholarship, without regard to the quality or significance of their contribution'.[42] I agree.

To advocate for a pluralistic tolerance of different perspectives can at first sight appear underwhelming. It might be taken as one of three inadequate positions, which I must mention since I am endorsing none of them: first, a both-side-ism that recognises strong views and fails or refuses to commit to one; second, a nihilism that there are no ultimately right answers, so no one is right;

[38] Conaghan (n 3).

[39] See generally W Twining, 'Reflections on Law in Context' in W Twining, *Law in Context: Enlarging a Discipline* (Clarendon Press, 1997); W Twining, 'Jurisprudence, Law in Context, Realism and Doctrine' in W Twining, *Jurist in Context: A Memoir* (Cambridge University Press, 2019); D Sugarman, 'William Twining: The Man Who Radicalised the Middle Ground' (2020) 16 *International Journal of Law in Context* 475.

[40] Twining, 'Jurisprudence' (n 39) 169.

[41] Conaghan (n 3) 573.

[42] ibid 581.

and, third, a mental rope-a-dope, or whataboutery, where one's own position is un-pin-down-able.

None of these would be a satisfactory starting point (or conclusion) for academic discourse, as they do not facilitate meaningful academic debate. We should avoid entrenched views, which can lead to disagreement becoming self-perpetuating. Rather, good argument depends upon recognising (rather than hiding or dismissing) the strengths of the other side, and then developing one's own account. This was one of the qualities in Rob, and in his work, that I so admired. In the opening chapter of his textbook, Rob cautioned that 'selection of scholars from only one, or a limited set of, legal tradition(s) can lead to a skewed view, which is incompatible with what an inclusive approach to international criminal law requires'.[43] That chapter, and the book as whole, surveys, and is informed by, a range of literature and methods. Exposure to such different perspectives enhances one's own work and the reader's experience. Intellectual collegiality does not, of course, mean agreeing with everything a colleague says, or giving up one's principles; it asks only that we engage seriously and generously with other perspectives.[44]

As I mentioned in the introduction, a significant feature of Rob's influence as a colleague was his desire to engage colleagues from across the school, and indeed the wider academy, in discussions around their research. Whatever one's methodology, tradition or subject area, Rob was always willing to chat. He would offer not only advice but also rigorous debate around one's aims and the point one was trying to make. I would emerge from such conversations with arguments refined and horizons broadened, and, as a result, the quality of my work improved. Rob was particularly valuable in advising on journal publishing – of course, he had a distinguished record of publications himself, and he was finely attuned to the question of audience for each piece. He thought carefully about who his interlocutors were for a specific argument and article, and chose his target journal, generalist or specialist, accordingly.

An editorial for the *Journal of Conflict and Security Law*, drafted by Rob but published after his death, spoke of the value of diversity, which extended to:

> [T]he Journal's approach to theoretical traditions (whether explicit, subtextual or sublimated). We seek open, non-aggressive scholarly debate. We do not encourage polemics, but reasoned discussions. Our broad approach though has been to be ecumenical, we would not refuse to publish a piece because we disagree with it, individually or collectively as editors, as long as it is thoughtful, and an original contribution to debate.[45]

[43] Cryer, Robinson and Vasiliev (n 1) 12.

[44] P Birks, 'Rights, Wrongs and Remedies' (2000) 20 *OJLS* 1, 37: 'University life has many blessings, never to be taken for granted. Of them, one of the greatest, perhaps the greatest, is that in a university disagreement, even serious disagreement about things which really matter, is never taken to be incompatible with admiration and affection. Many things are changing, but not that.'

[45] 'Editorial' (2021) 26 *Journal of Conflict and Security Law* 1, 5.

It is this appreciation of the 'ecumenism' of the universe of rigorous legal research, what Conaghan has called its 'catholicity'[46] and what I have termed intellectual collegiality, that I have celebrated here.

COLLEGIALITY

I said earlier that I learnt many things from Rob, including more about the ways in which one could be, and in which he was, collegial. Alongside his frequent co-authorship of academic articles (as well as, of course, the textbook), Rob's contributions in this respect could be seen in the intense interest he took in the emergence of new scholars. He offered valuable support to doctoral students: in developing their research or collaborating with them, as well as when it came to teaching. He would often advise his supervisees in international criminal law to develop an interest in teaching core private law subjects. This point was not just a tactical one, for their individual future employability; it was part of Rob's commitment to the value of good doctrinal scholarship and how it can complement and influence one's other work. He would also see it as part of his commitment to the importance of contributing to the law school in the round.

Rob also strongly believed in paying forward the generosity which he himself had received earlier in his career from those who had influenced him. In a memorial note, Rob paid tribute to his 'truly supportive mentor', the late Professor Peter Rowe, whom he described as 'a lodestar, as a scholar and a person'.[47] The value of leading scholars leading was never lost on Rob: whether he was serving as Acting Head of Birmingham Law School or journal editing. Rob would make an effort to accept invitations to speak at conferences where he thought his presence would assist the organisers with the success of their programme. Those of us contributing to this collection would be able to fill several volumes with individual instances of Rob himself making a difference and being inspirational.

CODA: FINAL THOUGHTS

This chapter has aimed to be a tribute to a scholar and to scholarship. When I speak and think of Rob as a 'scholar', I mean it in the widest sense, for he was a scholar in his own special, idiosyncratic way – he had a twinkling, almost impish kind of intelligence, underpinned by rare depth and breadth of knowledge and interest. He had a prodigious memory and ability to recall fine details from his encyclopaedic reading of books in his legendary personal library. He

[46] Conaghan (n 3) 581; see also BR Cheffins, 'Using Theory to Study Law: A Company Law Perspective' (1999) 58 *Cambridge Law Journal* 197.

[47] R Cryer, 'In Memoriam: Professor Peter J. Rowe (1947–2018)' (2018) 23 *Journal of Conflict and Security Law* 167, 169.

made all-round contributions to his discipline of the kind that I have argued is to be commended in modern scholarship. For scholarship is not just the list of research outputs or the number of degrees one has; it is a state of being and a way of acting.

As a scholar, Rob wore his learning lightly, which was no mean feat, since it was learning made from heavy metal. Conversations with him would be littered with gleeful references to international legal scholars or musical heroes I had never heard of, but I could always tell they were directly in tune with the topic and smiled accordingly. Sometimes he combined his love of music and law books. One of Rob's first-ever publications was a book review in the journal he would go on to edit. With scholarly precision, he commended the relevant book's strengths and critiqued what he saw as limitations. He concluded that:

> [I]t may be thought that the criticisms raised herein either stem from, or evidence a dislike for this book. This would not be correct, this book is amongst the best currently available and certainly merits inclusion in any library, the criticisms noted are no more than scratches on a much enjoyed album. The authors are to be congratulated for a serious analysis of the law and practice of international criminal law.[48]

This distinctive style of respectful yet insightful critique was typical of Rob's own work: revealing an intellectual collegiality that characterises the best of legal scholarship more broadly. Where Rob led, many others now follow.

[48] R Cryer, 'Book Review: SR Ratner and JS Abrams, *Accountability for Human Rights Atrocities in International Law: Beyond the Nuremberg Legacy*' (1998) 3 *Journal of Conflict and Security Law* 288, 291.

19

Rob and Bert in Tokyo

SERGEY VASILIEV*

PROLOGUE

IT HAPPENED SO that I never got to visit Rob in Birmingham, where he taught for over 14 years. Although he and I talked about it a few times, academic life decided otherwise. Regular events in The Hague or in Amsterdam, the more self-evident places of encounter, provided enough occasions for us to catch up. I felt that it was particularly fitting then – compulsory even – for me to pay my first, albeit belated, visit to Birmingham for a memorial conference organised by his university colleagues and friends in June 2023. A debt to Rob, it was equally a debt I owed to myself. I relished the chance to spend a couple of days in the same space with Rob's family, close colleagues and common friends in international law and in life beyond the law, as well as people whom I only knew by name or not at all, who loved, appreciated and were close to him. Celebrating Rob's life, intellectual legacy and contributions to international law scholarship, but, even more importantly, also reminiscing about the person that he was could help bring some sense of closure – or so I was hoping.

The conference was akin to a *séance* of group therapy. Each of us carried splinters of knowledge, recollections and anecdotes about Rob. They could now be pieced together to answer questions and fill the voids left by his premature passing.[1] It was a uniquely organic, beautifully eclectic, sincerely sentimental and at times emotionally raw gathering that provided the necessary space for ruminations, tears and laughter, chatter and silences, and more. Rob was ever-present, looking on and smiling faintly from a black-and-white photo on the screen.

The conference panel entitled 'Rob in Tokyo' put into the spotlight Rob and Neil Boister's highly influential and deservedly celebrated oeuvre on the

* The author is grateful to the organisers and participants of the conference 'Rob Cryer: A Life in Law and a Law unto Himself' (Birmingham, 29–30 June 2023), where the remarks on which this chapter is based were delivered. He also thanks Emma Breeze, Mark Drumbl, Gerry Simpson and Marianne Wade for their gentle and inspired, yet firm, stewardship of this project.

[1] N Boister et al, 'In Memoriam' (2021) 19 *Journal of International Criminal Justice* 235; N White and E Myjer, 'In Memory of Professor Rob Cryer' (2021) 26(1) *Journal of Conflict & Security Law* 1; G Simpson, 'Robert Cryer' (2023) *British Yearbook of International Law* 6.

International Military Tribunal for the Far East (IMFTE) or Tokyo IMT, their preferred nomenclature.[2] The legal analysis of the functioning and contributions of the Tokyo IMT, unsurpassed in its quality and depth, is one of the many areas of international (criminal) law where Rob left an indelible mark. For this chapter, I chose to revisit his solo piece on Bernard (Bert) Röling which appeared in the *Journal of International Criminal Justice* back in 2010.[3] The idea behind this re-read is to reconnect and get reacquainted with Rob-the-person by gaining an insight into the character of the writer behind the text. In the article, which built on research Rob had done for his and Boister's 2008 monograph, Rob assessed Röling's legacy and contributions to the Tokyo judgment by the 'member for the Netherlands', as he signed his separate opinion. However, Rob also used these texts to infer what kind of person Röling-the-judge was and what values informed his positions and interactions with colleagues on the Tokyo bench. I will try and do the same for Rob. Extrapolating his personality traits from one short article, I admit, is not a foolproof enterprise, and I do not intend it to be so. There is already a considerable body of registered oral histories of Rob. With this chapter, I merely hope to add a few strokes to his portrait, both intellectual and personal.

READING ROB READING BERT

Rob Cryer's 'Röling in Tokyo: A Dignified Dissenter' appeared in the *Journal of International Criminal Justice* symposium dedicated to the Dutch member of the Tokyo IMT, Judge Bert VA Röling (1906–85), alongside four other contributions.[4] With all his critical disposition, Rob had a sympathetic view of Röling and assessed his judicial service in Tokyo in distinctly positive terms. Rob appreciated Bert's judicial acumen and had intellectual affinity with him more than with any of the other Tribunal members. In a sense, both were interdisciplinarians who were modest about their credentials as such. Rob was both an international *and* a criminal lawyer, and he was widely read beyond the law; Röling was not an international lawyer, but a criminologist who after the Tokyo

[2] N Boister and R Cryer, *The Tokyo International Military Tribunal: A Reappraisal* (Oxford University Press, 2008); N Boister and R Cryer (eds), *Documents on the Tokyo International Military Tribunal, Charter, Indictment, and Judgments* (Oxford University Press, 2008).

[3] R Cryer, 'Röling in Tokyo: A Dignified Dissenter' (2010) 8(4) *Journal of International Criminal Justice* 1109. A modified version of this article was published as 'Justice Röling (The Netherlands)' in Y Tanaka, T McCormack and G Simpson (eds), *Beyond Victor's Justice? The Tokyo War Crimes Trial Revisited* (Brill, 2011) 109–26.

[4] Three were authored by Dutch international (and/or) criminal law academics Nico Schrijver, Constantijn Kelk, and Harmen van der Wilt, and one by Antonio Cassese, who had written previously about Röling and famously published book-length personal interviews with him: A Cassese, 'Röling, Bernardus' in A Cassese et al (eds), *The Oxford Companion to International Criminal Justice* (Oxford University Press, 2009) 491–92; BVA Röling and A Cassese (eds), *The Tokyo Trial and Beyond: Reflections of a Peacemonger* (Polity Press, 1993).

trial went on to write academically on international law and polemology. There are countless indications scattered throughout Rob's text that, much like for Cassese (whom Rob also admired),[5] namely Röling was Rob's 'favourite' judge in Tokyo.[6] Röling, he wrote, 'sought to … craft a judgment that would prove to be of lasting value to both the West and to much of Japan'.[7]

Rob was generous yet razor-sharp as always, and by no means hagiographic in his evaluations. As in all of his work, Rob leaves no stone unturned. To measure Röling's influence on the Tokyo judgment as scrupulously as possible, Rob delved into the Tokyo IMT and Röling's personal archives. Rob understood these materials like no one else did. In the article, he zeroes in and parses Röling's judicial pronouncements on the Tokyo IMT's jurisdiction, on crimes against peace, on the murder charges, on command responsibility and on facts adduced to sustain the charges of conspiracy. To use Rob's own words about Röling, every remark is 'thought through to its conclusion'. What aspects of Röling's legacy did Rob choose to foreground and which judicial and personal qualities did he value most? What can we learn about Rob while 'reading Rob reading Bert'? I will limit myself to highlighting three core traits or values that come to the fore and unmistakably mean a great deal to Rob-the-person.

FAIRNESS AND FAIRMINDEDNESS

What catches the eye from the first pages is the emphasis Rob places on Röling's fairness as an adjudicator and, relatedly, his fairmindedness in assessing the trial from an intellectual distance, despite his past personal and direct involvement. Rob vigorously defends Röling against the insinuations that he was too emotionally invested in and accordingly unable to disavow the Tokyo IMT despite its undeniable shortcomings, which ostensibly anguished him.[8] No, Rob argued, this reproach was not convincing: Bert proved more than willing and able to criticise the aspects of the trial he found underwhelming. He did so with poise and in a considered way, with 'the integrity he brought to all of his endeavours'.[9]

Fairmindedness threads through Rob's evaluation of Röling's judicial writing, which was distinguished, in Rob's view, by a genuine effort to 'transcend the parochial view' of the parties and of some of Bert's judicial brethren on both the law and the facts. In particular, he credited Bert with a fact-based rejection of the majority's self-serving and all-too-convenient narrative of the Japanese leaders' grand conspiracy against peace from 1928 onwards encompassing the

[5] R Cryer, 'International Criminal Tribunals and the Sources of International Law: Antonio Cassese's Contribution to the Canon' (2012) 10(5) *Journal of International Criminal Justice* 1045.

[6] For example, Cryer, 'Röling in Tokyo' (n 3) 1110–11, 1119, 1125.

[7] ibid 1111.

[8] ibid 1125, referring to U Kei, *Beyond the 'Judgment of Civilization'* (International House of Japan, 2003) 133.

[9] Cryer, 'Röling in Tokyo' (n 3) 1125, referring to Röling and Cassese (n 4).

commission of war crimes ('simplistic "wheel conspiracy"').[10] By contrast, Justice Pal saw no conspiracy at all, only the legitimate plan to free Asia from the Western yoke, with war crimes not attributable to the defendants, thus coming too close, for Rob's taste, to 'accepting uncritically the Defence submissions'.[11] Rob praised Röling's taking the *via media* in drawing up a more objective account of the relevant historical events as 'transcending the time in which he wrote', while taking due account of the prosecution and defence evidence, unlike the majority and Justice Pal.[12] There was a conspiracy, Judge Röling held, but only from 1940 onwards, and Hirota and Kido would have been acquitted if it had been up to him.

Rob was eager to highlight that, more than once and in spite of the peer pressure (from the majority), Judge Röling demonstrated fairness by choosing not to be unduly dismissive towards the 'underdog', the defence, whether in his memoranda to the colleagues or in his opinion. Thus, Röling attempted to convince the majority that intentional killings of military personnel, even if committed during an illegal or unjust war, were permissible under the law of armed conflict and did not amount to the crime against humanity of murder under Article 5(c) of the IMTFE Charter, as argued by the prosecution. Rob pointed out that shortly before the indictment had been received by the Tribunal, the Supreme Commander for the Allied Powers, General Douglas MacArthur, had removed the formula 'against the civilian population' from the definition specifically in order to accommodate the prosecution.[13] Röling insisted – to Rob's delight – on a strict interpretation of crimes against humanity in accordance with the generally applicable international law and the principle of legality. This was in line with his position that the Charter only conferred jurisdiction over the *existing* crimes as opposed to writing crimes into existence at a mere whim of the Supreme Commander. Yet, the majority regarded itself bound by the Charter's black-letter text as it had been handed down. Fortunately, the majority refrained from upholding charges for murder under crimes against humanity for the intentional killings, albeit for the wrong reason: it deemed the same to be covered sufficiently by the charges of crimes against peace, which Judge Röling also (rightly) rejected, evoking Rob's approving comment.[14]

Another example of fairmindedness which Rob flagged up was Judge Röling's rejection of 'cabinet liability', or civilian superior responsibility on steroids.[15] For the majority, membership in the government sufficed to establish responsibility for ill-treatment of prisoners of war or civilian internees if the

[10] Cryer, 'Röling in Tokyo' (n 3) 1122. See also R Cryer, 'Tokyo International Military Tribunal' in Cassese et al (n 4) 536 ('His approach to the facts was more nuanced than that of the majority').

[11] ibid.

[12] ibid 1122–23.

[13] ibid 1118, discussing 'Memorandum, Undated, to Members of the Tribunal from Member from Holland, *Some Points of Law*'.

[14] ibid 1119 ('It is difficult to deny the salience of almost all of what Röling said on point').

[15] ibid 1120–22.

person had knowledge of the practices and did not step down from the cabinet. Judge Röling deemed this too far-reaching and unjust because omission liability must not be imposed lightly. Convictions of cabinet members for the crimes, he argued, are justified only if there was (or should have been) knowledge of ill-treatment, there was a duty and power of those superiors to prevent or punish, and the person failed in that duty. On this issue, Rob sides with Bert's 'rather more sophisticated and nuanced view than the Majority, one which commended itself to history more favourably than others'.[16] He also cites Röling approvingly as having the 'upper hand' over the majority and endorsing as 'almost certainly correct' his standpoint that Hirota and Shigemitsu had been convicted inappropriately.[17]

Parenthetically, Röling's position on this issue may have primarily reflected Western European priorities of the moment and can be placed in the context of his own country's bloody campaign to suppress anti-colonial insurgency in Indonesia.[18] Elsewhere in this book, Judge Röling is mentioned as part of a fictitious exchange during a Nagasaki atomic bombing trial that never was ('But there's no way even he would have any stomach for looking into Dutch colonialism in Java. No way').[19] I would like to think that, of all people, Judge Röling did have the stomach for that.[20] I would have loved to hear from Rob whether he might agree. If Judge Röling had, on the contrary, been unable to vocally and unequivocally condemn the colonialist atrocities during the Netherlands' dark chapter at the time, it is certain at least that he firmly rejected the one-sided application of a lowered threshold of superior responsibility to the Japanese (but not anyone else).

HUMILITY AND COLLEGIALITY

Rob's appreciation of Judge Röling's genuine humility and collegiality clearly shows through in his analysis of the judge's input in the deliberations and his conduct while on the bench. Röling's attitude towards his colleagues and his own role at the tribunal contrasted sharply with those of his more notorious – (in)famous, as Rob wrote – members of the Tokyo IMT, such as Justice Pal,

[16] ibid 1120.

[17] ibid 1122.

[18] K Sellars, 'Revisiting Röling and Cassese's Appraisal of the Tokyo Tribunal' (2024) 35 *European Journal of International Law* 279, 287–88.

[19] See Drumbl and Mouthaan, ch 16 in this volume.

[20] Röling's assessment of European imperialism in Asia could be inferred from his 'Letter from the Member from the Netherlands to the President' dated 23 January 1947: 'Nor do I feel I can quote Grotius, Gentili and Vattel in the trial of Japanese aggression … I hesitate to approach the Far East in our effort to determine the criminality of aggression with quotations from idealists and philosophers of the very period when our heroes and soldiers were conquering its territories in what could hardly be called a defensive war.' Boister and Cryer (n 2) 292.

Prosecutor Joseph Keenan and, one might add, President William Webb.[21] Rob is adamant in reminding the Tokyo IMT's detractors that the 'dignified dissenter' Röling was as much a part of the IMT's history as those other figures.[22]

Bert Röling was one of the five IMTFE justices (out of nine in total) to write separately and one of three, alongside Judges Henri Bernard (France) and Radhabinod Pal (India), to pen a dissenting opinion.[23] He was not planning on doing it from the outset. He worked towards the unitary judgment in line with the Dutch tradition where judges do not write separately. But after Justice Pal announced early on that he would be issuing a dissenting opinion and the panel split, the judges who were unable to join the majority for various reasons chose to register their dissents too, lest their silence be interpreted as agreement with the majority's reasoning or conclusions. The decision to part ways with his colleagues did not come easy for Röling. His judicial rebellion was an act of professional bravery rather than fame-seeking. By making his individual voice heard, not only did he break the Dutch custom, as the opening paragraph of his dissent candidly acknowledges, but he also went against the express wishes of his government, which had attempted to suppress the dissent.[24] Moreover, Judge Röling knew that he would become a renegade to the majority for going along with Justice Pal and contributing to the public unravelling of judicial unanimity.

Cognisant of Judge Röling's dilemma, Rob commended the 'balanced and erudite' way in which he justified the unpopular step of parting ways with the majority.[25] Röling overcame his initial reluctance to issue a dissenting opinion primarily because he had been hoping that it could be relevant for General MacArthur's consideration of the requests for clemency, although the latter in all likelihood read neither the judgment nor the opinions.[26] For judicial economy considerations, Judge Röling did not voice all of his criticisms of the majority's views publicly. Some appeared only in internal memoranda he sent to other judges, including reasons for his unwillingness to punish intentional killings of

[21] Cryer, 'Röling in Tokyo' (n 3) 1110 fn 4 (noting Justice Pal's well-known excoriation of the majority and his belief in the innocence of all defendants, as well as Keenan's 'bombastic rhetorical style and personal and professional failings'); Röling and Cassese (n 4) 30 (Röling later characterised Presiding Judge William Webb as arrogant and dictatorial).

[22] Cryer, 'Röling in Tokyo' (n 3) 1110.

[23] Contesting the nature of his opinion as dissenting and attributing this misapprehension to the fact that the majority characterised the published part of it as such: Sellars (n 18) 287 (Röling's separate opinion was 'essentially in accord' with the majority judgment on the 'most politically sensitive substantive issues').

[24] Röling threatened to resign and the government fortunately backed down. Röling and Cassese (n 4) 61; Cryer, 'Röling in Tokyo' (n 3) 1125. See G Sluiter, 'Unity and Division in Decision Making: The Law and Practice on Individual Opinions at the ICTY' in B Swart et al (eds), *The Legacy of the International Criminal Tribunal for the Former Yugoslavia* (Oxford University Press, 2011) 195, referring to L van Poelgeest, *Nederland en het Tribunaal van Tokio: Volkenrechtelijke polemiek en internationale politiek rond de berechting en gratiëring van de Japanse oorlogsmisdadigers* (Gouda Quint BV, 1989) 82–95.

[25] Cryer, 'Röling in Tokyo' (n 3) 1110.

[26] ibid 1111 fn 11.

combatants as the crime against humanity of murder.[27] It was unclear whether those had any impact on the majority's analysis, and Rob deemed it unfortunate that the wrong ('at best, confused') legal position remained unchallenged by Bert-the-judge.[28] While remarking upon Judge Röling's 'great humility', Rob lamented that this trait had not permitted him to make public his detailed legal takedown of 'these rather dangerous charges' during his lifetime.[29] Rob held collegiality and humility, both personal and 'disciplinary', in high regard, and his academic work and service attest amply to his commitment to these values.[30] However, he also believed that humility, collegiality and courtesy should not stand in the way of the truth.[31] Dissensus on fundamental issues must not remain closeted, but must roam free: it enriches academic and judicial debate and sets the record straight.

INDEPENDENCE AND INTEGRITY

The third leitmotif in Rob's portrait of Judge Röling is the independence and integrity with which he exercised his functions at the Tokyo IMT. He was 'the judge who left Tokyo with his integrity and independence of mind most firmly intact'.[32] In relation to the well-known fact that the Dutch government exerted pressure on 'their' judge, Rob notes with relief and admiration, that he just 'ploughed his own furrow'.[33] His independence manifested itself in multiple episodes that Rob highlights.

On the contentious issue of the IMTFE jurisdiction, Rob credits Judge Röling with standing up to the majority.[34] The majority dismissed the defence's objection that war crime charges for the Lake Khassan (1938) and Khalkin-Gol (1939) episodes, which had been settled by separate agreements between Japan and the USSR, were outside of the Tokyo IMT's jurisdiction. By contrast, Judge Röling held that its jurisdiction was delimited by the Japanese Instrument of Surrender relating to the Asia-Pacific War and did not cover incidents from another war theatre. And yet, the majority convicted some defendants on those charges. Rob praised the dissenter's principled and consistent defence of his position and did not hold back about what he thought of the majority, which, 'showing national

[27] ibid 1117 fn 57.

[28] But not in his interview given to Cassese: Röling and Cassese (n 4) 56–57.

[29] Cryer, 'Röling in Tokyo' (n 3) 1119.

[30] Cryer and Boister (n 4) 2 ('with all due disciplinary humility, we must leave those questions to those more qualified to pronounce on them').

[31] R Cryer, 'International Law and the Illusion of Novelty: Georg Schwarzenberger and British International Law' in R McCorquodale and J-P Gauci (eds), *British Influences on International Law, 1915–2015* (Brill, 2016) 259 ('Matters of substance at least ought to trump questions of infelicity in expression').

[32] Cryer, 'Röling in Tokyo' (n 3) 1110.

[33] ibid 1125.

[34] ibid 1112.

loyalty rather than independence of spirit or mind, wrote [those USSR-driven charges] into their overall narrative of conspiracy'.[35]

On the legality in respect of the aggression charges, Rob was again keen to point out Röling's 'perhaps foremost of his disagreements' with the majority, which refused to submit the Tokyo Charter to a substantive legality check as far as crimes against peace were concerned.[36] For Justices Northcroft, Jaranilla, Patrick and Webb, the bench was bound by the Charter's text, which rendered the crimes against peace punishable. Accordingly, judges had to presume the validity of the Charter by virtue of their acceptance of the judicial appointment. However, Röling saw no paradox in their judicial competence to satisfy themselves that the imputed conduct was indeed criminal under the law applicable at the time. The Charter drafters were not allowed to create new crimes under international law, but only decided which of the existing crimes came within the IMTFE jurisdiction.

To Rob, Röling 'had a better argument'.[37] Judges were not bound by ultra vires enactments and had the responsibility to determine the applicable international law to which the Charter merely made reference. Unlike for the somewhat different challenges to the legality of the establishment of the Tokyo IMT as such, the need and duty of the judges to independently ascertain and apply the law as it stands did not run counter to their appointment to the bench; judges still operated within the boundaries of the Charter. Rob had sympathy for Röling's objection that he and his colleagues were a court, not a fact-finding body. Judges are not cogs or automatons in an administrative process, applying whatever is force-fed to them as the law.[38] As Rob points out with gusto, Röling's stance on misapplication of the ultra vires substantive criminal law was principled, brave and novel back in 1948.[39] Röling was a criminal justice scholar who was sensitive to legality concerns, and Rob – a public international lawyer as much as a criminal lawyer – fully shared that sensitivity.

The fundamental legality concern was visible in Judge Röling's 'unassailable' (per Rob) finding that the crimes against peace had no basis in the international law prior to and during the Second World War.[40] Aggression was a violation of international law, yet not a crime, and the Kellogg-Briand Pact (1928) was no criminal statute. Next comes the move in the reasoning on which Rob voices a rare criticism of Röling, manifesting an absolute – less typical for international as opposed to criminal lawyers – commitment to legality. Rob observes that, instead of joining Justice Pal in acquitting the defendants on the aggression charges, which would have been logical given his finding of the illegality

[35] ibid.
[36] ibid 1113–15.
[37] ibid 1114.
[38] ibid 1114.
[39] ibid 1113.
[40] ibid 1115.

of the charges, Röling paradoxically voted to convict along with the majority. Röling justified this view by the victorious powers' prerogative to 'prevent the recurrence of gravely offensive conduct' and 'to seek and retain the custody of the pertinent persons'. Röling's invocation of 'Napoleon's elimination' as the relevant precedent even earned him a caustic remark from Justice Pal.[41]

This punitive twist may appear as an incoherent compromise with the majority on the part of Röling, but it was a genuine, if mistaken, belief which he held until his death.[42] Rob does not attribute it to the deficit of independence or integrity, instead framing it as a fundamental disagreement on the (im) permissibility of 'preventive detention as a means of quelling threats to a new peaceful world'.[43] To Röling, the principle of legality in international law was not a legal principle, but a rule of policy, and aggression was akin to a political crime making perpetrators enemies, not villains. Reflecting on this more than 60 years later, Rob argued that preventive detention as a means of incapacitating offenders and neutralising threats to peace was unacceptable. He drew a parallel with the modern practice of preventive detention in the War on Terror, with the deplorable consequences for human rights.[44] Rob also rejected as unproven Röling's claim that this position was supported by the practice of the Nuremberg IMT, which did not sentence defendants convicted of crimes against peace to death. As Rob and Neil Boister argued previously, 'Röling cannot escape his own implied criticism of the Majority; without prior warning, preventive detention is as arbitrary as punishment'.[45]

Nonetheless, what is revealing about this episode is *how* Rob chose to deliver a fundamental criticism of Röling's standpoint which he found underwhelming. Where less merciful commentators would not hold back in expressing their criticism, Rob was firm yet gracious and gentle, as seen from the turns of speech he chose to use, such as 'perhaps unfortunate' and 'less than convincing'.[46] Rob then went out of his way to qualify his critique by offering counterpoints in Röling's defence – for example, that he had nevertheless adopted a high standard for the mental element required for crimes against peace.[47] As many of his colleagues know, Rob's kindness and generosity were unparalleled.[48] Even when

[41] ibid 1116.

[42] ibid 1117, referring to Röling and Cassese (n 4) 66–68.

[43] Cryer, 'Röling in Tokyo' (n 3) 1116.

[44] ibid 1117.

[45] Boister and Cryer (n 2) 134.

[46] Cryer, 'Röling in Tokyo' (n 3) 1117. See, eg, Cassese (n 4) 492 ('Röling often lacked profundity; he also tended to be rather eclectic and not to pursue his views and intuitions to their logical conclusions, thus failing to set out his arguments in fully developed constructs').

[47] Cryer, 'Röling in Tokyo' (n 3) 1117.

[48] 'His generosity, humanity and sense of humour marked him out as special to those who were taught by or worked with him.' White and Myjer (n 1); see also KJ Heller, 'Vale, Rob Cryer', *Opinio Juris*, 4 January 2021, https://opiniojuris.org/2021/01/04/vale-rob-cryer; and MA Drumbl, 'Godspeed, Rob', *Opinio Juris*, 4 January 2021, https://opiniojuris.org/2021/01/04/godspeed-rob.

he had a point and felt strongly about it, he carefully measured his words. On this, as well, he led by example.

ROB, THE BENEVOLENT CRIT

Rob is typically associated with the doctrinal positivist streak of the discipline of international criminal law, and rightly so. For instance, he praised Nino Cassese's masterful 'presentational positivism' – a type of argumentation advancing progressive interpretations of international law while bringing states along with him – while being clearly more critical of those who 'partake of the heady brew of pure naturalist argumentation'.[49] This also appears from how he viewed the Tokyo IMT and how he assessed Judge Röling's contributions to its judgment. He certainly appeared more drawn to Judge Röling than to, say, Justice Pal, who was best known for his 'radically critical', proto-Third World Approaches to International Law (TWAIL), take on the whole affair.[50] Rob was convinced by Judge Röling's reading of the historical context of Japan's actions in Asia, and its efforts to replace the West in colonising Asia, although not from as early as the prosecution and the majority would have it (1928). To Rob, Judge Röling had a clear edge over his Indian colleague, who he found 'far too sanguine' about Japan's plan to liberate Asia. Röling understood that slogan 'Asia for Asians' actually meant 'Asia for Japan' – this ultimately being about the grandeur of the (other) empire, as opposed to the liberation from imperialism.[51] Rob concurred with Röling on this, concluding that his version of history 'stands up better today than either the Majority's or Judge Pal's'.[52]

An astute and rigorous critical commentator as he were, Rob inhabited the mainstream space and worked in the international legal positivist tradition. His critiques are decidedly of a 'benevolent' rather than a 'radical' genre. He is at times seen as a transitional and roaming figure oscillating between the doctrinal and critical approaches – in other words, a maverick sitting on the fence. This characterisation has some basis, yet I doubt its accuracy. It is true that, as Ioannis Kalpouzos observed, Rob's scholarship was infused by a tongue-in-cheek scepticism (not cynicism!) about the international (justice) politics and a keen understanding of the institutional realities and related constraints. This, in turn, provided many others working with or on international criminal law with a rich ground for the construction of the more-than-benevolent critiques.[53]

[49] Cryer (n 5) 1048.

[50] For example, S Xavier, 'Locating and Situating Justice Pal: TWAIL, International Criminal Tribunals, and Judicial Powers' (2022) 12(2) *Asian Journal of International Law* 292.

[51] Cryer, 'Röling in Tokyo' (n 3) 1124.

[52] ibid.

[53] I Kalpouzos, 'Remembering Rob' in Boister et al (n 1) 245 ('while Rob consistently wrote from the field's mainstream, his rigorous and decidedly non-celebratory exploration of the intersections

With his toes touching the admittedly porous border line, Rob, in my view, never really crossed it from the 'benevolent' to the 'radical crithood' territory.

Like Bert Röling, who was a man of his time and not without blind spots, Rob was a consistent defender of international criminal justice. He advocated for the promotion of its core principles and the equal application of the law to all parties to a conflict, regardless of their geopolitical status and ideological or political leanings. A realist as he was, Rob was by no means starry eyed about the challenges and the difficult progress of international criminal justice, which he tellingly called an '*ambivalent* revolution in international law' (emphasis added).[54] He was perfectly aware of the formidable obstacles to 'realizing the utopia' of international criminal law,[55] which have remained essentially the same since Tokyo. Just like Röling, Rob was strongly opposed to the selective enforcement and one-sidedness of justice as undermining the legitimacy of international criminal law.[56] This was all the more the reason for him to stick with the project and keep pushing for the more even-handed enforcement of the law, including in respect of the powerful actors. Throwing the baby out with the bathwater was not an option for Rob. The final plea he attributed to Judge Röling in the conclusion of his article – namely, not to abandon international criminal law, but to guarantee that it can be applied equally and impartially – fully reflects Rob's own vision as well.[57]

GOODBYE, ROB

As I am writing this, more than three and a half years have gone by since Rob went silent. I sorely miss his *viva voce* and am still getting used to his absence. Even if the raw emotions on account of the loss have subsided somewhat, the Rob-shaped void in the international (criminal) law discipline and in many people's quotidian life in it is not going anywhere. For many colleagues, and I certainly speak for myself, Rob was an intellectual tuning fork or, more fittingly, a foolproof chromatic guitar tuner.[58] What remains is Rob's prolific

of doctrine and (institutional) politics constitutes … an incredibly rich resource for understanding and critiquing international criminal law, the law of war, and international law in general').

[54] Cryer, 'Röling in Tokyo' (n 3) 1126.

[55] On 'realistic utopia', see A Cassese, 'Introduction' in A Cassese (ed), *Realizing Utopia: The Future of International Law* (Oxford University Press, 2012) xxi.

[56] Cryer, 'Röling in Tokyo' (n 3) 1126, citing BVA Röling, 'The Nuremberg and Tokyo Trials in Retrospect' in M Cherif Bassiouni and VP Nanda (eds), *A Treatise on International Criminal Law* (Thomas, 1973) 600 ('That one-sidedness indeed annoys the lawyer and is repulsive to the defeated. Every army commits war crimes. On the allied side one needs only to remember the mass bombings (Dresden, Tokyo). As a matter of fact, from World War II above all two things are remembered: The German gas chambers and the American atomic bombings').

[57] Cryer, 'Röling in Tokyo' (n 3) 1126.

[58] On Rob's relationship with (heavy metal and punk rock) music, see Jachec-Neale, ch 14 in this volume, as well as obituaries by Darryl Robinson and me in Boister et al (n 1).

and impactful scholarship, the oral histories and our memories of him. Then there will be this book and more.

Almost on a daily basis, as I try to wrap my head around the ceaseless stream of atrocity news from Ukraine, Gaza, South Sudan, Yemen and elsewhere, or when making sense of the international justice events and accountability initiatives (or imitations thereof) amidst all the hope and despair, I catch myself asking: 'This now. What do you say, Rob?' 'The special tribunal for the crime of aggression in Ukraine … South Africa's Gaza genocide case at the ICJ … The Putin and Shoigu arrest warrants … The Oslo Accords issue messing up ICC jurisdiction over Israeli leadership? … Waiting for your takes!' Rob would have certainly had those takes on the ready with ironclad arguments up his sleeve, all supported by doctrine and case law going back to the eighteenth century and peppered with uniquely Rob-style mischievous jokes bound to make people chuckle against their will.

Years lapse. International law developments keep sticking and stacking on top of each other, marking progress and struggles, compromises and setbacks. If my memories of Rob remain intact, the imaginary conversations with him are getting increasingly monological. Echoes of his voice grow more distant as they soar freely and drift away to fill the ever-expanding empty spaces. Goodbye, dear friend.

Index

www.ingramcontent.com/pod-product-compliance
Ingram Content Group UK Ltd.
Pitfield, Milton Keynes, MK11 3LW, UK
UKHW021909150926
475560UK00003B/268

9 781509 983377